Accounting for Business

Accounting
for Business

Second edition

Peter Scott

OXFORD

UNIVERSITY PRESS

OXFORD

UNIVERSITY PRESS

Great Clarendon Street, Oxford, OX2 6DP,
United Kingdom

Oxford University Press is a department of the University of Oxford.
It furthers the University's objective of excellence in research, scholarship,
and education by publishing worldwide. Oxford is a registered trade mark of
Oxford University Press in the UK and in certain other countries

First edition 2012

Impression: 1

Published in the United States of America by Oxford University Press
198 Madison Avenue, New York, NY 10016, United States of America

British Library Cataloguing in Publication Data

Data available

Library of Congress Control Number: 2015948891

ISBN 978-0-19-871986-1

Printed in Italy by L.E.G.O. S.p.A.

Contents in brief

Contents in full

Part 1   Financial accounting

Acknowledgements

Thanks are due to many individuals. Firstly, to all the staff at Oxford University Press who have been involved with this project: to Sarah Iles, Commissioning Editor, who first proposed a second edition of the book in November 2013 before handing over to Amber Stone-Galilee; special thanks must go to Development Editor Nicola Hartley, who was entrusted with the unenviable task of teasing out the chapters one by one, patiently suggesting improvements and adding constant encouragement to ensure the task was completed by the deadline; and to Fiona Goodall, who was responsible for updating the online resource material. Secondly, a big thank you to all the reviewers for their positive and constructive comments and their input into the revision process. Thirdly, thanks must go to the innumerable students who have, over the years, been the guinea pigs for much of the material presented here; their ability to grasp concepts, ideas and techniques presented in various different ways has helped guide me in the formulation of my ideas on the most effective ways in which to present introductory material to the target audience. Fourthly, thanks go to my colleagues at De Montfort University for their constant encouragement and enthusiasm for the project and their very positive response to the first edition. Finally, the deepest debt of gratitude must go to my family and above all to my wife, Christine, for their forbearance, patience and encouragement during the time it took to revise and improve this book.

Peter Scott, June 2015

The author and publisher would like to sincerely thank all those people who gave their time and expertise to review draft chapters throughout the writing process. Your help was invaluable.

- Mahmoud Al-Sayed, University of Southampton
- Tracy Clewlow, Staffordshire University
- Rachel Holmes, Edinburgh Napier University
- Octavian Ionescu, University of East Anglia
- Henk Jager, *Hanzehogeschool, Groningen*
- Martin Kelly, Queen's University Belfast
- David McAree, Ulster University
- Rennie Tjerkstra, University of Kent at Canterbury
- Androniki Triantafylli, Queen Mary University of London
- Andy Turton, University of Sunderland

Thanks are also extended to those who wished to remain anonymous.

Preface

Why is accounting relevant to me?

Welcome to your accounting studies. You are probably wondering why you are required to study accounting when you have come to university to study marketing, economics, strategy or human resource management. Your first reaction might well be to say that you are not interested in accounting, so why is this subject a compulsory part of your course of study? In both the book and the online workbook, we will be showing you why a knowledge of accounting and its integral role in all organisations are of vital importance to you in your career in business.

This package is designed to be used as an introduction to the practice and techniques of accounting in the business world. It is aimed specifically at you as a non-specialist studying an introductory accounting module as part of your degree in a business related subject. The book thus aims to provide ongoing and constant illustration of the value of accounting as part of a wider business qualification. Throughout both the book and the online workbook, you are invited to engage actively in the study of accounting as one of the foundations for your role as a business professional. In your aspirations for your future career, you will find that a working knowledge of accounting terminology and techniques and an ability to interpret financial information will be essential in your day-to-day working life and in your career progression.

The approach to the subject adopted in this package is unashamedly practical: accounting is a 'doing' subject and the best way to learn how it works and what it does is to practice the various techniques and approaches as frequently as possible. You are provided with careful step-by-step guides showing you how to construct and evaluate various accounting statements. You are then given numerous further opportunities to apply what you have learnt with a view to enhancing your understanding and ability to produce and interpret accounting information.

How this package works

Alongside this textbook, you will have received access to your free online workbook (for details on how to access this, please refer to the 'Guided tour of the online workbook'). The aim of this integrated provision is to provide the supportive learning environment necessary to assist you as a non-specialist in the reinforcement of your learning and understanding of the subject.

The online workbook

You are offered numerous opportunities to revisit, reinforce and revise your understanding through the provision in the online workbook of exercises and examples that are fully integrated with the material in each chapter. You are thus able to strengthen your understanding of the material covered as approaches and techniques are regularly reviewed and recapped through the use of running examples across both the financial and management accounting sections.

The textbook

The first part of the textbook focuses on financial accounting. You are initially introduced to the three key financial accounting statements (the income statement, statement of financial position and statement of cash flows) and shown how these are constructed from first principles. You are then provided with an in-depth and detailed guide to interpreting these statements to show what information these statements provide about an entity's profitability and performance and its ability to survive into the future.

The second part of the book deals with cost and management accounting and the ways in which accounting can be used in decision making and in controlling a business's future development through planning and forecasting. The key techniques of costing, budgeting and capital investment appraisal are covered in the requisite depth and detail to provide you with a ready guide to the production of meaningful information for use both in the running of a business and in the evaluation of its performance.

A note on terminology

Business is increasingly international in its focus. As a result, the accounting terminology adopted throughout this book is that of international accounting standards rather than that of UK standards or legislation. Where different terms for the same statements are in common usage, these are noted throughout the book as they arise.

Guided tour of the book

Identifying and defining

Learning outcomes

Clear, concise learning outcomes begin each chapter and help to contextualise the chapter's main objectives. This feature can help you plan your revision to ensure you identify and cover all the key concepts.

Key terms and glossary

Key terms are highlighted where they first appear in the chapter and are also collated into a glossary at the end of the book. This provides an easy and practical way for you to revise and check your understanding of definitions.

Control purposes: businesses, as we shall see in Chapter 11, set budgets prior to the start of an accounting period (usually 12 months) which set out what they aim to achieve in terms of sales, profits and cash flows. A comparison of actual outcomes with the budget will enable managers to decide where the budget was met, where the budget was exceeded and where the budget failed to reach expectations. Then the causes of the last two outcomes can be investigated and action taken to address the reasons behind the underperformance or to take advantage of better than expected results. The future is uncertain, but businesses will still plan by predicting to the best of their ability what they expect to occur in the fol...

Production cost The total direct costs of producing one product or one unit of service plus the proportion of fixed production overheads allocated to products and services on the basis of the normal level of production.

Profit The surplus remaining after all expenses are deducted from sales revenue.

Profit after tax The profit that remains once all the expenses and charges have been deducted from sales revenue and any other income for the accounting period added on.

accounting periods subsequent to year 1. The re... balance method allocates a smaller charge for... ciation to each successive accounting period ben... from a non-current asset's use. Residual value is... when calculating reducing balance depreciation.

Relevance A requisite quality of financial infor... To be relevant, information must possess the... to influence users' economic decisions and be... Relevant information may be predictive and assis... in making predictions about the future or it...

Understanding accounting principles

Illustrations

The illustrations display accounting statements and documents, and serve to set out the numbers discussed in the text in an easily readable format. This enables you to closely follow the explanations and to become familiar with the layout of such documents.

Illustration 2.3 Misfits Limited: statement of financial position at 31 December 2016

	£000	Note
Assets		
Non-current assets		
Intangible assets	1,000	1
Property, plant and equipment	17,500	2
	18,500	3
Current assets		
Inventories	2,750	4
Trade receivables	2,000	4
Cash and cash equivalents	50	4
	4,800	5

In-text examples

Regular examples are presented throughout each chapter and illustrate how accounting material is used in a variety of different contexts from the world of business. The diversity in cases demonstrates how accounting information can be interpreted in different ways to achieve different ends according to business needs.

EXAMPLE 2.2

How does liability recognition work in practice? Let us take the example of Bunns the Bakers above. When the company bought the city centre shop from the property developer ten years ago, the purchase was financed by a loan from the bank of £500,000. This loan is currently repayable in full in 15 years' time. Does this loan constitute a liability of the business? Applying our criteria above:

· Does Bunns the Bakers have a present obligation at the statement of financial position date? Yes: the loan exists and is outstanding at the current year end. The obligating event (taking out the loan) had taken place by the statement of financial position date.

· Is the obligation to repay the loan unavoidable? Yes: the bank will hold signed documentation from the company agreeing that the loan was taken out and there will be entries in the relevant account at the bank and in bank statements to show the loan being received by the company. Should the company try to avoid repaying the loan, the bank will be able to enforce its legal rights against the company for repayment of the loan.

· Is there a past event giving rise to the obligation? Yes: a loan agreement was signed by Bunns the Bakers at the time the loan was taken out and the money transferred to the company with which to buy the shop.

· Will there be an outflow from Bunns the Bakers of resources embodying economic benefits? Yes: the company will have to transfer cash to settle the obligation. If the company is unable to meet the obligation in cash, the bank will accept the shop as a suitable substitute

Accounting in practice

'Give me an example' boxes

Topical examples taken from the *Financial Times*, BBC and other news outlets will help your understanding of how the theory being discussed in the chapter relates to a real-world case. There are also numerous references to financial statements from real companies which highlight how the accounting theory discussed plays out in business practice.

> **GIVE ME AN EXAMPLE 9.3 Outsourcing at Toyota**
>
> The Japanese car company, Toyota, prizes high quality at a low price. However, the company outsources 70% of the components for its cars to suppliers and produces just 30% of the components in its own production facilities. In order to ensure the quality of the products produced by its suppliers, Toyota adopts a policy of strong relationships and collaboration with its suppliers through the Toyota Production System. Toyota's high quality has been achieved as a result of the collaborative advantage it enjoys with its suppliers. Toyota regularly evaluates its suppliers' performance and provides suggestions on how they could improve their operations. However, this is not a one way relationship: the company also invites its suppliers to evaluate Toyota and to provide their suggestions for operational improvement. This continuous improvement approach enables the Toyota Production System to deliver the high quality products demanded by both Toyota and its customers despite the fact that most of its car parts are not manufactured in-house.
>
> Source: www.scribd.com/doc/53016595/Vertical-Integration-or-Outsourcing-Nokia-Ford-Toyota-IBM-Intel-Toshiba-Matsushita#scribd

'Why is this relevant to me?' boxes

These short and frequent explanations demonstrate exactly how the accounting material under discussion will be relevant to business professionals and decision makers, not just to those aiming for a career in accounting. They are an important reminder of how integral accounting knowledge is to successful business professionals.

> **WHY IS THIS RELEVANT TO ME? The timing of payments and the shortcomings of the current and quick ratios**
>
> To enable you as a business professional and user of accounting information to:
> - Appreciate that an entity's current liabilities will never all be due for payment at the same time unless that entity is in liquidation
> - Calculate the amounts due for payment on the day after the statement of financial position date as part of your assessment of an entity's liquidity
> - Forecast monthly cash outgoings for the next year to determine whether entities can meet those monthly outgoings from current trading
> - Appreciate how timing of payments analysis helps to overcome the shortcomings of the current and quick ratios in liquidity analysis

Testing and applying understanding

End-of-chapter questions

There is a set of questions at the end of every chapter designed to test your knowledge of the key concepts that have been discussed. They are divided into two tiers according to difficulty allowing you track your progress. Use them during your course to ensure you fully understand the accounting principles before moving on, or for revision to make sure you can confidently tackle the more difficult questions. The answers can be found in the back of the book.

> **END-OF-CHAPTER QUESTIONS**
>
> Solutions to these questions can be found at the back of the book from page 413.
>
> › *Develop your understanding*
>
> Question 2.1
>
> Using the criteria outlined in the summary in Figure 2.1, explain why the following items are assets that entities recognise on the statement of financial position:
>
> (a) Motor vehicles purchased by an entity
> (b) Inventory received from suppliers
> (c) Cash and cash equivalents
>
> Using the criteria outlined in the summary in Figure 2.1, explain why the following items are not assets and why they are not recognised on entities' statements of financial position:
>
> (a) Redundant plant and machinery that has been replaced by faster, more technologically advanced machinery. This redundant plant and machinery is no longer used in the business or industry and has no resale or scrap value.
> (b) A trade receivable from a customer who is bankrupt and from whom no payment is expected.
> (c) A highly skilled workforce.
>
> Question 2.2
>
> The directors of Oxford Academicals Football Club Limited are discussing whether player registrations can be recognised as assets on the club's statement of financial position. There are

Chapter summary

Each chapter concludes with a bulleted list linking to the learning outcomes, outlining the key points you should take away from the chapter.

> **CHAPTER SUMMARY**
>
> *You should now have learnt that:*
> - An asset is a resource controlled by an entity as a result of past events from which future economic benefits are expected to flow to the entity and whose monetary cost or value can be measured reliably
> - A liability is a present obligation arising from past events the settlement of which is expected to result in an outflow from the entity of resources embodying economic benefits and whose monetary value can be measured at a best estimate if reliable measurement is not possible

Guided tour of the online workbook

Access the interactive online workbook by visiting the Online Resource Centre at www.oxfordtextbooks.co.uk/orc/scott2e/ and entering the following username and password:

Username: scottonline2e
Password: Business123

The resources in the online workbook have been specifically designed to support you throughout your accounting studies. References within the textbook indicate the relevant resource accompanying that section or topic, thereby allowing you to reinforce your learning and ensuring you take full advantage of this fantastic package.

Student resources

Summaries of key concepts

Key glossary terms are provided in interactive flashcard format.

Multiple-choice questions

Interactive multiple-choice questions for every chapter give you instant feedback, as well as page references, to help you focus on the areas that need further study.

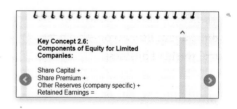

Numerical exercises

These exercises, often based in Excel, give you the opportunity to calculate accounting information from given sets of data, thereby practising what is discussed in the book.

Go back over this again

Containing a mixture of further examples, written exercises, true or false questions and annotated accounting information, this section provides the perfect opportunity for you to revise and revisit any concepts you might be unsure of.

Show me how to do it

Video presentations, accompanied by a voice-over, allow you to watch practical demonstrations of how more complex accounting tasks are dealt with by the author.

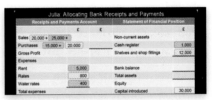

Web links

Arranged by chapter, these web links will take you directly to the websites of the companies and organisations covered in the book, as well as websites of more general accounting interest. Follow the links to learn more about how accounting plays out in the real world of business.

Further reading

Arranged by chapter, this section provides you with a list of additional resources you may wish to consult if you'd like to take your learning further, or simply consider a topic from a different perspective.

Guided tour of Dashboard

Simple. Informative. Mobile.

Dashboard is a cloud-based online assessment and revision tool. It comes pre-loaded with self-test questions for students, a homework course if your module leader has adopted Dashboard and additional resources as listed below.

Visit www.oxfordtextbooks.co.uk/dashboard for more information.

Simple: With a highly intuitive design, it will take you less than 15 minutes to learn and master the system.

Mobile: You can access Dashboard from every major platform and device connected to the internet, whether that's a computer, tablet or smartphone.

Informative: Your assignment and assessment results are automatically graded, giving your instructor a clear view of the class's understanding of the course content.

Student resources

Dashboard offers all the features of the online workbook, but comes with additional questions and practice material for you to take your learning further.

Lecturer resources

Pre-loaded homework assignments and test bank

A pre-loaded homework course structured around the book is available, supported by a test bank containing a wealth of additional multiple-choice questions. Your students can follow the pre-loaded course, or you can customize it, allowing you to add questions from the test bank or from your existing materials to meet your specific teaching needs.

Gradebook

Dashboard will automatically grade the homework assignments that you set for your students. The Gradebook also provides heat maps for you to view your students' progress which help you to quickly identify areas of the course where your students may need more practice, as well as the areas they are most confident in. This feature helps you focus your teaching time on the areas that matter.

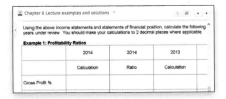

The Gradebook also allows you to administer grading schemes, manage checklists and administer learning objectives and competencies.

Lecturer examples and solutions

Additional exercises which can be used alongside the Powerpoint slides in lectures or seminars.

Group tutorial exercises

This feature includes a range of more detailed workshop-based activities: shorter lecture-based in-class exercises and suggestions for assessment approaches.

Lecturer examination questions and answers

Additional essay-based questions for you to set for examinations with accompanying answers.

PowerPoint slides

Accompanying each chapter is a suite of customisable and illustrated PowerPoint slides for you to use in your lectures. Arranged by chapter theme, the slides may also be used as handouts in class and can be easily adapted to suit your teaching style.

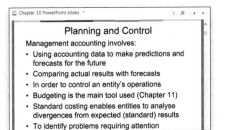

Part 1

Financial accounting

Introduction to accounting

LEARNING OUTCOMES

Once you have read this chapter and worked through the questions and examples in both this chapter and the online workbook, you should be able to:

- Define accounting and explain what role it plays in business
- Understand the fundamental role that accounting plays in informing all business decisions
- Define and discuss the qualities of useful accounting information
- Distinguish between the two branches of accounting, financial accounting and management accounting
- State the main users of accounting information and identify what they need from accounting information
- Explain what accounting does not do and the limitations of accounting information
- Understand why a knowledge of accounting is important to you

1

Introduction

Welcome to your accounting studies. You are probably wondering why you are required to study accounting when you have come to university to study business, marketing, strategy or human resource management. Thus your first reaction might be to say that you are not interested in accounting, so why is this a compulsory part of your course of study? In this book we will show you why a knowledge of accounting and its integral role in all organisations are of vital importance to you in your career in business. We will take a good look at the three key accounting statements you will encounter in your career in business to provide you with a working knowledge of how these are put together and how you can interpret the information they present. We will also consider how accounting is a valuable tool in planning for the future and in evaluating outcomes and the ways in which these techniques can help you become a much more rounded, much more valuable part of your organisation.

What skills do I need?

Many students find the thought of accounting worrying as they do not feel they have the necessary mathematical ability to be able to understand or apply the subject in practice. However, do be assured that accounting needs no particular mathematical strengths, just some basic arithmetical applications and an ability to reason. As long as you can add up, subtract, multiply and divide figures you have all the arithmetical skills you will need to undertake the calculations and apply this subject. The ability to reason is a skill that you will need in every subject of study and it will be fundamental to the success of any career, not just to your accounting studies.

Once you have learnt how to apply the basic techniques, accounting is much more about understanding what the figures are telling you and about interpreting the data in front of you—this requires you to think in a logical fashion and to investigate the meaning beneath the surface. Therefore, it is more accurate to say that accounting requires the ability to communicate and express your ideas in words rather than being dependent upon mathematical skills. As we shall see in this chapter, no matter what particular specialist area of business you are studying and no matter what your career aims are, a working knowledge of accounting will be essential to your success in both your studies and in business life.

WHY IS THIS RELEVANT TO ME?   Skills needed to study accounting

- To reassure you that the study of accounting requires no further special skills than those you already possess
- To enable you to appreciate that the study of accounting is merely an extension of your other studies in your business degree

What is accounting?

Let's start with a definition.

Accounting summarises numerical data relating to past events and presents this data as information to managers and other interested parties as a basis for both deci-sion making and control purposes, as presented in Figure 1.1.

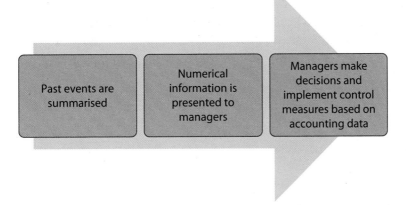

Figure 1.1 What is accounting? Diagram showing how accounting information leads to managerial decision making

This is quite a lot to take in, so let's unpick the various strands of this definition.

1. Numerical data: accounting information is mostly but not always presented in money terms. It could just as easily be a league table of football teams with details of games won, games lost and games drawn, goals for and goals against and points gained, all of which is numerical information. Or it could be a list of schools in a particular area with percentages of pupils gaining five GCSEs grades A*–C and average A level points at each school. In a business, it could be the number of units of product produced rather than just their cost, or the number of units sold in a given period of time. The critical point here is that accounting data is presented in the form of numbers.

2. Relating to past events: accounting systems gather data and then summarise these data to present details of what has happened. A league table is a summary of past results. Similarly, a total of sales for the month will be a summary of all the individual sales made on each day of that month and relating to that past period of time.

3. Information presented to managers: managers have the power and author-ity to use accounting information to take action now to maintain or improve future outcomes. In the same way, if a team is in the middle of the league table but aspires to a higher position, the team manager can take steps to hire bet-ter coaches, buy in the contracts of players with higher skill levels and sell the

contractual rights of underperforming players. If a school wants to improve their examination results, they will take steps to determine what is preventing better performance and try to correct these deficiencies.

4. As a basis for decision making: accounting information is used to determine what went well and which events did not turn out quite as anticipated. For example, demand for a business product over the past month might not have reached the levels expected. If this is the case, managers can take steps to determine whether the selling price is too high and should be reduced, whether there are defects in the products that require rectification or whether the product is just out of date and no longer valued by consumers. Whereas, if demand for a product is outstripping supply, then managers can take the decision to divert business resources to increase production to meet that higher demand.

5. Control purposes: businesses, as we shall see in Chapter 11, set budgets prior to the start of an accounting period (usually 12 months) which set out what they aim to achieve in terms of sales, profits and cash flows. A comparison of actual outcomes with the budget will enable managers to decide where the budget was met, where the budget was exceeded and where the budget failed to reach expectations. Then the causes of the last two outcomes can be investigated and action taken to address the reasons behind the underperformance or to take advantage of better than expected results. The future is uncertain, but businesses will still plan by predicting to the best of their ability what they expect to occur in the following months and then compare actual outcomes with what they expected to happen as a means of controlling operations.

WHY IS THIS RELEVANT TO ME?   Accounting definition

To enable you as a business professional and user of accounting information to:

• Understand what accounting is

• Appreciate that the production of accounting information is not an end in itself but is a tool to enable you to understand, direct and control business or other activities

---

SUMMARY OF KEY CONCEPTS   How well have you remembered the definition of accounting given above? Revise this definition with Summary of key concepts 1.1.

GO BACK OVER THIS AGAIN!   If this all still seems very complicated and not relevant to you, visit the **online workbook** Exercises 1.1 and 1.2 to enable you to appreciate that you are working with accounting data on a daily basis.

GO BACK OVER THIS AGAIN!   Quite sure you can define accounting? Go to the **online workbook** Exercises 1.3 to make sure you can say what accounting is and what role it performs in a business context.

Control, accounting and accountability

The function of accounting information as a mechanism through which to control outcomes and activities can be illustrated further. Representatives are accountable for their actions to those people who have placed them in positions of power. Accounting information is thus provided so that individuals and organisations can render an account of what they have done with the resources placed in their care.

EXAMPLE 1.1

Your employer pays your salary into your bank account while various payments are made out of your account to pay your bills and other outgoings. Your bank then provides you with a statement (either online or in paper copy) on a regular basis so that you can check whether they have accounted for your money correctly or not.

In the same way, company directors present accounts to shareholders and other interested parties on an annual basis to give an account of how they have looked after the money and other resources entrusted to them and how they have used that money to invest and generate income for shareholders. Local and national governments regularly publish information on the taxes collected and how those taxes have been spent. This information enables politicians to render an account of how taxes collected have been used to provide goods and services to citizens.

Where power and resources are entrusted to others, it is important that they are accountable for what they have done with that power and those resources. If your bank makes mistakes in the management of your account or charges you too much for managing your account, then you can change banks. If shareholders are unhappy with their directors' performance, they will not reappoint them as directors of their company. Instead, they will elect other directors to replace them in the expectation that these new directors will manage their investment much more carefully and profitably. Alternatively, they can sell their shares and invest their money in companies that do provide them with higher profits and higher dividends. If voters are unhappy with how their local and national politicians have taxed them or how they have spent their taxes, they will vote for different representatives with different policies more to their liking.

Persons entrusted by others with resources are in the position of stewards, looking after those resources for the benefit of other parties. Providing an account of their stewardship of those resources helps those other parties control the actions of their stewards. At the same time, accounts enable these other parties to make decisions on whether to continue with their current stewards or to replace them with others who will perform more effectively and provide them with a more efficient and profitable service. These relationships are summarised in Figure 1.2.

1

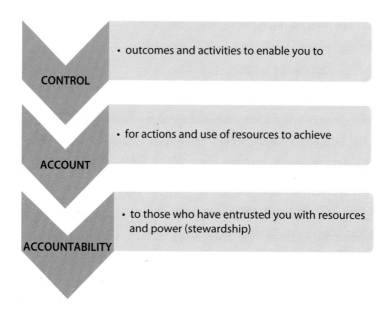

- outcomes and activities to enable you to

CONTROL

- for actions and use of resources to achieve

ACCOUNT

- to those who have entrusted you with resources and power (stewardship)

ACCOUNTABILITY

Figure 1.2 Control, accounting and accountability.

WHY IS THIS RELEVANT TO ME?   Control, accounting and accountability

To enable you as a business professional and user of accounting information to:

- Appreciate that accounting functions as a control on the actions of others
- Understand how you will be entrusted with a business's resources and that you will be accountable for your stewardship of those resources

GO BACK OVER THIS AGAIN!   Do you really understand how accounting helps with control and accountability? Go to the **online workbook** Exercises 1.4 to make sure you understand the links between accounting, accountability and control.

The role of accounting information in business decision making

Businesses are run to make a profit. Businesses that do not make a profit fail and are closed down. In order to achieve this profit aim, businesses need to make and implement decisions on a daily basis. Such decisions might comprise, among others, some or all of the following:

- What products should we produce?
- What services should we provide?
- How much do our products cost to make?

- How much do our services cost to provide?
- What price should we charge for our products or services?
- Should we be taking on more employees?
- How much will the additional employees cost?
- Will the cost of the new employees be lower than the income they will generate?
- Should we be expanding into bigger premises?
- Will the costs of the bigger premises be outweighed by the increase in income?
- How will we finance our expansion?
- Should we take out a bank loan or ask the shareholders to buy more shares?

All of these decisions will require accounting input:

- The marketing department can use reports from sales personnel and consumer evaluations to tell us what the demand for a product is, but it will be up to the accounting staff to tell us what the product costs to make and what the selling price should be in order to generate a profit on each sale.
- The personnel department can tell us about hiring new staff and the legal obligations incurred in doing so, the training required and the market rates for such workers, but it will be the accounting staff who can tell us what level of productivity the new employees will have to achieve in order to generate additional profit for the business.
- The strategy department can tell us what sort of premises we should be looking for, how these new premises should be designed and what image they should present, but it will be the accounting staff who can tell us how many products we will have to make and sell for the new premises to cover their additional costs and the best way in which to finance this expansion.

Accounting is thus at the heart of every decision and every activity that a business undertakes as shown in Figure 1.3.

At this early stage of your studies, it is easy to think of each department in a business just sticking to its own special field of expertise, operating in isolation from all the others, concentrating on their own aims and goals. You might reply that you would never think of a business as just a loose grouping of separate departments all doing their own thing

Figure 1.3 The central role of accounting in business activity and business decision making

with no thought for the big picture. But pause for a moment and ask yourself whether you treat all your current year study modules as interlinked or as totally separate subjects? You should see them as interlinked and look to see how all the subjects interact, but it is too easy to adopt a blinkered approach and compartmentalise your studies.

As the above decisions and discussion illustrate, all business decisions require input from different departments and information from one department has to be integrated with information from other departments before an overall plan of action is put into operation. Businesses operate as cohesive entities, with all departments pulling in the same direction rather than each following their own individual pathway. Management make decisions and implement strategies, but underpinning all these decisions and strategies is accounting information.

This central role for accountants and accounting information puts accounting staff under pressure to perform their roles effectively and efficiently. After all, if the information presented by the accounting staff is defective in any way, the wrong decision could be made and losses rather than profits might result. Therefore, accountants have to ensure that the information they provide is as accurate and as up to date as possible to enable management to make the most effective decisions. Ideally, accounting staff will always be striving to improve the information they provide to management as better information will result in more informed and more effective decisions.

To illustrate the importance of the accounting function, take a moment to think what would happen if we did not have accounting information. Businesses would be lost without the vital information provided by accounting. If accounting did not exist, there would be no information relating to costs, no indication of what had been achieved in the past as a point of comparison for what is being achieved now, no figures on which to base taxation assessments, no proof that results are as companies claim they are. In short, if accounting did not exist, someone would have to invent it.

WHY IS THIS RELEVANT TO ME? The role of accounting information in business decision making

To enable you as a business professional to:

- Appreciate that business decisions depend upon input from different departments and that decisions are not made in isolation by one department alone

- Appreciate the importance of accounting information in business decision making

- Persuade you that you should see your studies as an integrated, coherent whole rather than as a collection of disparate, unrelated subjects

MULTIPLE CHOICE QUESTIONS Convinced that you understand what role accounting plays in business decision making? Go to the **online workbook** Multiple choice questions 1.1 to make sure you can suggest how accounting and accounting information would be used in the context of a business decision.

What qualities should accounting information possess?

Given the pivotal role of accounting information in business decision making, what sort of qualities should such information possess for it to be useful in making these decisions? Helpfully, the International Accounting Standards Board (IASB) in its *Framework for the Preparation and Presentation of Financial Statements* provides guidance in this area. The IASB states that financial information should possess the following qualities:

- Relevance
- Reliability
- Comparability
- Understandability

What characteristics do each of the above qualities represent? Table 1.1 considers the characteristics of each of the four qualities of financial information.

Table 1.1 The qualities of accounting information

Quality	Characteristics
Relevance	• To be relevant, information must possess the ability to influence users' economic decisions otherwise there is no point in producing this information. • Relevant information may be predictive and assist users in making predictions about the future or it may be confirmatory by assisting users to assess the accuracy of past predictions. • The more accurate that past predictions of, for example, profits have been, the more likely it is that users will be able to rely on current predictions of future profits. • To be relevant, information must be timely: that is, it must be presented quickly enough for users to be able to make use of it in making economic decisions.
Reliability	• Accounting information, like all information, should be free of significant error or bias. • Information is reliable if it can be depended upon to represent faithfully the transactions or events it claims to represent.

→

1

Table 1.1 The qualities of accounting information

Quality	Characteristics
Comparability	• Accounting information should be comparable over time. • To achieve this, the same items should be presented in the same way in financial statements relating to different accounting periods. • Presentation of items in financial statements should thus be consistent across different accounting periods.
Understandability	• This characteristic should not be confused with simplicity. • Accounting information should be presented in such a way that those making use of it can understand what it represents. • Readers of financial reports are assumed to have sufficient knowledge of business and economic events in order to make sense of what they are presented with.

EXAMPLE 1.2

Let's think about how the qualities considered above apply to accounting information. Taking the bank statement example considered under Control, accounting and accountability earlier in this chapter, our thoughts might be as shown in Table 1.2.

Table 1.2 How your bank statement fulfils the qualities of accounting information

| Relevant? | • Your bank statement is able to influence your economic decisions as you are able to decide to spend less, increase the income into your bank account or decide to invest surplus funds in high interest accounts.
• Looking at your current income and expenditure, you can predict what is likely to happen in the future in your bank account. Where you have made predictions about what cash you would have left at the end of each month, you can then assess how accurate or inaccurate those predictions were and make future predictions about how much you will have left at the end of the next month to decide what you should do with these surplus funds.
• Accurate predictions in the past will enable you to be confident that your future predictions will be accurate too.
• Your bank statement is received each month (or you can access it instantly online), so it is presented in time for you to make economic decisions. If your bank statement were to be sent annually, this would not be relevant information as it would be seriously out of date by the time you received it. |

Table 1.2 How your bank statement fulfils the qualities of accounting information   (*continued*)

Reliable?	• Your bank statement is presented by your bank, so this is reliable information, free of error and bias; any errors can be notified to your bank for correction. • Your bank statement is a summary of transactions and faithfully represents what has happened in your account over the past month.
Comparable?	• Presentation of your bank statement does not differ over time and is presented in the same format every month so this information is comparable over different months.
Understandable?	• You can certainly understand your bank statement as it shows you the money going into and out of your account.

GO BACK OVER THIS AGAIN!   Certain you can define relevance, reliability, comparability and understandability? Go to the **online workbook** Exercises 1.5 to make sure you can define these qualities of accounting information accurately.

SUMMARY OF KEY CONCEPTS   Can you state and define the four qualities of financial information? Check your grasp of these qualities with Summary of key concepts 1.2–1.5.

Materiality

A further requirement of financial information for decision making purposes is that it should not be overloaded with unnecessary detail. This leads us on to the concept of materiality. The IASB defines materiality as follows:

Information is material if its omission or misstatement could influence the economic decisions of users taken on the basis of the financial statements.

Source: (IASB Framework)

EXAMPLE 1.3

An item could be material by size. If a shop makes £2 million of sales a year, then the sale of a 50p carton of milk missed out of those sales will not be material. However, in a steel fabrication business making £2 million of sales a year, the omission of a £250,000 sale of a steel frame for a building would be material as it makes up 12.5% of the sales for the year.

As well as size, items can be material by nature. The theft of £5 from the till by a member of staff would be unlikely to be material. However, the theft of £5 from the till by the managing director would be: if you are an investor in the business, this tells you that your investment might not be very safe if the managing director is willing to steal from the business.

MULTIPLE CHOICE QUESTIONS   Totally confident you can decide whether a piece of information is material or not? Go to the **online workbook** Multiple choice questions 1.2 to make sure you can determine whether information is material or not.

SUMMARY OF KEY CONCEPTS   Can you define materiality? Check your grasp of this definition in Summary of key concepts 1.6.

Cost v. benefit

Information should only be presented if the benefits of providing this information outweigh the costs of obtaining it.

EXAMPLE 1.4

You know that there is a wonderful quote in a book that you have read that would really enhance your essay and provide you with a brilliant conclusion. However, you have forgotten where to find this quote and you have not written down the name of the book or the page reference. Your essay must be handed in by 4.00 pm today and it is already 3.40 pm. You still have to print off your essay before handing it in. If your essay is handed in after 4.00 pm you will be awarded a mark of 0% and so fail the assignment.

The costs of searching for the quote outweigh the benefits of finding it as you will not receive any marks if your essay is late so you print off your essay and hand it in on time and, when it is returned, you have scored 65% and gained a pass on this piece of coursework.

WHY IS THIS RELEVANT TO ME?   The qualities of accounting information

To enable you as a business professional and user of accounting information to:

- Understand what qualities useful accounting information should possess
- Appreciate the constraints imposed upon useful accounting information by the materiality concept and the cost/benefit consideration

GO BACK OVER THIS AGAIN!   Quite sure you understand how cost v. benefit works? Visit the **online workbook** Exercises 1.6 to reinforce your understanding.

SUMMARY OF KEY CONCEPTS   Can you define cost v. benefit? Check your grasp of this definition in Summary of key concepts 1.7.

The users of accounting information

As we have seen, accounting is all about providing information to interested parties so that they can make decisions on the basis of that information. But who are the users of this accounting information and what decisions do they make as a result of receiving that information?

There are two branches of accounting which we will consider in this book and which you will meet in your studies and your career in business. One of these branches provides information to external users and the other provides information to internal users. The information needs of both these user groups differ in important ways as we shall see.

Accounting branch 1: financial accounting

Financial accounting is the reporting of past information to users outside the organisation. This information is presented in the annual report and accounts that all companies are obliged to produce by law, publish on their websites and lodge with the Registrar of Companies at Companies House. Even if a business entity is not a company and there is no legal obligation to produce accounts, it will still produce financial statements to provide evidence of what it has achieved over the past year. These accounts will also be used as a basis for enabling the business managers or owners and its lenders and advisors to make decisions based upon them.

What is the aim of these financial accounts and what do they provide? The IASB states that the objective of financial accounting statements is as follows.

> The objective of financial statements is to provide information about the financial position, financial performance and cash flows of an entity that is useful to a wide range of users in making economic decisions.
>
> Source: (IASB Framework, paragraph 12)

In this book we will be studying all three of the financial statements outlined by the IASB in that paragraph. Chapter 2 will consider the financial position of entities and how this is represented in the statement of financial position, while Chapter 3 will look at how entities' financial performance is measured and reported in the income statement and Chapter 4 will provide an overview of the statement of cash flows. Ways in which users can evaluate these particular financial statements and what they tell them about the performance, the financial stability and the investment potential of entities will be the subject of Chapters 6 and 7. However, our concern at this point is with the wide range of users of financial accounts and reports, so let us return to the different user groups and the economic decisions for which they might use financial accounting statements.

The IASB Framework lists seven categories of external users of financial statements:

1. Investors and their advisors
2. Employees and their representative groups

3. Lenders

4. Suppliers and other trade payables

5. Customers

6. Governments and their agencies

7. The public

What information would each of the above user groups expect to find in external financial statements that would enable them to make economic decisions? Table 1.3 provides examples of some of the questions that the seven categories of user will ask when looking at financial statements: can you think of additional questions that each user group will ask?

Table 1.3 The external users of financial statements

User group	Examples of questions asked by each user group
Investors and their advisors	• What profit has the company made for me in my position as a shareholder? • What financial gains am I making from this company? • Would it be worthwhile for me to invest more money in the shares of this company? • If the company has not done well this year, should I sell my shares or hold onto them?
Employees and their representative groups	• How stable is the company I work for? • Is the company I work for making profits? • If the company is making losses, will it survive for the foreseeable future? • What about the continuity of my employment? • Should I be looking for employment elsewhere? • If the company I work for is profitable, will I be awarded a pay rise or a bonus? • What retirement benefit scheme does my company offer to employees? • Is my employer investing in the future prosperity of the business?
Lenders	• Will this company be able to repay what has been lent? • Will this company be able to pay loan instalments and interest as they fall due? • Is this company in danger of insolvency? • What cash resources and cash generating ability does this company have?
Suppliers and other trade creditors	• Will I be paid for goods I have supplied? • Will I be paid on time so that I can pay my suppliers? • Will my customer expand so that I can expand, too?

Table 1.3 The external users of financial statements   *(continued)*

User group	Examples of questions asked by each user group
Customers	• Will the entity survive in the long term so that it can continue to provide me with goods and services?
Governments and their agencies	• What taxation does this entity pay? • What contribution does this entity make to the economy? • Does this entity export goods to other countries?
The public	• What contribution does this entity make to society? • Does this entity make donations to charity? • If this entity is a major local employer, will they survive into the future to ensure the health of the local economy?

Many questions that users of financial statements ask will be common to all categories of user. For example, investors might ask questions about the ethical and environmental record of the company and whether this is the kind of organisation they would want to be involved with and be seen to be involved with. But ethically and environmentally concerned employees might also ask the same questions and lenders, concerned about their reputation and being seen to do business with unethical organisations, might be looking for the same information. Suppliers and customers will have similar concerns as their image and reputation will be shaped by those with whom they do business.

Similarly, all user groups will want to know about the availability of cash with which to pay dividends (investors), salaries (employees), loan interest and loans (lenders), goods supplied on credit (suppliers) and taxes due (governments). Even customers and the public will be concerned about the availability of cash, as, without sufficient inflows of cash from trading, companies will collapse.

While users of external financial statements might legitimately ask the above questions, the extent to which such reports provide this information varies. Some financial reports are very detailed in their coverage, others less so. As you gradually become familiar with the contents of published financial reports and accounts, your awareness of shortcomings in these documents will increase.

WHY IS THIS RELEVANT TO ME?   The users of accounting information

To enable you as a business professional and user of accounting information to:

• Gain an awareness of the external parties interested in the financial information provided by business entities

• Understand the kinds of answers users of external financial reports expect from the information provided

---

GO BACK OVER THIS AGAIN! Convinced that you understand what information particular user groups are looking for in published financial reports? Go to the **online workbook** Exercises 1.7 to check your understanding in this area.

SUMMARY OF KEY CONCEPTS Can you state the seven user groups of financial accounting information? Check your knowledge of these users with Summary of key concepts 1.8.

SUMMARY OF KEY CONCEPTS Quite sure you can say what the objective of financial statements is? Check your knowledge of this objective with Summary of key concepts 1.9.

Accounting branch 2: cost and management accounting

Cost and management accounting is concerned with reporting accounting and cost information to users within an organisation. As the name suggests, management accounting information is used to help managers manage the business and its activities. Cost and management accountants are first concerned with the costs that go into producing products and services to determine a selling price for those products and services that will generate a profit for the business. Management accounting information is then used to plan levels of production and activity in the future as well as deciding what products to produce and sell to maximise profits for the business. As well as planning what the business is going to do, management accounting produces reports to evaluate the results of past plans to see whether they achieved their aims and the ways in which improvements could be made.

While financial accounting reports what has happened in the past, management accounting is very much concerned with both the present and the future and how accounting information can be used for short-term decision making and longer-term planning. In this book we will be looking at costs and cost behaviour in Chapter 8, while Chapter 9 will show you how costs and cost behaviour can be used in making short-term decisions. Chapter 10 then considers the technique of standard costing as an aid to quick decision making and performance evaluation. Chapter 11 focuses on the key short-term planning technique of budgeting, while Chapter 12 extends the time horizon to look at the ways in which long-term business planning determines whether a capital project is worth investing in or not.

As we shall see, the format of financial accounting statements is very much prescribed by legislation and the requirements of the IASB, whereas management accounting statements are presented in the format most appropriate for managers to aid them in their decision making. The distinction between financial and management accounting information will be dealt with in greater detail at the start of Chapter 8.

WHY IS THIS RELEVANT TO ME?   The two branches of accounting

To enable you as a business professional and user of accounting information to:

- Appreciate the wide range of internal and external users of accounting information
- Distinguish quickly between financial and management accounting

The structure and regulation of the accounting profession

Professional accounting bodies have been set up in many countries around the world. These professional accounting bodies are responsible for admitting individuals to membership and for regulation and oversight of their conduct as professional people once they have been accepted as members. Admission to the professional bodies is achieved through a combination of examinations and practical experience. The main professional accounting bodies in the United Kingdom and Ireland are:

- The Association of Chartered Certified Accountants (ACCA)
- The Chartered Institute of Management Accountants (CIMA)
- The Chartered Institute of Public Finance and Accounting (CIPFA)
- The Institute of Chartered Accountants in England and Wales (ICAEW)
- The Institute of Chartered Accountants in Ireland (ICAI)
- The Institute of Chartered Accountants in Scotland (ICAS)

Qualified accountants undertake the preparation of financial statements, the audit of financial statements and the provision of taxation and business advice to individuals and organisations. As professionals, qualified accountants are expected to adhere to certain standards of conduct to maintain the standing of the profession and to provide a professional service to their clients and the public. Accountants are expected to behave with integrity, being honest in their professional and business relationships. They are also expected to be objective, to carry out their duties with due care and competence, to maintain the confidentiality of information acquired in the course of fulfilling their duties and to comply at all times with relevant laws and regulations. Where accountants breach these ethical rules of conduct, their professional bodies will take action to punish them with warnings, fines and, in the most serious cases, exclusion from membership.

As well as adhering to the professional bodies' expected standards of behaviour and ethical conduct, qualified accountants are expected to ensure that accepted accounting standards have been applied correctly in the presentation of financial information. In the European Union (including the UK) accounting standards are set by the IASB for companies listed on a Stock Exchange and by the UK Accounting Standards Board (ASB) for smaller companies. Failure to apply these accounting standards correctly will also result in an accountant's professional body taking disciplinary action against a member.

Poor management and dishonest behaviour on the part of directors in the past led to investors losing a lot of money. Governments and stock exchanges around the world responded by setting up various committees to report on the state of corporate governance, the way in which large companies were run, and to make recommendations for improvement. As a result of these recommendations, corporate governance codes were formulated to enshrine best practice and to ensure that large companies were run in an open and honest manner to safeguard shareholders' and the general public's interests in those companies. Professional accountants are expected to adhere to and apply these corporate governance codes in businesses in which they work to ensure the transparency of information presented by these companies. Further consideration of the regulation of the accounting professional and corporate governance is beyond the scope of this present book. However, your future studies will encompass consideration of the legal and ethical aspects of business management and the ways in which good corporate governance is promoted throughout the business sector.

WHY IS THIS RELEVANT TO ME?   Structure and regulation of the accounting profession

To provide you as a business professional with:

- A quick overview of the accounting profession and the ways in which it is regulated

- An indication of the standards of behaviour to be expected from professional accountants and other persons holding positions of responsibility in companies

The limitations of accounting information

We have seen that accounting information plays an anchor role in decision making for businesses and other users. However, there are various aspects of business performance that accounting does not cover. While it is important to know what accounting is and what it does, it is just as important to be aware of what accounting does not do.

First, accounting does not provide you with measures of the quality of an organisation's performance. The quality of what an entity produces or provides is measured by its customers and their level of satisfaction with goods and services delivered, their willingness to recommend an organisation's products and the number of times they return to buy more goods or use more services. While measures can be devised to assess recommendations and repeat business, this is not a function that accounting would normally fulfil.

Similarly, a business entity may make a profit, but accounting does not tell us the time, effort and thought that went into delivering the products and services to generate that profit. In the same way, your team may win, draw or lose, but the bare result does not tell you about the quality of entertainment on offer, whether your team played badly but still managed to scrape a vital goal or whether they played brilliantly and were just unlucky.

Second, accounting does not tell you about the pollution and environmental or social damage an entity has caused. Organisations will report redundancies as an internal cost-saving opportunity for the business while ignoring the wider external effects of their action. Thus, businesses do not report the destruction of communities built around an organisation's operations and all the burdens that this imposes upon families, social services, the National Health Service and the state. Similarly, while companies use air, water and other natural resources in their production processes, there is no requirement that they should report on the damage they cause to these resources.

Finally, accounting does not provide any valuation or measure of the skills base and knowledge of organisations. Boards of directors will thank their staff for all their hard work and efforts during the previous financial year, but the value of the employees to the business does not feature in financial statements. This is attributable to the fact that valuing staff is impossible due to the subjective nature of such valuations. Thus, you might think your accounting lecturer is the most organised and most informative tutor you have seen on your course so far, while your friend is grumbling about how uninteresting the lectures and tutorials are and how they cannot follow them. In the same way, while employees, their skills, knowledge and abilities are the most valuable resources in a business, these resources cannot be measured in money or any other numerical terms and so do not appear in financial statements. As accounting is about measuring items in financial statements, you might find this omission rather odd given the importance of employees to the success or failure of a business. However, it is important to remember that Albert Einstein's famous dictum is just as applicable to accounting as it is to many other disciplines: 'Not everything that can be counted counts. Not everything that counts can be counted.'

WHY IS THIS RELEVANT TO ME?   The limitations of accounting information

To enable you as a business professional and user of accounting information to:

- Gain an awareness of the aspects of business performance that accounting does not cover
- Appreciate the limitations of accounting and accounting information
- Understand that accounting and accounting information will not necessarily provide you with all the information you need to make decisions

---

SUMMARY OF KEY CONCEPTS   Certain you can state the limitations of accounting and accounting information? Check your knowledge of these limitations with Summary of key concepts 1.10.

Why is accounting relevant to me?

This chapter has considered accounting information and its role in decision making, along with the two branches of accounting and how they present information that is useful to users. As a result of reading this far, you should now have some idea of why accounting is relevant not just to accountants but to all people concerned with business. In this section, we will consider how a knowledge of accounting is a key ingredient to a successful career in business and how a lack of this knowledge will seriously hinder your progress.

As we saw earlier, information generated by the accounting system is the bedrock on which all business decisions are built. Business decisions are governed by the monetary or other measurable effect that those decisions will have in the future, whether they will result in profits or losses for organisations, whether investments will generate increased sales and whether entities will be able to generate the cash they need to survive.

Employees' performance assessments and rewards will also be based upon accounting measures. Thus, the pay of sales staff will be linked to the monetary value of the sales they generate. Companies that reward their workers on the basis of what they produce will use accounting information to determine levels of production and hence levels of pay. Bonuses for production staff will be calculated on the degree to which they exceed certain levels of production in a given time period. In the same way, bonuses for management will be determined on the basis of achieving higher levels of profits and exceeding key performance indicators. All this information for deciding on levels of reward is based upon information produced by the accounting system. However you look at it, accounting is going to have a very big impact upon the organisations in which you work and the rewards you gain from your employment.

Accounting has been called the language of business (Michael Jones: *Accounting*, John Wiley & Sons, 2013, page 2). It is worth exploring this analogy further. When you visit a foreign country, it is always helpful to know some of the language so that you can communicate with local people. If you do not know the language and you are unwilling to learn it you are soon cut off from others. This may not be a problem if you are returning to the UK within a week or so, but if you are staying for the long term you will soon become very isolated. In the same way, if you do not learn about and understand the basics of accounting, you will become isolated in business. You will thus not be able to:

- Communicate fully with other members of the organisation
- Understand accounting reports put in front of you
- Draw up financial plans for the future

- Prepare simple reports to evaluate performance and outcomes
- Understand the financial effects of decisions made
- Check and evaluate the accuracy of what you are being told
- Understand how the figures you are presented with have been put together, what they are telling you and the limitations of the information given
- Provide potential employers with the full range of skills needed for a successful career in business
- Rise up the career ladder in your organisation as you lack the fully rounded business personality that employers require in their high level employees

Thus, a full understanding of business requires you to understand all the different aspects of the commercial world, not just your own particular specialism. Therefore, knowledge of accounting will be essential to the ultimate success of your career in business.

WHY IS THIS RELEVANT TO ME?   Knowledge of accounting

- To enable you as a business professional to appreciate the all-pervading role that accounting plays in the workings of business
- To encourage you to get to grips with accounting now so that you can use this knowledge to your benefit later on in your studies and in your career

CHAPTER SUMMARY

You should now have learnt that:

- Accounting summarises numerical data relating to past events and presents this data as information to managers and other interested parties as a basis for both decision making and control purposes
- Accounting information is the bedrock upon which all business decisions are based
- Useful accounting information possesses the characteristics of relevance, reliability, comparability and understandability
- Financial accounting is prepared for users external to the business
- Financial accounting information is used by shareholders, employees, lenders, suppliers, customers, governments and the public as a basis for making economic decisions
- Management accounting is prepared for internal users in a business to help them manage the business's activities
- Accounting does not measure, among other things, quality, pollution, social and environmental damage, human resources and the skills and knowledge base of organisations
- A knowledge of accounting is essential to the success of any career in business

END-OF-CHAPTER QUESTIONS

Solutions to these questions can be found at the back of the book from page 410.

> *Develop your understanding*

Question 1.1

What accounting and other information would the managers of the following organisations require in order to assess their performance and financial position?

• A charity

• A secondary school

• A university

• A manufacturing business

Question 1.2

A premier league football club has received an offer for its star striker from Real Madrid. The star striker is eager to leave and join the Spanish team and the board of directors has reluctantly agreed to let him go for the transfer fee offered. The team now needs a new striker and the manager has been put in charge of identifying potential new centre forwards that the club could bid for. You have been asked by the manager to draw up a chart listing the numerical information about potential targets that the manager should take into account when evaluating possible replacements.

The statement of financial position

LEARNING OUTCOMES

Once you have read this chapter and worked through the questions and examples in both this chapter and the online workbook, you should be able to:

- Define assets and liabilities
- Determine whether an entity should or should not recognise specific resources and obligations on its statement of financial position
- Distinguish between non-current and current assets and liabilities
- State the accounting equation
- Draw up a statement of financial position for organisations in compliance with the International Accounting Standards Board's requirements
- Explain how assets and liabilities are measured in monetary amounts at the statement of financial position date
- State what the statement of financial position does and does not show
- Understand how transactions affect two or more accounts on the statement of financial position
- Correctly record the effect of transactions on the assets, liabilities and equity in the statement of financial position

Introduction

All financial statements contain a statement of financial position. This is a summary, in money terms, of the assets an organisation controls and the liabilities an organisation owes to outside parties. Illustration 2.1 shows the statement of financial position of Bunns the Bakers plc, a regional baker with a bakery and 20 shops in the East Midlands. At first glance, this might look complicated as there are all kinds of seemingly complex words and jargon. However, don't worry as, after working your way through this chapter and the materials in the online workbook, you will soon have a much clearer idea of what the words and jargon mean.

Notice that there are various headings provided and that these headings contain the words 'assets', 'liabilities' and 'equity'. In this chapter we will be looking at what constitutes an asset and a liability and how equity is calculated. We shall also review the criteria for recognising assets and liabilities and how those assets and liabilities are classified as current or non-current. Just as assets and liabilities can be recognised in an organisation's statement of financial position so, once assets have been used up or liabilities discharged, they are derecognised. This just means that they are removed from the statement of financial position as they are no longer controlled or owed by the entity.

Once the definitions are clear, we shall move on to constructing simple statements of financial position from given data. We shall then consider what the statement of financial position shows us and, equally importantly, what it does not show us. There are many misconceptions about what a statement of financial position represents. This chapter will dispel these misconceptions and provide you with a very precise idea of what the statement of financial position provides by way of information and what it does not.

Finally, at the end of the chapter, we will have a quick look at how new transactions affect the statement of financial position. Double entry bookkeeping is not dealt with in any depth or detail in this book, but a quick appreciation of how this works will give you an insight into the logic of accounting and how new transactions have a two-fold effect on figures in the statement of financial position.

Terminology: statement of financial position/balance sheet

International Financial Reporting Standards use the term statement of financial position for what has traditionally been called the balance sheet. In keeping with the international focus of this book, the term statement of financial position will be used throughout. However, you will find the two terms used interchangeably in your wider reading, so you should understand that the terms balance sheet and statement of financial position refer to the same summary statement of assets, liabilities and equity.

Illustration 2.1 Bunns the Bakers plc: statement of financial position at 31 March 2016

	2016	2015
	£000	£000
Assets		
Non-current assets		
Intangible assets	50	55
Property, plant and equipment	11,750	11,241
Investments	65	59
	11,865	11,355
Current assets		
Inventories	60	55
Trade and other receivables	62	75
Cash and cash equivalents	212	189
	334	319
Total assets	12,199	11,674
Liabilities		
Current liabilities		
Current portion of long-term borrowings	300	300
Trade and other payables	390	281
Current tax liabilities	150	126
	840	707
Non-current liabilities		
Long-term borrowings	2,700	3,000
Long-term provisions	200	200
	2,900	3,200
Total liabilities	3,740	3,907
Net assets	8,459	7,767
Equity		
Called up share capital (£1 ordinary shares)	2,500	2,400
Share premium	1,315	1,180
Retained earnings	4,644	4,187
Total equity	8,459	7,767

GO BACK OVER THIS AGAIN! A copy of this statement of financial position is available in the **online workbook**: you might like to keep this on screen or print off a copy for easy reference while you work your way through the material in this chapter. There is also an annotated copy of this statement of financial position in the **online workbook** to go over the relevant points again to reinforce your knowledge and learning.

Assets

Illustration 2.1 shows you the statement of financial position for Bunns the Bakers plc. As noted in the introduction, the first part of this statement of financial position shows you the assets that an entity controls. However, the first questions to ask are: 'What is an asset?' and 'What does an asset represent?'

The International Accounting Standards Board's *Framework for the Preparation and Presentation of Financial Statements* provides the following definition of an asset:

> A resource controlled by the entity as a result of past events and from which future economic benefits are expected to flow to the entity.
>
> Source: (IASB Framework, paragraph 49(a))

This sounds complicated. However, once we consider the words carefully and analyse what they mean, we will find that this definition is actually very simple and presents a very clear set of criteria to determine whether an asset exists or not. So what does this definition tell you? Let's look at the key points:

- Control: the resource is owned or leased (rented) by an organisation: a resource is controlled by an entity when it can legally prevent everyone else from using that resource.

- As a result of past events: to gain control of a resource it is likely that a contract has been signed transferring or granting the right to use that resource to the current owner and money has been paid to other parties in exchange for the transfer or rights to use that resource.

- Future economic benefits: the resource will be used within a business to generate cash and profit from the sale of goods or services to other persons.

From this definition it follows that an asset represents a store of future economic benefits, the ability to use the asset to generate cash and profit for a business.

EXAMPLE 2.1

How does this work in practice? Let us take the example of Bunns the Bakers. The company bought a city centre shop from a property developer ten years ago for £500,000, with both the seller and the buyer of the shop signing a contract transferring legal title in the shop to Bunns the Bakers. The shop sells bread, cakes, hot and cold snacks, drinks and sandwiches. Does this constitute an asset of the business? Applying our criteria above:

- Do Bunns the Bakers *control* the shop (the resource)? Yes: the company *owns* the shop and, by virtue of the contract signed at the time the shop was purchased from the property developer, Bunns the Bakers can go to court to assert their legal rights to the shop and to prevent anyone else from using that shop for their own purposes.

- Is there *a past event*? Yes: Bunns the Bakers' representatives signed the contract and paid £500,000, so this is the *past event* giving rise to the resource (the shop).

- Will *future economic benefits* flow to the company? Yes: Bunns the Bakers is using the shop to sell goods produced by the company and bought in from suppliers to customers in order to generate cash and profits from those sales.

Thus, the shop represents an asset to the business as it meets the IASB criteria for recognition of an asset.

You can also view the shop as a store of future economic benefits for Bunns the Bakers. The company can continue to use the shop to make sales, profits and cash into the future. Alternatively, that store of future economic benefits could be realised by selling the shop to another company. This would still generate future economic benefits as the sale of the shop would release the cash (= the economic benefits) tied up in that shop. Even if Bunns the Bakers did not sell the shop but chose to rent it out to another party, the shop would still represent future economic benefits as monthly rental payments would be received in cash from the person renting the shop.

Assets: reliable monetary measurement

Our definition of what constitutes an asset now seems very clear. However, there is one further barrier to cross before an asset can be recognised in the statement of financial position. The IASB has laid down the rule that an asset can only be recognised in the statement of financial position when the cost of that asset can be measured reliably in monetary terms. Can the cost of the shop be measured reliably in monetary terms? Yes, as the cost of the shop was £500,000 this is a reliable monetary measurement and so the shop can be recognised in Bunns the Bakers' statement of financial position as an asset.

Asset recognition: summary of the steps to follow

Diagrammatically, the steps to follow to determine whether an asset can be recognised on the statement of financial position are shown in Figure 2.1.

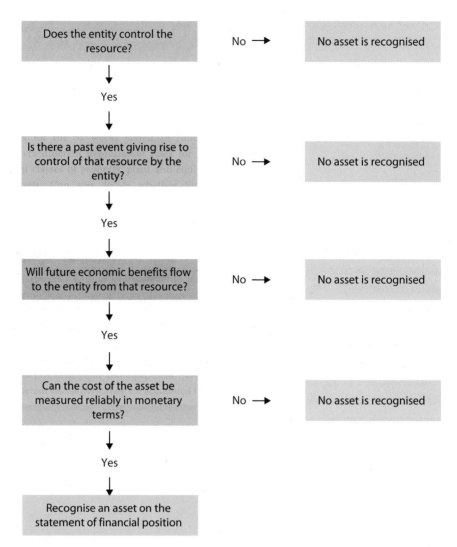

Figure 2.1 Steps in determining whether an asset can be recognised on the statement of financial position or not

WHY IS THIS RELEVANT TO ME? Definitions: assets

To enable you as a business professional and user of accounting information to:

• Understand what assets on the statement of financial position actually represent

• Understand the strict criteria that must be met before an asset can be recognised on the statement of financial position

• Provide you with the necessary tools to determine whether an asset should be recognised on the statement of financial position or not

SUMMARY OF KEY CONCEPTS   Convinced that you can define an asset? Revise this definition with Summary of key concepts 2.1 to reinforce your knowledge.

GO BACK OVER THIS AGAIN!   Sure that you have grasped the asset recognition criteria? Go to the **online workbook** Exercises 2.1 to make sure you understand how the asset recognition criteria are used in practice.

Assets in the statement of financial position

Now we have found out what assets are and the criteria for their recognition, let's look again at the statement of financial position of Bunns the Bakers plc to see what sort of assets a company might own and recognise.

Illustration 2.1 shows that Bunns the Bakers has two types of assets, non-current assets and current assets. Non-current assets are split into intangible assets, property plant and equipment and investments. Current assets are split into inventories, trade and other receivables and cash and cash equivalents. Total assets are calculated by adding together non-current and current assets as shown in Figure 2.2. What is the distinction between current and non-current assets? Let us look in more detail at these two types of assets and then the categorisation of assets as non-current or current will readily become apparent.

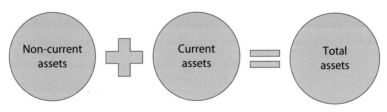

Figure 2.2 Diagram showing the calculation of total assets

Non-current assets

Non-current assets are those assets that are:

- Not purchased for resale in the normal course of business: this means that the assets are retained within the business for periods of more than one year and are not acquired with the intention of reselling them immediately or in the near future.
- Held for long-term use in the business to produce goods or services.

An example of a non-current asset would be the shop we considered earlier. This shop was not purchased with the intention of reselling it, but is held within the business for the long-term purpose of selling bakery goods to customers over many years.

SUMMARY OF KEY CONCEPTS   Totally confident that you can define non-current assets? Revise this definition with Summary of key concepts 2.2 to check your understanding.

Intangible assets are those assets that have no material substance (you cannot touch them). Examples of such assets would be purchased goodwill, patents, trademarks and intellectual property rights. Tangible assets are those assets that do have a material substance (you can touch them) and examples of these would be land and buildings, machinery, vehicles and fixtures and fittings.

Intangible assets are represented on Bunns the Bakers' statement of financial position in Illustration 2.1 and these probably relate to trademarks for the company's products. You would, however, need to consult the notes to the accounts to find out precisely what assets were represented by these figures, as shown in Give me an example 2.1.

GIVE ME AN EXAMPLE 2.1   Intangible assets

Premier Foods plc is the owner of some of the best known grocery brands in the UK, with Mr Kipling, Sharwoods and Oxo among them. On its statement of financial position at 4 April 2015 the company records an amount of £528.4 million under the heading 'Other intangible assets'. The reader of the report and accounts is then referred to Note 14 for further information. Note 14 shows that the intangible assets recognised are Software and Licences at £43.1 million, Brands, Trademarks and Licences at £474.2 million and Assets under Construction at £11.1 million.

Source: *Premier Foods annual report and accounts for the financial period ended 4 April 2015* www.premierfoods.co.uk

---

Property, plant and equipment represents the tangible assets of the business. As this is a bakery retail business, these tangible assets will consist of shops, bakeries, delivery vans, counters, tills and display cabinets in the shops and any other necessary non-current, long-term assets that the company requires to conduct its business.

Investments are just that: holdings of shares or other financial assets (such as loans to other entities) in other companies. These investments might be in companies that form part of the Bunns the Bakers group of companies or they could just as easily be long-term investments in non-group companies that are held in order to realise a long-term capital gain when they are eventually sold.

GO BACK OVER THIS AGAIN!   Do you think you can distinguish between intangible non-current assets, property, plant and equipment and investments? Go to the **online workbook** and complete Exercises 2.2 to make sure you can make these distinctions.

GIVE ME AN EXAMPLE 2.2   Non-current assets

What other categories of non-current assets do companies present in their financial statements? The consolidated balance sheet (= statement of financial position) at 31 December 2014 for Rolls-Royce Holdings plc shows the following non-current assets.

	31 December	
	2014	**2013**
Non-current assets	£m	£m
Intangible assets	4,804	4,987
Property, plant and equipment	3,446	3,392
Investments – joint ventures and associates	539	601
Investments – other	31	27
Other financial assets	107	674
Deferred tax assets	369	316
Post-retirement scheme surpluses	1,740	248
	11,036	10,245

Source: *Rolls-Royce Holdings annual report 2014* www.rolls-royce.com

Current assets

Current assets, by contrast, are short-term assets that are constantly changing. On Bunns the Bakers' statement of financial position the following items are found:

- **Inventory**: inventory is another word for stock of goods. Inventory represents goods held for production or sale. As Bunns the Bakers is a baker, inventories held for production will consist of raw materials such as flour, sugar, eggs and other bakery ingredients. As such raw materials deteriorate rapidly, these inventories will be used and replaced on a regular basis as bakery activity takes place, goods are produced, delivered to the shops and sold to the public. Inventory goods for sale might be bread and cakes produced today and held in cool storage ready for next day delivery to the shops. All inventories thus represent potential cash that will be generated from the production and sales of goods.

- Trade and other receivables: where organisations make their sales on credit terms to customers, customers are given time in which to pay so that the money due from these customers is recognised as money receivable. A moment's thought will convince you that, as Bunns the Bakers sells food products to the public for cash, there will be very few trade receivables. Any trade receivables that there are might arise from a business-to-business contract to supply large quantities of goods to another retailer such as a supermarket. As well as small amounts of trade receivables from such contracts, the company will also have other amounts receivable such as tax refunds or amounts paid in advance for services that have yet to be provided (these are called prepayments—see Chapter 3 for a detailed discussion of prepayments). While trade and other receivables represent the right to cash in the future, they are not cash yet and so are recognised in this separate category of current assets. You will find some sets of accounts that refer to trade and other receivables as debtors.

- Cash and cash equivalents: this category of current assets comprises of amounts of cash held in tills at the end of the year, cash held in the company's current account at the bank and cash held in short-term deposit accounts with bankers and other financial institutions.

MULTIPLE CHOICE QUESTIONS   Reckon that you can distinguish between different types of current assets? Go to the **online workbook** and have a go at Multiple choice questions 2.1 to make sure you can make these distinctions.

GIVE ME AN EXAMPLE 2.3   Current assets

What other categories of current assets do companies present in their financial statements? The consolidated balance sheet (= statement of financial position) at 31 December 2014 of Nestlé shows the following current assets.

	31 December	
	2014	2013
Current assets	CHFm	CHFm
Cash and cash equivalents	7,448	6,415
Short-term investments	1,433	638
Inventories	9,172	8,382
Trade and other receivables	13,459	12,206
Prepayments and accrued income	565	762

→

	31 December	
	2014	**2013**
Derivative assets	400	230
Current income tax assets	908	1,151
Assets held for sale	576	282
Total current assets	33,961	30,066

Source: *Nestlé financial statements 2014* www.nestle.com

The distinction between non-current and current assets

The distinction between non-current and current assets comes down to one of time. As we have seen, non-current assets are held by businesses to provide benefits in accounting periods exceeding one year. On the other hand, current assets are held only for a short time in order to produce goods to be sold to convert into cash which can then be used to buy in more raw materials to produce more goods to convert into more cash in a short but constantly repeating trading cycle.

However, to decide whether a resource is a non-current or current asset it is also important to determine the business in which an entity is engaged. For example, you might think that a car would be a non-current asset in any business, an asset to be used for the long term. But if that car is parked on the premises of a motor trader, is this car an item of inventory, held in stock for resale, a car owned by the motor trading business for long-term use in the business or the property of a member of staff who drives to work each day (and so not a business asset at all)? Further enquiries would have to be made to determine whether the car is a business asset and, if it is, the exact statement of financial position classification of this vehicle.

WHY IS THIS RELEVANT TO ME?   Non-current and current assets

To enable you as a business professional and user of accounting information to:

- Appreciate the different types of assets entities recognise on their statement of financial position
- Distinguish between the two types of assets
- Use the different types of assets in evaluating entities' efficiency and working capital management (discussed in further detail in Chapters 6 and 7)

GO BACK OVER THIS AGAIN! How easily can you distinguish between current and non-current assets? Go to the **online workbook** Exercises 2.3 to make sure you can make this distinction.

2

Liabilities

Liabilities appear lower down the statement of financial position and represent amounts that are owed to parties outside the business. As with assets, the first questions to ask are: 'What is a liability?' and 'What does a liability represent?'

The International Accounting Standards Board's *Framework for the Preparation and Presentation of Financial Statements* provides the following definition of a liability:

> A present obligation of an entity arising from past events, the settlement of which is expected to result in an outflow from the entity of resources embodying economic benefits.
>
> Source: (IASB Framework, paragraph 49(b))

While this definition again might seem complex, your experience gained in unravelling the meaning of the definition of assets above will certainly help you in understanding the various terms employed here. To put it simply, liabilities are the contractual or legal claims of outside parties against an entity. These contractual or legal claims may be short term (current liabilities) or long term (non-current liabilities). Again, let's break down this definition into its constituent parts in order to enable us to apply it in determining whether an entity has a liability or not:

- Present obligation: the obligation must exist at the financial year end date in order for any liability arising under that obligation to be recognised in the statement of financial position. Therefore, entities cannot recognise just any liability that they think they might incur at any time in the future. The event giving rise to the obligation must have taken place by the statement of financial position date to enable the entity to recognise that liability.

- Arising from past events: to give rise to an obligation, it is likely that a contract has been signed agreeing to pay for goods delivered but not yet paid for from a supplier or to take out a loan or an overdraft at the bank that will have to be repaid at some point in the future.

- Economic benefits: the obligation will result in the entity transferring cash to an outside party in order to settle the liability or, possibly, transferring other assets by way of settlement.

Importantly, the obligation must be unavoidable: if the entity can avoid transferring cash or other economic benefits then there is no obligation and no liability exists.

Interestingly, the IASB framework is not as strict in applying the 'reliable measurement in monetary terms' requirement to liabilities as it is in applying this criterion to the recognition of assets. If it is not possible to make a reliable monetary measurement of a liability, the best estimate of that liability is recognised. Thus, the criteria for asset recognition are rather stricter in this respect than the requirements for liability recognition.

EXAMPLE 2.2

How does liability recognition work in practice? Let us take the example of Bunns the Bakers above. When the company bought the city centre shop from the property developer ten years ago, the purchase was financed by a loan from the bank of £500,000. This loan is currently repayable in full in 15 years' time. Does this loan constitute a liability of the business? Applying our criteria above:

- Does Bunns the Bakers have a present obligation at the statement of financial position date? Yes: the loan exists and is outstanding at the current year end. The obligating event (taking out the loan) had taken place by the statement of financial position date.

- Is the obligation to repay the loan unavoidable? Yes: the bank will hold signed documentation from the company agreeing that the loan was taken out and there will be entries in the relevant account at the bank and in bank statements to show the loan being received by the company. Should the company try to avoid repaying the loan, the bank will be able to enforce its legal rights against the company for repayment of the loan.

- Is there a past event giving rise to the obligation? Yes: a loan agreement was signed by Bunns the Bakers at the time the loan was taken out and the money transferred to the company with which to buy the shop.

- Will there be an outflow from Bunns the Bakers of resources embodying economic benefits? Yes: the company will have to transfer cash to settle the obligation. If the company is unable to meet the obligation in cash, the bank will accept the shop as a suitable substitute for repayment of the loan. The shop embodies economic benefits as we saw above, so taking the shop instead of repayment will still be a transfer of economic benefits.

- Is the liability measurable in monetary terms? Yes: the loan is measured at £500,000 as a result of the cash transferred and this is a reliable measurement rather than a best estimate as the obligation due to the bank is clearly known.

Thus, the loan represents a liability of the business as it meets the IASB criteria for recognition of a liability.

Liability recognition: summary of the steps to follow

Diagrammatically, the steps to follow to determine whether a liability should be recognised on the statement of financial position are shown in Figure 2.3.

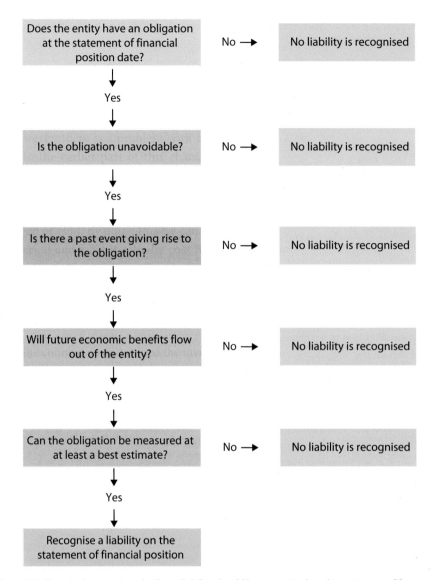

Figure 2.3 Steps in determining whether a liability should be recognised on the statement of financial position or not

---

WHY IS THIS RELEVANT TO ME?   Liabilities

To enable you as a business professional and user of accounting information to:

- Understand what liabilities on the statement of financial position actually represent
- Understand the strict criteria that must be met before a liability can be recognised on the statement of financial position
- Provide you with the necessary tools to determine whether a liability should be recognised on the statement of financial position or not

Liabilities in the statement of financial position

Now that we have considered what the term 'liabilities' means and the criteria for li-ability recognition in the statement of financial position, let us look again at the state-ment of financial position of Bunns the Bakers plc in Illustration 2.1 to consider what sort of liabilities a company might recognise.

Liabilities, just as in the case of assets, are split into non-current and current. Total liabilities are calculated by adding current and non-current liabilities together, as shown in Figure 2.4.

Non-current liabilities are long-term liabilities that the entity will only have to meet in more than one year's time while current liabilities will have to be paid within the course of the next year. Current liabilities are not due on the day immediately after the statement of financial position date but they will be due for settlement over the course of the next 12 months.

Current liabilities

Just as with current assets, current liabilities are short-term liabilities that are con-stantly changing. Looking at Bunns the Bakers' statement of financial position the fol-lowing liabilities are shown:

- Current portion of long-term borrowings: these are the loan instalments due to be repaid to lenders within the next 12 months.

Figure 2.4 Diagram showing the calculation of total liabilities

- Trade and other payables: any organisation that is involved in business will trade on credit with their suppliers, ordering goods that are delivered but not paid for immediately. Customers then either use the goods received to produce more goods to sell to the public and businesses or just resell those goods. Suppliers are paid from the proceeds of the sales of goods produced or resold. Normal trading terms are that suppliers are (usually) paid within 30 days of receipt of goods by the customer. Clearly, suppliers will not wait a long time for payment for goods delivered as they have their own suppliers and employees to pay. Therefore, suppliers will expect their cash to be returned to them quickly so trade and other payables are short-term, current liabilities. In the case of Bunns the Bakers, trade payables will consist of amounts of money owed to suppliers for flour, eggs, sugar, salt and other bakery ingredients as well as services provided by, for example, their legal advisors or their accountants.

- Current tax liabilities: Bunns the Bakers plc has made a profit over the course of the year. This profit is subject to tax and the tax liability on this year's profit is recognised as an obligation on the statement of financial position. The government will want the tax due reasonably quickly so that it can meet its own obligations to provide services to the public and contribute to the running of government departments so this, too, is a short-term, current liability.

Non-current liabilities

On Bunns the Bakers' statement of financial position, the following non-current liabilities are represented:

- Long-term borrowings: these are loans and other finance provided by lenders to finance the long-term non-current assets of the business. In the case of Bunns the Bakers, these could be loans used to finance the acquisition of shops (as in Example 2.2 in this chapter), the building of a new state of the art bakery or the purchase of new plant and equipment with which to produce goods. Other companies may take out loans to finance the acquisition of other companies. Long-term borrowings are repayable in accounting periods beyond the next 12 months.

- Long-term provisions: these are liabilities that the entity knows it must meet but which will not be due in the next accounting period but in accounting periods beyond the next 12 months. An example of such a long-term provision would be deferred taxation, but this is a very technical subject that is beyond the scope of this book.

GIVE ME AN EXAMPLE 2.4   Non-current and current liabilities

What other categories of non-current and current liabilities do companies present in their financial statements? The consolidated balance sheet (= statement of financial position) at 31 December 2014 of Persimmon plc shows the following non-current and current liabilities.

	31 December	
	2014	**2013**
Non-current liabilities	£m	£m
Trade and other payables	265.3	163.7
Deferred tax liabilities	17.8	22.4
Partnership liability	47.4	50.1
Retirement benefit obligations	0.5	–
	331.0	236.2
Current liabilities	£m	£m
Trade and other payables	731.5	637.9
Partnership liability	5.3	5.3
Current tax liabilities	95.9	98.0
	832.7	741.2
Total liabilities	1,163.7	977.4

Source: Persimmon Plc. Annual Report http://corporate.persimmonhomes.com/

WHY IS THIS RELEVANT TO ME?   Current and non-current liabilities

To enable you as a business professional and user of accounting information to:

- Appreciate the different types of liabilities an entity recognises on its statement of financial position
- Distinguish between the two types of liabilities
- Use the different types of liabilities in assessing an entity's financial position, short-term liquidity and long-term solvency (discussed in further detail in Chapter 7)

GO BACK OVER THIS AGAIN!   Quite convinced that you can distinguish between current and non-current liabilities? Go to the **online workbook** Exercises 2.5 to make sure you can make this distinction.

The accounting equation

Before we think about the third element on Bunns the Bakers' statement of financial position, equity, we need to think about the accounting equation. Looking at the statement of financial position, we notice that the net assets and the total equity are the same figure. What does this tell us about the relationship between the assets, liabilities and equity in an entity? From this observation, we can draw up the following equations that express the link between the three elements in the statement of financial position:

Either

Total assets = total liabilities + equity

Or:

Total assets − total liabilities = equity

Equity is thus the difference between the total assets (the sum of the current and non-current assets) and the total liabilities (the sum of the current and non-current liabilities). As the two equations add to the same figure, the statement of financial position is said to balance.

WHY IS THIS RELEVANT TO ME? **The accounting equation**

To enable you as a business professional and user of accounting information to:

- Appreciate how the two halves of the statement of financial position balance
- Balance your own statements of financial position when you draw these up in the future

SUMMARY OF KEY CONCEPTS Can you state the accounting equation? Revise this equation with Summary of key concepts 2.4.

Equity

The International Accounting Standards Board defines equity as follows:

The residual interest in the assets of the entity after deducting all its liabilities.

Source: (IASB Framework, paragraph 49(c))

This is exactly the same as the accounting equation above that says assets − liabilities = equity. In theory, equity represents the amount that owners of the entity should receive if the assets were all sold and the liabilities were all settled at their statement of financial position amounts. The cash received from these asset sales less payments made to discharge liabilities would belong to the owners and they would receive this cash on the winding up of the business.

The components of equity

1. Limited companies and public limited companies (plcs)

Bunns the Bakers' equity is made up of the following elements:

(a) Called up share capital: this is the number of shares issued multiplied by the par value (face value) of each share.

(b) Share premium: where each share is issued for an amount greater than its par value, then any amount in excess of par value is entered into the share premium account (we shall be looking at how share capital and share premium are determined in much greater detail in Chapter 5).

(c) Retained earnings: these are profits that the business has earned in past accounting periods that have not been distributed to shareholders as dividends.

You will see many company statements of financial position in practice that have many different accounts (other reserves) under the equity heading. Many of these accounts arise from statutory requirements governing transactions entered into by the company and, due to their specialised nature, consideration of these accounts does not form part of this book. However, when you come across these accounts at later stages of your studies and during your career in business, you should be aware that these accounts exist and form part of equity. The basic calculation of equity for limited companies and plcs is shown in Figure 2.5.

GIVE ME AN EXAMPLE 2.5   Equity

The consolidated balance sheet (= statement of financial position) of First Group plc at 31 March 2015 provides an illustration of the many different accounts that can make up equity.

	31 March	
	2015	2014
Equity	£m	£m
Share capital	60.2	60.2
Share premium	676.4	676.4
Hedging reserve	(55.5)	7.8
Other reserves	4.6	4.6

→

	31 March	
	2015	**2014**
Own shares	(1.9)	(1.8)
Translation reserve	241.7	17.8
Retained earnings	533.1	446.4
	1,458.6	1,211.4

Source: *First Group annual report and accounts for the year ended 31 March 2015* www.firstgroupplc.com

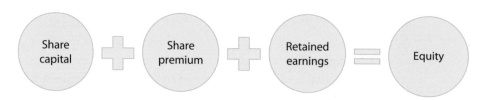

Figure 2.5 Diagram showing the calculation of equity in limited companies and plcs

2. Sole traders and unincorporated entities

Not all businesses are incorporated as limited companies. Such businesses do not, therefore, have issued share capital, but they still have an equity section. For sole traders and unincorporated entities, this is called the capital account. This comprises of the following headings:

(a) Capital at the start of the year: this is the capital account balance at the end of the previous accounting period. At the beginning of the first accounting period, the first year of trading, the balance at the start of the year is £nil.

(b) Capital introduced: this is the owner's own money that has been introduced into the business during the current accounting period.

(c) Retained profits for the year: any profit retained in the business during the year is added to the capital account as this profit belongs to the business's owner.

(d) Capital withdrawn: the business's owner will draw money out of the business to meet personal rather than business expenses during the year. This is treated as a repayment of part of the capital of the business to the owner. These withdrawals of capital are called drawings and are a deduction from the capital account. This is an application of the business entity convention that states that the business and its owner(s) are totally separate individuals. Only business transactions are included in the financial statements of the business with any non-business, personal transactions excluded.

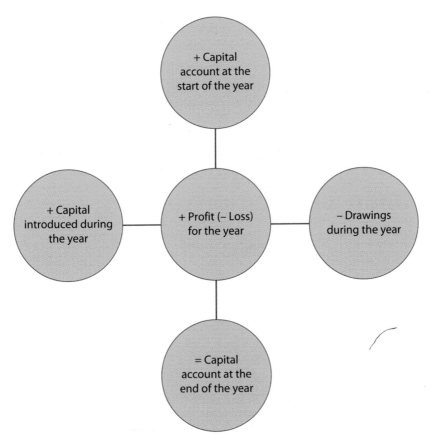

Figure 2.6 Diagram showing the calculation of the capital account for sole traders and unincorporated entities

Just as in the case of limited companies and plcs, the amount in the capital account is the amount that would, in theory, be paid out to the owner(s) of the business if all the assets of the business were sold at the amounts in the statement of financial position and all the liabilities of the business were settled at their statement of financial position amounts. The calculation of the capital account (equity) for sole traders and unincorporated entities is shown in Figure 2.6.

WHY IS THIS RELEVANT TO ME?   **Equity and the components of equity**

To enable you as a business professional and user of accounting information to:

- Understand that equity is the difference between an entity's total assets and total liabilities
- Appreciate the different components of equity in incorporated and unincorporated businesses
- Distinguish elements of equity from assets and liabilities

MULTIPLE CHOICE QUESTIONS Confident that you could calculate the equity of a business from a given set of information? Go to the **online workbook** and have a go at Multiple choice questions 2.2 to make sure you can make these calculations.

SUMMARY OF KEY CONCEPTS Sure you can state the components of equity? Revise these components with Summary of key concepts 2.5 and 2.6.

Drawing up the statement of financial position

We now know what assets and liabilities are and how they relate to equity, but what steps should we follow in drawing up the statement of financial position? This section provides a step-by-step approach to preparing the statement of financial position from the account balances at the end of the financial year.

EXAMPLE 2.3

The following is a list of balances for Misfits Limited at 31 December 2016. You are required to draw up the statement of financial position from this list of balances.

Illustration 2.2 Misfits Limited: account balances at 31 December 2016

	£000
Trade receivables	2,000
Trade payables	1,500
Bank loan repayable 31 December 2022	10,000
Bank overdraft	200
Land and buildings	15,000
Trademarks	1,000
Fixtures and fittings	2,500
Share capital	1,800
Retained earnings	7,500
Share premium	2,300
Inventories	2,750
Cash in the tills	50

Guidelines on the approach to adopt in drawing up the statement of financial position

1. First, decide whether each of the balances is an asset, a liability or an element of equity.

2. Once you have categorised the balances, think about whether the assets and liabilities are current or non-current.

3. Some of the balances might need adding together to produce one figure in the statement of financial position. For example, there might be cash in hand or in the safe, cash in the bank current account and cash on deposit in an investment account at the bank. All of these balances would be added together and shown as one figure for cash and cash equivalents.

4. Once you have made all your decisions, slot the figures into the relevant headings (use the headings in Illustration 2.1, adding any additional headings you might need and removing headings you do not need), add it all up and it should balance.

Illustration 2.3 Misfits Limited: statement of financial position at 31 December 2016

	£000	Note
Assets		
Non-current assets		
Intangible assets	1,000	1
Property, plant and equipment	17,500	2
	18,500	3
Current assets		
Inventories	2,750	4
Trade receivables	2,000	4
Cash and cash equivalents	50	4
	4,800	5
Total assets	23,300	6

→

	£000	Note
Liabilities		
Current liabilities		
Bank overdraft (you could call this short-term borrowings)	200	7
Trade payables	1,500	7
	1,700	8
Non-current liabilities		
Bank loan (you could call this long-term borrowings)	10,000	7
Total liabilities	11,700	9
Net assets (total assets – total liabilities)	11,600	10
Equity		
Called up share capital	1,800	11
Share premium	2,300	11
Retained earnings	7,500	11
Total equity	11,600	12

Notes to the above statement of financial position for Misfits Limited:

1. Trademarks are intangible assets, as we noted above.

2. Land and buildings and fixtures and fittings are both classified under the heading 'Property, plant and equipment'. The land and buildings are property and the fixtures and fittings are plant and equipment. £15,000,000 for the land and buildings + £2,500,000 for the fixtures and fittings give the total figure of £17,500,000 for Property, plant and equipment.

3. This is the total of the two non-current asset headings £1,000,000 + £17,500,000 = £18,500,000.

4. These figures are as given in the list of balances.

5. £4,800,000 is the total of all the current assets added together.

6. £23,300,000 is the total non-current assets of £18,500,000 added to the total current assets of £4,800,000 to give the figure for total assets.

7. These figures are as given in the list of balances. If you were in any doubt that the loan is a non-current liability, look at the date for repayment: 31 December 2022 is six years away from the current statement of financial position date so this liability is repayable more than 12 months after the statement of financial position date. Remember that current liabilities include all obligations payable within 12 months so that any liability payable after this is a non-current liability.

8. £1,700,000 is the total of the bank overdraft of £200,000 and of the trade payables of £1,500,000.

9. £11,700,000 is the total of the current liabilities of £1,700,000 and of the non-current liabilities of £10,000,000.

10. The figure for net assets is given by deducting the total liabilities figure of £11,700,000 from the total assets figure of £23,300,000 to give you net assets (total assets – total liabilities) of £11,600,000.

11. Called up share capital, Share premium and Retained earnings are all as given in the list of balances.

12. This is the total of the three elements of equity added together.

WHY IS THIS RELEVANT TO ME?   Drawing up the statement of financial position

To enable you as a business professional and user of accounting information to:

• Understand how the statement of financial position is put together from the balances at the year end date

• Draw up your own statements of financial position

SHOW ME HOW TO DO IT   Did you understand how Misfits Limited's statement of financial position was drawn up? View Video presentation 2.1 in the **online workbook** to see a practical demonstration of how this statement of financial position was put together.

NUMERICAL EXERCISES   Are you sure that you could draw up a statement of financial position from a list of year end balances? Go to the **online workbook** Numerical exercises 2.1 to practice this technique.

How are assets and liabilities valued?

Historic cost v. current value

How should we value assets and liabilities for inclusion in the statement of financial position? At their cost price? Selling price? Market value? Or some other amount?

Accounting has traditionally dictated that the value of all assets and liabilities recognised in the statement of financial position should be based on their original cost:

this is called the historic cost convention. Thus, for example, inventory is valued at its cost to the business, not its selling price or current market value, while trade payables are valued at their invoice amount and loans are valued at the amount borrowed less any repayments made.

However, this accounting convention has been relaxed over the past 40 years and entities are now allowed to value different classes of assets either at cost or at fair value. Fair value is equivalent to market value, the amount at which an asset could be sold or a liability settled in the open market. Although the cost or fair value option exists, organisations rarely choose the fair value alternative. The only class of assets that entities might wish to present at their fair value is land and buildings as these assets tend to rise in value over time. For all other assets and liabilities historic cost is preferred.

But there is one exception to this option. The International Accounting Standards Board has made market valuations mandatory for all investments held by organisations. This is often called the 'mark to market' approach to valuation of these assets.

A mixture of original cost and current valuation: problems

So, users can be presented with a mixture of assets at cost and at fair value. Does this failure to present all assets and liabilities consistently at fair/market values cause any problems for users of the statement of financial position?

Historic cost is seen as objective as it is verifiable by reference to a transaction at a fixed point in time. It is thus a reliable measure as it was determined by the market at the date of the transaction. With short-term current assets and liabilities this is not a problem as these assets and liabilities are, as we have seen, always changing and being replaced by new assets at more recent, up-to-date values. However, when long-term, non-current assets and liabilities are measured at historic cost these costs gradually become more and more out of date as time moves on. As a result, these costs become less and less relevant in decision making as the market moves forward and asset and loan values rise and fall in real terms with the onward march of the economy.

We will not consider this problem any further in this text, but it is a difficulty of which you should be aware. The cost v. fair/market value debate has been raging for well over a century and an acceptable solution is no nearer than it was when the problem was first pointed out. It is therefore going to be a continuing shortcoming of the statement of financial position for the indefinite future and a limitation that you will need to take into account whenever you are looking at these statements in your career in business.

WHY IS THIS RELEVANT TO ME?   Historic cost, valuation and market values

To enable you as a business professional and user of accounting information to:

• Understand the basis upon which the figures in the statement of financial position are determined

• Provide you with an awareness of the limitations of continuing to value non-current assets and liabilities at historic cost

• Appreciate that there are alternative valuation bases for non-current assets and liabilities, but that companies rarely make use of these alternatives

What does the statement of financial position show?

This leads us neatly on to a discussion of what the statement of financial position shows and what it does not show.

Put simply, the statement of financial position shows the financial situation of an entity on the last day of its accounting year. However, it is important to remember that the statement of financial position just shows the financial situation on that one day in the year and it is thus a snapshot of the entity at this one point in time. A totally different view would be shown if the picture were taken on any other day in the year. It is true to say that, at this one point in time, the statement of financial position does show the financially measurable resources (assets) and financially measurable obligations (liabilities) of the business in money terms, but this might seem to present a rather limited view.

In order to gain a better understanding of what the statement of financial position represents, it is useful to consider what the statement of financial position does not show.

What the statement of financial position does not show

The statement of financial position does not show:

• All the assets of the organisation. The statement of financial position does not include or value the most valuable assets of an organisation. These comprise the skills and knowledge of the employees, goodwill, brands, traditions and all the other intangible but impossible to value assets that make an organisation what it is. All entities are so much more than the sum of the financial assets and liabilities.

- All the liabilities of a business. There might be liabilities for damage caused to the environment or to consumers as a result of product liability legislation, claims for damages or breaches of contract, none of which have come to light by the year end date: as a result, they will not be reflected in the statement of financial position at the accounting year end.

- The market value of an entity. This is a common misconception about the statement of financial position. The monetary value of any entity is determined by the amount a third party would be willing to pay not only for all the known assets and liabilities but also for the unrecognised assets of the organisation noted above. However, the amount an outside party would be willing to pay will change on a daily basis as more information comes to light about hidden liabilities or the true value of assets or as the economy moves from a boom to a recession or vice versa.

You should therefore remember that what the statement of financial position does not recognise is just as or even more important than what it does include.

EXAMPLE 2.4

A moment's thought will show you that this is equally true of your own circumstances. You might know the monetary value of the cash you hold in various bank and savings accounts and you might have a collection of various assets such as a tablet, a mobile phone, digital music and clothing, all of which you could value in money terms. But these assets are not the sum total of what represents you. There are your friends, family, memories and achievements, none of which can be valued or quantified, but which are just as or even more important to you than those tangible items that can be given a monetary value. Give me an example 2.6 demonstrates this further.

GIVE ME AN EXAMPLE 2.6   The statement of financial position does not show the true value of an entity

Balfour Beatty plc's published report and accounts for the year ended 31 December 2013 showed a net assets (total assets less total liabilities) figure of £1.035 billion. In August 2014, Carillion plc made a bid for Balfour Beatty plc that valued the Balfour Beatty group of companies at £2.1 billion. Carillion plc was bidding not just for Balfour Beatty's net assets but also for their reputation, customer base, future contracts and workforce, all of which represent value over and above the value of the net assets.

Source: *Balfour Beatty's report and accounts for the year ended 31 December 2013* www.balfourbeatty.com/; *The Guardian 19 August 2014* www.theguardian.com/business/2014/aug/19/carillion-raises-balfour-beatty-merger-proposal

WHY IS THIS RELEVANT TO ME? What the statement of financial position shows and does not show

To enable you as a business professional and user of accounting information to:

- Appreciate the limitations of the monetary information presented in the statement of financial position

- Provide you with the necessary awareness of what the statement of financial position includes and does not include

- Make you aware that the statement of financial position will not provide all the answers needed to evaluate an entity's financial and economic position

- Think outside the parameters of the statement of financial position when assessing an entity's standing in the business world

GO BACK OVER THIS AGAIN! Do you think that you can say clearly what the statement of financial position does and does not show? Go to the **online workbook** Exercise 2.6 to test your knowledge of this area.

The dual aspect concept

The statement of financial position for Misfits Limited was drawn up from a list of balances at a given point in time. But businesses are not static and new transactions will change the figures on the statement of financial position as they occur. These transactions have an effect on two or more accounts and may cause the balances on those accounts to rise or fall as new assets or liabilities are created or as assets are used up or liabilities settled. Accountants describe this dual aspect as double entry and the entries to the accounts affected by transactions as debits and credits. You might prefer to think of these transactions as pluses and minuses or increases and decreases in the various accounts in the following examples and in the online workbook. We are not going to look at double entry in any great depth in this book and you will not need a detailed knowledge of double entry bookkeeping for your career in business. However, an awareness of accountants' terminology and what this means in practice will be useful to you.

As an example, think about how you would record the receipt of goods from a supplier that are to be paid for in 30 days' time. This receipt of goods will increase the inventory that is held by the business, but also increase the amounts owed to trade payables. If the goods were bought for cash, this would still increase the inventory but reduce the cash held in the bank account if the company has a positive balance in their account. In both of these examples, two accounts were affected, inventory and trade payables or cash.

The following examples will show you how the dual aspect concept works and how the statement of financial position will still balance after each transaction is completed.

EXAMPLE 2.5

Misfits Limited's statement of financial position at 31 December 2016 is reproduced below in the left hand column. On 2 January 2017 the company receives a £50,000 payment from one of its trade receivables. This payment is paid into the bank account. How would this transaction be recorded in the statement of financial position? Trade receivables go down by £50,000 as this receivable has paid what was owed. The money has been paid into the bank so the bank overdraft (money owed to the bank) also goes down as less money is now owed to the bank. Recording the transactions as follows gives us the new statement of financial position at 2 January 2017:

Illustration 2.4 Misfits Limited: the effect on the statement of financial position of cash received from a trade receivable

Misfits Limited	Statement of financial position at 31 December 2016	Increase (plus)	Decrease (minus)	Statement of financial position at 2 January 2017
Non-current assets	£000	£000	£000	£000
Intangible assets	1,000			1,000
Property, plant and equipment	17,500			17,500
	18,500			18,500
Current assets				
Inventories	2,750			2,750
Trade receivables	2,000		– 50	1,950
Cash and cash equivalents	50			50
	4,800			4,750
Total assets	23,300			23,250
Current liabilities				
Bank overdraft	200		– 50	150
Trade payables	1,500			1,500
	1,700			1,650
Non-current liabilities				
Bank loan	10,000			10,000
Total liabilities	11,700			11,650
Net assets	11,600			11,600

→

Misfits Limited	Statement of financial position at 31 December 2016	Increase (plus)	Decrease (minus)	Statement of financial position at 2 January 2017
	£000	£000	£000	£000
Equity				
Called up share capital	1,800			1,800
Share premium	2,300			2,300
Retained earnings	7,500			7,500
	11,600			11,600

Current assets have been reduced by £50,000 and current liabilities have been reduced by £50,000 so the statement of financial position still balances.

EXAMPLE 2.6

Let's try another example. On 3 January 2017, the company receives £100,000 of inventory from a supplier, the invoice to be paid in 30 days' time, and acquires a new piece of property, plant and equipment for £75,000 paid for from the bank. How will these transactions be shown in the statement of financial position? Illustration 2.5 shows the account headings affected.

Illustration 2.5 Misfits Limited: the effect on the statement of financial position of cash paid to buy new plant and equipment and inventory acquired on credit

Misfits Limited	Statement of financial position at 2 January 2017	Increase (plus)	Decrease (minus)	Statement of financial position at 3 January 2017
	£000	£000	£000	£000
Non-current assets				
Intangible assets	1,000			1,000
Property, plant and equipment	17,500	+ 75		17,575
	18,500			18,575
Current assets				
Inventories	2,750	+ 100		2,850
Trade receivables	1,950			1,950
Cash and cash equivalents	50			50
	4,750			4,850
Total assets	23,250			23,425

→

Misfits Limited	Statement of financial position at 2 January 2017	Increase (plus)	Decrease (minus)	Statement of financial position at 3 January 2017
	£000	£000	£000	£000
Current liabilities				
Bank overdraft	150	+ 75		225
Trade payables	1,500	+ 100		1,600
	1,650			1,825
Non-current liabilities				
Bank loan	10,000			10,000
Total liabilities	11,650			11,825
Net assets	11,600			11,600
Equity				
Called up share capital	1,800			1,800
Share premium	2,300			2,300
Retained earnings	7,500			7,500
	11,600			11,600

Non-current assets increase by £75,000 and the overdraft also increases by £75,000 as a result of the acquisition of the new piece of equipment paid for by cheque from the bank: assets have risen, but more is now owed to the bank as more has been drawn out so the bank overdraft goes up. Similarly, inventory has increased by £100,000, but more is now owed to trade payables so this has also risen by £100,000.

GO BACK OVER THIS AGAIN! Do you understand how the dual aspect concept applies to new transactions? Go to the **online workbook** Exercises 2.7 to look at further examples of the dual aspect and the effect of new transactions on the statement of financial position.

NUMERICAL EXERCISES Are you quite convinced that you could record new transactions accurately in the statement of financial position? Go to the **online workbook** Numerical exercises 2.2 to test out your abilities in this area.

MULTIPLE CHOICE QUESTIONS Are you confident that you could state the correct double entry for a transaction in the statement of financial position? Go to the **online workbook** and have a go at Multiple choice questions 2.3 to test your knowledge in this area.

This is probably the first time you have come across double entry, so if you are finding this confusing this should not surprise you. Further practice at more examples will help to reduce this confusion and you will gradually appreciate how double entry works and how transactions affect two or more accounts on the statement of financial position. However, do remember that you do not need to understand double entry to be able to evaluate sets of accounts, so do not give up at this early stage of your accounting studies.

CHAPTER SUMMARY

You should now have learnt that:

- An asset is a resource controlled by an entity as a result of past events from which future economic benefits are expected to flow to the entity and whose monetary cost or value can be measured reliably

- A liability is a present obligation arising from past events the settlement of which is expected to result in an outflow from the entity of resources embodying economic benefits and whose monetary value can be measured at a best estimate if reliable measurement is not possible

- Non-current assets are resources not purchased for resale in the normal course of business and are held for long-term use in the business to produce goods or services

- Current assets consist of inventory, trade and other receivables and cash and cash equivalents whose economic benefits will be used up within 12 months of the statement of financial position date

- Current liabilities are obligations that will be settled within 12 months of the statement of financial position date, while non-current liabilities are obligations that will be settled in accounting periods beyond the next 12 months

- The accounting equation states that total assets – total liabilities = equity

- Some assets in the statement of financial position may be shown at historic cost, while some may be shown at fair (current) value

- The statement of financial position only presents figures for resources (assets) whose economic benefits have not yet been consumed and figures for obligations that have not yet been settled

- The statement of financial position does not show all the assets and liabilities of an entity nor does it give a market value for an entity

- Under the dual aspect concept, new accounting transactions affect two or more statement of financial position account headings

QUICK REVISION Test your knowledge with the online flashcards in Summary of key concepts and attempt the Multiple choice questions, all in the **online workbook**. www.oxfordtextbooks.co.uk/orc/scott/

END-OF-CHAPTER QUESTIONS

Solutions to these questions can be found at the back of the book from page 413.

> *Develop your understanding*

Question 2.1

Using the criteria outlined in the summary in Figure 2.1, explain why the following items are assets that entities recognise on the statement of financial position:

(a) Motor vehicles purchased by an entity

(b) Inventory received from suppliers

(c) Cash and cash equivalents

Using the criteria outlined in the summary in Figure 2.1, explain why the following items are *not* assets and why they are not recognised on entities' statements of financial position:

(a) Redundant plant and machinery that has been replaced by faster, more technologically advanced machinery. This redundant plant and machinery is no longer used in the business or industry and has no resale or scrap value.

(b) A trade receivable from a customer who is bankrupt and from whom no payment is expected.

(c) A highly skilled workforce.

Question 2.2

The directors of Oxford Academicals Football Club Limited are discussing whether player registrations can be recognised as assets on the club's statement of financial position. There are two groups of players. The first group consists of those players whose contracts have been bought by the club from other teams in the transfer market. The second group is made up of players who have come up through the youth scheme and who have been playing at various levels for the club since the age of 12. The accounts department has informed the directors that the transfer fees for the bought in contracts amount to £25 million. The directors, however, cannot agree on a valuation for the players that have been developed by the club. The managing director thinks these players should be valued at £30 million, while the finance director thinks this is far too high a figure and would value these players at £15 million. Various offers have been received from other clubs to sign the players developed by the club and the combined values of these offers have ranged from £10 million to £25 million. Advise the directors on whether any of the players' registrations can be recognised in the statement of financial position and, if they can be so recognised, the category of assets that these registrations would appear under and the value that can be recognised.

Question 2.3

The following balances have been extracted from the books of the limited companies Alma, Bella, Carla, Deborah and Eloise at 30 April 2016. Using the statement of financial position format presented in this chapter, draw up the statement of financial positions for the five companies at 30 April 2016.

	Alma £000	Bella £000	Carla £000	Deborah £000	Eloise £000
Share capital	1,000	5,000	2,500	3,000	4,500
Cash at bank	—	800	—	550	200
Goodwill	—	—	400	250	500
Inventory	1,000	700	800	750	900
Trade payables	1,450	4,000	1,750	5,600	5,800
Plant and machinery	2,000	9,500	3,750	4,250	5,000
Trade receivables	1,750	3,000	2,750	2,950	3,100
Bank overdraft	800	—	1,250	—	—
Loans due on 30 April 2023	1,000	10,000	1,500	—	—
Loans due by 30 April 2017	200	400	300	—	—
Land and buildings	4,500	17,100	10,200	8,750	15,000
Taxation payable	540	1,100	800	—	—
Cash in hand	10	25	15	8	12
Trademarks	—	—	200	100	450
Motor vehicles	—	1,500	1,950	1,250	1,600
Tax repayment due	—	—	—	250	800
Retained earnings	2,770	4,625	7,465	5,508	8,262
Share premium	1,500	7,500	4,500	5,000	9,000

Question 2.4

Maria runs a small corner shop. Her statement of financial position at 31 October 2016 is shown below.

	£
Non-current assets	
Property, plant and equipment	15,000
Current assets	
Inventory	20,000
Other receivables	3,000
Cash and cash equivalents	500
	23.500
Total assets	38,500

→

	£
Current liabilities	
Bank overdraft	7,000
Trade and other payables	8,000
Taxation	3,000
Total liabilities	18,000
Net assets	20,500
Capital account	
Balance at 31 October 2016	20,500

The following transactions took place in the first week of November 2016:

- Trade payables of £3,500 were paid from the bank account.
- Maria paid £10,000 of her own money into the bank account.
- Inventory of £1,200 was sold for £2,000 cash, a profit of £800 for the week.
- New inventory of £2,500 was purchased on credit from trade payables.
- Maria withdrew £300 from cash for her own personal expenses.

Required

Show how the above transactions would increase or decrease the various balances on the statement of financial position and draw up and balance the new statement of financial position at 7 November 2016.

» Take it further

Question 2.5

Given below is the statement of financial position for Andy Limited at 30 June 2016. The following transactions took place in the first week of July 2016:

- 1 July 2016: paid a trade payable with a cheque from the bank for £2,500 and received a cheque for £3,000 from a trade receivable.
- 2 July 2016: took out a bank loan (full repayment is due on 30 June 2019) with which to buy a new vehicle costing £20,000. The vehicle purchase agreement was signed on 2 July 2016.
- 4 July 2016: sold goods costing £7,500 to a customer on credit terms, the customer agreeing to pay for those goods on 3 August 2016. The goods were sold for a selling price of £10,000.
- 5 July 2016: sold goods costing £2,500 to a customer for £3,250. The customer paid cash for the goods.
- 6 July 2016: received new inventory from a supplier. The new inventory cost £15,000 and Andy Limited has agreed to pay for the inventory on 5 August 2016.
- 7 July 2016: paid tax of £3,000 and a trade payable of £7,000 from the bank account.

Required

Show how the above transactions would increase or decrease the various balances on the statement of financial position and draw up and balance the new statement of financial position at 7 July 2016.

Andy Limited

Statement of financial position at 30 June 2016

ASSETS	£
Non-current assets	
Property, plant and equipment	320,000
Current assets	
Inventories	50,000
Trade receivables	75,000
Cash and cash equivalents	20,000
	145,000
Total assets	465,000
LIABILITIES	
Current liabilities	
Trade payables	80,000
Taxation	20,000
	100,000
Non-current liabilities	
Bank loan (long-term borrowings)	250,000
Total liabilities	350,000
Net assets	115,000
EQUITY	
Called up share capital	20,000
Retained earnings	95,000
Total equity	115,000

Question 2.6

(a) The following balances have been extracted from the books of Frankie Limited at 31 December 2016.

	£000
Cash at bank	600
Land and buildings	15,500
Loans due for repayment by 31 December 2017	850
Share premium	4,000
Loans due for repayment on 31 December 2025	8,500
Cash in hand	5
Share capital	2,000
Goodwill	1,000
Taxation payable	1,380
Fixtures and fittings	1,670
Trade receivables	4,910
Plant and machinery	10,630
Trade payables	6,720
Retained earnings	13,365
Inventory	2,500

Required

Using the statement of financial position format presented in this chapter, draw up the statement of financial position for Frankie Limited at 31 December 2016.

(b) During January 2017, the following transactions took place:

• Bought £12,200,000 of inventory on credit from suppliers.

• Made sales on credit to customers of £15,500,000. The inventory cost of the sales made was £11,450,000.

• Took out a loan of £2,500,000 with which to purchase new plant and machinery for £2,500,000. The new loan is due for repayment on 31 December 2021.

• Held a share issue, which raised cash of £1,500,000. £500,000 of the total amount raised represents share capital while the remaining £1,000,000 represents share premium.

• Made a tax payment from the bank account of £690,000.

• Received £6,450,000 from trade receivables.

• Paid trade payables £8,210,000.

• Sold a surplus piece of land that had cost £2,000,000 for £2,500,000.

• Made a short-term loan repayment of £200,000.

Required

Using the statement of financial position for Frankie Limited drawn up at 31 December 2016, show how the above transactions would increase or decrease the various balances on the statement of financial position and draw up and balance the new statement of financial position at the end of January 2017.

The income statement

LEARNING OUTCOMES

Once you have read this chapter and worked through the questions and examples in both this chapter and the online workbook, you should be able to:

- Define income and expenses
- Understand the different expense categories and profit figures that are presented in published financial statements
- Understand that income statement revenue and costs represent income earned and expenditure incurred in an accounting period and not just the cash received and cash paid in that period
- Apply the accruals basis of accounting in determining income earned and expenditure incurred in an accounting period
- Calculate prepayments and accruals at the end of an accounting period
- Define and calculate depreciation using both the straight line and reducing balance methods
- Make accounting adjustments to the income statement to reflect the effect of bad debts, doubtful debts, sales returns, purchase returns, discounts allowed and discounts received
- Prepare an income statement for an accounting period together with the statement of financial position at the end of that accounting period from a given set of information

Introduction

In the last chapter we looked at the statement of financial position. We noted that this statement just presents an entity's financial position on one day in the year, the financial year-end date. However, many users of financial information turn first of all not to the statement of financial position but to the income statement. This statement shows the income and expenditure of the entity for the year. The difference between total income and total expenditure represents the profit or loss that the entity has made during that financial year. It is this profit or loss figure that initially tends to be of most interest to financial statement users. A quick skim through the financial press on any day of the week will show you that profit or loss is one of the most discussed numbers in any set of financial statements. It is this figure, in many people's (and shareholders' and the stock market's) view, that determines whether a company has had a successful or unsuccessful year as shown by the two examples in Give me an example 3.1.

GIVE ME AN EXAMPLE 3.1   The importance of profits for businesses

Compare the stock market's reactions to two differing announcements from Greggs plc regarding its profits for the year ended 28 December 2013 and its forecast profits for the year ended 27 December 2014.

26 February 2014: Greggs' shares fall 9% after profits drop

Greggs' shares have fallen more than 9% after the bakery chain reported a sharp drop in annual profit for 2013. In the year to 28 December, pre-tax profits fell to £33.2m, down from £52.4m the previous year. The cost of changes to Greggs' strategy, pressures from competition and bad weather all contributed to the slump.

Source: Reproduced with permission from the BBC news team: www.bbc.co.uk/news/business-26351756

16 September 2014: Greggs' shares hit record high

BRITAINS's biggest high street purveyor of sausage rolls and pasties, Greggs, has said it expects profits 'materially ahead of expectations' after reporting accelerating sales. The update has led to a round of broker upgrades, sending shares more than 12pc higher yesterday. The strong performance also comes amid falling wholesale food prices which should mean greater profits for the bargain baker. The trading update marks an excellent turnaround, after a miserable run of profit warnings and stodgy sales hit the shares last year.

Source: www.telegraph.co.uk/finance/markets/questor/11097810/Questor-share-tip-Greggs-shares-hit-record-high.html

Illustration 3.1 shows the income statement for Bunns the Bakers plc for the years ended 31 March 2016 and 31 March 2015. This statement begins with income (**revenue**) and then deducts various categories of expenditure to reach the retained profit for the year. However, income and expenditure are not just simply money received and money spent during the year. There are various accounting conventions that have to be applied in the determination of income and costs for a period. How these conventions are applied to individual items of revenue and expenditure will determine the profit for each accounting period. The application of these conventions will form a large part of this chapter. Careful study of these applications will enable you to understand how income and expenditure are calculated and how, in turn, the profit or loss for a period is determined.

Terminology: income statement/ profit and loss account

The income statement is also known as the profit and loss account. In keeping with the International Financial Reporting Standards approach adopted in this book, the term 'income statement' is used throughout, but you will still find entities presenting a 'profit and loss account'.

Note: income and profit figures are shown without brackets while items of expenditure are shown in brackets. This is to help you understand which items are subtracted and which items are added to determine the result (profit or loss) for the year. Taking sales and finance income as positive figures, subtract the expenses to ensure you understand the relationships between the figures and to make sure that:

- Revenue – **cost of sales** = gross profit
- Gross profit – distribution and selling costs – administration expenses = operating profit
- Operating profit + finance income – finance expense = profit before tax and
- Profit before tax – income tax = profit for the year.

Illustration 3.1 Bunns the Bakers plc: income statement for the years ended 31 March 2016 and 31 March 2015

	2016	2015	
	£000	£000	
Revenue	10,078	9,575	
Cost of sales	(4,535)	(4,596)	
Gross profit	5,543	4,979	The trading part of the income statement
Distribution and selling costs	(3,398)	(3,057)	
Administration expenses	(1,250)	(1,155)	
Operating profit	895	767	
Finance income	15	12	The financing part of the income statement
Finance expense	(150)	(165)	
Profit before tax	760	614	
Income tax	(213)	(172)	
Profit for the year	547	442	

GO BACK OVER THIS AGAIN! A copy of this income statement is available in the **online workbook:** you might like to keep this on screen or print off a copy for easy reference while you work your way through the material in this chapter. There is also an annotated copy of this income statement in the **online workbook** to go over the relevant points again to reinforce your knowledge and learning.

Definitions

Illustration 3.1 shows the income statement for Bunns the Bakers plc. As noted in the introduction, the income statement contains items of revenue (income) and expenditure (costs incurred in making goods and selling them and in running and financing the company). Before we look at these different items of income and expenditure in more detail, let's start with some definitions.

Income

The International Accounting Standards Board defines income as 'increases in economic benefits during the accounting period' (IASB Framework, paragraph 70(a)). This is logical as, if you make a sale for cash or earn interest on cash deposited in a bank account, you have increased the cash available to yourself and so you have an increase in economic benefits. Similarly, making a sale on credit to a customer who will pay at some later date also increases economic benefits as you have the right to receive cash in the future. In the same way, people earn income from their employment. Receiving their salaries on pay day gives them an increase in economic benefits as they then have more cash available.

Expenses

As you might have expected, given the definition of income, the International Accounting Standards Board defines expenses as 'decreases in economic benefits during the accounting period' (IASB Framework, paragraph 70(b)). Paying a bill reduces the cash available so that an entity suffers a decrease in economic benefits as a result of the payment of cash. In the same way, incurring a liability by buying goods on credit also reduces your economic benefits as you now have an obligation to transfer economic benefits in the form of cash in the future. Just as receiving your salary in your bank account increases your economic benefits, so using your salary to pay for everyday necessities such as heating and lighting, food, rent and credit card payments decreases your economic benefits.

WHY IS THIS RELEVANT TO ME?   Definitions: income and expenses

To enable you as a business professional and user of accounting information to:

• Understand what income and expenditure in the income statement represent

• Appreciate how entities meet the definitions by generating income and paying expenses,

---

SUMMARY OF KEY CONCEPTS   Can you remember the income and expenses definitions? Revise these definitions with Summary of key concepts 3.1 to reinforce your knowledge.

Income in the income statement

The first line in Illustration 3.1 refers to Revenue. Revenue represents sales income earned in an accounting period (usually one year) and may be referred to in some sets of accounts as sales or turnover as well as by the term revenue. These three terms all refer to the same type of income, income from trading or providing services.

Revenue appears as the first item in the income statement and arises from sales made by an entity in the ordinary (everyday) course of business. For Bunns the Bakers plc this will mean selling bread, sandwiches, cakes, hot snacks, drinks and other products associated with their primary (everyday) activity, selling bakery and related goods. Were Bunns the Bakers to sell one of their shops, this would not be a transaction in the ordinary course of business and would not be recorded as part of revenue: selling shops is not what a bakery company would be expected to do on a regular basis. Instead, the profit or loss on the sale of the shop would be recorded in a separate line for exceptional income in the income statement below operating profit. The way in which entities record exceptional income in their financial statements is illustrated in Give me an example 3.2.

GIVE ME AN EXAMPLE 3.2 Recording exceptional income in the income statement

The following extract from the consolidated income statement of Roll-Royce Holdings plc for the year ended 31 December 2013 shows exceptional income recorded below the oper-ating profit line. Note that such exceptional income is not included in Revenue.

Source: *Rolls-Royce Holdings annual report 2013* www.rolls-royce.com

	£m
Operating profit	1,535
Profit on transfer of joint ventures to subsidiaries	119
Profit on disposal of businesses	216
Profit before financing and taxation	1,870

The first six lines in the income statement (from Revenue down to Operating profit) thus consist of items relating to the everyday trading activity of the organisation. Therefore, items of income and expense that do not relate to trading are excluded from the revenue, cost of sales, distribution and selling costs and administration expenses categories in the income statement.

Not all income will arise from an entity's regular or trading activities. The other element of income shown in Bunns the Bakers plc's income statement above is Finance income. This will consist of interest income received and receivable from the company's bank on deposits of surplus cash held in Bunns' account(s). As Bunns the Bakers is not a bank, earning interest is not part of its trading activities in the ordinary course of business, so any interest earned in the period is disclosed on a separate line. This income is disclosed outside the trading part of the income statement in its own separate section. Figure 3.1 summarises the three different types of income in the income statement.

WHY IS THIS RELEVANT TO ME? Income categorised under different headings

To enable you as a business professional and user of accounting information to:

• Read a published income statement and to understand what each category of income represents

• Appreciate that not all income arises from sales made in the ordinary course of business

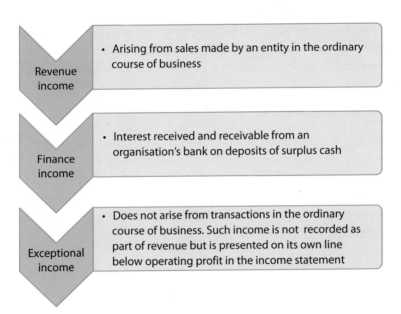

Figure 3.1 The different types of income in the income statement

---

GO BACK OVER THIS AGAIN!   Are you confident that you understand how revenue in the income statement is split into income from sales made in the ordinary course of business, finance income and exceptional income? Go to the **online workbook** and complete Exercises 3.1 to make sure you can distinguish between these different types of income.

Expenditure in the income statement

Expenditure in Bunns the Bakers' income statement falls under various headings. Let's look at each of these in turn.

Cost of sales

This heading comprises those costs incurred directly in the making or buying in of products. In the case of Bunns the Bakers, there will be the cost of the raw materials such as flour, fat, salt, cream, sugar and all the other ingredients that go into the bread, cakes, hot snacks and sandwiches, as well as goods bought in ready made from other manufacturers such as soft drinks and chocolate bars. In addition, the wages of the bakers, the electricity or gas used in heating the ovens and all the other associated costs of making or buying in the products will be included in cost of sales.

Determining the cost of making the products is important. The cost of the product is usually the starting point for setting a selling price at which customers will buy and to cover all the other costs of the operation so that a profit is made (see Chapter 8).

In smaller entities, as we shall see shortly, cost of sales is usually calculated as: opening inventory of goods at the start of the accounting period + purchases during the accounting period – closing inventory of goods at the end of the accounting period.

Distribution and selling costs

These costs will comprise all those costs incurred in the distribution and selling of the products. For Bunns the Bakers, advertising would fall under this heading, as would the transport of bakery goods produced from the main bakery to each of the individual shops. The wages of shop staff would be part of selling costs, too, as would the costs of running the shops, including shop expenditure on goods and services such as cleaning, repairs, electricity, maintenance, rent, rates and water.

Administration expenses

This heading covers all the costs of running the trading operation that do not fall under any other heading. Examples of such costs for Bunns the Bakers (and many other entities) would be legal expenses, accountancy and audit costs, directors' salaries, accounting department costs, bank charges and human resource department expenditure. Such costs are essential in running the business, but they cannot be allocated to the costs of making and producing or distributing and selling the goods sold by the organisation. Figure 3.2 summarises the different types of trading expenditure incurred in running a business.

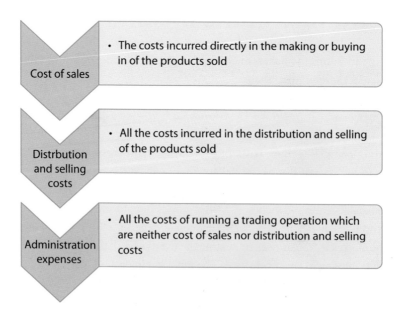

Figure 3.2 The different types of trading expenditure incurred in running a business

GO BACK OVER THIS AGAIN!   Are you convinced that you can distinguish between items that belong in the cost of sales, selling and distribution, and administration sections of the income statement? Go to the **online workbook** and complete Exercises 3.2 to make sure you can make these distinctions.

Finance expense

As with finance income, this expense is not incurred as part of the trading activities of the business. Finance expense is made up of interest paid on the borrowings used to finance the business. Look back at Illustration 2.1: Bunns the Bakers' statement of financial position shows that the company has borrowings under current and non-current liabilities. The finance expense will be the interest charged on these borrowings.

Income tax

The final expense to be deducted in Bunns the Bakers' income statement is income tax. All commercial entities have to pay tax on their profits according to the tax law of the country in which they are resident and in which they operate. The income tax charge is based on the profits of the entity for the accounting period and the entity would expect to pay this tax at some point in the coming financial year. Figure 3.3 represents these five different strands of costs.

Figure 3.3 The different types of costs (expenditure) in a typical income statement

> **WHY IS THIS RELEVANT TO ME?   Expenditure categorised under different headings**
>
> To enable you as a business professional and user of accounting information to:
> * Appreciate that expenses are categorised according to different types of expenditure
> * Read a published income statement and understand what each category of expenditure represents

MULTIPLE CHOICE QUESTIONS   Are you certain that you can distinguish between items that belong in the various categories of income and expenditure in the income statement? Go to the **online workbook** and complete Multiple choice questions 3.1 to make sure you can make these distinctions.

Different categories of profit

Bunns the Bakers' income statement presents several different lines describing various different numbers as 'profit'. Why are there so many different figures for profit and what does each of them tell us about the profits of the company? The following observations can be made:

* Gross profit = revenue – cost of sales: this is the profit that arises when all the direct costs of production of the goods sold are deducted from the sales revenue earned in the accounting period.

* Operating profit = gross profit – distribution and selling costs – administration expenses: the profit remaining when all the other operating costs not directly associated with the production or buying in of goods are deducted from the gross profit. Alternatively, this is the profit after all the costs of trading, direct (cost of sales) and indirect (distribution and selling costs and administration expenses), are deducted from sales revenue.

* Profit before tax = operating profit + finance income – finance expense: the profit that remains once the costs of financing operations have been deducted and any finance or other income has been added onto operating profit.

* Profit for the year = profit before tax – income tax (also called the profit after tax or the net profit): this is the profit that is left once the tax on the profits for the accounting period has been deducted from the profit before tax. Alternatively, this is the profit that remains once all the expenses have been deducted from the sales revenue and any other income for the accounting period added on. This profit is now available to the company to distribute to the shareholders as a dividend or to retain within the business to finance future expansion. Figure 3.4 presents the different categories of profit.

Figure 3.4 The different categories of profit in a typical company income statement

---

WHY IS THIS RELEVANT TO ME?   Different categories of profit

To enable you as a business professional and user of accounting information to:

• Understand the accounting terminology describing the various categories of profit

• Understand how trading and financing activities have contributed to the results for the accounting period

---

GO BACK OVER THIS AGAIN!   Quite sure that you can remember how each different profit figure is calculated and what it means? Go to the **online workbook** and complete Exercises 3.3 to reinforce your learning.

SUMMARY OF KEY CONCEPTS   Can you state the different profit figure calculations? Revise these calculations with Summary of key concepts 3.2 to check your understanding.

Income statement: simplified format

The income statement for Bunns the Bakers plc (Illustration 3.1) is presented in the format that you will find in published financial statements for limited and public limited companies. However, to simplify matters, the rest of this chapter will use examples and exercises based on the format in Illustration 3.2 for the income statement, the format that is used every day by traders and companies as a simple way to present income and expenditure to determine whether a profit or loss has been made. Study this format now along with the notes below.

Illustration 3.2 A trader: simplified income statement for the year ended 31 March 2016

	£	£
Sales		347,250
Opening inventory	13,600	
Purchases	158,320	
Closing inventory	(17,500)	
Cost of sales (opening inventory + purchases – closing inventory)		154,420
Gross profit (sales – cost of sales)		192,830
Expenses (can be listed in any order required)		
Heat and light	9,500	
Motor expenses	12,250	
Rent and rates	25,685	
Wages and salaries	48,345	
Administration expenses	10,050	
Accountancy	2,000	
Legal expenses	1,950	
Bank interest	6,000	
Depreciation of non-current assets	24,000	
Insurance	7,500	
Miscellaneous	1,890	
Total expenses (all expenses items added together)		149,170
Bank interest received		950
Net profit (gross profit – total expenses + bank interest received)		44,610

GO BACK OVER THIS AGAIN!   How would the income and expenditure in Illustration 3.2 be presented in the published financial statements format? Go to the **online workbook** Exercises 3.4 to see how the above information would be summarised ready for publication.

Notes to the income statement in Illustration 3.2

- The simplified income statement consists of three sections: sales, cost of sales and expenses.

- Just as in the case of published income statements, sales are made up of all the revenue derived from the ordinary activities of the business.

- Cost of sales is the opening inventory of unsold goods at the start of the year, plus purchases of goods during the year, less the closing inventory of unsold goods at the end of the year.

- Expenses are listed in any order: there is no set order in which expenses have to be presented.

- Expenses would include finance expense if an entity has incurred any interest costs relating to money borrowed to finance the business (Bank interest in Illustration 3.2) while finance income (interest receivable) is shown on a separate line below total expenses (Bank interest received in Illustration 3.2).

- Note the format of the statement: the component parts of Cost of sales and Expenses are listed in the left hand column and then the total figures for Cost of sales and Expenses are totalled in the right hand column and deducted from Sales and Gross profit respectively.

- As in Bunns the Bakers' income statement, sales − cost of sales = gross profit and gross profit − total expenses = net profit for the accounting period.

3

WHY IS THIS RELEVANT TO ME?   Income statement: simplified format

To enable you as a business professional and user of accounting information to understand:

- That income statements for internal use within businesses adopt a simpler format than published income statements

- How to draw up simplified income statements for presentation to interested parties

- What the income and two categories of expenditure represent

---

NUMERICAL EXERCISES   Do you think that you could prepare simplified income statements from a given set of information? Go to the **online workbook** and complete Numerical exercise 3.1 to test out your ability to prepare these simplified statements.

SUMMARY OF KEY CONCEPTS   Reckon that you can state how cost of sales is calculated? Revise this calculation with Summary of key concepts 3.3 to check your knowledge.

Now that we have looked at the presentation of the income statement and what it contains, it is time to find out how income and expense are determined in an accounting period.

Determining the amount of income or expense

At the start of this chapter we noted that income and expenditure are not just simply money received and money spent, though cash received and cash paid are the starting point for any set of financial statements. Revenue for an accounting period consists of all the sales made during that period, whether the cash from those sales has been received or not. Where a sale has been made but payment has not been received the entity recognises both a sale and a trade receivable at the end of the accounting period. This trade receivable is money due to the entity from a customer to whom the entity has made a valid sale. Thus, the entity recognises this sale in the income statement as part of sales for the period and as a trade receivable in the statement of financial position. Where a sale has been made and the cash received, the entity recognises the sale in the income statement and the increase in cash in the statement of financial position.

Diagrammatically, the above transactions can be represented as shown in Table 3.1.

Table 3.1 Cash and credit sales: income statement and statement of financial position effects

	Income statement effect	Cash received?	Statement of financial position effect
Sale made for cash	Increase revenue	Yes	Increase cash
Sale made on credit, payment due in 30 days	Increase revenue	No	Increase trade receivables
Cash received from trade receivable	No effect: no new revenue	Yes	Increase cash, decrease trade receivables

GIVE ME AN EXAMPLE 3.3   When do commercial organisations recognise revenue in their financial statements?

The following accounting policy regarding the timing of revenue recognition is taken from Nestlé's financial statements for the year ended 31 December 2014

Revenue

Sales represent amounts received and receivable from third parties for goods supplied to the customers and for services rendered. Revenue from the sales of goods is recognised in the income statement at the moment when the significant risks and rewards of ownership of the goods have been transferred to the buyer, which is mainly upon shipment.

Source: *Nestlé financial statements 2014* www.nestle.com, p.67.

Note that revenue comprises both cash received ('amounts received') and cash receivable (amounts 'receivable'). Revenue is thus not just the cash received in an accounting period, it represents all the revenue that an entity has generated during an accounting period whether the cash has been received or not.

Similarly, expenses are not just the money paid during an accounting period for goods and services received but *all* the expenses incurred in that period whether they have been paid for or not. Where an entity has incurred an expense during an accounting period but not paid this amount by the statement of financial position date, then the entity records the expense along with a trade payable. This trade payable represents an obligation owed by the entity at the end of the accounting period for an expense validly incurred during that accounting period. If the expense has been paid then the expense is recognised along with a reduction in cash.

Diagrammatically, these transactions can be represented as shown in Table 3.2.

Table 3.2 Cash and credit expenses: income statement and statement of financial position effects

	Income statement effect	Cash paid?	Statement of financial position effect
Expense paid for with cash	Increase expenses	Yes	Decrease cash
Expense incurred on credit, payment due in 30 days	Increase expenses	No	Increase trade payables
Cash paid to trade payable	No effect: no new expense	Yes	Decrease cash, decrease trade payables

3

GIVE ME AN EXAMPLE 3.4 When do commercial organisations recognise costs and expenses in their financial statements?

The following accounting policy regarding the timing of expense recognition is taken from Nestlé's financial statements for the year ended 31 December 2014.

Expenses

Cost of goods sold is determined on the basis of the cost of production or of purchase, adjusted for the variation of inventories. All other expenses, including those in respect of advertising and promotions, are recognised when the Group receives the risks and rewards of ownership of the goods or when it receives the services.

Source: *Nestlé financial statements 2014* www.nestle.com

Note that expenses are recognised not when cash is paid but when goods and services are received and when the company has an obligation to pay for those goods and services (the point at which the risks and rewards of ownership are received, i.e. when the goods are delivered to the company).

GO BACK OVER THIS AGAIN! Totally convinced that you understand how to determine the correct amount of income or expense for a given period? Go to the **online workbook** and complete Exercises 3.5 to reinforce your learning.

The accruals basis of accounting

The principle that all income and expenditure incurred in a period is recognised in that period is referred to as the accruals basis of accounting. Under this basis, the timing of cash payments and receipts is irrelevant as transactions are matched (allocated) to the period in which they occur not to the periods in which they are paid for or in which cash is received.

Why is the accruals basis of accounting applied to financial statements? If the accruals basis of accounting did not exist, entities could time their cash receipts and payments to manipulate their cash-based income statements to show the picture they wanted to show rather than the portrait of the income actually generated and the expenses actually incurred during an accounting period. Thus, some accounting periods would show high sales receipts, low expense payments and high profits, while other accounting periods would show low sales receipts, high expense payments and low profits or even losses. Results would depend upon money received and money paid out rather than reflecting all the business activity that had actually taken place within a given period of time.

An ability to manipulate the accounts in this way would lead to a lack of comparability between different accounting periods and between different organisations. We saw in Chapter 1 that comparability is an essential quality of accounting information. Lack of comparability makes it very difficult for users to gain an understanding of how the entity is making (or failing to make) progress in terms of profits earned or increases in sales made.

WHY IS THIS RELEVANT TO ME?   **The accruals basis of accounting**

To enable you as a business professional and user of accounting information to appreciate that:

- The timing of cash received and cash paid is irrelevant in the preparation of financial statements

- Transactions are reflected in financial statements on the basis of when they took place not on when the cash was received or paid

---

SUMMARY OF KEY CONCEPTS   Can you say what the accruals basis of accounting means? Revise this definition with Summary of key concepts 3.4 to check your learning.

The accruals basis of accounting looks like a difficult concept to grasp, but with practice you will soon be able to apply this concept readily to accounting problems. Let's look at some examples to show how the accruals basis of accounting works in practice. Think about the outcomes you would expect and compare your expectations to the actual answers. Remember that income and expenditure is allocated to an accounting period on the basis of income earned and expenditure incurred in that accounting period not on the timing of cash receipts and payments.

EXAMPLE 3.1

The Traditional Toy Company has an accounting year end of 30 June. On 1 January 2015, the company paid its annual insurance premium of £1,000, giving the company and its activities cover up to 31 December 2015. On 1 January 2016, the company paid its annual insurance premium of £1,200, which covers the company and its activities up to 31 December 2016. What expense should the Traditional Toy Company recognise for insurance for its accounting year 1 July 2015 to 30 June 2016?

The answer is £1,100. How did we arrive at this figure?

The premium paid on 1 January 2015 relates to the 12 months to 31 December 2015. Six of the months for the accounting period 1 July 2015 to 30 June 2016 are covered by this insurance premium, namely July, August, September, October, November and December 2015. Therefore 6/12 of the £1,000 belong in the accounting year to 30 June 2016, the other 6/12 of this payment belong in the accounting year 1 July 2014 to 30 June 2015.

Similarly, the premium paid on 1 January 2016 covers the whole calendar year to 31 December 2016. However, as the Traditional Toy Company's accounting year ends on 30 June 2016, only six months of this insurance premium belong in the financial year ended on that date, namely January, February, March, April, May and June 2016. Therefore 6/12 of £1,200 belong in the accounting year to 30 June 2016, the other 6/12 of this payment belong to the accounting year 1 July 2016 to 30 June 2017.

The total insurance expense recognised in the income statement for the 12 months accounting year to 30 June 2016 is thus:

$$£1,000 \times 6/12 + £1,200 \times 6/12 = £1,100$$

Figure 3.5 will help you understand how the amounts paid in the above example have been allocated to the different accounting periods.

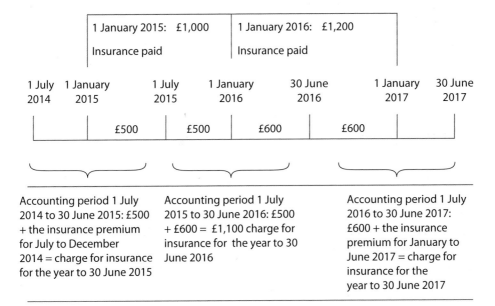

Figure 3.5 The accruals basis of accounting: insurance expense recognised in the Traditional Toy Company's accounting year 1 July 2015 to 30 June 2016

Hand Made Mirrors Limited has an accounting year end of 30 September. On 1 July 2015, the company paid its annual rates bill of £3,000 covering the period 1 July 2015 to 30 June 2016. On 1 July 2016, Hand Made Mirrors Limited received its annual rates bill for £3,600 covering the year to 30 June 2017 but did not pay this bill until 30 November 2016. What expense should the company recognise for rates for its accounting year 1 October 2015 to 30 September 2016?

The answer is £3,150. How did we arrive at this figure?

The rates paid on 1 July 2015 relate to the 12 months to 30 June 2016. Nine of the months for the accounting period 1 October 2015 to 30 September 2016 are covered by this rates bill, namely October, November and December of 2015 and January, February, March, April, May and June of 2016. Therefore 9/12 of this £3,000 belong in the accounting year to 30 September 2016.

Similarly, the rates paid on 30 November 2016 cover the whole year from 1 July 2016 to 30 June 2017. However, as Hand Made Mirrors Limited's accounting year ends on 30 September 2016, only three months of this rates bill belong in the accounting year ended on that date, namely July, August and September 2016. Therefore 3/12 of £3,600 belong in the accounting year to 30 September 2016.

The total rates expense recognised in the income statement for the year to 30 September 2016 is thus:

$$£3,000 \times 9/12 + £3,600 \times 3/12 = £3,150$$

Again, a diagram as shown in Figure 3.6 will help you understand how the amounts paid in the above example have been allocated to the different accounting periods.

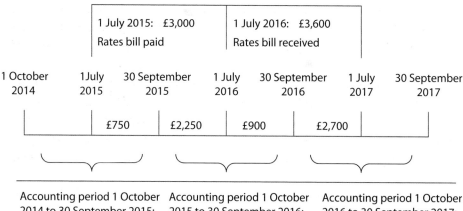

Figure 3.6 The accruals basis of accounting: Hand Made Mirrors Limited's rates expense recognised in the accounting year 1 October 2015 to 30 September 2016

MULTIPLE CHOICE QUESTIONS   Do you think you can allocate costs to accounting periods on an expense incurred basis under the accruals basis of accounting? Go to the **online workbook** and have a go at Multiple choice questions 3.2 to make sure you can make these allocations.

Prepayments and accruals: recording transactions in the income statement and statement of financial position

The two scenarios above provide us with one example of a **prepayment** and one example of an **accrual** at the end of an accounting period.

Prepayments

A prepayment is an expense paid in advance of the accounting period to which it relates. As this expense has been paid in advance, it is an asset of the entity. At 30 June 2016, in the case of the Traditional Toy Company, there is a prepaid insurance premium of £1,200 × 6/12 = £600. This prepayment is an asset as it gives rise to future economic benefits (the right to enjoy the protection provided by payment of the insurance premium in the next six months) and it is a resource controlled by the entity as a result of past events, the payment of the premium. While recognising the insurance expense of £1,100 for the accounting year to 30 June 2016, the entity also recognises a prepayment of £600 at the statement of financial position date of 30 June 2016.

At the end of the previous accounting period, at 30 June 2015, the Traditional Toy Company also had an insurance prepayment amounting to £1,000 × 6/12 = £500 (covering the months of July to December 2015 and paid in advance at 30 June 2015) so the insurance expense charge for the year is the £500 prepayment at the end of last year plus the £1,200 paid in the year less the prepayment at the end of the year of £600, thus:

£500 (prepayment at the end of last year) + £1,200 (payment in the year) − £600 (prepayment at the end of this year) = £1,100 insurance expense charge for the year

When attempting the multiple choice questions and exercises in the online workbook (and in real life situations), you can apply the rule presented in Figure 3.7 when you have an expense prepayment at the start and at the end of the financial year.

Accruals

An accrual is an expense owing at the end of the financial year for goods and services received but not yet paid for. As this expense is owed at the end of the year it represents a liability. At 30 September 2016, Hand Made Mirrors Limited has a liability for unpaid

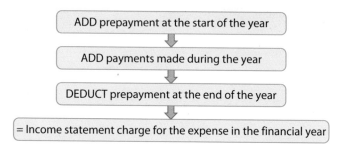

Figure 3.7 Calculating the income statement expense for the financial year when there is a prepayment at the start and at the end of the accounting period

rates of £3,600 × 3/12 = £900. This is a liability of the company at 30 September 2016 as it is a present obligation of the entity arising from the consumption of past services that will result in the outflow of economic benefits (in the form of a cash payment to the local council on 30 November 2016) in order to settle the obligation. While recognising the total expense of £3,150 in the income statement, Hand Made Mirrors Limited also recognises a £900 liability under trade and other payables in its statement of financial position at 30 September 2016. Remember that this is an expense incurred but not yet paid for, so you should increase the expense and increase the trade payables.

There was no accrual at the end of the previous accounting year. Had there been such an accrual this would be treated as a deduction in arriving at the expense charge for the current accounting year. This is because an accrual at the end of the previous accounting period is a liability for a cost that was incurred in the previous accounting period but which will be paid in the current accounting period. The payment to discharge this liability has no bearing on the current accounting period's charge for this expense, so it is a deduction from the total payments made in the current accounting period.

When attempting the multiple choice questions and exercises in the online workbook (and in real life situations), you can apply the rule presented in Figure 3.8 when you have an expense accrual at the start and at the end of the financial year to find the amount you should recognise in the income statement for that particular expense in the current financial year.

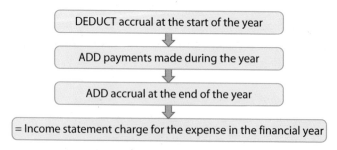

Figure 3.8 Calculating the income statement expense for the financial year when there is an accrual at the start and at the end of the accounting period

WHY IS THIS RELEVANT TO ME?   Prepayments and accruals

To enable you as a business professional and user of accounting information to understand how:

- Costs are allocated to accounting periods as they are incurred
- To calculate simple accruals and prepayments at the end of an accounting period
- Assets and liabilities arise as a result of prepaid and accrued expenses

MULTIPLE CHOICE QUESTIONS   Are you totally convinced that you can calculate income statement expenses when there are prepayments and accruals at the start and end of the financial year? Go to the **online workbook** and have a go at Multiple choice questions 3.3 to test your ability to make these calculations.

Depreciation

When we looked at the statement of financial position in Chapter 2, we noted that there are various types of non-current assets such as property, plant and equipment, patents and copyrights, among others. These assets are purchased by business organisations with a view to their long term employment within the business to generate revenue, profits and cash. Businesses pay money for these assets when they buy them and then place these assets initially on the statement of financial position at their cost to the business.

A problem then arises. How should the cost of these non-current assets be allocated against income generated from those assets? The total cost of these assets is not allocated immediately against the income and profits made from those assets. Instead, the total cost is posted to the statement of financial position when the non-current asset is first acquired. Should we then allocate the cost of the asset to the income statement at the end of the asset's life when the asset is worn out and of no further use to the business? Again, this will not happen. Setting the total cost of the asset against profit at the start or at the end of the asset's life would result in a very large one-off expense against profit in the year in which the asset is either bought or scrapped, so there has to be a better way to allocate the cost of non-current assets to accounting periods benefiting from their use. This is where depreciation comes in. Depreciation allocates the cost of a non-current asset to all those accounting periods benefiting from its use.

EXAMPLE 3.3

Suppose that Pento Printing Press has bought a printing machine for £100,000 and expects this non-current asset to be used within the business for the next five years. By simply dividing the asset's cost by the number of years over which the asset will be used in the business, this will give us an annual allocation of the cost of this asset of £100,000 ÷ 5 years = £20,000 per annum. This means that there will be a charge in Pento's income statement in year 1 of £20,000 for use of the asset in the business, a charge in the income statement of £20,000 in year 2 for use of the asset and so on until the end of the five years when the asset is scrapped and a replacement asset is purchased.

The allocation of depreciation in this way has a dual effect: part of the cost of the asset is charged to the income statement each year and at the same time the unallocated cost of the asset on the statement of financial position reduces each year. Table 3.3 shows how the annual depreciation is allocated to each accounting period benefiting from the printing machine's use and the effect that this will have on Pento's statement of financial position figure for this asset at the end of each financial year. In accounting terminology, this is expressed as follows: the original cost of the asset – the depreciation charged to the income statement each year = the **net book value** of the asset shown on the statement of financial position at the end of each financial year.

The £20,000 depreciation on the asset is charged as an expense in the income statement of each annual accounting period in which the asset is used within the business.

The accumulated depreciation charged rises each year as the printing machine ages. At the end of the first year, the accumulated depreciation is the same as the annual depreciation charge. By the end of the second year the accumulated depreciation of £40,000 is made up of the first year's charge of £20,000 plus the second year's charge of £20,000. Then, by the end of year 3, the accumulated depreciation of £60,000 is made up of three years' charges of £20,000 each year and so on until the end of the printing machine's useful life. At the end of year 5, the accumulated depreciation of £100,000 is the same as the original cost of £100,000. As each year progresses, the net book value of the printing machine (cost – the accumulated depreciation) gradually falls. Thus, the net book value reduces as more of the original cost is allocated against profit each year.

Table 3.3 Straight line depreciation on Pento Printing Press' printing machine costing £100,000 with £nil value at the end of five years

Year	Income statement: annual charge for depreciation on printing machine	Accumulated depreciation	Statement of financial position: net book value of printing machine at the end of each financial year
	£	£	£
1	20,000	20,000	80,000
2	20,000	40,000	60,000
3	20,000	60,000	40,000
4	20,000	80,000	20,000
5	20,000	100,000	Nil

WHY IS THIS RELEVANT TO ME?   Depreciation

To enable you as a business professional and user of accounting information to understand how:

- The use of non-current assets within a business results in an annual depreciation expense in the income statement
- The cost of non-current assets is allocated to the income statement each year
- The net book value of non-current assets is calculated at the end of each financial year

MULTIPLE CHOICE QUESTIONS   How well do you understand the calculation of accumulated depreciation and net book value? Go to the **online workbook** and have a go at Multiple choice questions 3.4 to test your understanding of how to make these calculations.

Residual value and the annual depreciation charge

In Example 3.3 we assumed that all of the cost of the printing machine would be consumed over the five-year period and that it would have no value at the end of its projected five-year life. This might be a realistic scenario in the case of assets such as computers, which will be completely superseded by advancing technology and so have no value at the end of their useful lives within a business. However, it is just as likely that assets could be sold on to another buyer when the business wishes to dispose of them. A car, for example, will usually have some resale value when a company comes to dispose of it and, in the same way, second-hand machinery will find willing buyers.

It is thus normal practice, at the time of acquisition, to estimate a residual value for each non-current asset. Residual value is the amount that the original purchaser thinks that the asset could be sold for when the time comes to dispose of it. When calculating the annual depreciation charge, the residual value is deducted from the original cost so that the asset is depreciated down to this value. If the residual value is estimated at £nil, then the full cost of the asset is depreciated over its useful life.

EXAMPLE 3.4

The directors of Pento Printing Press now decide that their new printing machine will have an estimated residual value of £10,000 at the end of its five-year life. The annual depreciation charge will now fall to (£100,000 original cost − £10,000 residual value)/5 years = £18,000. Charging £18,000 depreciation each year will depreciate the asset down to its residual value as shown in Table 3.4.

Table 3.4 Pento Printing Press: straight line depreciation of a printing machine costing £100,000 with a £10,000 residual value

Year	Income statement: annual charge for depreciation on printing machine	Accumulated depreciation	Statement of financial position: net book value of printing machine at the end of each financial year
	£	£	£
1	18,000	18,000	82,000
2	18,000	36,000	64,000
3	18,000	54,000	46,000
4	18,000	72,000	28,000
5	18,000	90,000	10,000

WHY IS THIS RELEVANT TO ME? Residual value

To enable you as a business professional and user of accounting information to understand that:

• The estimated residual value of an asset at the end of its useful life reduces the annual depreciation charge

• Residual value is just an estimate of expected resale value at the end of a non-current asset's useful life

Profits and losses on disposal of non-current assets

You might now wonder what will happen if Pento Printing Press does not sell the asset at the end of the five years for £10,000. If the asset were to be sold for £8,000, £2,000 less than its net book value at the end of year 5, then Pento Printing Press would just record a loss (an additional expense) of £2,000 on disposal of the printing machine in the income statement. Profits would be reduced by that additional expense of £2,000. If, on the other hand, the asset were to be sold for £11,000, £1,000 more than the net book value at the end of the five years, Pento Printing Press would recognise a profit (an additional surplus) on the disposal of that asset in the income statement. Profits on disposal of non-current assets are recorded as a deduction from expenses and are not recorded as additional revenue in the income statement.

There would be no need for Pento Printing Press to go back and recalculate the depreciation for each of the five years in either of these cases as companies accept that the estimation of residual value is just that, a best guess at the time of acquisition of the asset of what the asset might be sold for at the end of its useful life within the business. It is quite normal for companies to recognise small gains and losses on the disposal of assets when they are sold on or scrapped either at the end of their useful lives or during the time that they are being used within the business.

3

WHY IS THIS RELEVANT TO ME? Profits and losses on disposal of non-current assets

To enable you as a business professional and user of accounting information to understand that:

- Profits on the disposal of non-current assets are recognised as income (a deduction from expenses) in the income statement in the year of the asset's disposal
- Losses on the disposal of non-current assets are recognised as an expense in the income statement in the year of the asset's disposal
- The profit or loss on disposal is calculated as the difference between the sale proceeds and the net book value of the asset at the date of disposal

MULTIPLE CHOICE QUESTIONS Can you calculate profits and losses arising on the disposal of non-current assets? Go to the **online workbook** and have a go at Multiple choice questions 3.5 to test your ability to make these calculations.

Methods of depreciation: straight line and reducing balance

The approach used in the Pento Printing Press examples (Examples 3.3 and 3.4) to calculate depreciation resulted in the same depreciation charge for each year of the printing machine's useful life. This is the straight line basis of depreciation as it allocates an equal amount of depreciation to each year that the asset is used within the business.

An alternative method of depreciation that is also used is the reducing balance basis. This approach uses a fixed percentage of the cost in year 1 and the same fixed percentage of the net book value in subsequent years to calculate the annual depreciation charge. When using the reducing balance basis, residual value is ignored as the percentage used will depreciate the original cost down to residual value over the number of years in which the asset is used within the business.

EXAMPLE 3.5

Continuing with the Pento Printing Press example, a suitable percentage at which to depreciate the new printing machine on a reducing balance basis would be 36.90%. Let's see how this will work in Table 3.5.

The annual depreciation figures were calculated as follows:

- In year 1, depreciation is calculated on cost. This gives a figure of £100,000 × 36.90% = £36,900. This depreciation is then deducted from the original cost of £100,000 to leave a net book value at the end of year 1 of £100,000 − £36,900 = £63,100.

- In years 2 and onwards, depreciation is calculated on the net book value at the end of the preceding financial year. Net book value at the end of year 1 is £63,100, so depreciation for year 2 is £63,100 × 36.90% = £23,284 (rounding to the nearest £). This then gives a net book value at the end of year 2 of £63,100 − £23,284 (or £100,000 − £36,900 − £23,284) = £39,816.

- In year 3, depreciation is calculated on the net book value at the end of year 2. This gives an annual depreciation charge of £39,816 × 36.90% = £14,692 and a net book value at the end of year 3 of £39,816 − £14,692 = £25,124.

Work through the figures for years 4 and 5 to make sure that you understand how reducing balance depreciation works and to reinforce your learning.

Figure 3.9 visually represents the annual depreciation charge under both the reducing balance (the blue line) and the straight line (the red line) methods. The straight line method of depreciation charges exactly the same depreciation each year, £18,000 (Table 3.4), so this is a straight line drawn across the graph through the £18,000 mark on the y axis. Reducing balance depreciation charges a high level of depreciation in the first year of the asset's life and this then gradually reduces each year, thereby producing the curved blue line on the graph.

Table 3.5 Pento Printing Press: reducing balance depreciation of a printing machine costing £100,000 with a £10,000 residual value

Year	Income statement: annual charge for depreciation on printing machine	Accumulated depreciation	Statement of financial position: net book value of printing machine at the end of each financial year
	£	£	£
1	36,900	36,900	63,100
2	23,284	60,184	39,816
3	14,692	74,876	25,124
4	9,271	84,147	15,853
5	5,850	89,997	10,003

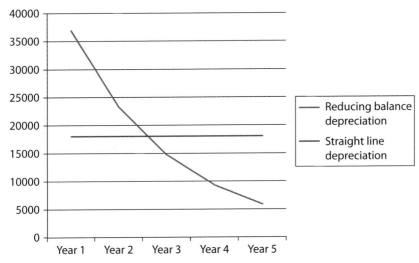

Figure 3.9 Graph representing the annual depreciation charges under both the reducing balance and straight line methods of depreciation for Pento Printing Press' printing machine costing £100,000 with a residual value of £10,000

Which depreciation method is most appropriate in practice?

When selecting a method of depreciation, entities should always ask themselves how the economic benefits of each asset will be consumed. If most of the economic benefits that the asset represents will be used up in the early years of an asset's life, then reducing balance depreciation would be the most suitable method to use. Reducing balance would charge a higher proportion of the cost to the early years of the asset's life, thereby reflecting the higher proportion of economic benefits used up in these early years. Where benefits from the asset's use will be used up evenly over the asset's life, then straight line depreciation is the most appropriate method to use.

WHY IS THIS RELEVANT TO ME?   Methods of depreciation: straight line and reducing balance

To enable you as a business professional and user of accounting information to understand:

- The two main methods of depreciation that are applied in practice

- How to undertake depreciation calculations to assess the impact of depreciation upon profits in the income statement and upon the net book values of assets in the statement of financial position

- The criteria to be used in the selection of the most appropriate depreciation method for non-current assets

3

What sort of depreciation rates and methods do companies use in practice? The following extract from the accounting policies detailed in the report and accounts of Finsbury Foods plc for the 52 weeks ended 28 June 2014 gives different depreciation rates for different classes of property, plant and equipment assets. Can you decide whether Finsbury Foods plc uses the straight line or the reducing balance basis to calculate the annual depreciation charge?

Depreciation

Depreciation is provided to write off the cost, less estimated residual value, of the property, plant and equipment by equal instalments over their estimated useful economic lives to the Consolidated Statement of Profit and Loss. When parts of an item of property, plant and equipment have different useful lives, they are accounted for as separate items (major components) of property, plant and equipment.

The depreciation rates used are as follows:

Freehold buildings 2% – 20%	Plant and equipment 10% – 33%
Leasehold property Up to the remaining life of the lease	Assets under construction Nil
Fixtures and fittings 10% – 33%	Motor vehicles 25% – 33%

Did you notice the words 'equal instalments' in the extract above? Equal instalments means that Finsbury Food plc uses the straight line basis of depreciation when allocating the cost of non-current assets to the consolidated statement of profit and loss (= the income statement). Equal instalments = the same charge each year, i.e. the straight line basis.

Source: *Finsbury Foods plc annual report and accounts 2014* http://www.finsburyfoods.co.uk

---

MULTIPLE CHOICE QUESTIONS Are you totally confident you can calculate depreciation charges on both the straight line and the reducing balance bases? Go to the **online workbook** and have a go at Multiple choice questions 3.6 to test your ability to make these calculations.

What depreciation is and what depreciation is not

There are many misconceptions about what depreciation is and what it represents. The following notes will help you distinguish between what depreciation is and what it is not:

- Depreciation is a deduction from the cost of a non-current asset that is charged as an expense in the income statement each year.

- This depreciation charge represents an allocation of the cost of each non-current asset to the accounting periods expected to benefit from that asset's use by an organisation.

- Depreciation is another application of the accruals basis of accounting. Just as the accruals basis of accounting matches income and expenditure to the periods in which they occurred, so depreciation matches the cost of non-current assets to the periods benefiting from their use.
- Depreciation is NOT a method of saving up for a replacement asset.
- Depreciation does NOT represent a loss in value of a non-current asset.
- Depreciation does NOT represent an attempt to provide a current value for non-current assets at each statement of financial position date.

3

EXAMPLE 3.6

Think about these last two points. Suppose you were to buy a car today for £15,000 and expect to use that car for five years before buying a replacement. The resale value of that car the next day would not be £15,000 less one day's depreciation, the original cost less a very small charge for the asset's economic benefits used up by one day's travelling. The showroom that sold you the car the day before would probably offer you half of the original cost of £15,000. The car is now second-hand and so worth much less on the open market than you paid for it the day before even if it only has five miles on the clock and is still in immaculate condition. Thus, the net book value of non-current assets on a company's statement of financial position is just the original cost of those assets less the depreciation charged to date. This net book value represents the store of economic benefits that will be consumed by the entity over the remaining useful lives of those assets rather than presenting the current market value of those non-current assets.

WHY IS THIS RELEVANT TO ME? What depreciation is and what depreciation is not

To enable you as a business professional and user of accounting information to understand:

- The function of depreciation in accounting statements
- What depreciation does not represent

GO BACK OVER THIS AGAIN! How firmly have you grasped the ideas of what depreciation is and what it is not? Go to the **online workbook** and complete Exercises 3.6 to reinforce your understanding.

Further adjustments to the income statement

We have now looked at how the income statement reflects the actual income and expenditure incurred in an accounting period rather than just the receipts and payments of cash during that accounting period together with the subject of depreciation. There are some further adjustments that are made to figures in the income statement and statement of financial position that you should be aware of before we work through a comprehensive example.

Bad debts

Where entities trade with their customers on credit, providing customers with goods now and allowing them a period of time in which to pay, there will inevitably be times when some customers are unable or refuse to pay for whatever reason. When this situation arises, an administrative expense is recognised for the amount of the trade receivable that cannot be collected and trade receivables reduced by the same amount. Note that these bad debts are not deducted from sales but are treated as an expense of the business.

Bad debts are recognised as an expense and a deduction from trade receivables when there is objective proof that the customer will not pay. Usually, this objective proof is in the form of a letter from the customer's administrator advising the company that no further cash will be forthcoming to settle the trade receivable owed.

Doubtful debts

As well as known bad debts, organisations will also calculate a provision for doubtful debts, trade receivables that may not be collected rather than bad debts, receivables that will definitely not pay. A provision for doubtful debts is an application of the prudence principle, being cautious and avoiding over optimistic expectations, making a provision for a potential loss just in case. Provisions for doubtful debts thus build up a cushion against which future bad debts can be set when they arise.

Provisions for doubtful debts are calculated as a percentage of trade receivables after deducting known bad debts. The provision for doubtful debts is deducted in its entirety from trade receivables in the statement of financial position while only the increase or decrease in the provision over the year is charged or credited to administrative expenses (not sales) in the income statement. An example will help you understand how doubtful debt provisions are calculated and the accounting entries required.

EXAMPLE 3.7

Gemma runs a recruitment agency. She has year-end trade receivables at 30 September 2016 of £300,000. She knows that one trade receivable owing £6,000 will not pay as that company is now in liquidation. Gemma's experience tells her that 5% of the remaining trade receivables will not pay. Her doubtful debt provision at 30 September 2015 was £12,000. What is the total charge for bad and doubtful debts that she should recognise in her income statement for the year to 30 September 2016? What figure for net trade receivables will appear in her statement of financial position at that date?

Bad and doubtful debts charge in the income statement

	£	£
Bad debts charged directly to the income statement		6,000
Movement in the provision for doubtful debts:		
Year-end trade receivables (total)	300,000	
Less: known bad debts charged directly to the income statement	(6,000)	
Net trade receivables on which provision is to be based	294,000	
Provision for doubtful debts on £294,000 at 5%	14,700	
Less: provision for doubtful debts at 30 September 2015	(12,000)	
Increase in provision charged to the income statement this year		2,700
Total income statement charge for bad and doubtful debts for the year ended 30 September 2016		8,700

Trade receivables in the statement of financial position

	£
Total trade receivables at 30 September 2016	300,000
Less: known bad debts charged directly to the income statement	(6,000)
	294,000
Less: provision for doubtful debts at the start of the year	(12,000)
Less: increase in the provision for doubtful debts during the year	(2,700)
Net trade receivables at 30 September 2016	279,300

The total provision for doubtful debts is made up of the provision at the end of last year and the increase (or decrease) during the current year. The total provision of £14,700 is deducted from trade receivables at the end of the year. The charge (or credit) for doubtful debts for the year in the income statement, however, is just the increase (or decrease) during the year.

MULTIPLE CHOICE QUESTIONS Do you reckon that you can calculate doubtful debt provisions and the amounts to charge or credit to the income statement? Go to the **online workbook** and have a go at Multiple choice questions 3.7 to test your ability to make these calculations.

Discounts allowed

To persuade customers to settle what they owe early or by way of reward for buying large quantities of goods over a given period of time, entities often allow their customers a discount, a reduction in the amount owed. This is again treated as an administrative expense and a reduction in trade receivables. Note that this expense is not deducted from sales.

Discounts received

Similarly, suppliers will reward their customers with discounts for the same reasons, early payment or bulk discounts. These are a source of income in the income statement, a deduction from cost of sales and a deduction from trade payables.

Sales returns

Sometimes, goods are just not suitable, are not of the requisite quality or they are faulty. In this case, customers will return these goods to the supplier. These returns are treated as a deduction from sales, as the return of goods amounts to the cancellation of a sale and a deduction from trade receivables.

Purchase returns

Similarly, when entities return goods to their suppliers, suppliers will reduce the amount that is owed to them by the issue of a credit note. As this is the cancellation of a purchase, the purchases part of cost of goods sold and trade payables are reduced.

Closing inventory

At the end of the financial year, entities count up the goods in stock and value them at cost price to the business. To value closing inventory at selling price would be to anticipate profit. This would contravene the realisation principle of accounting which says that profits should not be anticipated until they have been earned through a sale. The cost of these goods is carried forward to the next accounting period by deducting the cost of this inventory in the income statement and recognising an asset in the statement of financial position. This is a further application of the accruals basis of accounting, carrying forward the cost of unsold goods to a future accounting period to match that cost against sales of those goods when these arise.

WHY IS THIS RELEVANT TO ME?   Further adjustments to the income statement

To provide you as a business professional and user of accounting information with:

- Knowledge of additional figures that affect both income and expenditure and the statement of financial position
- Details of how these adjustments are treated in practice
- An ability to apply these adjustments in business situations

We will look at how these adjustments are applied in practice in our comprehensive example and in Numerical exercises 3.2.

Preparing the income statement

We have now considered all the building blocks for the income statement. It is time to look at a comprehensive example to see how the income statement is put together from the accounting records and how it relates to the statement of financial position. You will need to work through this comprehensive example several times to understand fully how all the figures are derived, but this is quite normal. Even those at the top of the accountancy profession today would have struggled with this type of problem when they first started out on their accounting studies. It is just a case of practice and familiarising yourself with the techniques involved in putting a set of accounts together.

The following list of points is a quick summary of how to prepare an income statement and the statement of financial position, starting with a simple list of receipts and payments presented by a business:

- First, summarise the receipts into and payments out of the entity's bank account: this will give you the basic sales receipts and expenses as well as any non-current assets that the entity may have purchased.

- Once you have completed the bank account you will have a difference between the receipts and payments in the period: if receipts are greater than payments, you have a positive cash balance in the bank account, a current asset. If the payments are greater than the receipts, you have a negative balance in the bank account, an overdraft, and this will be recorded as a current liability.

- Using the cash received and paid you should then adjust income and expenditure for the accruals basis of accounting. Add to sales any income earned in the accounting period for which cash has not yet been received and recognise a trade receivable for the outstanding balance due. For expenses, determine what the expense should be based on, the time period involved and then add additional expenditure where a particular cost is too low (and add to current liabilities as an accrual, an obligation incurred but not yet paid for) and deduct expenditure where a particular cost is too high (and add to current assets as a prepayment of future expenditure that relates to a later accounting period). .

- Remember to depreciate any non-current assets at the rates given, provide for any bad debts that might have been incurred, make an adjustment for the increase or decrease in the provision for doubtful debts, adjust sales and purchases for returns, deduct discounts received from purchases and add discounts allowed to expenses.

EXAMPLE 3.8

Your friend Julia started a business on 1 April 2016 buying and selling sports equipment from a shop on the high street. It is now 30 June 2016 and Julia is curious to know how well or badly she is doing in her first three months of trading. She has no idea about accounts and presents you with the following list of balances of amounts received and paid out of her bank account.

Illustration 3.3 Julia's bank account receipts and payments summary

Date		Receipts £	Payments £
1 April 2016	Cash introduced by Julia	30,000	
1 April 2016	Three months' rent paid on shop to 30 June 2016		5,000
1 April 2016	Cash register paid for		1,000
1 April 2016	Shelving and shop fittings paid for		12,000
30 April 2016	Receipts from sales in April 2016	20,000	
5 May 2016	Sports equipment supplied in April paid for		15,000
12 May 2016	Rates for period 1 April 2016 to 30 September 2016 paid		800
19 May 2016	Cash withdrawn for Julia's own expenses		2,000
30 May 2016	Receipts from sales in May 2016	25,000	
5 June 2016	Sports equipment supplied in May paid for		20,000
10 June 2016	Shop water rates for the year 1 April 2016 to 31 March 2017 paid		400
30 June 2016	Receipts from sales in June 2016	30,000	
30 June 2016	Balance in bank at 30 June 2016		48,800
		105,000	105,000

Julia is very pleased with her first three months' trading and regards the additional £18,800 cash in the bank as her profit for the three months. Is she right? Has she really made £18,800 profit in the three months since she started trading? Her argument is that she started with £30,000 and now has £48,800 so she must have made a profit of £18,800, the difference between her opening and closing cash figures. Let us have a look and see how her business has really performed in its first three months of operations.

Our first job is to split the receipts and payments down into trading receipts and payments and statement of financial position (capital) receipts and payments. Have a go at this on your own before you look at the answer below. You will need to add up the receipts for sales and payments for purchases and other expenses: make a list of these individual totals.

You should now have the following totals:

Illustration 3.4 Julia's receipts and payments account for the three months ended 30 June 2016

	£	£
Sales £20,000 (April) + £25,000 (May) + £30,000 (June)		75,000
Purchases £15,000 (May) + £20,000 (June)		35,000
Gross surplus (sales – purchases)		40,000
Expenses		
Rent £5,000 (April)	5,000	
Rates £800 (May)	800	
Water rates £400 (June)	400	
Total expenses		6,200
Net surplus for the three months		33,800

Illustration 3.5 Julia's statement of financial position based on her receipts and payments for her first three months of trading at 30 June 2016

	£
Non-current assets	
Cash register	1,000
Shelves and shop fittings	12,000
	13,000
Bank balance at 30 June 2016	48,800
Total assets	61,800
Equity	
Capital introduced by Julia	30,000
Drawings (cash withdrawn from the business for personal expenses)	(2,000)
Surplus for the three months	33,800
	61,800

All we have done here is restated the figures from Julia's bank account, splitting them into income statement and statement of financial position items on a purely receipts and payments basis. Sales and expenses have been entered into the income statement, while non-current assets (the cash register and the shelving and shop fittings: those assets that are used long term in the business) have been entered into the statement of financial position. The statement of financial position also shows the cash in the bank, the asset remaining at the end of the financial period, along with the capital introduced by Julia less her drawings in the three-month period plus the surplus the business has made during that period.

3

However, there is a problem with receipts and payments accounts. As we have seen in the earlier part of this chapter, what we need to do now is adjust these receipts and payments for the accruals basis of accounting, matching all the income and expenses to the three months in which they were earned and incurred rather than just allocating them to the three-month period on the basis of when cash was received or paid. By doing this we can then determine the actual sales made during the period and what it actually cost Julia to make those sales. This will give her a much clearer idea of the profits she has actually earned in her first three months of trading.

You mention this problem to Julia, who provides you with the following additional information:

- She counted up and valued the inventory at the close of business on 30 June 2016: the cost of this inventory came to £10,000.

- At 30 June 2016, Julia owed £25,000 for sports equipment she had purchased from her suppliers on credit in June. She paid this £25,000 on 5 July 2016.

- While her main business is selling sports equipment for cash, Julia has also made sales to two local tennis clubs in June on credit. At 30 June 2016, the two clubs owed £2,500, although one club disputes £50 of the amount outstanding, saying that the goods were never delivered. Julia has no proof that these goods were ever received by the club and has reluctantly agreed that she will never receive this £50.

- During the month of June, Julia employed a part time sales assistant who was owed £300 in wages at the end of June 2016. These wages were paid on 8 July 2016.

- On 5 July 2016, Julia received a telephone bill for £250 covering the three months 1 April 2016 to 30 June 2016 together with an electricity bill for £200 covering the same period.

- Julia expects the cash register and shelving and shop fittings to last for five years before they need replacement. The level of usage of these assets will be the same in each of the next five years. She also expects that the assets will have no residual value at the end of their useful lives and that they will just be scrapped rather than being sold on.

- The cash register contained £500 in cash at 30 June 2016 representing sales receipts that had not yet been banked.

- On 29 June 2016, one of the tennis clubs she trades with on credit returned goods with a sales value of £400. These goods were faulty. Julia returned these goods to her supplier: the goods had originally cost Julia £250.

Taking into account the additional information, together with the transactions through the bank account and our receipts and payments account, Julia's income statement and statement of financial position are shown in Illustrations 3.6 and 3.7.

Illustration 3.6 Julia's income statement for the three months ended 30 June 2016

	£	£	Note
Sales £75,000 (cash received) + £2,500 (sales invoiced but cash not yet received) – £400 (goods returned: no sale or trade receivable recognised) + £500 (cash in till representing unrecorded sales)		77,600	1
Purchases £35,000 (cash paid) + £25,000 (goods received not yet paid for) – £250 (faulty goods returned to supplier: no cost or liability recognised)	59,750		2
Less: closing inventory (inventory of goods not yet sold at 30 June 2016)	(10,000)		3
Cost of sales (purchases – closing inventory)		49,750	4
Gross profit (sales – cost of sales)		27,850	5
Expenses			
Rent	5,000		6
Rates £800 – (£800 × 3/6) (payment is for a six-month period, therefore three months out of six are prepaid)	400		7
Water rates £400 – (£400 × 9/12) (12-month period, so nine months are prepaid)	100		8
Bad debt £50 (sale made but no cash will be received)	50		9
Wages £300 (work performed for wages in June but paid in July)	300		10
Telephone £250 (service received but paid in July)	250		11
Electricity £200 (electricity received but paid in July)	200		12
Cash register depreciation (£1,000/5 years × 3/12 months)	50		13
Shelving and fittings depreciation (£12,000/5 years × 3/12 months)	600		14
Total expenses		6,950	15
Net profit for the three months		20,900	16

Illustration 3.7 Julia's statement of financial position at 30 June 2016

	£	Notes
Non-current assets		
Cash register £1,000 – (£1,000/5 years × 3/12 months)	950	13
Shelves and shop fittings £12,000 – (£12,000/5 years × 3/12 months)	11,400	14
	12,350	
Current assets		
Inventory (inventory of goods not yet sold at 30 June 2016)	10,000	3
Trade receivables £2,500 (sales invoiced but cash not yet received) – £50 (sale made but no cash will be received) – £400 (goods returned: no sale or trade receivable recognised)	2,050	1, 9
Rates prepayment £800 × 3/6 (6 month period, therefore 3/6 prepaid)	400	7
Water rates prepayment £400 × 9/12 (12 month period, 9 months prepaid)	300	8
Bank balance at 30 June 2016	48,800	
Cash in cash register at 30 June 2016 (£500 cash in till representing unrecorded sales, increase sales and increase cash)	500	1
	62,050	
Total assets (£12,350 non-current assets + £62,050 current assets)	74,400	
Current liabilities		
Trade payables £25,000 (goods received not yet paid for) – £250 (goods returned to supplier: no cost or liability recognised)	24,750	2
Wages accrual	300	10
Telephone accrual	250	11
Electricity accrual	200	12
Total liabilities	25,500	
Net assets (total assets (£74,400) – total liabilities (£25,500))	48,900	
Equity (capital account)		
Capital introduced by Julia	30,000	
Drawings (cash paid from the business for personal expenses)	(2,000)	
Net profit for the three months	20,900	
Capital account at 30 June 2016	48,900	

Notes to Julia's income statement and statement of financial position:

1. This figure consists of the sales represented by cash banked (£75,000) + the additional sales made on credit of £2,500 + the unrecorded cash of £500 representing sales made on 30 June 2016. The £2,500 credit sales are recognised now as they are sales that occurred in the three-month period to 30 June 2016 and so are

matched to this accounting period even though the cash from these sales will not be received until after the end of the three-month period. Similarly, the £400 goods returned are recognised as a deduction from the sales total as this sale was cancelled during the three-month period. Money owed by trade receivables is £2,100 (£2,500 credit sales made – £400 selling price of goods returned) while cash rises by £500 as these sales had already been realised in cash. Note that the bad debt of £50 is not deducted from sales but is disclosed as a separate expense in the income statement.

2. Goods purchased on credit in the period and not paid for are likewise matched to the period in which the transaction occurred. Failure to recognise this expense in the period would incorrectly increase the profit for the period and give a completely false picture of how well the business is performing. The receipts and payments account initially showed purchases of £35,000. Once we have added in the additional purchases in the period and deducted the £250 of faulty goods returned to the supplier, the purchases figure has risen to £59,750, a significant increase on the original figure, but one that is required by the accruals basis of accounting. Just as the purchases expense has risen by £24,750 (£25,000 – £250), trade payables have risen by the same amount to reflect the amount owed by the business at 30 June 2016.

3. Closing inventory of goods is treated as a deduction in the income statement as the cost of these unsold goods is carried forward to match against future sales of these goods. While cost of sales is thus reduced by £10,000, the statement of financial position reflects the same amount as an asset, a store of value the business owns which it can sell in future periods to generate further economic benefits for the organisation.

4. Cost of sales, as we noted earlier in the chapter, is calculated as opening inventory (= last year's closing inventory) + purchases during the period – closing inventory. In Julia's case, there is no opening inventory as this is her first trading period, so opening inventory is £nil.

5. Gross profit is calculated as: sales – cost of sales, income earned less the costs incurred in generating that income. Gross profit is an important figure in assessing the performance of an entity as we shall see in Chapter 6.

6. Rent is one figure that does not need adjusting. As stated in the bank receipts and payments, the rent paid is for the months of April, May and June 2016 and is paid right up to 30 June, so there is no prepayment (money paid in advance for services still to be received) or accrual (unpaid amount for services already received) of rent at the end of the three-month accounting period.

7. The rates are for the half year from 1 April 2016 to 30 September 2016. The whole amount due for the six months has been paid during the period. At 30 June 2016, the payment for July, August and September 2016 has been made in advance so

half the £800 is a prepayment at 30 June 2016. The true cost of rates for the three months to 30 June 2016 is 3/6 of £800, so that only £400 is matched as an expense for the quarter.

8. Similarly, the water rates are paid for the whole year from 1 April 2016 to 31 March 2017, so that only three of the twelve months represented by this payment have been used up by 30 June 2016 (April, May and June 2016) leaving the nine months 1 July 2016 to 31 March 2017 prepaid. Again, the water rates expense for the period is only 3/12 of the total paid and this is the expense to match to the three-month period to the end of June 2016. The remainder of this expense is carried forward at the end of the three-month period to match against water usage in future accounting periods.

9. The bad debt is recognised as an expense and not as a deduction from sales. As well as being charged as an expense in the period to which it relates, it is also deducted from trade receivables. As this £50 will not be received, it no longer represents an asset generating future economic benefits so it is deducted from trade receivables in the statement of financial position and charged as an expense in the income statement.

10. The £300 wages cost has been incurred by 30 June 2016 and, while this amount is not paid until after the end of the three-month period, it is matched with the income that those wages helped to generate during June 2016. Expenses increase by £300 and, as this amount has not been paid by the period end, it is recognised as a liability.

11. Similarly, the telephone service has been received over the three-month accounting period so there is a liability at the end of the period together with an expense of £300 matched to the period in which it was incurred.

12. Again, the electricity has been consumed during the three-month period to 30 June 2016, so that a liability exists at the period end for this amount and this, too, is recognised as an expense matched to the accounting period in which it was incurred.

13. As we saw earlier in this chapter, depreciation is charged on non-current assets to reflect the economic benefits of those assets consumed during each accounting period. Julia expects the same level of usage each year from the cash register and the shelving and shop fittings, so this implies the straight line basis of depreciation, an equal amount charged to the periods benefiting from their use. As there is no residual value, the total cost is used to calculate the depreciation charge for the three-month period. In the case of the cash register, £1,000 divided by five years gives an annual depreciation charge of £200. However, as the accounting period is less than a year, the depreciation charge is spread out over the relevant months to give an expense of $£200 \times 3/12 = £50$.

14. In the same way, the straight line basis of depreciation gives an annual charge of £12,000/5 = £2,400 on the shelving and shop fittings. As the accounting period is only three months long, only 3/12 of this annual depreciation is matched to the current accounting period, so that £2,400 × 3/12 = £600 charged to reflect the economic benefit of these assets used up in the accounting period.

15. Total expenses are the sum of all the expenses from rent down to shelving and fittings depreciation.

16. Net profit for the period is given by the gross profit − total expenses.

Drawings and the business entity assumption

Julia's drawings for her personal expenditure have been deducted from equity. Why are these costs not treated as part of the business's expenditure? The answer is that the business's affairs and the owner's affairs are kept entirely separate as the business and the owner are treated as two separate entities. Therefore, there is a need to distinguish the personal affairs of the owner from the affairs of the business and not to mix the two together. Where the owner takes money out of the business for non-business, personal expenditure, any such expenditure is deducted from the owner's interest in the business as it is not expenditure incurred on behalf of the business. The owner's interest in the business is represented by the amounts in the capital account, as we saw in Chapter 2 (The components of equity). All expenditure shown in the business's accounts must be business expenditure only. Thus any personal expenditure charged to the business's bank account is treated as a repayment of the amounts owed to the owner rather than being charged as an expense of the business.

SHOW ME HOW TO DO IT   Are you certain you understand how Julia's income statement and statement of financial position were put together? View Video presentation 3.2 in the **online workbook** to see a practical demonstration of how these two statements were drawn up.

WHY IS THIS RELEVANT TO ME?   Comprehensive example: income statement and statement of financial position

To enable you as a business professional and user of accounting information to appreciate:

- How the income statement and statement of financial position are drawn up from the receipts and payments for an accounting period together with the application of the accruals basis of accounting

- How you should approach income statement and statement of financial position preparation problems

NUMERICAL EXERCISES Are you totally confident that you could prepare income statements and statements of financial position from a given set of information? Go to the **online workbook** and complete Numerical exercises 3.2 to test out your ability to prepare these two statements.

CHAPTER SUMMARY

You should now have learnt that:

- Income statements and statements of financial position are drawn up on the accruals basis of accounting

- Income statement income and expenditure represent income earned and expenditure incurred during an accounting period

- Income statement income and expenditure do not just represent cash received and cash paid during an accounting period

- Accruals are expenses incurred in an accounting period but not yet paid

- Accruals give rise to additional expenditure in the income statement and a current liability in the statement of financial position

- Prepayments are expenses paid in advance of the accounting period to which they relate

- Prepayments reduce current period expenditure and represent a current asset on the statement of financial position

- Depreciation is the allocation of the cost of non-current assets to the accounting periods benefiting from their use

- Depreciation does not represent a loss in value of non-current assets

- Depreciation is not a way of presenting non-current assets at market values

QUICK REVISION Test your knowledge with the online flashcards in Summary of key concepts and attempt the Multiple choice questions, all in the **online workbook**. www.oxfordtextbooks.co.uk/orc/scott/

END-OF-CHAPTER QUESTIONS

Solutions to these questions can be found at the back of the book from page 429.

> *Develop your understanding*

Question 3.1

Abi runs a market stall selling fashion clothing for cash. Her business bank account balance at 1 September 2015, the start of her most recent trading year, was £7,342. She also had

Chapter 3 The income statement   **105**

inventory of £2,382 and trade payables of £3,445 on that date. She rents her market stall at an annual cost of £6,000 payable quarterly in advance from 1 September each trading year. Abi paid all the rent that was due during the year to 31 August 2016. Her cash receipts from sales to customers for the year to 31 August 2016 totalled up to £157,689, but she also gave refunds to customers for returned goods of £3,789. She paid the outstanding trade payables at 1 September 2015 on 5 September 2015. Her purchases for the year totalled up to £120,465, of which she paid £116,328 during the year to 31 August 2016. At 31 August 2016 Abi valued her inventory of clothing at a cost of £4,638. From 1 September 2015 she employed a part time assistant, Kate, agreeing to pay her £100 a week for the year. At the end of August 2016, while Abi had paid Kate all the amounts due for the first 50 weeks of the year, she still owed her £200 for the last two weeks of August 2016. To improve the presentation of her fashion clothing ranges, Abi paid £600 to buy some display stands on 1 September 2015. Abi reckons that these display stands will last her for three years and that they will have a scrap value of £30. On 31 August 2016, Abi had £650 in cash representing sales that had not yet been banked. Abi withdrew £1,500 a month for her own personal expenses from the business bank account.

Required

1. Calculate Abi's opening capital account (equity) balance (remember the accounting equation) at 1 September 2015.

2. Draw up Abi's bank account for the year to 31 August 2016.

3. Prepare Abi's income statement for the year ended 31 August 2016 together with a statement of financial position at that date.

Question 3.2

Alison runs an online gift shop, trading for cash with individual customers and offering trading on credit terms to businesses. She presents you with the following account balances for the year ended 31 December 2016:

	£
Purchases of goods for resale	225,368
Accumulated depreciation on racks, shelving and office furniture at 31 December 2016	14,650
Trade receivables	27,400
Administration expenses	15,265
Racks, shelving and office furniture at cost	33,600
Telephone expenses	5,622
Capital account at 1 January 2016	52,710
Sales	439,429

→

	£
Accumulated depreciation on computers at 31 December 2016	13,850
Inventory at 1 January 2016	27,647
Discounts allowed (already deducted from trade receivables)	1,439
Purchase returns (already deducted from trade payables)	5,724
Bank balance (asset)	52,315
Trade payables	24,962
Rent on warehouse and office unit	15,000
Business rates	9,325
Computer equipment at cost	20,775
Discounts received (already deducted from trade payables)	2,324
Delivery costs	36,970
Electricity and gas	8,736
Insurance	3,250
Drawings	40,000
Depreciation charge for the year on non-current assets	13,255
Sales returns (already deducted from trade receivables)	17,682

Alison provides you with the following additional information.

• Alison valued the inventory at 31 December 2016 at a cost of £22,600.

• All depreciation charges on non-current assets for the year to 31 December 2016 are included in the depreciation figures above.

• Rent on the trading unit prepaid at 31 December 2016 amounted to £3,000.

• Rates prepaid at 31 December 2016 amounted to £1,865.

• Accountancy costs of £1,250 had not been paid by the year end and are not included in the figures above.

• There were no other prepaid or accrued expenses at the year end.

• Alison would like to include a provision for doubtful debts of 10% of year-end trade receivables. There was no provision for doubtful debts at 31 December 2016.

Required

Using the list of balances and the additional information prepare Alison's simplified income statement for the year ended 31 December 2016 together with a statement of financial position at that date.

Question 3.3

The following balances have been extracted from the books of Volumes Limited, a book binder, at 30 September 2016:

	Assets and expenses	Income and liabilities
	£000	£000
Plant and machinery: cost	2,000	
Plant and machinery: accumulated depreciation at 30 September 2016		800
Sales		4,750
Trade receivables	430	
Administration expenses	300	
Selling and distribution costs	200	
Production costs	2,600	
Finance expense	100	
Cash at bank	175	
Loan (due 30 September 2025)		500
Trade payables		300
Finance income		25
Called up share capital		250
Share premium		125
Retained earnings at 30 September 2015		155
Inventory at 1 October 2015	100	
Production wages	1,000	
	6,905	6,905

Additional information

- Inventory at 30 September 2016 was valued at a cost of £150,000.
- Taxation on the profit for the year has been estimated to be £250,000.
- All depreciation charges for the year to 30 September 2016 have been calculated in the balances above.

Required

Using the list of balances and the additional information prepare the income statement and statement of financial position for Volumes Limited in a form suitable for publication.

You will need to produce a working to calculate cost of sales.

You may find that consulting Illustrations 2.1 and 3.1 will assist you in the preparation of the income statement and statement of financial position.

› Take it further

Question 3.4

The following balances have been extracted from the books of Textiles Limited, a cloth manu-facturer and wholesaler, at 30 June 2016:

	Assets and expenses £000	Income and liabilities £000
Plant and machinery: cost	3,000	
Plant and machinery: accumulated depreciation at 30 June 2015		1,200
Motor vehicles: cost	800	
Motor vehicles: accumulated depreciation at 30 June 2015		400
Trade receivables	1,050	
Cost of sales	4,550	
Sales returns (already deducted from trade receivables)	150	
Issued share capital		200
Trade payables		300
Finance expense	110	
Purchase returns (already deducted from trade payables)		80
Administration expenses	700	
Bank overdraft		200
Selling and distribution costs	1,000	
Sales		7,750
Discounts received (already deducted from trade payables)		125
Loan (due for repayment on 30 June 2024)		1,000
Discounts allowed (already deducted from trade receivables)	200	
Retained earnings at 30 June 2015		545
Inventory at 30 June 2016	300	
Provision for doubtful debts at 30 June 2015		60
	11,860	11,860

Additional information

- Audit and accountancy fees (to be charged to administration expenses) of £10,000 have not been taken into account at 30 June 2016.

- Administration expenses include payments for insurance premiums of £30,000 for the 12 months to 31 December 2016.

- Since the year end, a customer of Textiles Limited has gone into liquidation owing £50,000. Textiles Limited does not expect to receive any cash from this trade receivable.

- The provision for doubtful debts is to be adjusted to 4% of trade receivables after deducting known bad debts. All bad and doubtful debts are to be charged to administration expenses.

- Depreciation for the year to 30 June 2016 still has to be calculated. Plant and machinery is to be depreciated at 20% straight line and motor vehicles are to be depreciated at 25% reducing balance. Plant and machinery depreciation should be charged to cost of sales and motor vehicle depreciation should be charged to distribution and selling expenses.

- Taxation on the profit for the year is to be calculated as 25% of the profit before tax.

Required

Prepare the income statement and statement of financial position in a form suitable for publication in accordance with International Financial Reporting Standards.

Question 3.5

Laura was made redundant on 1 July 2015 and received £50,000 in redundancy pay. With this money, she opened a business bank account and set up a small building company undertaking household and small industrial construction work. She commenced her business on 1 September 2015 and she has now reached her year end of 31 August 2016. She has produced a summary of payments and receipts into her business bank account along with additional information that she thinks will be useful in preparing the income statement and statement of financial position for her first year of trading. The details she has presented you with are as follows:

1. Laura's customers usually pay cash at the end of each job. Cash received and banked totals up to £112,000. However, her small industrial clients keep her waiting for payment. She invoiced her small industrial customers £48,000 during the year, but she had only collected £36,000 of this amount by 31 August 2016.

2. Laura buys her construction materials on credit from a local wholesaler. Her total spending on materials this year has been £45,000 of which she had paid £38,000 by 31 August 2016. Her annual trading summary from the wholesaler received on 5 September 2016 tells her that she has qualified for a bulk purchase discount of £1,000, which she can deduct from her next payment in September 2016.

3. Since 31 August 2016, a small industrial customer has gone into liquidation, owing Laura £2,500. The liquidator has told Laura that no payment towards this trade receivable will be made. This liquidation of her customer has made Laura think about the solvency of her

other trade receivables: she decides that she would like to create a doubtful debt provision of 10% of her remaining trade receivables.

4. Laura bought a second-hand van for £6,000 on 1 September 2015. She reckons this van will last for three years before she has to replace it. She anticipates that the trade-in value of this van will be £600 in three years' time. Laura expects the van to do 5,000 miles each year.

5. Van running expenses and insurance for the year amounted to £4,000. All of these expenses were paid from the business bank account. There were no outstanding or prepaid van running expenses at 31 August 2016.

6. On 1 September 2015, Laura paid £5,000 for various items of second-hand construction equipment. These assets should last four years and fetch £60 as scrap when they are replaced. Laura expects to make the same use of these assets in each of the four years.

7. Two part-time helpers were employed for 13 weeks during June, July and August 2016. By 31 August 2016, Laura had paid both these helpers 12 weeks of their wages amounting to £9,600 out of the business bank account.

8. Comprehensive business insurance was taken out on 1 September 2015. As a new business customer, Laura took advantage of the discount scheme to pay £1,800 for 18 months cover.

9. Laura counted up and valued her stock of building materials at 31 August 2016. She valued all these items at a cost to her of £4,500.

10. £400 in bank charges was deducted from her bank account during the year. The bank manager has told her that accrued charges to the end of August 2016 amount to an additional £75.

11. Laura's bank account was overdrawn in the early part of her first year of trading. The bank charged her £200 interest on this overdraft. Since then, her bank account has been in credit and she has earned £250 in interest up to 31 July 2016. The bank manager has told her that in August 2016 her interest receivable is a further £50 and this will be added to her account in October 2016.

12. Laura withdrew £2,500 each month from the bank for personal expenses. As she had so much cash in the bank in August 2016, on 31 August 2016 she used £90,000 from her business bank account to repay half of the mortgage on her house.

Required

1. Prepare Laura's bank account for the year ended 31 August 2016.

2. Prepare a simplified income statement for Laura's business for the year to 31 August 2016 and a statement of financial position at that date.

The statement of cash flows

LEARNING OUTCOMES

Once you have read this chapter and worked through the questions and examples in both this chapter and the online workbook, you should be able to:

- Understand that profit does not equal cash
- Appreciate that without a steady cash inflow from operations an entity will not be able to survive
- Describe the make up of operating, investing and financing cash flows
- Prepare simple statements of cash flows using both the direct and indirect methods
- Explain the importance of statements of cash flows as the third key accounting statement alongside the income statement and statement of financial position
- Understand why statements of cash flows on their own would be insufficient to present a clear picture of an entity's performance and financial position
- Summarise and describe the conventions upon which accounting is based

Introduction

The last two chapters have considered two of the three main accounting statements that entities publish relating to each accounting period. The statement of financial position gives us a snapshot of an entity's assets and liabilities at the end of each accounting period, while the income statement shows us the profit or loss based on the income generated and expenditure incurred within each accounting period. This chapter will consider the third key accounting statement, the statement of cash flows, which presents users of financial information with details of cash inflows and outflows for an accounting period. As we shall see, the statement of cash flows links together the income statement and statement of financial position to demonstrate changes in an entity's financial position over each accounting period arising from operating, investing and financing activities.

Without a steady inflow of cash, businesses cannot survive. Thus, if cash is not generated from sales, there will be no money with which to pay liabilities owed, to pay wages to employees to produce or sell goods, to pay rent on facilities hired, to pay returns to investors or to finance growth and expansion. Over time, cash inflows must exceed cash outflows in order for an entity to remain a **going concern**, a business that will continue into the foreseeable future. The ability of a business to generate cash is thus critical to its survival as, without a steady inflow of cash, the business cannot carry on, no matter how profitable. It is hugely important to appreciate that profit does not represent cash. To illustrate this fact, Give me an example 4.1 presents the case of Salesforce.com, a loss making company with a very positive cash position.

GIVE ME AN EXAMPLE 4.1   Salesforce.com

Yes, but look at the cash. That is the response from Salesforce.com bulls when some spoilsport notes that the software-as-a-service company makes no net profit. And indeed, in the past 12 months, the company had a net loss of $260m, and free cash flow (cash from operations less capital spending) of $760m – a $1bn gap.

A happy feature of the Salesforce model is that the company gets paid largely in advance, when a contract is signed, while revenues and profits are recognised over the life of the contract. As long as the company is signing up new customers, cash outruns accounting profits.

Source: The Lex column, *Financial Times*, 8 July 2014 (© The Financial Times Limited 2014. All Rights Reserved.)

To enable you as a business professional and user of financial information to understand that:

- Turning profits into cash is a most important task for businesses
- Without cash, businesses will not be able to meet their commitments or fund their expansion plans and will fail

GO BACK OVER THIS AGAIN! Do you really appreciate how important cash and cash inflow are? Go to the online workbook Exercises 4.1 to make sure you have grasped this critical lesson.

4

Statement of cash flows: format

What format does the statement of cash flows take? Illustration 4.1 shows the statement of cash flows for Bunns the Bakers plc for the years ended 31 March 2016 and 31 March 2015. Consider this statement of cash flows for a moment and then we will look at how it is constructed and what the terminology means.

Note: cash inflows (money coming in) are shown without brackets while cash outflows (money going out) are shown in brackets. Work through the statement of cash flows, adding the figures without brackets and deducting the figures in brackets to help you understand how the cash inflows and outflows add up to the subtotals given.

The net increase in cash and cash equivalents for the year ended 31 March 2016 of £23,000 is given by adding the net cash inflow from operating activities (+ £1,219,000) and then subtracting the net cash outflow from investing activities (– £891,000) and subtracting the net cash outflow from financing activities (– £305,000). Check back to the statement of financial position for Bunns the Bakers plc (Illustration 2.1, Chapter 2) to make sure that the figure given for cash and cash equivalents at 31 March 2016 is £212,000. Repeat the calculations for 2015 to make sure you understand how the figures in the statement of cash flows are derived.

SUMMARY OF KEY CONCEPTS Do you think that you know how to calculate the net increase/(decrease) in cash and cash equivalents? Check your knowledge with Summary of key concepts 4.1.

GO BACK OVER THIS AGAIN A copy of this statement of cash flows (Illustration 4.1) is available in the **online workbook**. You might like to keep this on screen or print off a copy for easy reference while you work your way through the material in this chapter. There is also an annotated copy of this statement of cash flows in the **online workbook** to go over the relevant points again to reinforce your knowledge and learning.

Illustration 4.1 Bunns the Bakers plc statement of cash flows for the years ended 31 March 2016 and 31 March 2015

	2016	2015
	£000	£000
Cash flows from operating activities		
Cash generated from operations (see below)	**1,408**	1,142
Taxation paid	**(189)**	(154)
Net cash inflow from operating activities	**1,219**	988
Cash flows from investing activities		
Acquisition of property, plant and equipment	**(910)**	(600)
Acquisition of investments	**(6)**	(11)
Proceeds from the sale of property, plant and equipment	**10**	47
Interest received	**15**	12
Net cash outflow from investing activities	**(891)**	(552)
Cash flows from financing activities		
Proceeds from the issue of ordinary share capital	**235**	148
Dividends paid	**(90)**	(72)
Repayment of the current portion of long-term borrowings	**(300)**	(300)
Interest paid	**(150)**	(165)
Net cash outflow from financing activities	**(305)**	(389)
Net increase in cash and cash equivalents	**23**	47
Cash and cash equivalents at the start of the year	**189**	142
Cash and cash equivalents at the end of the year	**212**	189

Cash generated from operations	2016	2015
	£000	£000
Operating profit for the year	**895**	767
(Increase)/decrease in inventories	**(5)**	8
Decrease in trade and other receivables	**13**	9
Increase/(decrease) in trade and other payables	**109**	(15)
Amortisation of intangible non-current assets	**5**	7
Depreciation of property, plant and equipment	**394**	362
(Profit)/loss on the disposal of property, plant and equipment	**(3)**	4
Cash from operating activities	**1,408**	1,142

Constructing the statement of cash flows

Illustration 4.1 shows that Bunns the Bakers' statement of cash flows consists of three sections:

- Cash flows from operating activities
- Cash flows from investing activities
- Cash flows from financing activities

These three sections represent the inflows and outflows of cash for all entities. Let us look at each of these categories in turn.

Cash flows from operating activities

All entities operate with a view to generating cash with which to finance their day-to-day operations, their operating activities, and with the intention and expectation of generating surplus cash for future investment and expansion. This cash generated will consist of the cash from sales less the cash spent in both generating those sales and in running the organisation.

As we have already seen, Bunns the Bakers produces bakery goods and buys in other goods for resale in the shops. Operating cash inflows will thus consist of money received from sales in the shops while operating cash outflows will be made up of the money spent on:

- Producing the goods
- Buying goods in for resale
- Distributing the goods to shops
- Selling those goods in the shops
- Administration expenses incurred in the running of the business

The difference between the trading and operating cash flowing into the business and the trading and operating cash flowing out of the business will give the net operating cash inflows or outflows for each accounting period, the cash generated from operations. Any taxation paid by the entity will also be deducted from operating cash flows. Tax arises as a consequence of profits made from operating activities, so any tax paid in an accounting period will be deducted from the cash generated from operations.

Bunns the Bakers' statement of cash flows is an example of the indirect method of cash flow preparation. This approach requires that the operating profits for the year be subjected to certain adjustments: these adjustments are given in the 'Cash generated from operations' note. These adjustments to the operating profit represent the effect of non-cash entries into the income statement alongside movements in working capital (changes in inventory, trade and other receivables and trade and other payables over the course of the accounting period) and are made in order to work back to the cash generated from operating activities. These adjustments and how they are derived are explained in more detail later in this chapter, The indirect method.

GIVE ME AN EXAMPLE 4.2   Cash flows from operating activities

What sort of cash flows from operating activities do companies present in their annual reports and accounts? The following extract is taken from the statements of cash flows of Greggs plc for the 52 weeks ended 28 December 2014 and the 52 weeks ended 29 December 2013.

Cash flow statement – cash generated from operations

	2014	2013
	£000	£000
Profit for the financial year	37,556	24,189
Amortisation	100	161
Depreciation	37, 463	33,225
Impairment	414	5,252
Loss/(profit) on sale of property, plant and equipment	3,576	1,390
Release of government grants	(473)	(470)
Share-based payment expenses	529	592
Finance expense	(175)	206
Income tax expense	12, 187	8,963
Decrease/(increase) in inventories	115	2,253
Decrease/(increase) in receivables	(1,079)	1,905
Increase/(decrease) in payables	17,089	1,220
Increase/(decrease) in provisions	1,250	3,607
Cash from operating activities	108,552	82, 493

Source: *Greggs plc annual report and accounts 2014* www.corporate.greggs.co.uk/investor-centre

---

GO BACK OVER THIS AGAIN!   Are you totally convinced that you can distinguish between cash inflows and cash outflows from operating activities? Go to the **online workbook** and complete Exercises 4.2 to make sure you can make these distinctions.

Cash flows from investing activities

In order to expand a business, entities must invest in new capacity in the form of non-current assets. Any cash paid out to buy new property, plant and equipment or intangible assets such as trademarks will appear under this heading as this represents investment of cash into new long-term assets with which to generate new income by expanding and improving the business. Where an entity has surplus funds that cannot currently be used to invest in such assets, it will place those funds in long-term investments to generate interest or dividend income that will increase the profits of the organisation. Thus, any investment in non-current asset investments will also appear under this heading. Note that both of these uses of cash represent outflows of cash as cash is leaving the business in exchange for new property, plant and equipment or new long-term investments.

In addition to these outflows of cash, investing activities also give rise to inflows of cash. When buying new property, plant and equipment, it is quite likely that some other non-current assets will be sold or scrapped at the same time, as these are now worn out or surplus to requirements. Selling or scrapping these assets will result in a cash inflow and any cash raised in this way will be classified under investing activities. Likewise, any interest or dividends received from investing surplus funds in current or non-current asset investments are also cash inflows under investing activities: the investments were made with a view to generating investment income, so such cash inflows are logically included under this heading. Cash inflows and outflows from investing activities are summarised in Figure 4.1.

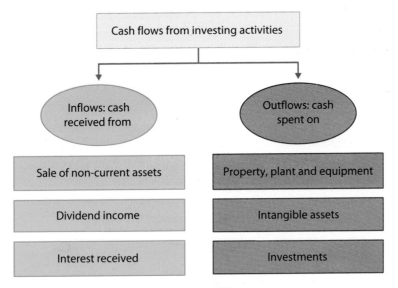

Figure 4.1 Cash inflows and outflows from investing activities

GIVE ME AN EXAMPLE 4.3   Cash flows from investing activities

What sort of cash flows from investing activities do companies present in their annual reports and accounts? The following extract is taken from the statements of cash flows of Greggs plc for the 52 weeks ended 28 December 2014 and the 52 weeks ended 29 December 2013.

Investing activities	2014	2013
	£000	£000
Acquisition of property, plant and equipment	(44, 456)	(47,808)
Acquisition of intangible assets	(3,809)	(785)
Proceeds from sale of property, plant and equipment	2,231	3,194
Interest (paid)/received	173	(24)
(Acquisition)/redemption of other investments	(7,000)	(3000)
Net cash outflow from investing activities	(52,861)	(48, 423)

Source: *Greggs plc annual report and accounts 2014* www.corporate.greggs.co.uk/investor-centre

GO BACK OVER THIS AGAIN!   Quite sure that you could say whether a transaction is a cash inflow or cash outflow from investing activities? Go to the **online workbook** and complete Exercises 4.3 to make sure you can make these decisions correctly.

Cash flows from financing activities

There are three main sources of finance for a business. The first of these is cash generated from operations. This source of cash has already been dealt with earlier under 'Cash flows from operating activities'.

The second source of finance for business is from the issue of share capital. Bunns the Bakers have issued shares during the year for cash and so this is recorded as a cash inflow to the business: money has been paid into the company in return for new shares. Shareholders expect a return on their investment in the company: the cash outflows related to share capital are the dividends paid out to shareholders. The payment of dividends is an outflow of cash and is recorded under financing activities as it relates to the cost of financing the business through share capital.

The third source of finance is provided by lenders, money borrowed from banks or the money markets to finance expansion and the acquisition of new non-current assets. As the expansion/new non-current assets generate cash from their operation, these cash inflows are used to repay the borrowings over the following years, much as a taxi driver might borrow money to buy a taxi and then repay that loan from monthly fares earned. This is the case for Bunns the Bakers this year. While no new borrowings have been taken out (this would be an inflow of cash) part of the money previously borrowed has now been repaid from cash generated from operations in the current year. Repayments of borrowings are an outflow of cash. Any interest paid that arises from borrowing money is recorded as an outflow of cash under financing activities. Just as dividends are the cost of financing operations or expansion through the issue of share capital, interest is the cost of financing operations or expansion through borrowing and so is matched to the financing activities section of the statement of cash flows. Figure 4.2 summarises the cash inflows and outflows from financing activities.

GIVE ME AN EXAMPLE 4.4   Cash flows from financing activities

What sort of cash flows from financing activities do companies present in their annual reports and accounts? The following extract is taken from the Consolidated cash flow statement of Next plc for the financial years ended January 2015 and January 2014.

Cash flows from financing activities

	2015	2014
	£m	£m
Repurchase of own shares	(137.9)	(295.8)
Purchase of shares by ESOT	(79.8)	(97.5)
Proceeds from disposal of shares by ESOT	45.0	42.9
Bonds issued	–	250.0
Bonds redeemed	–	(85.5)
Interest paid	(29.7)	(21.5)
Interest received	0.9	0.5
Payment of finance lease liabilities	(0.2)	(0.1)
Dividends paid	(434.4)	(164.8)
Net cash from financing activities	(636.1)	(371.8)

Source: *Next plc annual report and accounts January 2015* www.nextplc.co.uk

Note: ESOT = Employee share ownership trust.

GO BACK OVER THIS AGAIN!   How easily can you distinguish between cash inflows and cash outflows from financing activities? Go to the **online workbook** and complete Exercises 4.4 to make sure you can make these distinctions.

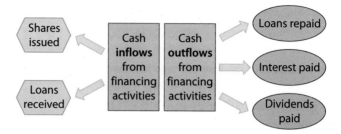

Figure 4.2 Cash inflows and cash outflows from financing activities

Cash and cash equivalents

The sum of all three cash flow sections will equal the movement in cash and cash equivalents during the accounting period. The meaning of cash is quite clear, but you might be puzzled by the phrase cash equivalents. Is there really an equivalent to cash?

What this means is anything that is close to cash, a source of cash that could be called upon immediately if required. Such a source might be a bank deposit account rather than money held in the current account for immediate use. Where money held in bank deposit accounts is readily convertible into cash then this is a cash equivalent. Thus, cash held in a deposit account requiring 30 days' notice would be a cash equivalent as the cash can easily be converted to a fixed sum of cash in a maximum of 30 days. However, cash currently held in a bond with a maturity date in two years' time would not be a cash equivalent as it cannot be converted easily to cash now or in the very near future. The International Accounting Standards Board allows any deposit of cash with a notice term of 90 days or less to be classified as a cash equivalent alongside money held in current accounts and held as cash on the business premises.

WHY IS THIS RELEVANT TO ME?   Cash flows from operating activities, investing activities and financing activities

To enable you as a business professional and user of financial information to:

• Understand the different sources from which cash flows into and out of an entity

• Read statements of cash flows and understand what the various cash inflows and outflows of an organisation represent, along with the transactions behind them

MULTIPLE CHOICE QUESTIONS   Do you think that you can say to which category of cash flows a cash inflow or outflow belongs? Go to the **online workbook** and complete Multiple choice questions 4.1 to make sure you can identify these accurately.

Profit ≠ cash

We have already touched upon the idea at the start of this chapter that profit does not equal cash. It is now time to show how true this statement is with a detailed example.

4

EXAMPLE 4.1

Start Up begins a wholesale trading business on 1 January and makes sales of £20,000 in January, £30,000 in February and £40,000 in March. The cost of purchases is £15,000 in January, £22,500 in February and £30,000 in March. All goods purchased each month are sold in that month so that cost of sales equals cost of purchases.

The income statement for Start Up for each month and in total for the three months will be as follows:

	January £	February £	March £	Total £
Sales	20,000	30,000	40,000	90,000
Cost of sales	15,000	22,500	30,000	67,500
Gross profit	5,000	7,500	10,000	22,500

Start Up makes a profit each month. Profit is rising so the owners of Start Up will be pleased. However, to show that profit is not cash, let's look at two alternative scenarios for the way in which Start Up collects its cash from customers and pays cash to its suppliers.

Start Up: cash flow: scenario 1

Start Up is unable to gain credit from its suppliers and so pays for goods in the month of purchase. In order to build up trade with its customers, Start Up offers generous credit terms and allows its customers to pay for goods delivered two months after sales are made. There is no cash in the bank on 1 January and each month that the company is overdrawn a charge of 1% of the closing overdraft is incurred on the first day of the following month. Each month that the company is in credit (has a surplus in its account) the bank pays interest of 0.5% on the credit balance at the end of the month on the first day of the following month. The cash flow for the three months ended 31 March will be as follows:

	January £	February £	March £	Total £
Opening cash balance	—	(15,000)	(37,650)	—
Cash receipts from sales	—	—	20,000	20,000
Cash paid to suppliers	(15,000)	(22,500)	(30,000)	(67,500)
Interest received	—	—	—	—
Overdraft charges (1%)	—	(150)	*(377)	(527)
Closing cash balance	(15,000)	(37,650)	(48,027)	(48,027)

* Rounded to the nearest whole £.

Despite the profit made according to the income statement, look how poorly trading has turned out from a cash flow point of view. All the purchases have been paid for in the month in which they were made, but the company is still owed £70,000 by customers (£30,000 for February + £40,000 for March: might any of these debts become bad debts?) at the end of March. In addition, Start Up has incurred overdraft charges of £527 in February and March with the prospect of another £480 to pay in April (£48,027 × 1%).

Clearly, the £22,500 gross profit for the three months has not translated into surplus cash at the end of the three-month period. Start Up's bank manager might begin to worry about the increasing overdraft and put pressure on the company to reduce this. But, with cash being paid out up front to suppliers while customers enjoy a two-month credit period in which to pay, a reduction in the overdraft in the near future looks highly unlikely. Many small businesses when they start up offer generous credit terms to customers while being forced to pay quickly by their suppliers, so it should come as no surprise that many small businesses collapse within a year of starting to trade as their cash flow dries up and banks close them down to recover what they are owed.

Start Up: cash flow: scenario 2

Facts are as in Scenario 1, except that this time Start Up pays for its supplies one month after the month of purchase and collects cash from its customers in the month in which sales are made. The three-month cash flow will now be as shown in the table below.

	January	February	March	Total
	£	£	£	£
Opening cash balance	—	20,000	35,100	—
Cash receipts from sales	20,000	30,000	40,000	90,000
Cash paid to suppliers	—	(15,000)	(22,500)	(37,500)
Interest received	—	100	*176	276
Overdraft charges	—	—	—	—
Closing cash balance	20,000	35,100	52,776	52,776

*Rounded to the nearest whole £.

What a difference a change in the terms of trade makes. By requiring customers to pay immediately for goods received and deferring payments to suppliers for a month, the cash flow has remained positive throughout the three months and additional interest income has been received from the bank by keeping cash balances positive. Suppliers are still owed £30,000, but there is more than enough cash in the bank to meet this liability and still have money available with which to keep trading.

Notably, the cash in the bank again bears no relationship to the gross profit of £22,500, so, once again, this example illustrates the key point that profit does not equal cash. The lesson to learn here is clear: if you can make sure that your customers pay before cash has to be paid to suppliers, the business will survive. In situations in which customers pay what is owed after suppliers have been paid, then the business will struggle to maintain cash inflows and be in danger of being closed down by banks to which the business owes money.

WHY IS THIS RELEVANT TO ME? Profit ≠ cash

To enable you as a business professional and user of financial information to:

- Appreciate that profit does not equal cash in an accounting period
- Realise that the timing of cash inflows and cash outflows has to be finely balanced to ensure that positive cash inflows are achieved
- Understand that positive cash inflows are critical to a business's ability to survive

---

NUMERICAL EXERCISES   Are you quite convinced that you could calculate cash flows from given terms of trade? Go to the **online workbook** Numerical exercises 4.1 to test out your abilities in this area.

Cash is cash is cash: the value of statements of cash flows

The income statement and the two cash flows for Start Up earlier also illustrate the advantages and the true value of the statement of cash flows when making comparisons between entities. If two companies presented exactly the same income statement figures, it would be very difficult, if not impossible, to choose between the two and to say which company enjoyed the more stable, cash generative financial position. However, by looking at the statements of cash flows, we could say instantly that the company that presented the cash flow shown in scenario 2 was in a much better position financially compared to the company presenting the cash flow in scenario 1. Without the statement of cash flows we would not see that one company is doing very well from a cash management point of view while the other is doing very poorly. Hence the value of the statement of cash flows in enabling users to determine the financial position of an entity, information that is not available from just the income statement.

However, the two statements of cash flows above illustrate further advantages of this statement. As we saw in Chapter 3, the income statement is drawn up on the accruals basis of accounting, which requires income and expenditure to be recognised in the period in which it was earned and incurred. The statement of cash flows just presents the cash inflows and outflows relating to that period. As we have seen, profit, the difference between income earned and expenditure incurred, does not equate to cash. Therefore, the provision of a statement of cash flows enables users to see much more clearly how quickly profit is turned into cash: in scenario 2 cash is clearly being generated very effectively while in scenario 1 the company looks as though it is about to collapse. While the accrual of expenses and income into a period can produce the impression of an excellent result from a profit point of view, since cash is cash is cash it does not suffer from any distortion that might arise in the timing of income and expenditure recognition.

WHY IS THIS RELEVANT TO ME?   The value of statements of cash flows

To enable you as a business professional and user of financial information to appreciate how statements of cash flows:

• Enable users to discriminate between different entities with the same levels of profit

• Are not distorted by the effect of the accrual of income and expenditure into different accounting periods

GO BACK OVER THIS AGAIN Quite sure that you appreciate why statements of cash flows are so valuable? Go to the **online workbook** Exercises 4.6 to test your grasp of their value.

Is the statement of cash flows enough on its own?

If statements of cash flows are so useful, why do entities have to present the income statement and the statement of financial position as well? Why not just require all organisations to produce the statement of cash flows only? This is a valid question and it leads us into thinking about why the statement of cash flows in isolation does not actually tell us very much beyond the cash generated and spent during an accounting period. Let's think first about how useful the statement of financial position and the income statement are.

In Chapter 2 we saw that the statement of financial position provides us with details of:

- Liabilities to be paid
- Assets employed within the organisation.

Users of financial statements can look at an entity's assets and make an assessment of whether they will be able to generate the cash necessary to meet the liabilities as they fall due. If only a statement of cash flows were to be presented, then there would be no details of either assets or liabilities and so no assessment of an entity's cash generating potential would be possible.

In Chapter 3 we saw that the income statement presents details of:

- Income earned
- Expenditure incurred.

Users of financial statements can then assess how profitable an organisation is and, in conjunction with the statement of cash flows, how effectively it can turn profits into cash with which to meet operating expenses and liabilities as they fall due. Without an income statement, the statement of cash flows cannot tell us how profitable an organisation is or how quickly profits are being turned into cash.

A statement of cash flows on its own could be subject to manipulation. Entity owners or directors could time their cash inflows and outflows to present the most flattering picture of their organisation (Chapter 3, The accruals basis of accounting). Therefore, just as an income statement or statement of financial position in isolation does not tell us very much, so a statement of cash flows presented as the

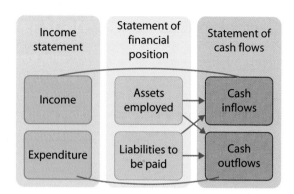

Figure 4.3 The three main financial statements and the ways in which they interact

sole portrait of performance would also be much less informative without its fellow financial statements.

This is why the IASB requires preparers of financial statements to present all three statements as 'users are better able to evaluate this ability to generate cash and cash equivalents if they are provided with information that focuses on the financial position [the statement of financial position], performance [the income statement] and changes in financial position [statement of cash flows] of an entity' (IASB Framework, paragraph 15). Any one (and indeed any two) of the three statements on their own will not provide all the information that users will need to make the necessary evaluations. Figure 4.3 summarises the three main financial statements and the figures they present.

WHY IS THIS RELEVANT TO ME?   **Is the statement of cash flows enough on its own?**

To enable you as a business professional and user of financial information to appreciate how:

- Statements of cash flows would not on their own provide sufficient useful information about an entity's financial position and performance

- How the three main financial statements link together to provide useful information to users

---

GO BACK OVER THIS AGAIN!   Are you convinced that you understand how statements of cash flows work with the other two financial statements? Go to the **online workbook** Exercises 4.7 to test your grasp of the value of cash flow statements.

GO BACK OVER THIS AGAIN!   Can you see how the statement of cash flows explains the changes in the financial position of an entity? Go to the **online workbook** Exercises 4.8 to see how the one statement explains the changes in the other.

Preparing the statement of cash flows

The direct method

Illustration 4.2 Julia's bank account receipts and payments summary (= Illustration 3.3)

Date		Receipts £	Payments £
1 April 2016	Cash introduced by Julia	30,000	
1 April 2016	Three months rent paid on shop to 30 June 2016		5,000
1 April 2016	Cash register paid for		1,000
1 April 2016	Shelving and shop fittings paid for		12,000
30 April 2016	Receipts from sales in April 2016	20,000	
5 May 2016	Sports equipment supplied in April paid for		15,000
12 May 2016	Rates for period 1 April 2016 to 30 September 2016 paid		800
19 May 2016	Cash withdrawn for Julia's own expenses		2,000
30 May 2016	Receipts from sales in May 2016	25,000	
5 June 2016	Sports equipment supplied in May paid for		20,000
10 June 2016	Shop water rates for the year 1 April 2016 to 31 March 2018 paid		400
30 June 2016	Receipts from sales in June 2016	30,000	
30 June 2016	Balance in bank at 30 June 2016		48,800
		105,000	105,000

EXAMPLE 4.2

There are two approaches to preparing the statement of cash flows, the direct and indirect methods. We will use the example of Julia from Chapter 3 to illustrate both methods. Julia's bank summary for the three months ended 30 June 2016 from Chapter 3 (Example 3.8, Illustration 3.3) is shown again in Illustration 4.2.

While Illustration 4.2 is already almost a complete statement of cash flows, showing cash received and cash paid out, all these transactions (together with the cash not yet banked from sales on 30 June 2016) would be presented in the required format as shown in Illustration 4.3.

Illustration 4.3 Julia: statement of cash flows for the three months ended 30 June 2016 using the direct method

	£	£
Cash flows from operating activities		
Receipts from sales banked 20,000 + 25,000 + 30,000	75,000	
Cash sales not yet banked	500	
Payments to trade payables for sports equipment 15,000 + 20,000	(35,000)	
Payments for expenses 5,000 (rent) + 800 (rates) + 400 (water)	(6,200)	
Net cash inflow from operating activities		34,300
Cash flows from investing activities		
Payments to acquire shop fittings and shelving	(12,000)	
Payments to acquire cash register	(1,000)	
Net cash outflow from investing activities		(13,000)
Cash flows from financing activities		
Cash introduced by Julia	30,000	
Cash withdrawn by Julia	(2,000)	
Net cash inflow from financing activities		28,000
Net increase in cash and cash equivalents		49,300
Cash and cash equivalents at the start of the period		—
Cash and cash equivalents at the end of the period		49,300

The figure for cash and cash equivalents at the end of the period is exactly the same as the bank balance plus the cash in the till at 30 June 2016 as shown in Julia's statement of financial position in Chapter 3, Illustration 3.7.

NUMERICAL EXERCISES   Are you certain that you could prepare statements of cash flows using the direct method? Go to the **online workbook** Numerical exercises 4.2 to test out your ability to prepare these statements.

The indirect method

The statement of cash flows for Julia in Illustration 4.3 represents an example of the direct method of cash flow preparation: this takes all the cash inflows and outflows from operations and summarises them to produce the net cash inflow from operating activities. Thus, receipts from sales are totalled up to give the cash inflow from sales and payments to suppliers and for expenses are totalled up to give a figure for payments to trade payables in the period. The difference between the inflows of cash from sales and the outflows of cash for expenses represents the operating cash inflows for the three months.

However, as we noted in this chapter in the Cash flows from operating activities section above, the example of Bunns the Bakers' statement of cash flows in Illustration 4.1 represents an example of the indirect method of cash flow preparation. Under this method, the total inflows and outflows from operations are ignored and the operating profit for a period is adjusted for increases or decreases in inventory, receivables, prepayments, payables and accruals and for the effect of non-cash items such as depreciation. As we saw in Chapter 3, depreciation is an accounting adjustment that allocates the cost of non-current assets to the accounting periods benefiting from their use.

Illustration 4.4

	£	£
Cash flows from operating activities		
Net profit for the 3 months to 30 June 2016 (Illustration 3.6)		20,900
Add: depreciation on shelving and fittings (Illustration 3.6)		600
Add: depreciation on the cash register (Illustration 3.6)		50
Deduct: increase in inventory		(10,000)
Deduct: increase in receivables		(2,050)
Deduct: increase in prepayments		(700)
Add: increase in payables		24,750
Add: increase in accruals		750
Net cash inflow from operating activities (= Illustration 4.3)		34,300
Cash flows from investing activities		
Payments to acquire shop fittings and shelving	(12,000)	
Payments to acquire cash register	(1,000)	
Net cash outflow from investing activities (= Illustration 4.3)		(13,000)
Cash flows from financing activities		
Cash introduced by Julia	30,000	
Cash withdrawn by Julia	(2,000)	
Net cash inflow from financing activities (= Illustration 4.3)		28,000
Net increase in cash and cash equivalents		49,300
Cash and cash equivalents at the start of the period		—
Cash and cash equivalents at the end of the period		49,300

Therefore, depreciation is NOT a cash flow. The actual cash flows associated with non-current assets are the cash paid to acquire the assets in the first place and the cash received on disposal of those assets when they are sold or scrapped at the end of their useful lives.

Let's look at how using the indirect method would affect the preparation of Julia's statement of cash flows. While the direct method of cash flow preparation is very easy to understand and put together from summaries of cash receipts and payments, most entities use the indirect method. For Julia, the cash flow for the three months ended 30 June 2016 under the indirect method would be as shown in the accounting statement in Illustration 4.4.

Not surprisingly, both the direct and the indirect method give the same answer for net cash inflow for the three months, £49,300. The only differences between the two cash flows are in the calculation of the cash flow from operating activities.

In the cash flow from operating activities section, depreciation on the shelving and fittings and on the cash register is exactly the same as the depreciation charged in the income statement for the three months ended 30 June 2016 (Chapter 3, Illustration 3.6). The changes in the amounts for inventory, receivables, prepayments, payables and accruals are usually the difference between the current period end's figures and the figures at the end of the previous accounting period. As this is Julia's first trading period, the figures for the changes in these amounts are exactly the same as the figures from her statement of financial position (Chapter 3, Illustration 3.7). The figures at the start of the business were all £nil. Thus, for example, in the case of inventory £10,000 – £nil = an increase of £10,000.

WHY IS THIS RELEVANT TO ME?   Preparing the statement of cash flows: direct and indirect methods

To enable you as a business professional and user of financial information to:

- Prepare simple cash flow statements for a given period using either the direct or indirect method

- Understand that the two different methods used to prepare statements of cash flows produce the same results

---

SHOW ME HOW TO DO IT   Are you certain that you understand how Julia's statement of cash flows using the indirect method was put together? View Video presentation 4.1 in the **online workbook** to see a practical demonstration of how this statement of cash flows was drawn up.

NUMERICAL EXERCISES   Do you reckon that you could prepare statements of cash flows using the indirect method? Go to the **online workbook** Numerical exercises 4.3 to test out your ability to prepare these statements.

The indirect method: cash flows from operating activities: inflows or outflows?

Why are the cash flows associated with Julia's inventory, receivables and prepayments treated as outflows of cash (appearing in brackets) while the cash flows associated with payables and accruals are all inflows of cash (appearing without brackets)? The answer lies in the fact that the income statement is prepared on the accruals basis of accounting, recognising income and expenses in the period in which they are earned or incurred rather than in the periods in which cash is received or paid. Some income has thus been recognised in the income statement that has not yet resulted in a cash inflow. Similarly, some expenses have been recognised in the income statement without the corresponding cash outflow. Therefore, adjustments for these 'non-cash' figures have to be made to operating profit to determine the actual cash flows from operating activities under the indirect method. Let's look at each of these adjustments in turn.

Inventory

An increase in inventory is an increase in an asset. This represents an outflow of cash as more money will have been spent on acquiring this additional inventory. Hence the deduction from operating profit. On the other hand, if the cost of inventory decreases over the year, this would mean that more inventory had been sold, resulting in larger cash inflows. Such a fall in inventory would result in an inflow of cash and be added to operating profit.

Receivables

An increase in receivables means additional sales have been recognised in the income statement, but that cash has not yet been received from this additional income. As no cash inflow relating to these additional sales has occurred, the increase in receivables is treated as a deduction from operating profit to reflect this lack of cash inflows. As in the case of inventory, if the amount of receivables falls, this means more money has come in from receivables so this is treated as an increase in cash inflows and is added to cash flows from operating activities.

Trade payables

On the other hand, if trade payables have increased, you have not spent money on paying your suppliers. The increase in trade payables means that cash has not flowed out of the business, so this reduction in payments is added to operating profit. Where trade payables have decreased, this means more cash has been spent on reducing liabilities, so this is treated as a decrease in cash and a deduction is made from operating profit to reflect this outflow of cash.

Prepayments and accruals

Prepayments represent expenses paid in advance so an increase in prepayments means that more cash has flowed out of the business due to an increase in payments made. This increase is deducted from operating profit. An increase in accruals on the other hand, as with the increase in payables, means that while an expense has been recognised no cash has yet been paid out so this increase is added to operating profit. Where prepayments fall, this is treated as an increase in operating cash flows as less cash has been spent on paying expenses, while a decrease in accruals would represent increased cash outflows as more money would have been spent on reducing these liabilities.

Initially these rules will seem confusing, but practice will enable you to become familiar with them and to apply them confidently in the preparation of statements of cash flows. To assist you in applying these rules, Table 4.1 shows which adjustments should be added and which adjustments should be deducted from operating profit in arriving at the cash flows from operating activities. Keep this table handy when you are working through the online examples and the questions at the end of this chapter.

Table 4.1 Figures to add to and figures to deduct from operating profit to determine the cash flow from operating activities when preparing statements of cash flows using the indirect method

Starting point: operating profit from the income statement	
Add	**Deduct**
Depreciation of non-current assets	
Amortisation of intangible non-current assets	
Loss on disposal of non-current assets	Profit on disposal of non-current assets
Decrease in inventory	Increase in inventory
Decrease in receivables	Increase in receivables
Decrease in prepayments	Increase in prepayments
Increase in payables	Decrease in payables
Increase in accruals	Decrease in accruals
Increase in provisions	Decrease in provisions

GO BACK OVER THIS AGAIN! How well can you remember Table 4.1? Go to the **online workbook** and complete Exercises 4.9 to check your recollection.

The only items in Table 4.1 that we have not dealt with in our cash flow studies to date are the profits and losses on the disposal of non-current assets. The actual cash flow associated with the disposal of non-current assets is the actual cash received. Just as depreciation, which was treated as an expense in arriving at operating profit, is added back to operating profit to determine the cash flows from operating activities, so losses on disposal are added as they, too, have been treated as an additional expense in arriving at operating profit. Profits on disposal, on the other hand, have been treated as income in determining operating profit and so have to be deducted in arriving at the cash flows from operating activities.

WHY IS THIS RELEVANT TO ME? The indirect method: cash flows from operating activities: inflows or outflows?

To enable you as a business professional and user of financial information to understand how:

- Adjustments under the indirect method of preparation have been calculated
- Movements in the working capital (inventory, receivables and payables) impact upon the cash flows from operating activities

MULTIPLE CHOICE QUESTIONS Could you calculate profits and losses on disposal? Say what the cash inflow or outflow was on a non-current asset disposal? Go to the **online workbook** and complete Multiple choice questions 4.2 to make sure you can make these calculations correctly.

Accounting conventions

We have now worked through the three key accounting statements: the income statement, statement of financial position and statement of cash flows. On our journey this far, we have noted various accounting conventions that apply in the preparation of these three financial statements. These conventions are listed below:

- Accruals (also known as matching)
- Business entity
- Consistency
- Dual aspect
- Going concern
- Historic cost
- Materiality
- Money measurement
- Periodicity

- Prudence
- Realisation

How well do you remember these conventions and what they say? We will not be discussing these conventions in any more detail at this point, but there are various activities upon which you can now test your knowledge.

WHY IS THIS RELEVANT TO ME?   Accounting conventions

To enable you as a business professional and user of financial information to understand the conventions:

- Upon which financial statements are based
- Which you will have to apply if you are ever required to produce your own financial statements

---

GO BACK OVER THIS AGAIN!   How well have you remembered what these conventions state and how they are applied? Go to the **online workbook** and complete Exercises 4.10 to check your recollection.

MULTIPLE CHOICE QUESTIONS   Do you think that you can distinguish between different accounting conventions? Go to the **online workbook** and complete Multiple choice questions 4.3 to test your ability to make these distinctions.

CHAPTER SUMMARY

You should now have learnt that:

- Organisations' cash flows are made up of cash flows from operating activities, cash flows from investing activities and cash flows from financing activities
- Cash generated during an accounting period is not the same as profit
- Cash flow is critical to the survival of an organisation
- Statements of cash flows can be prepared using both the direct and indirect methods
- A statement of cash flows is not sufficient on its own to provide users of financial statements with all the information they will need to assess an entity's financial position, performance and changes in financial position
- Various accounting conventions apply to the preparation of financial statements

---

QUICK REVISION   Test your knowledge with the online flashcards in Summary of key concepts and attempt the Multiple choice questions, all in the **online workbook**. www.oxfordtextbooks.co.uk/orc/scott/

END-OF-CHAPTER QUESTIONS

Solutions to these questions can be found at the back of the book from page 446.

> *Develop your understanding*

Question 4.1

Look up the answer to End-of-chapter questions 3.1. Using details of Abi's assets and liabilities at the start of the trading year, her income statement, her statement of financial position and her bank account summary for the year, present Abi's statement of cash flows using both the direct and the indirect method for the year ended 31 August 2016.

Question 4.2

Alison runs an online gift shop, trading for cash with individual customers and offering trading on credit terms to businesses. Alison provides you with the following list of statement of financial position balances at 31 December 2015:

	£
Non-current assets	
Computer equipment at cost	12,775
Less: accumulated depreciation on computer equipment at 31 December 2015	(7,245)
Racks, shelving and office furniture at cost	24,000
Less: accumulated depreciation on racks, shelving and office furniture at 31 December 2015	(8,000)
	21,530
Current assets	
Inventory	27,647
Trade receivables	27,200
Rent prepayment	2,500
Rates prepayment	1,965
Cash and cash equivalents	3,682
	62,994
Total assets	84,524
Current liabilities	
Trade payables	30,314
Telephone, electricity and gas accruals	1,500
Total liabilities	31,814
Net assets	52,710
Capital account	52,710

Alison provides you with the following additional information:

- During the year to 31 December 2016, Alison spent £8,000 on buying new computer equip-ment and £9,600 on new racks, shelving and office equipment as her business expanded.
- There were no disposals of non-current assets during the year.

Required

Using the statement of financial position at 31 December 2015 and the additional information above, together with the answer to Question 3.2, prepare Alison's statement of cash flows for the year ended 31 December 2016 using the indirect method.

Question 4.3

Look up the answer to End-of-chapter questions 3.5. Using the income statement and the statement of financial position, present the statement of cash flows for Laura using the indirect method.

» Take it further

Question 4.4

The statements of financial position for Potters Limited, together with relevant notes, are given below. Potters Limited produces crockery for sale to shops and through its site on the Internet.

Potters Limited: statements of financial position at 30 June 2016 and 30 June 2015

	2016	2015
	£000	£000
Assets		
Non-current assets		
Intangible assets: trademarks	100	120
Property, plant and equipment	10,200	8,600
	10,300	8,720
Current assets		
Inventories	1,000	1,100
Trade and other receivables	1,800	1,550
Cash and cash equivalents	200	310
	3,000	2,960
Total assets	13,300	11,680

→

| | 2016 | 2015 |
	£000	£000
Liabilities		
Current liabilities		
Trade and other payables	1,200	1,000
Current tax liabilities	300	250
	1,500	1,250
Non-current liabilities		
Long-term borrowings	3,200	2,600
Total liabilities	4,700	3,850
Net assets	8,600	7,830
Equity		
Called up share capital (£1 ordinary shares)	1,000	800
Share premium	2,500	2,150
Retained earnings	5,100	4,880
Total equity	8,600	7,830

During the year to 30 June 2016:

- Potters Limited paid £2,500,000 to acquire new property, plant and equipment
- Depreciation of £800,000 was charged on property, plant and equipment
- Plant and equipment with a net book value of £100,000 was sold for £150,000
- £20,000 amortisation was charged on the trademarks
- Dividends of £100,000 were paid
- Taxation of £275,000 was paid
- £200,000 interest was paid on the long-term borrowings
- Operating profit for the year was £845,000
- 200,000 new ordinary shares were issued for cash at a price of £2.75 each
- Potters Limited received no interest during the year to 30 June 2016

Required

Prepare the statement of cash flows for Potters Limited for the year ended 30 June 2016 using the indirect method.

Question 4.5

Statements of financial position for Metal Bashers plc, together with extracts from the income statement and relevant notes, are given below. Metal Bashers plc produces machine tools for industrial use.

Metal Bashers plc: statements of financial position at 30 September 2016 and 30 September 2015

	2016 £000	2015 £000
Assets		
Non-current assets		
Intangible assets: patents	200	150
Property, plant and equipment	21,800	18,850
	22,000	19,000
Current assets		
Inventories	1,400	1,200
Trade and other receivables	2,350	2,400
Cash and cash equivalents	750	400
	4,500	4,000
Total assets	26,500	23,000
Liabilities		
Current liabilities		
Current portion of long-term borrowings	500	500
Trade and other payables	2,000	2,300
Current tax liabilities	400	350
	2,900	3,150
Non-current liabilities		
Long-term borrowings	6,500	7,000
Total liabilities	9,400	10,150
Net assets	17,100	12,850
Equity		
Called up share capital (£1 ordinary shares)	3,600	2,000
Share premium	5,600	2,400
Retained earnings	7,900	8,450
Total equity	17,100	12,850

1. Prepare the statement of cash flows for Metal Bashers plc for the year ended 30 June 2016 using the indirect method.

2. If total cash received from sales amounted to £9,550,000, total cash paid to trade payables for raw materials and expenses was £5,100,000 and total cash paid to employees was £1,280,000, show how the cash flow from operating activities would appear under the direct method of statement of cash flow preparation.

...ions
...e financing
...siness

...G OUTCOMES

...you have read this chapter and worked through the questions and examples in both this ...apter and the online workbook, you should be able to:

- Understand the different forms of business organisation and the advantages and disadvantages of each format

- Describe the various sources of finance available to the different forms of business organisation

- Discuss the costs of each source of finance

- Describe the features of ordinary and preference share capital

- Understand how cash is raised from an issue of shares

- Understand how bonus issues and rights issues function

- Understand how limited companies make dividend distributions and whether they have the capacity to make such distributions

Introduction

So far we have studied various examples of accounting statements produced by a variety of different organisations. While the financial statements of these organisations seem to adopt basically the same formats, we have not yet formally considered the different types of business entity and the ways in which they differ one from the other. Bunns the Bakers is a public limited company, while Julia set up her sports equipment shop and started trading as a sole trader. What are the distinctions between these two business formats? Are there any other business formats that are commonly adopted in practice? Why is one format preferable to another and why do all businesses not follow the same format? Quite commonly, what starts off as a small business trading as a sole trader becomes a limited company later on in that business's life. This chapter will deal with the different features of each type of business organisation and the advantages and disadvantages of each format.

At the same time, the two business formats we have looked at seem to adopt different methods through which to finance their operations. Julia introduced her own money into her sports equipment retailing business and was allocated all the profit from that activity at the end of the accounting year. Bunns the Bakers is financed by share capital, but how is the profit from that business allocated to its owners? In this chapter we will also be looking at how different businesses finance their operations and the requirements that each different financing method imposes upon each different business format.

> **WHY IS THIS RELEVANT TO ME?** Types of business organisation and organisational finance
>
> To enable you as a business professional and user of financial information to understand:
>
> - The various different types of business organisation you will be dealing with
> - How different types of business organisation are constituted and the powers that each type enjoys
> - The different types of finance that are available to different types of business organisation and how each type of organisation raises finance to fund their operations

Types of business organisation

Let's start with a review of each of the three main types of business organisation. These comprise sole traders, partnerships and limited companies.

Sole traders

Simple businesses require a simple format. As the name implies, sole traders run their businesses on their own. Sole traders set their businesses up and, while they might employ one or two other people to assist them in the day-to-day running of operations, they undertake all the business tasks themselves and assume total responsibility for the success or failure of their businesses. The sole trader format for organising a business is most effective where operations are straightforward and where there are no complexities that could be more efficiently dealt with by adopting a different structure. Examples of sole traders would be Julia, our stand alone retailer in Chapters 3 and 4, childminders, hairdressers, market traders, taxi drivers, sports coaches and barristers. All these people operate their businesses on their own and plough a lone furrow as they make their way in the world. There are no special requirements for setting up in business as a sole trader: just start trading.

GO BACK OVER THIS AGAIN!   Think you understand how sole traders operate? Go to the **online workbook** and have a go at Exercises 5.1 to reinforce your understanding of sole traders and how they operate.

Partnerships

Where two or more individuals own and run a business together, then a partnership structure will be adopted for that business. The Partnership Act 1890 limits the number of partners in a partnership to 20, although this limit has been relaxed for partnerships of accountants and solicitors. Partnerships are more complex undertakings than sole traders and reflect the fact that one person cannot know everything or be talented in every activity. Thus, in a building firm partnership, one partner might be skilled as a brick layer and plasterer, one as a plumber and heating engineer, one as an electrician. Similarly, in an accounting partnership, one partner might be knowledgeable in accounts preparation and audit, one in tax and one in insolvency.

The principle in a partnership is that all the partners take part in running the business and enjoy a share of the profits from that business. You might say that a partnership is two or more sole traders coming together to make a bigger business, with each partner enjoying a share of management and reward from that enlarged business. The problem in a partnership is that the partners have to be certain that they will all work together effectively and that no personality clashes or disputes will cause disruption to the business. Sole traders, of course, do not have this problem. Partnerships, like sole traders, can be set up informally and just start trading. However, given the possibility that there will be disagreements between the partners, it is usual to set out the key terms of the partnership in a written agreement signed by all the partners at the start of the partnership.

GO BACK OVER THIS AGAIN!   Confident you know how partnerships work? Go to the **online workbook** and have a go at Exercises 5.2 to reinforce your understanding of partnerships and how they operate.

Limited companies

Limited companies are much more complex organisations and are subject to much greater regulation and oversight. Given this complexity, let's look at the distinguishing features of limited liability companies one by one, comparing and contrasting limited companies with sole traders and partnerships.

Separate legal identity

Limited companies are regarded as separate legal entities with a distinct name and a perpetual life. Businesses that operate as sole traders or partnerships are considered to be an extension of those individuals and the businesses and their owners are not regarded as separate legal beings. This separate legal identity means that limited companies can sue and be sued, sign undertakings and enter into contractual obligations in their own name. Sole trader and partnership businesses tend to cease when the owners retire or die, but limited companies carry on indefinitely no matter how many of their directors or shareholders leave the company.

Share capital

Businesses can incorporate themselves as limited companies. Incorporation requires a detailed formal process (see Formation documents later). On incorporation of a business, shareholders subscribe for shares in the limited company. When individuals subscribe for shares, this gives limited companies a source of finance. While sole traders and partners provide the financing for their businesses and record this in their statements of financial position as capital introduced, shareholders pay money into the company's bank account and receive shares in proportion to the capital they have invested. This share capital is recorded as issued share capital in the limited company's statement of financial position.

Limited liability

The great advantage of limited companies over sole traders and partnerships is that the liability of the shareholders to meet the debts of the limited company is restricted to the amount they have subscribed for their shares. If a limited company were to fail and go out of business, then shareholders will not have to provide any more money towards clearing the debts of the company than they have already paid for their shares. Shareholders lose the money they have already paid to acquire their shares, but they have no further liability beyond this. Thus, if a shareholder agreed to purchase one hundred £1 shares on the formation of a company, then, once the £100 has been paid to the company, the shareholder has to make no further contribution to the company should it fail. Sole traders and partnerships have unlimited liability for the debts of their businesses and they could lose everything in a business failure. These losses would extend to personal assets such as houses, cars, investments, in fact anything that those sole traders or partners own.

The annual general meeting

Sole traders and partners own their businesses. Limited companies are owned by the shareholders. Sole traders and partners make major decisions about their organisations during the year. However, every year each and every limited company must hold an **annual general meeting (AGM)** at which the shareholders come together to consider and vote on various significant resolutions affecting the company. Shareholders have voting rights at the AGM. The size of these voting rights and the power of each shareholder depend upon the number of shares held. For each share held, a shareholder has one vote. The more shares that a shareholder owns, the more power that shareholder can exercise when voting on company resolutions.

Appointment of directors

One of the resolutions voted on at the AGM concerns the appointment of directors of the company. Limited companies, although owned by their shareholders, are run by directors appointed by the shareholders at the AGM. The directors are elected by the shareholders to run the company on their behalf. If shareholders are not happy with the performance of the current directors, they have the power to vote them out of office at the AGM and appoint different directors in their place. Directors are employees of limited companies placed in a position of trust by the shareholders. Ownership (by shareholders) and management (by directors) are thus separated, a situation that does not apply in sole traders and partnerships.

Annual accounts

Because of this separation of ownership and management, the directors of limited companies have a statutory obligation under the Companies Act 2006 to present annual accounts to the shareholders at the AGM. These accounts are a financial record of how the directors have managed the monies and other resources entrusted to them by the shareholders and how they have used that money to invest and generate profits for shareholders during the past year. As we noted in Chapter 1, the directors present this account of their stewardship of the resources entrusted to them to help shareholders control the directors' actions and prevent them from exceeding their powers. All limited company accounts are filed at Companies House and are available for public consultation.

Auditors and annual accounts

As shareholders do not take part in the day-to-day running of the company, they do not know whether the accounts presented by the directors are a true and fair summary of the financial achievements during the year or not. Therefore, shareholders appoint independent auditors to check the annual report and accounts for inaccuracies, omissions and misrepresentations. These auditors then report to the shareholders on whether the annual report and accounts present a true and fair view of the company's profit or loss and cash flow for the year and of the state of the company's affairs (the statement of financial position) at the year-end date. Shareholders are empowered by the Companies Act 2006 to choose the auditors they want to conduct the annual audit rather than the auditors that the directors would like to appoint. Auditors of limited companies enjoy various protections against removal by the directors and this enables them to perform their audits efficiently and effectively without fear or favour to the shareholders' benefit.

Sole traders and partnerships prepare annual accounts, but these are to determine any tax that is due on profits and to present to banks to support applications for loan and other borrowing facilities. There is no obligation upon sole traders or partnerships to publish their accounts publicly so that the financial affairs of sole traders and partnerships remain private and confidential.

Formation documents

When limited companies are formed, they are registered with the Registrar of Companies. This registration comprises the name of the company and the names of the first directors (the names of the company and the directors can be changed at any time by the submission of the appropriate documentation to Companies House). In addition, two important documents are filed when a company is registered. The first is the **Memorandum of Association**. This document covers the limited company's objectives and its powers and governs the relationship of the company with the outside world. The second document is the **Articles of Association**, which covers the internal regulations of the company and governs the shareholders' relationships with each other.

WHY IS THIS RELEVANT TO ME?   Types of business organisation

To enable you as a business professional and user of financial information to:

- Appreciate the different types of business organisation
- Understand how the different types of business organisation operating in the economy today are set up and run
- Compare and contrast the different types of business organisation you will be dealing with

GO BACK OVER THIS AGAIN!   Sure you can describe the different features of the various types of business organisations and distinguish between them? Go to the **online workbook** and have a go at Exercises 5.3 to make sure you can describe and distinguish between the different types of business organisation.

SUMMARY OF KEY CONCEPTS   Are you quite happy that you can describe the main features of each of the three different types of business organisations? Revise these main features with Summary of key concepts 5.1–5.3.

Public limited and private limited companies

The Companies Act 2006 regulates all limited liability companies. However, there are two types of limited company covered in the Act: private limited companies and public limited companies. Private limited companies are prohibited from selling their shares to the public and usually have very few shareholders. Public limited companies can issue shares to the public and have many shareholders. The shares of public limited companies are traded on recognised stock exchanges such as those of London, New York, Paris, Hong Kong and Tokyo. Many of the businesses or websites you visit each day are run by public limited companies and these include your bank and the shops in which you buy your food. Private limited companies have the word limited or Ltd after their names while the names of public limited companies are followed by the letters plc. Look out for these company designations as you browse the web or go out into town.

Public and private limited companies are subject to exactly the same rules in the Companies Act 2006. Both types of limited company produce annual reports and accounts (these are also referred to by the term financial statements). Public limited companies are also subject to stock exchange rules and regulations. A more complex financial reporting regime applies to public limited companies in that they also have to comply with various corporate governance codes, which seek to improve their ethics and accountability. Consideration of these codes is, however, outside the scope of this book.

WHY IS THIS RELEVANT TO ME?   **Public and private limited companies**

To enable you as a business professional and user of financial information to:

- Gain an awareness of the two types of limited company
- Appreciate the differences between public and private limited companies

GO BACK OVER THIS AGAIN! Are you completely certain that you can distinguish between private and public limited companies? Go to the **online workbook** and have a go at Exercises 5.4 to make sure you understand the differences between private and public limited companies.

SUMMARY OF KEY CONCEPTS Are you totally happy that you can describe the main features of private and public limited companies? Revise these main features with Summary of key concepts 5.4.

Financing business

All businesses have to raise finance at the start of their lives and at regular intervals as they expand. Providers of finance to businesses require some form of reward for providing that finance. So what sort of finance is raised by different businesses and what are the costs of each type of finance?

Capital introduced: sole traders and partnerships

We have already looked briefly at this method of financing for sole traders in Chapter 2. When a sole trader or a partnership is set up, the owners pay money into the new venture. It will take a little time for trading income to begin to flow into the business so this start-up capital is needed to buy non-current assets with which to set up the operations of the business and to provide cash to ensure the continuity of trading in the early stages of the business' life.

As an example, look back to Chapter 3, Illustration 3.3. Julia paid £30,000 into her business bank account and then used this cash to pay the initial rent of £5,000 and to buy the cash register and the shelves and fittings for her shop for £11,000 on the same day. No trading had taken place at this point so Julia had made no cash profits from which to pay for these non-current assets. Without her initial payment into the business, Julia would not have had the cash with which to make these necessary investments to run her retail operation. Many businesses start up in the same way with the owners paying in cash to buy assets and meet initial expenses from their own resources.

Sole traders and partners do not charge their businesses interest on this capital introduced. Instead, they draw on this capital and the profits made by the business as their source of income from which to meet their personal expenses and to finance their lifestyles. Chapter 2 noted that the term for these withdrawals is 'drawings', money taken out of the business by the owner(s) for their own personal use.

As sole traders and partners are considered to be an extension of their businesses, withdrawing money in this way from their businesses is perfectly acceptable. However, it is not possible for shareholders in limited companies to withdraw money from their companies in the same way as limited companies have a separate legal identity and are regarded as completely distinct from their owners.

WHY IS THIS RELEVANT TO ME?   **Capital introduced: sole traders and partnerships**

To enable you as a business professional and user of financial information to:

• Revise capital introduced from earlier chapters

• Understand how sole traders and partnerships finance their start-up capital

• Remember how the owner's capital account for sole traders and partnerships works

---

GO BACK OVER THIS AGAIN!   Are you sure that you understand capital introduced? Go to the **online workbook** and have a go at Exercises 5.5 to make sure you can describe capital introduced.

Bank finance: all businesses

Banks provide short- and medium-term finance to businesses in the form of overdrafts and loans. In Chapter 2 we noted that such overdrafts and loans are described as borrowings under current and non-current liabilities in the statement of financial position. The cost of both these sources of finance is interest that the bank charges on the amounts borrowed.

Bank overdrafts have the following features (summarised in Figure 5.1):

• Overdrafts are short-term finance.

• The overdraft amount varies each month depending on cash inflows and outflows during each month. The more cash received and the less paid out, the lower the overdraft and vice versa.

• There is usually a limit on the amount of the overdraft allowed by the bank. When customers reach or exceed this overdraft limit, the bank is entitled to refuse any further credit on that account.

• Overdrafts are subject to an annual review by the bank to determine whether the overdraft limit should remain the same, increase or decrease.

• Overdrafts are not contractual arrangements and banks can ask for overdrafts to be repaid immediately.

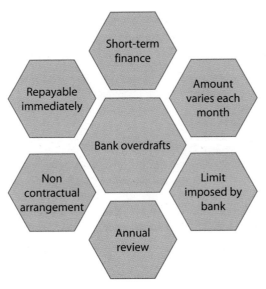

Figure 5.1 Features of bank overdrafts

GIVE ME AN EXAMPLE 5.1   Bank overdrafts

Details of overdrafts offered by Lloyds Bank on 22 February 2015:

Business Overdraft

- Make sure extra funds are there when you need them.

- Only pay interest on the funds you use.
- Apply for a limit that suits your business.

Source: www.lloydsbank.com/business/retail-business/loans-and-finance.asp

---

Bank loans operate as follows (the features of bank loans are summarised in Figure 5.2):

- A fixed amount is borrowed for a fixed term, usually a period of 5–10 years.

- Repayments are made on a regular basis, either monthly or quarterly.

- Each monthly repayment consists of an interest element and a repayment of part of the sum originally borrowed.

- Loans are contractual arrangements. Banks can only demand immediate repayment of loans when the borrower has failed to meet a contractual repayment by the due date.

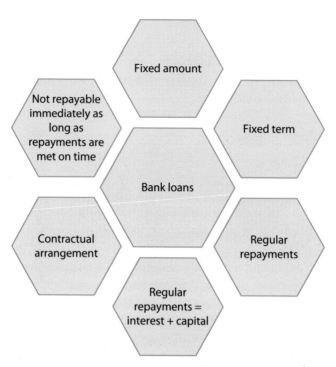

Figure 5.2 Features of bank loans

GIVE ME AN EXAMPLE 5.2 Bank loans

Table 5.1 Details of business loans offered by Lloyds Bank on 22 February 2015

Commercial Fixed Rate Loan	SME Fixed Rate Loan
• Interest Rate reduced by 1% as part of the Lloyds Bank Funding for Lending scheme.	• Interest rate reduced by 1% as part of the Lloyds Bank Funding for Lending Scheme.
• Borrow from £50,001.	• Borrow from £50,001 to £500,000.
• Choose a term from one to 25 years.	• Terms from five to 25 years.
• Fixed monthly repayments during the fixed rate period.	• Interest rate fixed for a five-year or a 10-year term, with a variable rate thereafter.
• Benefit from capital repayment holidays, available in certain circumstances.	• The fixed rate can be reserved for up to three months before booking.
• Borrow on a secured or unsecured basis.	• Maximum break costs are defined at the outset of your loan, giving you certainty around the maximum costs involved should you decide to repay early during the fixed rate period.
• Early repayment charge may be payable if a fixed rate loan is fully or partly repaid early.	• Capital repayment holidays may be available.

→

Base Rate Loan	Fixed Rate Loan
• Reduce your interest rate by 1% as part of the Lloyds Bank Funding for Lending Scheme.	• Reduce your interest rate by up to 1% as part of the Lloyds Bank Funding for Lending Scheme.
• Borrow from as little as £1,000.	• Borrow between £1,000 and £50,000.
• Available for one to 25-year terms.	• Choose a term from one to 10 years.
• Benefit from capital repayment holidays, available in certain circumstances.	• Repay a consistent monthly amount for the entire length of your loan term.
• Security may be required. If you wish to borrow on other terms we may still be able to help you.	• Benefit from capital repayment holidays, available in certain circumstances.
	• Borrow on a secured or unsecured basis.

Source: www.lloydsbank.com/business/retail-business/loans-and-finance.asp

5

WHY IS THIS RELEVANT TO ME? **Bank finance**

To enable you as a business professional and user of financial information to:

• Understand the difference between bank overdrafts and bank loans

• Appreciate the key features of overdraft and loan finance

GO BACK OVER THIS AGAIN! Do you reckon that you can distinguish between overdraft and loan finance? Go to the **online workbook** and have a go at Exercises 5.6 to make sure you do understand the differences.

SUMMARY OF KEY CONCEPTS Are you confident that you can describe the main features of overdraft and loan finance? Revise these main features with Summary of key concepts 5.5.

Other types of long-term finance: public limited companies

Debenture loans/bonds

Public limited companies can issue **debentures** or **bonds** to the public. Debentures and bonds are long-term loans with a fixed rate of interest and a fixed repayment date. Thus a plc might issue a £500 million debenture with an interest rate of 5.25% and a repayment date of 31 January 2025. Lenders would then receive an interest payment of £26.25 million (£500m × 5.25%) every year on the anniversary of the debenture's issue and full repayment of the £500 million plus any interest outstanding up to the date of repayment on 31 January 2025.

Next plc records the following corporate bond liabilities together with their associated interest rates and maturity dates in note 20 to the annual report and accounts for the financial year ended 24 January 2015.

Corporate bonds

	Nominal value	
	2015	**2014**
	£m	**£m**
Corporate bond 5.875% repayable 2016	212.6	212.6
Corporate bond 5.375% repayable 2021	325.0	325.0
Corporate bond 4.375% repayable 2026	250.0	250.0
	787.6	787.6

Source: http://www.nextplc.co.uk

How do lenders make sure they will be repaid the amounts they have lent? Companies often give security to lenders when debentures or bonds are issued or bank loans are taken out. This means that certain assets of the borrowing company are nominated for sale should the company become unable to repay the amounts borrowed. If the company is unable to repay the amounts borrowed, then these assets would be sold and the lenders repaid from the proceeds of these sales. Debentures and bonds are traded on stock exchanges around the world so lenders can sell their holdings in these long-term loans without waiting for the repayment date.

WHY IS THIS RELEVANT TO ME? Bond and debenture finance

To provide you as a business professional and user of financial information with:

- An awareness of bonds and debentures as a means of raising finance for large companies
- A brief overview of the features of bonds and debentures

GO BACK OVER THIS AGAIN! Are you totally convinced that you understand bonds and debentures? Go to the **online workbook** and have a go at Exercises 5.7 to make sure you can describe these sources of finance.

SUMMARY OF KEY CONCEPTS Do you think that you can describe the main features of bond and debenture financing? Revise these main features with Summary of key concepts 5.6.

Share capital: limited companies

All limited companies, whether public or private, issue share capital. Share capital is a source of very long-term finance for a business. Shares subscribed by shareholders will be in issue for as long as the company exists. Share capital financing is not available to sole traders or partnerships unless they choose to transfer their operations to a limited company set up for this purpose. As well as issues of ordinary share capital, some companies also issue preference share capital.

Companies distribute dividends to their shareholders. Dividends are a share of the profit earned in a financial year paid out to the shareholders. Whereas interest on loans and overdrafts has to be paid no matter what the circumstances of the business are, companies do not have to distribute a dividend if the directors decide that it is not in the company's best interests to do so. For example, if the company were about to make a large investment in new non-current assets, it would make more sense for the company to hold onto its cash to make this investment rather than paying a dividend.

Before we consider dividends further and how these are calculated, let's look at the two types of share capital that companies issue.

Preference share capital

Preference shares are so called because holders of preference shares receive preferential treatment from the issuing company in the following ways:

- Preference shareholders must receive their dividends from the company before ordinary shareholders are paid any dividend.
- Thus, if there are no profits left over for distribution after the preference dividends have been paid then the ordinary shareholders receive no dividend for that year.
- On the winding up/liquidation of a company, once all the claims of a company's creditors have been settled, any money left over and available to shareholders is repaid to preference shareholders before any payment is made to ordinary shareholders.

However, preference shareholders also suffer various restrictions as a result of this preferential treatment:

- The rate of dividend on preference shares is fixed. Thus, preference shareholders are not entitled to any further share of the profits available for distribution once their fixed rate of dividend has been paid.
- Preference shareholders have no right to vote in general meetings.

Preference shareholders' rights are restricted in the above ways as they take on a lower level of risk when compared to ordinary shareholders. Although the companies in

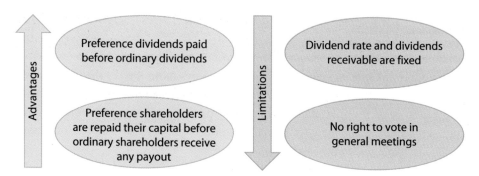

Figure 5.3 The characteristics of preference shares

which preference shareholders invest might still fail or not earn much profit, the fact that they are paid their dividends first and receive their money back in a liquidation before the ordinary shareholders means that they are taking less risk than ordinary shareholders who stand to lose everything. The advantages and limitations of preference shares are summarised in Figure 5.3.

Ordinary share capital

Ordinary share capital is the name given to the most common form of share capital issued by companies. Ordinary shareholders take on the highest risks when they buy shares in a company. Investors in ordinary shares might receive all of a company's profits as dividends and see the value of their shares rise many times above what they originally paid for them or they could receive no dividends and nothing when the company goes into liquidation, losing all of their investment. All limited companies must issue ordinary share capital. Ordinary shares are the only shares that carry voting rights at company meetings. The positive and negative aspects of ordinary shares are summarised in Figure 5.4.

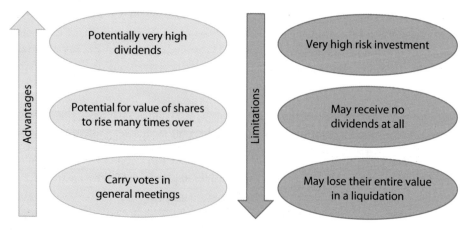

Figure 5.4 The characteristics of ordinary shares

Share capital: share issues at par value

Under the Companies Act 2006, every company can issue as many shares as it wishes. Share capital is increased simply by issuing more shares.

EXAMPLE 5.1

Printers Limited has share capital made up of ordinary shares of £1 each and preference shares of 50 pence each. Printers can issue any number of shares it wishes. However, companies only issue shares as and when they need to raise funds rather than raising all the cash they can from shareholders immediately.

In Example 5.1, the ordinary shares have a par value of £1. The par value is the face value or nominal value of each share. Par values can be of any amount. As well as the ordinary shares with a par value of £1 each, Printers also has preference shares with a par value of 50 pence each. However, par values could be 1 pence or 12½ pence or 25 pence or any other amount that the founders of the company decide. The par value of a company's shares is stated in the Memorandum and Articles of Association.

GIVE ME AN EXAMPLE 5.4 The par value of shares

As an example of par values of share capital, Balfour Beatty plc has ordinary shares with a par value of 50 pence each and preference shares with a par value of 1 pence each.

Source: *Balfour Beatty annual report and accounts 2014* www.balfourbeatty.com

At the start of a limited company's life, shares are issued at their par value. Thus, Printers' directors might decide to raise £20,000 on its first day to provide the company with sufficient capital to start operating. The directors decide to issue just ordinary shares. The ordinary shares have a par value of £1, so 20,000 £1 shares will need to be issued to raise the £20,000 required. Investors are said to subscribe for their shares and they pay cash to make this investment. After the share issue, the company will now have £20,000 cash in the bank and £20,000 in issued share capital.

MULTIPLE CHOICE QUESTIONS Confident that you could calculate the sums raised from a share issue? Go to the **online workbook** and have a go at Multiple choice questions 5.1 to make sure you can calculate these amounts.

Share capital: shares issued at a premium

As companies grow, their shares increase in value. Therefore, when companies want to issue shares at a later stage of their lives, these new shares are issued at par value plus a premium to reflect this increase in value.

EXAMPLE 5.2

Printers' directors decide to issue a further 30,000 £1 ordinary shares after one year of trading, but they now set the issue price for these additional shares at £1.25. The issue price for each share is made up of the £1 par value and a 25 pence premium. How much cash will be raised and how will this be recorded in Printers' financial statements?

The cash raised is given by multiplying the 30,000 shares by the £1.25 issue price for each share. This gives total cash raised of $30,000 \times £1.25 = £37,500$. This £37,500 comprises £30,000 of ordinary share capital (the par value of £1 × 30,000 shares) and a share premium of £7,500 (30,000 shares issued × 25 pence). The £30,000 is added to share capital and the £7,500 is added to the share premium account in the statement of financial position with the whole £37,500 raised being added to cash in the bank.

Example 5.2 tells us that the share premium is any amount raised from an issue of shares over and above the par value of the shares issued.

GIVE ME AN EXAMPLE 5.5 Shares issued at a premium to the par value

As an example of shares issued at a premium, note 17 in the Triodos Renewables 2012 annual report presents the following information: 'During the year, the company undertook a share issue in which it raised £3,546,730 (before costs) through the issue of 1,866,700 Ordinary shares of 50p each at a premium of £1.40 per share.'

Source: *Triodos Renewables annual report 2012* www.triodos.co.uk

WHY IS THIS RELEVANT TO ME?   **Share issues at par value and share issues at a premium**

To enable you as a business professional and user of financial information to understand:

- How limited companies raise cash from share issues
- The financial effect of issuing shares at a premium

MULTIPLE CHOICE QUESTIONS   Could you calculate the sums raised from a share issue when shares are issued at a premium? Go to the **online workbook** and have a go at Multiple choice questions 5.2 to see if you can make these calculations correctly.

SUMMARY OF KEY CONCEPTS   Can you define share premium? Revise this definition with Summary of key concepts 5.8.

Share capital: bonus issues

As well as issuing shares for cash, limited companies also make what are called **bonus issues** of shares. Bonus issues are made when a company has a large surplus on its retained earnings on the statement of financial position. These retained earnings have not yet been distributed to shareholders as dividends and the company wants to keep these earnings within the business as share capital. This process is known as capitalising reserves, turning distributable retained earnings into new non-distributable share capital. No cash is raised in a bonus issue, but the number of shares in issue increases while the retained earnings reduce by a corresponding amount. Bonus issues are only made to existing ordinary shareholders and the amount capitalised as share capital is the par value of the shares issued.

A bonus issue is always expressed as a certain number of bonus shares for a certain number of shares already held by ordinary shareholders. Thus, a one-for-four bonus issue means that one new bonus share is issued to ordinary shareholders for every four shares they already hold. A two-for-five bonus issue means that two bonus shares are issued for every five shares currently held. Let's illustrate how a bonus issue works with an example.

EXAMPLE 5.3

James plc currently has 12 million ordinary shares of £1 each in issue. The balance on retained earnings is currently £25 million. The directors propose a four for three bonus issue.

In this example, four bonus shares are issued for every three shares currently held. This means that 12m × 4 new shares ÷ 3 shares currently in issue = 16m new shares of £1 each issued to ordinary shareholders. This transaction would be presented as shown in Illustration 5.1: £16 million is added to ordinary share capital and £16 million is deducted from retained earnings.

Illustration 5.1 James plc: bonus issue of four £1 shares for every three £1 shares
already held by ordinary shareholders

	Before bonus issue	+ £	– £	After bonus issue
Equity	£m			£m
Ordinary share capital	12,000,000	16,000,000		28,000,000
Retained earnings	25,000,000		16,000,000	9,000,000
	37,000,000			37,000,000

James plc now has 28 million ordinary £1 shares in issue compared to the original 12 million before the bonus issue. These newly issued bonus shares will receive dividends in the future just as the ordinary shares currently do. Issuing bonus shares is a good way of increasing the number of shares in issue and strengthening the fixed capital base of a company. Once the bonus shares have been issued the retained earnings balance falls and this limits the retained earnings that can be paid out in future as dividends.

Share capital: rights issues

From time to time, public limited companies make new issues of shares to raise funds. However, companies cannot just issue new shares to anyone they want. The Companies Act 2006 prevents companies from issuing new shares to outside parties until those new shares have first been offered to current shareholders. Only when existing shareholders have turned down the opportunity to buy these new shares can the shares be offered to investors who are not currently shareholders of the company. These rights to subscribe for new issues of shares are known as pre-emption rights, the right to be offered first refusal on any new issue of shares.

Why does the Companies Act 2006 protect shareholders' rights in this way? Pre-emption rights prevent the dilution of existing shareholders' interests in a company. What this means and how **pre-emption rights** protect existing shareholders are illustrated in Example 5.4.

EXAMPLE 5.4

Joe and Bill each hold 50,000 ordinary shares in Painters Limited. Painters Limited has a total of 100,000 ordinary shares in issue, so Joe and Bill each own a 50% interest in the company. The directors decide that Painters needs to issue another 100,000 shares. If the directors were able to offer the shares to external investors, then Joe's and Bill's interest in Painters would fall to 25% each (50,000 shares ÷ (100,000 shares currently in issue + 100,000 new shares being issued)). They would thus suffer a 50% reduction in their interest in the company as a result of new shareholders being brought in. Whereas before they each controlled 50% of Painters, they now control only 25% each as a result of this new issue of shares to new investors. The Companies

Act 2006 thus requires the directors to offer the new shares to Joe and Bill first so that they can take up the new shares and each maintain their 50% holding in the company. Only when Joe and Bill have declined the right to buy these new shares can the shares be offered to outside parties.

Rights issues: pricing

Rights issues are priced at a discount to the current market price to encourage shareholders to take up the issue.

EXAMPLE 5.5

If the current market value of James plc £1 ordinary shares is £3, then the directors will price the rights issue at, for example, £2.20 to encourage shareholders to take up their rights. £2.20 is a discount to the current market price of 80 pence (£3.00 – £2.20). The number of shares will rise when the rights issue is complete. As you will know from studying economics, when supply increases, price goes down. Since there will be more James plc shares in issue after the rights issue the market price will fall. The discount to the current market price of the ordinary shares thus compensates James plc's shareholders for this anticipated fall in the market value of their shares.

Do note that the pricing of a rights issue at a discount to the market price is not the same as issuing shares at a discount. Issuing shares at a discount is illegal under the Companies Act 2006 and would involve, for example, selling shares with a par value of £1 for 75 pence. This is not allowed under company law.

How does a rights issue work? James plc's directors decide to make a rights issue of £1 ordinary shares, one for every four currently held. There are 28 million shares in issue after the bonus issue and the rights issue price is set at £2.20.

Your first task is to determine how many new shares will be issued. One new ordinary share is being issued for every four in issue, so this will give us 28,000,000 ÷ 4 = 7,000,000 new ordinary shares to issue.

How much money will this raise? Each share is being issued at £2.20, so an issue of seven million shares will raise 7,000,000 × £2.20 = £15,400,000.

You know from our discussions above that, with the par value of the shares being £1, there is a share premium to account for as well as the new addition to share capital. How much is this premium? Issuing £1 par value shares at £2.20 means that the premium on each share issued is £2.20 – £1.00 = £1.20. The total premium on the issue of seven million shares is then 7,000,000 × £1.20 = £8,400,000. Cash thus goes up by the £15,400,000 raised from the issue, ordinary share capital goes up by £7,000,000, while the share premium account rises by £8,400,000.

GIVE ME AN EXAMPLE 5.6   Rights issues of shares

On 4 March 2014, Premier Foods plc announced the proposed placing of 76,923,077 shares at 130 pence per placing share (this is where shares are sold to institutions at an agreed price) together with a proposed 8 for 5 rights issue of 506,824,531 new ordinary shares at 50 pence

→

each. The aim of the placing and rights issue was to raise cash to finance a joint venture in Premier Foods' bread business. Prior to the shareholders' meeting on 20 March 2014 to approve the placing and rights issue, shares in Premier Foods were trading on the stock market at prices between 125.50 pence and 160.75 pence per share. Note that the 50 pence rights issue price for each share was thus a large discount to the current market price of the shares, but not a discount to the par value of the shares of 10 pence each. Once the shareholders' meeting on

20 March 2014 had approved the transactions and the issue of the new shares and the placing shares, the share price fell to 72.25 pence per share on 24 March 2014 as the increase in the number of shares in issue resulted in a reduction in the price. The rights issue price of 50 pence thus compensated the ordinary shareholders for the anticipated fall in the market value of their shares following the approval of the new issue of shares.

Source: www.premierfoods.co.uk

WHY IS THIS RELEVANT TO ME?   Bonus and rights issues

To enable you as a business professional and user of financial information to understand:

• How bonus and rights issues work

• The financial effect of bonus and rights issues

MULTIPLE CHOICE QUESTIONS   Are you convinced that you understand how bonus and rights issues work? Go to the **online workbook** and have a go at Multiple choice questions 5.3 to make sure you can calculate the entries to the relevant accounts for bonus and rights issues.

SUMMARY OF KEY CONCEPTS   Quite certain that you can define bonus and rights issues? Revise these definitions with Summary of key concepts 5.9 and 5.10.

Dividends

We have already discussed the subject of dividends. It is now time to see how dividends for the year are calculated.

Dividends are distributions of profit to shareholders. They are not an expense of the distributing company in the way that wages, rent or electricity are expenses. Dividends are deducted directly from retained earnings in the statement of financial position and do not appear in the income statement.

When a company decides to pay a dividend to the shareholders, a figure of pence per share is quoted. Dividends are always paid on the number of shares in issue. How does a dividend distribution work?

EXAMPLE 5.6

James plc declares a dividend of 12 pence per ordinary share. How much dividend will be paid out? There are 35 million shares in issue after the rights issue (Example 5.5). This means that holders of the 35 million £1 ordinary shares will receive 12 pence for each share that they hold. The total dividend payment will thus be $35{,}000{,}000 \times £0.12 = £4{,}200{,}000$. When this dividend is paid, cash at the bank will fall by £4,200,000 and retained earnings will be reduced by £4,200,000.

EXAMPLE 5.7

When calculating preference dividends, the par value of the preference shares is simply multiplied by the dividend rate. Remember that preference dividends are paid at a fixed rate and preference shareholders receive nothing more than their contractually agreed preference dividend. James plc also has 10,000,000, 50 pence, 5% preference shares in issue. This tells us that every 50 pence preference share receives a dividend of 2.5 pence ($£0.50 \times 5\%$). The total preference dividend will thus be £250,000 (10,000,000 shares $\times$ £0.025).

Public limited companies paying dividends usually make two distributions in each financial year. These are known as the interim dividend, paid part way through the financial year, and a final dividend based on the profits for the financial year.

Distributable and non-distributable reserves

Dividends are paid from distributable reserves only. Ordinary share capital, preference share capital, share premium and revaluation reserves are all capital reserves and the funds in these capital reserves are not distributable to shareholders. To make a dividend distribution from any of these reserves would be illegal under the Companies Act 2006.

For our purposes, the only distributable reserve, the one that represents realised profits of the company, is retained earnings. Retained earnings are a revenue reserve and it is this reserve from which dividends can be paid. However, if a company has retained losses and a negative balance on retained earnings, no dividends can be paid. Only when a company has a positive balance showing that the company has made profits can a distribution be made from the retained earnings reserve.

WHY IS THIS RELEVANT TO ME?   Dividends

To enable you as a business professional and user of financial information to:

- Understand how dividends are calculated
- Distinguish between capital reserves and revenue reserves

MULTIPLE CHOICE QUESTIONS   Are you confident that you could calculate dividends correctly? Go to the **online workbook** and have a go at Multiple choice questions 5.4 to make sure you can calculate dividend distributions accurately.

CHAPTER SUMMARY

You should now have learnt that:

- Very small businesses organise themselves as sole traders or partnerships that take on unlimited liability for the debts of their businesses

- Larger businesses organise themselves as limited liability companies whose owners (share-holders) have no obligation to meet the debts of their company beyond their investment in their company's share capital

- Sole traders and partnerships raise money to finance their operations from their own capital resources, from the profits of their businesses, from bank loans and from bank overdrafts

- Limited liability companies raise money to finance their operations from the issue of ordi-nary and preference share capital and by borrowing from banks in the form of loans or overdrafts and by issuing bonds and debentures

- The par value of a share is the face value or nominal value of that share

- A bonus issue involves the reduction of retained earnings and an increase in the issued share capital

- A rights issue is the issue of shares to shareholders at a discount to the current market price

- Dividends can only be distributed from retained earnings

QUICK REVISION   Test your knowledge with the online flashcards in Summary of key con-cepts and attempt the Multiple choice questions, all in the **online workbook**. www.oxfordtext-books.co.uk/orc/scott/

END-OF-CHAPTER QUESTIONS

Solutions to these questions can be found at the back of the book from page 454.

〉 *Develop your understanding*

Question 5.1

Which business format would be most suitable for the following businesses? Can you say why your chosen format would be most suited to each business?

- An oil exploration company
- A taxi driver
- A family run knitwear manufacturing business
- Two friends setting up a dance school

Question 5.2

An investor has £200,000 to invest and has to choose between three different investments:

- An investment in a £200,000 bond paying 5% interest per annum
- An investment in preference shares with a par value of 50 pence paying an annual dividend of 3 pence per share
- An investment in ordinary shares with a par value of 25 pence paying an annual dividend of 2 pence per share.

How much will each investment return to the investor? Which investment would be preferable on the assumption that the investor wishes to maximise income from investing the £200,000?

Question 5.3

A printing company wishes to raise £3,000,000 to finance its expansion plans. It can do this in one of three ways: borrowing from the bank at an annual interest rate of 5%, by issuing ordinary shares at their par value of 40 pence, which will require an annual dividend payment of 1.9 pence per share, or by issuing preference shares with a par value of 60 pence, which requires a fixed dividend of 3.15 pence per share. Which financing option will require the lowest cash outlay for the printing company?

》 *Take it further*

Question 5.4

Plants Limited runs a garden centre business selling garden plants and products to the public from its busy edge of town site. In the year to 31 October 2016, Plants Limited's issued share capital consists of 100,000 ordinary shares of 50 pence each and 100,000 preference shares of £1 each. The preference share dividend rate is 6%. Preference dividends are payable on 31 October each year. An interim dividend of 10 pence per share was paid on the ordinary share capital on 15 May 2016 and the directors paid a final ordinary dividend of 20 pence per ordinary share on 15 October 2016.

Required

(a) Calculate the preference dividend that Plants Limited will pay for the year ended 31 October 2016.

(b) Calculate the total ordinary dividend for the year ended 31 October 2016.

(c) If retained earnings at 1 November 2015 were £45,000 and profit for the year to 31 October 2016 was £50,000, what is the balance on retained earnings after dividends have been paid at 31 October 2016?

Question 5.5

Plants Limited is looking to expand its operations in the year to 31 October 2017, but needs to raise additional finance to do so. The company is proposing to raise £500,000 by the issue of 200,000 ordinary shares on 1 May 2017. Profits for the year to 31 October 2017 are expected to be £90,000. An interim ordinary dividend of 15 pence per share will be paid on 15 April 2017 and a final ordinary dividend of 25 pence per share will be paid on 15 October 2017.

Required

Using the information above, the information from Question 5.4 and the answer to Question 5.4:

(a) Calculate the amounts to be added to ordinary share capital and share premium in the equity section of the statement of financial position in respect of the new issue of ordinary shares on 1 May 2017.

(b) Calculate the total dividends, both ordinary and preference, to be paid in the year to 31 October 2017.

(c) Calculate the expected balance on retained earnings at 31 October 2017 after dividends for the year have been paid.

Question 5.6

At 1 July 2016 Halyson plc had 500,000 ordinary shares of 25 pence each in issue together with 300,000 7½% preference shares of £1 each. The balance on Halyson's retained earnings at 1 July 2016 is £5,200,000.

Halyson plc is proposing a bonus issue of seven new ordinary shares for every two ordinary shares currently held. Once this bonus issue is complete, a rights issue will be made of five new ordinary shares for every three ordinary shares held at a price of £0.95. These transactions will take place on 1 April 2017.

On 28 June 2017, Halyson plc will pay the preference dividend for the year and a total ordinary dividend for the year of 30 pence per share. The loss for the year to 30 June 2017 is expected to be £1,500,000.

Required

Calculate for Halyson plc:

(a) The number of bonus shares to be issued

(b) The par value of the bonus shares to be added to ordinary share capital

(c) The number of ordinary shares to be issued in the rights issue

(d) The amount to be added to ordinary share capital and share premium as a result of the rights issue

(e) The preference dividend for the year to 30 June 2017

(f) The ordinary dividend for the year to 30 June 2017

(g) The balance on the ordinary share capital account on 30 June 2017

(h) The expected balance on retained earnings at 30 June 2017

5

6 Ratio analysis: profitability, efficiency and performance

LEARNING OUTCOMES

Once you have read this chapter and worked through the questions and examples in both this chapter and the online workbook, you should be able to:

- Understand the importance and advantages of using ratios to evaluate the profitability, efficiency, performance and liquidity of entities

- Understand how the financial statements and ratios interact in the interpretation of the profitability, efficiency, performance and liquidity of organisations

- Calculate profitability ratios for gross profit percentage, operating profit percentage, profit before tax percentage and profit after tax percentage

- Suggest economic reasons for the changes in profitability ratios year on year

- Calculate efficiency ratios for non-current asset turnover, revenue per employee and profit per employee

- Show how efficiency ratios help to explain changes in the profitability ratios

- Understand how increasing the revenue from each unit of fixed resource employed in the business will increase an entity's profits

- Calculate performance ratios for earnings per share, price/earnings ratio, dividends per share, dividend yield and dividend cover

- Explain what the performance ratios you have calculated mean from a shareholder's point of view

- Compare an entity's profitability, efficiency and performance ratios with the profitability, efficiency and performance ratios of other companies as a way of benchmarking an entity's financial outcomes

Introduction

In Chapters 2, 3 and 4 we looked at the three major accounting statements, how they are put together, how they integrate with each other and what they tell us individually about the results for each accounting period. However, the real skill in accounting lies not in an ability to produce these statements but in analysing and interpreting the information they contain. Such analysis and interpretation enable users to draw conclusions about how well an entity is performing and the strength of its financial position. Financial information as presented in the three major statements has to be analysed to determine the **profitability** of an entity, how efficiently its assets are being used, how well an organisation is performing to meet the expectations of its owners and how secure its future cash flows and financial stability are. These aspects are analysed under the headings of profitability, efficiency, performance and **liquidity** and we will consider each of these measures in turn in this and the next chapter.

When reading the business and financial pages, the importance of these indicators will readily become apparent as we see in Give me an example 6.1.

6

GIVE ME AN EXAMPLE 6.1   A selection of terms linked to the analysis of companies' results and position

- Profitability
- Earnings
- Dividend cover
- Dividend yield
- Dividend per share
- Earnings growth
- Leverage

- Return on capital
- Like-for-like sales growth
- Liquidity
- Earnings per share
- Profit margins

Source: taken from a quick skim read of the *Financial Times* Companies and Markets section on 14 February 2015.

What these terms mean and how they are used in evaluating entities' profitability, efficiency, performance and liquidity will become clear as you work through this chapter and the next. To appreciate how common the above terms are and how relevant they continue to be in assessing companies' performance and position, quickly read through the Companies and Markets section in today's *Financial Times* and see how many of the above terms, among others, continue to appear.

Evaluating financial statements: ratio analysis

How do users evaluate and assess financial statements? The technique most commonly used is ratio analysis. A ratio in its simplest form expresses the relationship between two different figures. The calculation of the same ratio over several different time periods enables comparisons to be made between those different time periods to determine whether that ratio is rising, falling or staying the same. In this way, the performance and position of entities can be evaluated by analysing the trends that emerge over time. Ratio analysis, however, is not just confined to financial information but can be applied to any sets of numbers where relationships can be established.

When grocery shopping you might be evaluating two different sizes of a particular product: one costs £1.50 for 100g and the other costs £4.00 for 250g: which one offers the better value? By calculating the per gram price, the ratio of cost for one unit of weight, you can determine that the 100g product costs 1.50 pence per gram, while the 250g product costs 1.60 pence per gram. Therefore, the smaller sized product offers better value. Bigger is not always cheaper!

GO BACK OVER THIS AGAIN!   Are you quite sure that you understand how ratios can be used to simplify the relationship between two figures to enable comparisons to be made? Go to the **online workbook** and look at Exercises 6.1 to show you how ratios can be used in this way.

WHY IS THIS RELEVANT TO ME?   Evaluating financial statements: ratio analysis

To enable you as a business professional and user of accounting information to:

- Understand how ratios simplify the relationships between two figures to enable meaningful comparisons to be made

- Appreciate the role of ratios in evaluating information used for making economic decisions

Why is ratio analysis needed?

Example 6.1 shows the value of ratios, expressing one figure in relation to another to highlight information critical to making an economic decision. However, why is ratio analysis needed in the interpretation and evaluation of financial statements? Again, a simple example will help to explain why ratios are such a useful tool in analysing financial performance and position.

EXAMPLE 6.2

A pottery company has sales of £110,376 in the year to 31 December 2015 and sales of £150,826 in the year to 31 December 2016. The company owners will see the year to 31 December 2016 as a great success in terms of the increase in sales achieved. Profit for the year to 31 December 2015 was £27,594 and £34,690 for the year to 31 December 2016. Again, you might say that the company has been successful in the most recent year as it has generated more profit than it did in the previous year. While it is true that profit has risen, the figures alone do not tell us whether the company is now more *profitable*. The figures for sales and profits have both increased, but is each sale in the year to 31 December 2016 generating as much, less or more profit as each sale in the year to 31 December 2015? A simple comparison, as shown in Table 6.1, of the profit to the sales in each year will tell us the answer to this question.

Table 6.1 Comparison of profit to sales in each year

	2016 Calculation	Ratio	2015 Calculation	Ratio
$\dfrac{\text{Profit}}{\text{Sales}} \times 100\%$	$\dfrac{£34,690}{£150,826} \times 100\%$	23%	$\dfrac{£27,594}{£110,376} \times 100\%$	25%

Calculating these two profitability ratios shows us that despite the rise in both sales and profits in 2016, each sale has generated less profit than sales in 2015. For every £1 of sales, 23 pence is profit in 2016 compared to 25 pence of profit per £1 of sales in 2015. Ratios thus provide a *relative* measure from which to determine simple relationships between the financial figures. Calculating the ratio for the two time periods has enabled us to highlight a variance in profitability that was not at all apparent from the raw figures as presented in the accounts.

GO BACK OVER THIS AGAIN! Convinced you could calculate ratios from a given set of data and draw valid conclusions? Go to the **online workbook** and have a go at Exercises 6.2 to check your understanding.

WHY IS THIS RELEVANT TO ME?   Why is ratio analysis needed?

To enable you as a business professional and user of accounting information to appreciate:

• That larger numbers do not necessarily indicate greater success or an improvement in relative terms

• How ratios can be used to determine changes relative to other figures

Now that we have this information showing reduced profitability in 2016 we can ask questions to determine why the pottery company's profitability has fallen this year. If the company had sold exactly the same goods at exactly the same prices to exactly the same customers in both years, then the profitability percentage, the pence of profit from each £1 of sales, should have been exactly the same. As the profitability percentage has fallen, financial statement users will want to know the reasons for the change and will ask questions with a view to identifying these reasons. Questions asked will focus on changes in the business and the economic climate with a view to explaining this fall. Examples of such questions (among others) might be as follows:

- Has the pottery business reduced selling prices to increase sales in an attempt to increase the company's share of local pottery sales?
- Has there been an increase in the price of clay used to make the pottery or has there been a rise in the potters' wages which the owner has chosen not to pass on to customers?
- Has the pottery business offered discounts to bulk buyers of its goods?
- Has a rival business opened in the area forcing selling prices down?
- Is an economic recession forcing the owner to reduce prices to attract customers?

GO BACK OVER THIS AGAIN! Are you sure that you understand how profitability would fall in the circumstances outlined in the questions above? Visit the **online workbook** Exercises 6.3 to see how profitability would fall as a result of the reasons suggested.

Ratios are thus a starting point in the interpretation and evaluation of financial information. Calculating the ratios gives us information about which relationships have changed. We can then seek out explanations for these changes to assist us in understanding the business and how it operates and then use this information in making decisions about the future prospects of the business.

WHY IS THIS RELEVANT TO ME? Why is ratio analysis needed?

As a business professional and user of accounting information you will be expected to:
- Calculate ratios for the business and compare these ratios to ratios from earlier accounting periods
- Use ratios to evaluate the performance of different parts of your organisation
- Use ratios to determine aspects of the business in which improvements could be made

Ratios, figures or both?

Given that ratios are so useful in interpreting an organisation's results, should we just ignore the financial statement figures once we have calculated the ratios? While ratios are an excellent interpretative tool, it is important to realise that the interpretation of financial statements relies on the figures presented in the income statement, the statement of financial position and the statement of cash flows *and* the ratios derived from these figures. Just taking the figures or the ratios on their own would be insufficient to enable users to form a full understanding of what the financial statements are telling them about the profitability, performance, efficiency and liquidity of an entity. Thus, an evaluation of an entity should look at both the figures presented in the financial statements and the ratios derived from those numbers. To understand why both the figures and the ratios are used together, consider the following two examples.

EXAMPLE 6.3

An entity has a profitability percentage of 20% compared to its competitor with a profitability percentage of 10%. Logically, based on just this ratio, users will prefer the company with a profitability percentage of 20% as this is higher. However, the entity with the 20% profitability has a profit of £50,000 and sales of £250,000 while its competitor has a profit of £10,000,000 and sales of £100,000,000. Which is the more preferable company now? Clearly the company with sales of £100 million and profit of £10 million will attract greater attention. This is a much larger company, probably very well established and with higher profits (if not higher profitability) from which to pay dividends to shareholders and with a longer, more stable and more firmly grounded trading record. Hence it is vital to look at the financial statement figures as well as the ratios when evaluating an organisation's financial performance and position.

EXAMPLE 6.4

A profit of £1 million sounds impressive. However, the £1 million figure has no context. If the profit of £1 million was generated from sales of £10 million, this would give a profitability percentage of 10% (£1 m/£10 m × 100%). Yet if the £1 million profit was generated from sales of £100 million this would give a profitability percentage of just 1% (£1 m/£100 m × 100%). Profitability of 10% is much more preferable to 1% profitability. Hence, it is vital to look at the ratios as well as the financial statement figures when evaluating an organisation's financial performance and position.

Even more useful would be information comparing the profitability percentage achieved in prior years: if the entity generating 10% profitability this year had achieved 20% profitability in each of the previous five years, the 10% profitability in the current year would be seen as a very poor performance, but might be understandable if those profits had been generated during a period of contraction in the economy. However, if the profitability percentage in the previous five years had been 5%, then doubling the profitability percentage to 10% would be seen as a very worthwhile achievement indeed.

6

WHY IS THIS RELEVANT TO ME?   Ratios, figures or both?

As a business professional and user of accounting information you should appreciate:

- That the figures and the ratios based on them are both equally valuable in analysing and interpreting financial statements
- The interlinking nature of both ratios and figures in the analysis of financial results
- The different perspectives that both ratios and financial statement figures bring to the analysis of financial results

GO BACK OVER THIS AGAIN!   Do you really understand how ratios and financial statement figures interact? Go to the **online workbook** and have a go at Exercises 6.4 to check your understanding.

The advantages of ratios: summary

The preceding pages have presented a lot of arguments, so let's just pause for a moment to summarise how ratios and ratio analysis are advantageous in the evaluation of financial statements:

- Ratios are easy to calculate and to understand.
- Ratios highlight trends and variances by simplifying data into key indicators.
- Ratios help to express relationships between different figures in the financial statements.
- Calculating ratios across different time periods helps us to build up a picture of the trend in a particular indicator.
- Because ratios are a proportion calculated on a consistent basis across different time periods, this helps to overcome the problem of figures changing from year to year.
- Ratios, of course, are not the final answer: changes in ratios over different accounting periods will just indicate that we need to investigate why those ratios have changed and to rationalise the changes by reference to different economic conditions prevailing in each accounting period, different product mixes or the strategy the organisation is pursuing in relation to its goals.
- Ratios are thus not an end in themselves; they are an indicator of change or movement that prompts further questions and further action to correct unfavourable movements or to take further actions to maintain the positive trend.

REFER BACK To illustrate the ratios discussed below and in the next chapter we will use the statement of financial position, income statement and statement of cash flows for Bunns the Bakers presented in Chapters 2, 3 and 4. You should refer to Illustrations 2.1, 3.1 and 4.1 in these chapters or refer to the copies available in the **online workbook** as you work through the rest of this chapter and the next.

Profitability ratios

Now that we have considered the role of ratios in conjunction with the financial statement figures, it is time to look at the specific ratios used in analysing organisations' profitability. While we have already looked at a simple example of a profitability ratio earlier in this chapter (Example 6.2), we will now think about profitability ratios in much more depth and detail and consider the ratios shown in Figure 6.1.

As we noted in Chapter 3, profit is one of the most discussed numbers in any set of financial statements. However, to put profit into context, we have to know whether profits are higher or lower and how these profits compare with results from previous accounting periods. In money terms: is the profit of an organisation rising or falling? In relative terms: is the entity making more or less profit per pound of sales than in previous years? Profitability ratios compare the various profit figures shown in the income statement to the revenue for the year in order to make this assessment.

Bunns the Bakers' income statement (Illustration 6.1) shows the revenue and profit figures for the years ended 31 March 2016 and 31 March 2015.

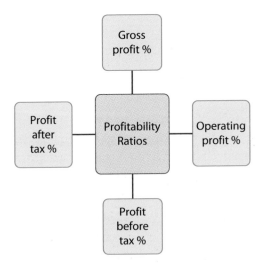

Figure 6.1 Profitability ratios

Illustration 6.1 Bunns the Bakers: revenue and profit figures for the years ended 31 March 2016 and 31 March 2015

	2016	2015
	£000	£000
Revenue	10,078	9,575
Gross profit	5,543	4,979
Operating profit	895	767
Profit before tax	760	614
Profit for the year	547	442

Following the principle above that we must consider ratios and the absolute figures together, we should first highlight the trends in the profits in Illustration 6.1 before we calculate any ratios. All the figures given for the different profits for 2016 are higher than the profits in 2015. This looks good: in money terms, profits are rising. However, as we have already noted, these raw figures only tell us that Bunns the Bakers has made more profit in the current year, but do not tell us whether the company is more *profitable*. To assess profitability, we would need to compare the various profit figures to the sales made by the organisation to see whether more or less profit is being generated per £ of sales through the calculation of various ratios.

Gross profit percentage

As we saw in Chapter 3, gross profit is the profit left over after deducting from sales the direct costs of production of the goods sold or, in Julia's case, after deducting the costs of buying in goods for resale. This ratio is very useful when assessing how effectively the organisation is controlling its costs of production or costs of buying in goods for resale. This ratio is calculated as follows:

$$\text{Gross profit \%} = \frac{\text{Gross profit}}{\text{Revenue}} \times 100\%$$

Looking at Illustration 6.1, the company has made a gross profit in the year to 31 March 2016 of £5,543,000 from revenue of £10,078,000. This gives the organisation a gross profit percentage for 2016 of:

$$\frac{£5,543,000}{£10,078,000} \times 100\% = 55.00\%$$

Conventionally, ratios are calculated to two decimal places.

Have Bunns the Bakers achieved a higher ratio in 2016 compared with 2015? Let's calculate the gross profit ratio for 2015 to see whether 2016's gross profit percentage is higher or lower than 2015's. Gross profit in the income statement (Illustration 6.1) for the year ended 31 March 2015 is £4,979,000 from revenue of £9,575,000, so this gives a gross profit percentage for 2015 of:

$$\frac{£4,979,000}{£9,575,000} \times 100\% = 52.00\%$$

WHY IS THIS RELEVANT TO ME?   Gross profit percentage

To enable you as a business professional and user of accounting information to:

- Find information relevant to the gross profit percentage calculation in the financial statements

- Calculate your own gross profit percentage figures

MULTIPLE CHOICE QUESTIONS   Totally confident that you can calculate a gross profit percentage from a given set of financial information? Go to the **online workbook** and have a go at Multiple choice questions 6.1 to test out your ability to calculate this ratio.

6

Interpretation of the results

The increase in gross profit percentage is encouraging. Bunns the Bakers are making 55 pence of gross profit from each £1 of sales in 2016 compared to a gross profit of 52 pence from each £1 of sales in 2015. However, as we noted earlier, just calculating the ratios is not enough: in your role as a business professional, you will be expected to investigate and explain why ratios have changed when compared with the previous year. The way to do this is to consider and investigate possible reasons for the changes or to rationalise these changes by reference to the economy in which the organisation operates.

Why might Bunns the Bakers be generating a higher gross profit percentage in the current year compared to the previous year? It is important to explain this change as it might be expected that each sale less the cost of sales will generate the same gross profit percentage every time (for this idea, see Chapter 9 and the assumption that the contribution (sales – variable costs) from each extra unit of sales will be the same as for all other units of sales).

There are two aspects to the gross profit of an organisation, the revenue and the cost of sales, so either or both of these figures might have been subject to certain changes to give a higher gross profit percentage. Therefore, possible reasons for the increase in 2016 might be as follows:

- An increase in selling prices that is higher than the rise in costs incurred in producing or buying in the goods for sale.

- A change in the types of sales made from lower profitability goods such as bread to higher profitability goods such as pies, pastries and ready-made sandwiches.

- A fall in the price of input materials thereby lowering the cost of sales.

- An increase in the productivity of the workforce, producing more goods per hour or selling more goods per shop than in the previous year.

- The company might have benefited from bulk discounts from suppliers: when goods are ordered in larger quantities, suppliers often give their customers a discount for placing larger orders. Bulk discounts received reduce the cost of raw materials in the production process thereby lowering the cost of sales and increasing the gross profit.

These are just some of the possible reasons for the change in the gross profit percentage and you can probably think of other perfectly valid reasons to explain this improvement. As a business professional you will be expected to calculate the ratios and then think about and offer reasons why ratios are changing in order to understand and explain the economic trends underlying the movements in these figures.

6

WHY IS THIS RELEVANT TO ME? Interpretation of the results

As a business professional and user of accounting information you should appreciate that:

- Senior managers will want to know why the gross profit percentage is changing: they will not just accept the changes without any explanation

- Business leaders do not have to be told that ratios are changing, they want to know why they are changing so that action can be taken to extend favourable or to correct unfavourable movements

GO BACK OVER THIS AGAIN! How easily could you determine the causes of rises and falls in the gross profit percentage? Go to the **online workbook** and have a go at Exercises 6.5 to make sure you can distinguish between factors that will cause the gross profit percentage to rise and factors that will cause it to fall.

MULTIPLE CHOICE QUESTIONS Quite confident that you could determine factors affecting the gross profit percentage? Go to the **online workbook** and have a go at Multiple choice question 6.2 to test out your ability to determine these factors.

Other profitability ratios

As well as the gross profit figure, Illustration 6.1 gives income statement figures for operating profit, profit before tax and profit for the year (= profit after tax). Profitability ratios can be calculated for these figures as shown in Table 6.2.

Using the figures for revenue and for profits in Illustration 6.1, we can calculate the other profitability percentages for Bunns the Bakers for the two years ending 31 March 2016 and 31 March 2015. These figures are shown in Table 6.3.

Table 6.2 Profitability ratios for operating profit, profit before tax and profit for the year

Ratio	Calculation	What does this ratio tell us?
Operating profit %	$\dfrac{\text{Operating profit}}{\text{Revenue}} \times 100\%$	Determines profitability on the basis of revenue less all operating costs, before taking into account the effects of finance income, finance expense and taxation
Profit before tax %	$\dfrac{\text{Profit before tax}}{\text{Revenue}} \times 100\%$	Bases the profitability calculation on profit before taxation to eliminate the distorting effect of changes in tax rates. The profit before tax percentage is the profitability of the entity after deducting all costs incurred and taking into account income earned from all sources, both trading and investment
Profit after tax %	$\dfrac{\text{Profit for the year}}{\text{Revenue}} \times 100\%$	Calculates profitability for the period after adding all income and deducting all expenses and charges for the period under review

Table 6.3 Other profitability percentages for Bunns the Bakers for the two years ending 31 March 2016 and 31 March 2015

	2016 Calculation	Ratio	2015 Calculation	Ratio
Operating profit %	$\dfrac{£895,000}{£10,078,000} \times 100\%$	8.88%	$\dfrac{£767,000}{£9,575,000} \times 100\%$	8.01%
Profit before tax %	$\dfrac{£760,000}{£10,078,000} \times 100\%$	7.54%	$\dfrac{£614,000}{£9,575,000} \times 100\%$	6.41%
Profit after tax %	$\dfrac{£547,000}{£10,078,000} \times 100\%$	5.43%	$\dfrac{£442,000}{£9,575,000} \times 100\%$	4.62%

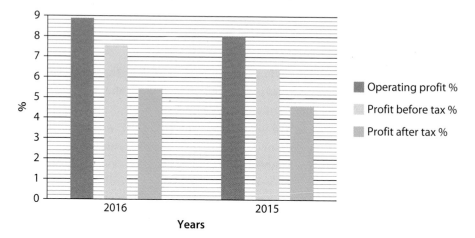

Figure 6.2 Bunns the Bakers' operating profit, profit before tax and profit after tax %s

These profitability ratios have risen, too, so it is quite clear that Bunns the Bakers is more profitable in 2016 than it was in 2015 as shown in Figure 6.2. The rise in gross profit is part of the explanation for the increase in the above ratios. There is now more gross profit from which to pay all the other operating and finance expenses and still leave a larger profit for the year. Cost control will also be a factor and we can investigate which costs are lower or higher than in the previous year and determine how these rises and falls have affected profits and profitability in the current year. However, we can also investigate the efficiency with which assets are being used within the business. The greater the efficiency and productivity of these assets, the higher the revenue and profits will be.

WHY IS THIS RELEVANT TO ME?   Profitability ratios

As a business professional and user of accounting information you will be expected to:

• Understand how ratios relevant to assessing profitability are calculated

• Calculate those ratios yourself

• Use the calculated ratios as a foundation on which to build explanations for changes in the ratios in comparison to previous years

MULTIPLE CHOICE QUESTIONS   Think that you can calculate operating profit, profit before tax and profit after tax percentages? Go to the **online workbook** and have a go at Multiple choice questions 6.3 to test your ability to calculate these ratios.

SUMMARY OF KEY CONCEPTS   How well have you grasped the formulae for gross profit percentage, operating profit percentage, profit before tax percentage and profit after tax percentage? Take a look at Summary of key concepts 6.1–6.4 to reinforce your understanding.

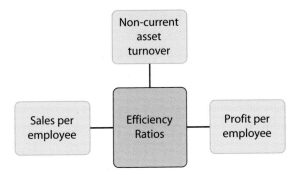

Figure 6.3 Efficiency ratios

Efficiency ratios

Efficiency ratios consider how effectively and productively the resources of the organisation are being used to create both revenue and profit. An organisation's resources fall into two categories. First, non-current assets used in the production of goods and sales and, second, the employees engaged within the business as illustrated in Figure 6.3. Various ratios can be calculated to demonstrate how efficiently these resources are being used within an organisation and these ratios should also help to explain the improved profitability of Bunns the Bakers in the year to 31 March 2016.

Non-current asset turnover

This ratio compares the sales achieved by an organisation with the non-current assets in use in that organisation to determine how many £s of sales are produced by each £ of non-current assets. Ideally, this ratio will rise over time as non-current assets are used more efficiently to generate increased revenue.

This ratio is calculated as follows:

$$\text{Non-current asset turnover} = \frac{\text{Revenue}}{\text{Non-current assets}}$$

We have already seen that Bunns the Bakers has revenue of £10,078,000 for the year ended 31 March 2016 and revenue of £9,575,000 for the previous financial year. From the statement of financial position in Illustration 2.1, total non-current assets at 31 March 2016 and 31 March 2015 are £11,865,000 and £11,355,000, respectively. This gives the following figures for non-current asset turnover:

$$2016\text{: Non-current asset turnover: } \frac{£10,078,000}{£11,865,000} = £0.85$$

$$2015: \text{Non-current asset turnover:} \frac{\pounds9,575,000}{\pounds11,355,000} = \pounds0.84$$

The figures show a slight improvement over the year. In 2015 each £1 of non-current assets generated revenue of 84 pence and in 2016 this has improved to 85 pence. Our conclusion from this ratio would be that non-current assets are being used more efficiently to generate revenue for the business as more revenue is being produced per £ of non-current assets.

However, a word of caution is needed at this point. As we saw in Chapter 2 (How are assets and liabilities valued?), users have to be careful when using information on assets employed within an organisation. The amount at which assets are recorded in the statement of financial position may be increased by restating these assets to current values. Conversely, this amount may be too low because assets bought many years ago are still being used within the business. When such assets are still recorded at their original cost less any depreciation charged, these figures will now be seriously out of date and produce much less meaningful comparisons.

Similarly, when an organisation leases assets, a situation common in the retail industry as shops are often rented from landlords, these leased assets will not currently appear on the statement of financial position at all as the organisation does not control them. Therefore, retailers' non-current assets might be misleadingly low on account of the absence of these leased assets from their statements of financial position. Despite the potential shortcomings in this ratio, the non-current asset turnover figure does present users with relevant information on how effectively the organisation is using its long-term assets to generate revenue.

MULTIPLE CHOICE QUESTIONS Sure that you can calculate non-current asset turnover ratios? Go to the **online workbook** and have a go at Multiple choice questions 6.4 to test your ability to calculate this ratio.

Revenue and profit per employee

Unlike non-current assets, employees cannot be given a monetary value within financial statements as they do not meet the definition of an asset (Chapter 2, Assets). However, employees are a vital part of every organisation and how they perform during their working hours will determine how successful and how profitable organisations are. Increased productivity on the part of employees, generating more output or selling more goods during the hours worked each week, will have a significant impact upon both revenue and profitability. Employees are usually paid a fixed weekly wage, so the more they produce for that fixed weekly wage, the more profit entities will make. As an example of this, think about Bunns the Bakers' shop employees. They will be paid the same amount each week for selling 10 sandwiches or 400 sandwiches, but the latter sales figure will lead to much higher profits in each shop. Increasing sales while keeping input costs the same inevitably leads to higher profits. This principle holds where any cost is fixed: the more production or the more sales that can be generated from this fixed cost, the more profitable organisations will be.

NUMERICAL EXERCISES Are you convinced you understand how increasing output while keeping input costs the same can lead to higher profits? Visit the **online workbook** Numerical exercises 6.1 to reinforce your understanding of how this is true.

If employees are not given a monetary value within financial statements, how can we assess whether they have been more or less productive during each accounting period? In many jurisdictions, organisations must report the average number of employees during each financial reporting period. You may have to search for this information in the notes to the financial statements, but it will be there and you will be able to use this information to make meaningful comparisons of the revenue and profit per employee across different years. The higher the revenue and profit per employee, the more efficiently organisations are working to generate returns to satisfy the business's objectives of profit and revenue growth. Where these ratios are falling, management can look into the reasons for declining revenue and profit per employee. Are operations overstaffed and is there scope to reduce employee numbers to improve the efficiency, productivity and profitability of operations?

These measures of employee efficiency are calculated as follows. While operating profit per employee is calculated below, you could just as easily calculate per employee figures for gross profit, profit before tax or profit after tax (= profit for the year). Whichever measure you use, you must be consistent in your calculation of the ratio so that you are comparing like with like across different accounting periods. Similarly, the measure calculated below is based on all employees, but the ratios could be calculated using just production employees or production plus retail employees or any other combination of employee numbers deemed suitable, provided that the calculation continues to be consistently applied.

$$\text{Revenue per employee} = \frac{\text{Total revenue}}{\text{Total number of employees}}$$

$$\text{Profit per employee} = \frac{\text{Operating profit}}{\text{Total number of employees}}$$

From the notes to the accounts, it can be determined that the average number of employees in the year to 31 March 2016 was 120 and 112 in the year to 31 March 2015.

Using these figures and the figures for revenue and operating profit in Illustration 6.1, the following efficiency ratios can be calculated:

$$2016: \text{Revenue per employee} = \frac{£10,078,000}{120} = £83,983$$

$$2015: \text{Revenue per employee} = \frac{£9,575,000}{112} = £85,491$$

$$2016: \text{Operating profit per employee} = \frac{£895,000}{120} = £7,458$$

$$2015: \text{Operating profit per employee} = \frac{£767,000}{112} = £6,848$$

While **revenue per employee** has fallen in 2016, operating profit per employee has risen by £610, a rise of 8.91% ((£7,458 − £6,848)/£6,848 × 100%). This increase suggests that costs have been well controlled this year and that the company's employees are working effectively to generate increased profit for the business. This increase in profit per employee might also go some way to explaining the increased profitability noted earlier in this chapter: more profit has been generated per unit of resource employed, possibly due to higher productivity, and, as a result, a higher profit and higher profitability percentages have been produced.

WHY IS THIS RELEVANT TO ME? Efficiency ratios

To enable you as a business professional and user of accounting information to:

- Understand ratios that are relevant to determining the effectiveness of asset utilisation
- Calculate these ratios yourself
- Appreciate that the more revenue and profit that can be generated from a fixed cost resource, the more profitable and successful an organisation will be

MULTIPLE CHOICE QUESTIONS Do you reckon you can calculate revenue and profit per employee ratios? Go to the **online workbook** and have a go at Multiple choice questions 6.5 to test your ability to calculate these ratios.

SUMMARY OF KEY CONCEPTS Certain you can remember the formulae for non-current asset turnover, revenue per employee and profit per employee? Take a look at Summary of key concepts 6.5–6.7 to reinforce your understanding.

Sales and profit per unit of input resource

One further aspect of efficiency merits our attention at this point. It is common practice in the retail sector to measure sales and profits per square metre or square foot of selling space (where shops differ greatly in size from superstores down to small high street outlets) or per shop (where shop size does not vary significantly). When these figures rise year on year, then more has been produced from the same unit of resource: input resources have been used more effectively and efficiently to produce more sales and hence more profits. Let's see if Bunns the Bakers are producing more sales and profits from their resources by calculating asset utilisation ratios (Figure 6.4).

Bunns the Bakers had 19 shops all of similar size open to the public in the year to 31 March 2015. During the year to 31 March 2016 an additional shop was opened on 1 October 2015, exactly six months into the current year. During the year to 31 March 2016, then, Bunns the Bakers had 19 + (1 × 6/12) = 19.5 shops selling the company's goods and products. Dividing the figures for the number of shops into the revenue for each year will give us the following results for revenue per shop:

6

$$2016: \text{Revenue per shop: } \frac{£10,078,000}{19.5} = £516,821$$

$$2015: \text{Revenue per shop: } \frac{£9,575,000}{19} = £503,947$$

These figures tell us that Bunns the Bakers has achieved higher sales per shop and so is using the company's resources much more efficiently, squeezing more output from

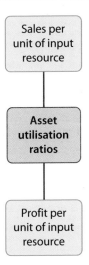

Figure 6.4 Asset utilisation ratios

the same unit of resource. A similar calculation can be undertaken to find out whether more profit has been generated from the resources used. The focus of our attention here will be the operating profit per shop, the sales less all the operating costs of the business.

$$2016: \text{Operating profit per shop: } \frac{\text{£}895,000}{19.5} = \text{£}45,897$$

$$2015: \text{Operating profit per shop: } \frac{\text{£}767,000}{19} = \text{£}40,368$$

Again, just as in the case of the employees, the shops have generated higher profits per shop in 2016 compared to 2015. More revenue and more profit have been generated from the same resources and so the business will be more profitable.

GO BACK OVER THIS AGAIN!   Quite sure you understand how increasing income per unit of input resource leads to higher profits? Visit the **online workbook** and look at Exercises 6.6 to prove to yourself that this is true.

A real-life example of increasing sales from the same inputs resulting in higher profits can be seen in Give me an example 6.2 (emphasis added). As can be seen, Domino's generated more sales from the same units of resource (the shops, delivery vehicles and employees), hence the increase in their profits for the six months under review. Like-for-like sales refers to the comparison between sales in the current six months compared to sales in the same six months in the previous year.

GIVE ME AN EXAMPLE 6.2   World Cup hunger boosts Domino's

Strong growth in its Internet business combined with a boost from the World Cup buoyed first-half sales at Domino's, the pizza chain ...

'Before any ball got kicked [in the World Cup finals], our like for likes going into the competition were already up 12.8 per cent, but it gave us a substantial boost when it started', said Chris Moore, chief executive.

'Interestingly enough, the biggest gain was for the Slovenia game [against England]—UK mature store sales on that day were up 65 per cent, and between 2 pm and 5 pm that afternoon our mature stores averaged 333 per cent ahead.'

'Sales across the group's franchisees in the UK and Ireland rose 21 per cent to £237m in the six months to June 27 [2010], with like for like sales in the 553 mature stores up 14 per cent ...'

First half pre tax profits rose 30 per cent to £17 m, on revenue ahead 24 per cent to £91 m.

John O'Doherty, *Financial Times* 13 July 2010, page 20

Source: *Financial Times* © The Financial Times Limited 2010. All Rights Reserved.

WHY IS THIS RELEVANT TO ME?   Sales and profit per unit of input resource

To enable you as a business professional and user of accounting information to:

- Appreciate that increasing sales per unit of input resource is often the key to improving an organisation's profitability

- Devise suitable efficiency ratios to measure output per unit of input resource to see if this is rising, falling or staying the same

GO BACK OVER THIS AGAIN!   Can you identify ways in which to increase sales and profit per unit of input resource? Go to the **online workbook** and have a go at Exercises 6.7 to test your understanding of how this works.

Performance ratios

These ratios , illustrated in Figure 6.5, are of particular interest to an entity's shareholders as they measure the returns to the owners of the business. As we saw in Chapter 5, the owners of incorporated entities are the shareholders. Shareholders invest money into the shares of a business with a view to earning dividends from the profits made by that business. The various ratios considered under this heading first compare the profits generated to the number of shares in issue and then think about the dividends paid out on each share. Comparisons of dividends to the market price of each share tell shareholders what their return is on that share. In this way they can assess whether they could earn more by investing their money in alternative investments, while comparing dividends paid with profits generated helps investors decide how safe their future dividend income will be.

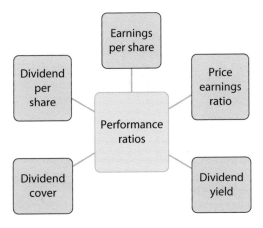

Figure 6.5 Performance ratios

Earnings per share (EPS)

The first **performance ratio** that shareholders consider is the **earnings per share** (this is frequently abbreviated to **EPS**). This figure is produced simply by dividing the profit for the year by the number of ordinary shares in issue. This figure represents the dividend that would result if all the profits for the period were paid out to ordinary shareholders as dividends. As we noted in Chapter 5, such a pay-out is most unlikely as the directors hold back some of the profits each year from which to finance future investment in the company.

EPS is calculated as follows:

$$\text{Earnings per share} = \frac{\text{Profit after taxation and after preference dividends}}{\text{Number of ordinary shares in issue}} \times 100 \text{ pence}$$

The profit after taxation is equivalent to the profit for the year. In situations in which an entity has preference shares in issue, any dividends paid on those preference shares will be paid out before any dividends are paid to ordinary shareholders. Therefore, this prior claim on the profits of an entity has to be deducted from profit for the year before the profits available for distribution to the ordinary shareholders can be determined. Note that EPS is always expressed in pence per share.

Looking at the figures for Bunns the Bakers, the profit after taxation (= profit for the year) for 2016 is £547,000 and £442,000 for 2015. The number of shares in issue can be observed in the statement of financial position. As shown in Illustration 2.1, Bunns the Bakers had 2,500,000 £1 shares in issue in the year to 31 March 2016, while in the previous year there were only 2,400,000 £1 ordinary shares. The increase in the number of shares indicates that additional shares have been issued during the year to 31 March 2016. The calculations for EPS for the two years under consideration are thus:

$$2016: \text{Earnings per share} = \frac{£547,000}{2,500,000} \times 100 \text{ p} = 21.88 \text{ pence}$$

$$2015: \text{Earnings per share} = \frac{£442,000}{2,400,000} \times 100 \text{ p} = 18.42 \text{ pence}$$

Bunns the Bakers has no preference shares in issue, so there are no preference dividends to deduct from the profit for the year before the EPS figures can be calculated. Therefore, the EPS calculation is simply based on the profit for the year divided by the number of ordinary shares in issue. Given the rise in EPS, shareholders will be pleased and the stock market will give the shares a higher valuation based on these increased returns.

MULTIPLE CHOICE QUESTIONS Are you quite confident that you can calculate earnings per share? Go to the **online workbook** and have a go at Multiple choice questions 6.6 to test your ability to calculate this ratio.

EPS is a key figure in the evaluation of an entity's performance by the stock market and by stock brokers and traders. A review of the financial press will show you that where EPS are expected to increase, the share price rises ahead of the announcement of earnings for the financial period under review. Similarly, where an entity's actual EPS do not meet market expectations, share prices of that entity are marked down by the market. This reduction in the market price of the shares arises first from the fact that the results are a disappointment and second because the flows of cash to shareholders in the form of dividends from that entity are likely to be lower than expected. Ideally, the EPS figure should keep rising each year. Where this is the case, the share price will keep rising too and a rising share price is a source of happiness to shareholders as such rises indicate increasing wealth. In reality, EPS rise and fall in line with the economy: during periods when the economy surges, profits, and hence EPS, rise, but when the economy contracts and slows down, profits reduce, causing EPS and share prices to fall. Similarly, when companies' results and EPS are better than expected, share prices rise, but when they fall or are expected to fall, then the share price falls, too. Give me an example 6.3 provides two examples to illustrate these share price movements.

6

GIVE ME AN EXAMPLE 6.3   The effect of profits on share prices

Shares of Toll Brothers climbed 5 per cent to $38.92 after financial first quarter earnings and sales topped Wall Street estimates. The luxury housebuilder reported profits of $81.3 million, or 44 cents per share, on sales of $853.5 million. Analysts had forecast earnings of 28 cents a share on sales of $777.8 million.

(*Financial Times*, 25 February 2015, page 29)

Ladbrokes [share price] dropped after its joint house broker said a big change of strategy was needed. Deutsche Bank forecast that the book-maker's 2015 earnings would miss market expectations by 15 per cent

(*Financial Times*, 24 February 2015, page 31)

Source: *Financial Times* © The Financial Times Limited 2015. All Rights Reserved.

WHY IS THIS RELEVANT TO ME?   Earnings per share

As a business professional and user of accounting information you will be expected to be aware of:

• How to calculate the earnings per share ratio
• The effects that profits or losses will have on the earnings per share of your employer
• How the stock market values companies' shares on the basis of earnings per share

Price/earnings ratio (the P/E ratio)

The **price/earnings ratio** is linked to the EPS. This ratio divides the EPS into the current market price of that share. This gives a number that is an indicator of how many years it would take for that share to pay back its owner in earnings if the share were purchased today and earnings remained the same for the foreseeable future. A quick glance at the financial pages will show you that every listed company has a different P/E ratio (as shown in Give me an example 6.4), some higher and some lower than others. Typically, shares in companies with steady profits have a higher P/E ratio as the cash flows from dividends are perceived to be more secure and enduring than from other shares. On the other hand, shares in companies whose earnings are expected to fluctuate a great deal have lower P/E ratios as the cash flow stream from dividends in these companies is expected to be less secure and so P/E ratios for shares in these companies are lower. You might say that the P/E ratio is an indicator of the market's confidence in a particular company: the more likely it is that a company will continue to produce profits, earnings and dividends for shareholders, the higher the P/E ratio of that company will be.

GIVE ME AN EXAMPLE 6.4   Differing price/earnings ratios

A glance at the *Financial Times* Share Service for Wednesday 25 February 2015 shows the following information for three companies:

Company	P/E ratio
Debenhams	11.43
Marks and Spencer	16.37
Ted Baker	34.96

Source: *Financial Times* for Wednesday 25 February 2015

Ted Baker has a very high P/E ratio, implying that shareholders would have to wait almost 35 years before their investment was fully repaid in earnings. Ted Baker markets itself as a global lifestyle brand that designs and sells clothing and fashion accessories to men and women who value something different. The company has very strong branding and doubled revenue and profits from 2010 to 2014. There is a very clear expansion strategy in place and the company's worldwide presence and strong products have encouraged investors to anticipate much bigger profits, earnings per share and dividends in the future. The share price reflects these future expectations and investors' confidence that the directors' long-term strategic goals will be achieved.

Marks and Spencer generate around 50% of their sales from general merchandise and 50% from food. The general merchandise side of the business has suffered some setbacks in recent years. Retailers of general merchandise are also subject to intense competition in the market place and the products of one general retailer are interchangeable with the products sold by other general retailers. Marks and Spencer lack the distinctive branding of Ted Baker and these factors are reflected in Marks and Spencer's lower share price and

→

consequently lower P/E ratio. As a mature business, Marks and Spencer is now a steady rather than an ambitious performer so that investors buying shares in Marks and Spencer today will expect their investment to repay itself in earnings in just over 16 years.

Debenhams is also a retailer of general merchandise. The company has suffered various problems in recent years, resulting in downgrades in profit expectations, and has lost sales and customers to other retailers owing to the interchangeability of the products it sells. As a result, the P/E ratio of the company suggests that investors will receive their money back in earnings within 11.5 years because of the reduced confidence that the future performance of the business will deliver high returns to shareholders.

The price/earnings ratio is calculated in the following way:

$$\text{Price/earnings ratio} = \frac{\text{Market value of one ordinary share}}{\text{Earnings per share}}$$

Share prices for Bunns the Bakers, when their results were released for the years ended 31 March 2016 and 31 March 2015, were 310.7 pence and 254.2 pence, respectively. These prices and the EPS calculated above give P/E ratios as follows:

$$\text{2016: Price/earnings ratio} = \frac{310.7}{21.88} = 14.2$$

$$\text{2015: Price/earnings ratio} = \frac{254.2}{18.42} = 13.8$$

The share price has risen as the EPS have increased in 2016. Given the rise in EPS in the current financial year, the stock market would expect future earnings to be more secure (and that a higher dividend will be paid from higher earnings) and so the price/earnings ratio has also risen. Given the nature of Bunns the Bakers' products, investors would also expect customers to continue buying such products in the foreseeable future. Indeed, they might even buy additional treats to cheer themselves up during a difficult economic period. A higher level of confidence in the shares to continue producing an enduring earnings and dividend stream is thus being shown by the higher P/E ratio.

GO BACK OVER THIS AGAIN! Do you really understand the relationship between price and earnings in the price/earnings ratio? Go to the **online workbook** and have a go at Exercises 6.8 to test your understanding of this relationship.

MULTIPLE CHOICE QUESTIONS How easily can you calculate price/earnings ratios? Go to the **online workbook** and have a go at Multiple choice questions 6.7 to make sure you can calculate this figure.

Dividend per share (DPS)

This ratio is used by shareholders to determine how much dividend is being paid on each share. As in the case of EPS, the ideal situation for shareholders is for the dividends to keep rising each year. Such increases indicate confidence in the company's ability to continue generating rising profits into the future. In addition, higher dividends result in rising share prices as expectations of future dividend increases feed into the market's valuation of the shares. The **DPS** can be compared to the EPS to calculate the pay-out ratio, the percentage of the EPS that have been distributed as dividend to the shareholders over the year.

The DPS figure is worked out in almost exactly the same way as EPS, but the total dividends paid out are substituted for the profits after taxation and after preference dividends. This ratio is calculated as follows:

$$\text{Dividend per share} = \frac{\text{Total ordinary dividends}}{\text{Number of ordinary shares in issue}} \times 100 \text{ pence}$$

From the statement of cash flows in Illustration 4.1, we can see that the dividends paid out in the year to 31 March 2016 were £90,000 compared with £72,000 in the year to 31 March 2015. This gives DPS figures for the two years as follows:

$$2016: \text{Dividend per share} = \frac{£90,000}{2,500,000} \times 100 \text{ p} = 3.60 \text{ pence}$$

$$2015: \text{Dividend per share} = \frac{£72,000}{2,400,000} \times 100 \text{ p} = 3.00 \text{ pence}$$

Comparing these figures to the EPS for the two years gives a pay-out ratio (dividend per share as a percentage of earnings per share for the year) of:

$$2016: \text{Payout ratio} = \frac{3.60 \text{ pence}}{21.88 \text{ pence}} \times 100\% = 16.45\%$$

$$2015: \text{Payout ratio} = \frac{3.00 \text{ pence}}{18.42 \text{ pence}} \times 100\% = 16.29\%$$

DPS has risen and this represents a higher pay-out ratio as well. The company has thus paid out more DPS this year as a percentage of EPS, but has still retained a significant proportion of the earnings (over 83% in both years under review) with a view to re-investing these into the business to generate further expansion in the future and to increase both sales and profits.

Dividend yield

Shareholders invest in companies firstly to generate income in the form of dividends and secondly to increase their wealth through the capital appreciation (the increase in the market price of a share over the year) of their shares' value. These same shareholders could just as easily invest their cash in the safety of bank or building society accounts and earn interest on their deposits. Is the dividend and capital appreciation they are earning on their shares sufficient compensation for the risk they are taking by investing in the stock market?

The dividend earned by shareholders is compared with the market price of a share to give the dividend yield. This figure is calculated as follows:

$$\text{Dividend yield} = \frac{\text{Ordinary dividends per share}}{\text{Current market price of one ordinary share}} \times 100\%$$

For Bunns the Bakers, the **dividend yield** for the financial years ended 31 March 2016 and 31 March 2015 is as follows:

$$2016: \text{Dividend yield} = \frac{3.60 \text{ pence}}{310.7 \text{ pence}} \times 100\% = 1.16\%$$

$$2015: \text{Dividend yield} = \frac{3.00 \text{ pence}}{254.2 \text{ pence}} \times 100\% = 1.18\%$$

The dividend yield does not appear to be very high at present, though it compares well with the Bank of England base rate of 0.50%. By investing in a building society account with a more favourable interest rate, shareholders could gain a much better monetary return of around 2.50% to 3.00%. However, using this building society interest rate as a benchmark would ignore the fact that the share price has risen from 254.2 pence a year ago to 310.7 pence today, a rise of 22.23% ((310.7 − 254.2)/254.2 × 100%). This capital appreciation, along with the dividends received, represent the total return to shareholders over the year. When looking at the dividend yield, it is important to remember that a low return does not necessarily indicate a poorly performing share. Both the capital appreciation in the share price and the dividend actually received have to be taken into account.

Dividend cover

This ratio measures how many times the current year ordinary dividend could be paid from the profit for the year. **Dividend cover** looks at the profit after taxation and after any preference dividends that have to be paid first. This ratio is a measure of the security of the dividend that has been paid: the higher the ratio, the more secure the dividend. A dividend cover of 1.0 would indicate that all the EPS were being paid out as dividends with no retention of profits within the entity to finance future expansion and development. Whereas a dividend cover of 3.0 would indicate that the current year dividend could be paid out three times and that two-thirds of the profit for the year is being retained within the business.

The dividend cover ratio is calculated in the following way:

$$\text{Dividend cover} = \frac{\text{Profit after tax and after preference dividends}}{\text{Total ordinary dividends}}$$

Looking at Bunns the Bakers, the dividend cover ratio for the two financial years that concern us is:

$$2016: \text{Dividend cover} = \frac{£547,000}{£90,000} = 6.08 \text{ times}$$

$$2015: \text{Dividend cover} = \frac{£442,000}{£72,000} = 6.14 \text{ times}$$

As Bunns the Bakers have no preference shares in issue, the relevant number to use in this calculation is the profit for the year as given in the income statement. From the results of the above calculations, the ratio has fallen slightly, but a dividend cover of over six times is very safe indeed and shareholders can anticipate that their dividend will continue to be paid for the foreseeable future.

WHY IS THIS RELEVANT TO ME?   **Performance ratios**

As a business professional and user of accounting information you will be expected to:

• Understand ratios relevant to investors and the stock market

• Understand how these ratios are calculated

• Be able to calculate these ratios yourself

GO BACK OVER THIS AGAIN!   Sure that you can distinguish between the five performance ratios? Go to the **online workbook** and have a go at Exercises 6.9 to test your understanding of which ratio does what.

MULTIPLE CHOICE QUESTIONS   Convinced that you can calculate dividend per share, pay-out, dividend yield and dividend cover ratios? Go to the **online workbook** and have a go at Multiple choice questions 6.8 to make sure you can calculate these figures.

SUMMARY OF KEY CONCEPTS   Can you remember the formulae for earnings per share, price/earnings ratio, dividend per share, pay-out ratio, dividend yield and dividend cover? Take a look at Summary of key concepts 6.8–6.13 to reinforce your understanding.

Will Bunns The Bakers' shareholders be happy with the company's performance?

How have Bunns the Bakers performed this year? Shareholders will consider the following factors:

- EPS and DPS are both higher than in 2015.

- The increase in the P/E ratio indicates the market's expectation that the company will continue producing earnings and dividends for shareholders into the foreseeable future.

- While the dividend yield fell very slightly from 1.18% to 1.16%, the increase in the share price over the year will have more than compensated for this reduction.

- Taken together, the dividend yield and the increase in the share price have comfortably exceeded the returns on what are perceived to be safer investments (bank and building society deposit accounts).

- Shareholders will therefore be happy with the dividends paid and the increase in the market value of their shares.

- The dividend cover indicates that future dividends should be easily affordable from profits.

- The low dividend pay-out ratio indicates that the company is keeping plenty of profit back with which to finance future growth and expansion.

- While shareholders might want profits, earnings, dividends and share price to be even higher, they can be satisfied with the company's performance in the year ended 31 March 2016 when comparing this performance with the previous year.

6

WHY IS THIS RELEVANT TO ME?   **Evaluation of performance ratios**

As a business professional and user of accounting information you will be expected to:

- Appreciate what factors shareholders and the stock market will take into account when assessing an entity's performance

- Be able to make an assessment of an entity's performance yourself

Return on capital employed

A common ratio that you will find in other introductory books on accounting is the return on capital employed (often abbreviated to ROCE). This ratio is calculated as follows:

$$\frac{\text{Profit before interest and tax}}{\text{Capital employed}} \times 100\%$$

Capital employed is defined as the equity of an entity plus the long-term borrowings. Looking at the statements of financial position of Bunns the Bakers at 31 March 2016 and 31 March 2015 (Illustration 2.1) equity totals up to £8,459,000 and £7,767,000, respectively. Long-term borrowings (included in non-current liabilities) at the two accounting dates are £2,700,000 and £3,000,000. Profit before interest and tax is equivalent to the operating profit line in Illustration 6.1 and this amounts to £895,000 for the year to 31 March 2016 and £767,000 for the year to 31 March 2015. This gives us the following figures for return on capital employed for the two years as follows:

$$2016: \text{ROCE} = \frac{£895,000}{(£8,459,000 + £2,700,000)} \times 100\% = 8.02\%$$

$$2015: \text{ROCE} = \frac{£767,000}{(£7,767,000 + £3,000,000)} \times 100\% = 7.12\%$$

What is this ratio trying to do? ROCE is used to compare the different profits of different companies that have different capital structures. As we saw in Chapter 5, some companies raise their finance solely through share capital while others rely on loans and still others use a mixture of both share and loan capital to finance their businesses. In this way, the operating profits generated by these different capital structures can be compared to determine which entities produce the highest returns from their capital structures. Investors can then determine which entities they will invest their money into to produce the highest returns. Return on capital employed is often used to compare returns available from companies with interest rates available from banks and building societies to decide whether it would be safer to invest in these much less risky investments rather than in a particular company.

However, the ROCE ratio suffers from a number of problems. We saw in Chapter 2 that not all the assets of an entity are reflected in organisations' statements of financial position. Similarly, the figures presented on the statement of financial position are not necessarily as up to date as they might be. The equity of an entity is made up of share capital that may have been issued many years ago along with retained earnings that have been accumulated over many different accounting periods. These figures would need to be adjusted for changes in the purchasing power of the pound to bring all the pounds tied up in equity up to current day values for this ratio to be meaningful. After all, the profit before interest and tax has been earned in the current year, but this is being compared to share capital and retained earnings from previous years when the value of each pound was very different from what it is today. As noted in Give me an example 6.5 dealing with Ryanair, this is tantamount to comparing apples and pears so that the comparison loses its validity.

It should be possible to restate all the share capital and retained earnings figures to current values (for example by multiplying the market value of each share by the total number of shares in issue) to produce a suitable figure for equity. However, this is a time-consuming exercise and users of accounts might prefer to look at the total share-holder return as represented by the dividend yield and the increase in the market value of shares over the year as the best indicator of the returns available from each company. Users are completely free to use the ROCE ratio as they see fit, but they must be fully aware of the severe limitations that this ratio presents and how these limitations will affect their perceptions of the returns available from each entity.

WHY IS THIS RELEVANT TO ME?   Return on capital employed

To enable you as a business professional and user of accounting information to understand:

• The way in which return on capital employed is used by entities

• The limitations of the return on capital employed ratio

• That total shareholder return presents a more effective way in which to distinguish between different investment opportunities

6

The importance of calculating and presenting ratios consistently

Emphasis has been placed throughout this chapter on the need to calculate and present ratios consistently year on year. Why is this consistency so important? Failure to calculate and present ratios consistently from year to year will mean that comparisons are distorted and figures misleading rather than being accurate portrayals of the financial position compared to previous accounting periods. The dangers of trying to compare information that is not consistently presented and the distortions that this gives rise to are illustrated in Give me an example 6.5.

GIVE ME AN EXAMPLE 6.5   Ryanair's Stansted spin

Michael O'Leary's ability to spin a tale has reached a new level this week. Along with the gullibility of parts of the media in accepting it. Hook, line and sinker.

'Ryanair cuts Stansted winter capacity by 40%,' claimed his press release. The assertion was patently rubbish. But it is almost universally already accepted as fact. On the most charitable assessment, he is planning to cut Stansted winter capacity by 14 per cent. The probability is that the year-on-year decline in Ryanair passenger numbers at Stansted will be much lower even than that. BAA, Stansted's owner, is forecasting a drop of 6–7 per cent.

To get to the claim of a drop of 40 per cent Mr O'Leary is comparing an apple with a pear. He is comparing the number of aircraft he is operating from Stansted, his biggest base, this summer (40) with the number he plans to deploy in the winter (24). But the airline industry is highly seasonal. Comparing Ryanair's summer capacity with its winter capacity at any airport is about as useful as saying 'ice-cream sales to fall by 40% this winter' or 'temperature to fall by 40 per cent'. Shock horror.

Last winter Ryanair operated between 26 and 28 aircraft at Stansted. This year it is planning to operate 24, a decline of at most 14 per cent year on year and a long way from the claimed fall of 40 per cent. The decline will doubtless be even less in the number of flights operated year on year. Mr O'Leary chose to describe only the number of aircraft overnighting at Stansted. He gave no numbers for the volume of weekly flights that includes services operating in and out of Stansted from other Ryanair bases.

The summer/winter capacity comparison is about as silly as comparing profits/losses between different quarters of the year rather than year on year. Not even Ryanair has yet adopted that approach as a new accounting standard.

This week's spin was egregious even by Mr O'Leary's standards. A year ago, when he staged the same show over cutbacks at Stansted, at least he had the good grace to compare an apple with an apple. But the result was much less impressive.

Brian Groom, Lombard

Financial Times 23 July 2009.

Source: *Financial Times* © The Financial Times Limited 2009. All Rights Reserved.

WHY IS THIS RELEVANT TO ME?   The importance of calculating and presenting ratios consistently

To enable you as a business professional and user of accounting information to:

• Understand why it is important to ensure your reports do not present misleading and biased data

• Appreciate that all data presented must be calculated consistently in order to produce fair and valid comparisons between different reporting periods

• Be aware of the dangers of not comparing like with like

How well are we doing? Comparisons with other companies

So far we have just looked at the financial statements and ratios of Bunns the Bakers. The company seems to be moving in the right direction with profits and profitability up, improved efficiency leading to rising revenue and shareholders who should be content with the returns they are receiving. However, we have looked only at internal information with no benchmark against which to compare our company's results. Therefore, we cannot say how well Bunns the Bakers is doing in comparison with the market, whether it is doing better, worse or just as well as its peer companies.

To determine the company's relative success in comparison to other bakery sector companies, we need to compare Bunns the Bakers' figures and ratios with those of a competitor or a series of competitors. In this way, we can benchmark the financial performance of our company against a company in the same line of business to decide whether Bunns' ratios are in line with the sector or whether they are lower or higher. Ratios are a relative measure and, as such, they can be compared with other relative measures from other companies to highlight differences and trends. Such comparisons make ratios especially useful in understanding the profitability, efficiency, performance and liquidity of several organisations and in providing individual business entities with a target to aim for.

Ideally, when making inter-company comparisons of ratios and financial statement figures, we should only compare:

- Similar businesses
- Of similar size
- In a similar industry
- In a similar location
- Over the same accounting period

in order to eliminate random variances arising from differences in activities, size, industry, geographical location and economic factors. All comparative data should be consistently prepared to avoid distortions and bias in the analysis. In addition, organisations can also compare:

- Budgeted or planned performance data to see where the plan went well or went off course (see Chapters 10 and 11)
- Industry data and averages for the same accounting period

when making assessments of their own profitability, efficiency and performance.

WHY IS THIS RELEVANT TO ME? How well are we doing? Comparisons with other companies

As a business professional and user of accounting information it is important for you to:

- Appreciate that a full evaluation of an entity's profitability, efficiency and performance cannot be made just from looking at data generated from internal sources
- Understand how comparative data from outside an entity can be used to evaluate that entity's profitability, efficiency and performance
- Source comparative data to make assessments of an entity's profitability, efficiency and performance

Undertaking comparisons

One company that is in the same industry as Bunns the Bakers is Greggs plc. Greggs is engaged in bakery retail throughout the United Kingdom and has 1,650 shops supplied by nine regional bakeries (Greggs Annual Report for the 53 Weeks Ended 3 January 2015, page 2). To test your knowledge and your ability to calculate and interpret the ratios of another company, you will now need to turn to the **online workbook**, Numerical exercises 6.2, to undertake the analysis of the financial statements of Greggs plc and to compare Bunns the Bakers' 2015 results with this competitor company.

NUMERICAL EXERCISES   Think you can calculate profitability, efficiency and performance ratios for Greggs Plc and interpret them in a meaningful way? Think you can use the ratios you have calculated to draw conclusions about Bunns the Bakers' profitability, efficiency and performance in comparison to a competitor? Have a look at Numerical exercises 6.2 dealing with the financial statements of Greggs Plc and then have a go at the various exercises linked to the two companies in the **online workbook**.

CHAPTER SUMMARY

You should now have learnt that:

- Financial statement figures are an absolute performance measure while ratios are a relative performance measure
- Financial statement figures and ratios interact in the interpretation of profitability, efficiency and performance
- Ratios are a very good way in which to understand the changing relationship between two figures
- Managers use ratios to understand and improve the operations of a business
- Profitability ratios are calculated by dividing revenue into gross profit, operating profit, profit before tax and profit after tax
- Ratios are just a starting point in identifying the reasons for changes in financial statement figures year on year
- Efficiency ratios comprise of non-current asset turnover, revenue per employee and profit per employee
- Efficiency ratios can be used to understand changes in profitability
- Increasing the revenue from each unit of fixed resource employed in the business will increase an entity's profits
- Performance ratios are calculated for earnings per share, dividends per share, dividend yield and dividend cover

- The price/earnings ratio compares the current price of a share with the earnings per share

- Performance ratios are used by shareholders to assess how well an organisation has performed over an accounting period

- Assessments of an entity's profitability, efficiency and performance should never take place in a vacuum but should be compared with measures from other companies in the same industry to provide a better understanding of how an entity's results compare to those of peer companies in the market

---

QUICK REVISION Test your knowledge with the online flashcards in Summary of key concepts and attempt the Multiple choice questions, all in the **online workbook**. www.oxfordtextbooks.co.uk/orc/scott/

END-OF-CHAPTER QUESTIONS

Solutions to these questions can be found at the back of the book from page 458.

6

› *Develop your understanding*

Question 6.1

Cuddles Limited produces teddy bears. The income statements for the years ended 30 April 2016 and 30 April 2015 are presented below.

	2016 £000	2015 £000
Revenue	34,650	29,360
Cost of sales	15,939	14,093
Gross profit	18,711	15,267
Distribution and selling costs	5,355	4,550
Administration expenses	3,654	3,083
Operating profit	9,702	7,634
Finance income	150	75
Finance expense	750	650
Profit before tax	9,102	7,059
Income tax	2,182	1,694
Profit for the year	6,920	5,365

Other information for the two years 30 April 2016 and 30 April 2015:

	2016	2015
Total dividends paid for the year	£4,400,000	£3,700,000
Number of shares in issue during the year	20,000,000	18,500,000
Number of employees during the year	275	250
Non-current assets at the financial year end	£21,655,000	£18,820,000

Cuddles Limited had no preference shares in issue in either of the two years ended 30 April 2016 and 30 April 2015.

For Cuddles Limited calculate the following ratios for the years ended 30 April 2016 and 30 April 2015 (all calculations should be made to two decimal places):

- Gross profit percentage
- Operating profit percentage
- Profit before tax percentage
- Profit after tax percentage
- Non-current asset turnover
- Revenue per employee
- Operating profit per employee
- Earnings per share
- Dividends per share
- Dividend pay-out ratio
- Dividend cover

Question 6.2

The following information has been extracted from the financial statements of DD Limited for the years ended 30 June 2016 and 30 June 2015:

	2016	2015
Profit for the year	£8,622,350	£7,241,330
Number of ordinary shares in issue during the year	37,192,500	36,197,500
Number of preference shares in issue during the year	22,000,000	20,000,000
Ordinary dividend for the year	3,347,325	2,895,800

Further information for the two years 30 June 2016 and 30 June 2015:

- The preference shares have a par value of 50 pence each and a dividend rate of 4%.
- Market values of one ordinary share:

30 June 2014	220 pence
30 June 2015	260 pence
30 June 2016	325 pence

For DD plc calculate the following ratios for the years ended 30 June 2016 and 30 June 2015:

- Earnings per share
- Dividends per share
- Dividend pay-out ratio
- Dividend cover
- Dividend yield
- Growth in the share price over the course of each year

You should make all your calculations to two decimal places.

› *Take it further*

Question 6.3

Below are extracts from the income statements, statements of financial position and notes to the accounts for Bovis Homes plc (years ended 31 December 2014 and 31 December 2013), Persimmon Homes plc (years ended 31 December 2014 and 31 December 2013) and Crest Nicholson plc (years ended 31 October 2014 and 31 October 2013). All three companies build residential housing in the UK.

	Bovis Homes Plc		Persimmon Homes Plc		Crest Nicholson Plc	
	2014	2013	2014	2013	2014	2013
	£m	£m	£m	£m	£m	£m
Revenue	809.4	556.0	2,573.9	2,085.9	636.3	525.7
Cost of sales	612.2	425.7	2,002.1	1,664.6	454.3	384.5
Gross profit	197.2	130.3	571.8	421.3	182.0	141.2
Operating profit	137.6	82.8	465.3	326.5	128.1	97.3
Profit before tax	133.5	78.8	467.0	323.0	116.7	86.8
Profit for the year	105.2	60.1	372.0	246.4	98.8	71.5
Non-current assets	67.8	71.5	506.1	538.9	59.8	64.7
Dividends paid (total)	46.9	18.1	213.9	227.9	35.9	16.3

	2014	2013	2014	2013	2014	2013
	Number	Number	Number	Number	Number	Number
Employees: average during the year	905	741	3,453	2,791	711	617
Shares in issue (million)	134.228	134.096	306.460	304.658	251.431	251.427
Houses sold in the year	3,635	2,813	13,509	11,528	2,530	2,172

None of the three companies had any preference shares in issue in either of the accounting periods shown above.

Required

For the three companies for both 2014 and 2013 calculate:

- Gross profit percentage
- Operating profit percentage
- Profit before tax percentage
- Profit after tax percentage
- Non-current asset turnover
- Revenue per employee
- Operating profit per employee
- Earnings per share
- Dividends per share
- Dividend pay-out ratio
- Dividend cover

Make your calculations to two decimal places other than for revenue per employee and operating profit per employee, which should be made to the nearest whole £.

Question 6.4

Using the ratios you have calculated in Question 6.3 for the three companies:

- Suggest reasons for the changes in profitability over the two years for all three companies.
- Evaluate the performance of the three companies from the point of view of the shareholders.

Question 6.5

From the financial press or Internet, track the share price of the three companies given above for one week and calculate the average share price for each company.

Using your average share price, the earnings per share and the dividends per share from the answers to Question 6.3, calculate:

- Dividend yield
- Price/earnings ratio

Using a share price tracker on the Internet, look back to the same week you have chosen a year ago and track the share price for that week. Average the share price for that week a year ago and then calculate the percentage increase in the share price over the past year. Which of the three companies has produced the best total return over the year?

Liquidity, working capital and long-term solvency

7

LEARNING OUTCOMES

Once you have read this chapter and worked through the questions and examples in both this chapter and the online workbook, you should be able to:

- Understand what is meant by the term 'liquidity'

- Appreciate that the length of the cash flow cycle varies for different types of business

- Calculate the current ratio and the quick ratio and explain what each of these ratios tells you about the short-term liquidity of an organisation

- Understand the shortcomings of current and quick ratios in the assessment of entities' short-term liquidity

- Define the term working capital and state its components

- Calculate ratios for inventory days/inventory turnover, receivables days and payables days and discuss what these ratios tell you about the short-term liquidity of an entity

- Calculate the cash conversion cycle and explain what this means for a particular entity

- Show how organisations manage to meet their liabilities as they fall due from year end cash and from future cash inflows from sales despite having current and quick ratios well below the expected norms

- Calculate the gearing ratio, debt ratio and interest cover and explain what these ratios tell us about the long-term solvency of an organisation

Introduction

The previous chapter considered profitability, efficiency and performance ratios in the interpretation and evaluation of the financial results of each accounting period's trading and operations. These ratios concentrated on the income statement as the source of data on which to build these ratios and the evaluations based upon them. Chapter 4 discussed the importance of cash flows and how cash flows and their timing are the key to the survival of any entity. The cash flows of an organisation are extremely important in your evaluation of the liquidity of that organisation and you should quickly go over the lessons of Chapter 4 again before reading further in this chapter. This is to ensure that you fully appreciate the importance of cash flow information in the assessment of an entity's financial position and its financial stability.

This chapter will look at liquidity ratios and the related analysis provided by working capital ratios. Liquidity ratios and working capital ratio assessments are built upon the information contained in the statement of financial position. In addition, we will consider how an entity's capital structure contributes to an assessment of that entity's long-term solvency. We saw in Chapter 5 that businesses issue shares and take out loans with which to finance their activities: the proportions in which share capital and borrowed funds finance an entity have a bearing on the ability of that entity to continue operating when economic conditions become less favourable. We will look at the key ratios in the assessment of entities' capital structures as well as evaluating organisations' ability to survive with high levels of borrowings.

The International Accounting Standards Board in its 'Framework for the Preparation of Financial Statements' recognises the critical importance of information on an organisation's liquidity, solvency, cash flow generating capacity and its ability to borrow to finance operations:

> The financial position of an entity is affected by the economic resources it controls, its financial structure, its liquidity and solvency, and its capacity to adapt to changes in the environment in which it operates. Information about the economic resources controlled by the entity and its capacity in the past to modify these resources is useful in predicting the ability of the entity to generate cash and cash equivalents in the future. Information about financial structure is useful in predicting future borrowing needs and how future profits and cash flows will be distributed among those with an interest in the entity; it is also useful in predicting how successful the entity is likely to be in raising further finance. Information about liquidity and solvency is useful in predicting the ability of the entity to meet its financial commitments as they fall due. Liquidity refers to the availability of cash in the near future after taking account of financial commitments over this period. Solvency refers to the availability of cash over the longer term to meet financial commitments as they fall due.
>
> Source: IASB Framework for the Preparation of
> Financial Statements, paragraph 16

Analysis of these aspects is critical to any assessment of an entity's survival prospects. It is these aspects and the analysis of this information that will form the main subject of this chapter.

REFER BACK   To illustrate the ratios discussed below we will use the statement of financial position, income statement and statement of cash flows for Bunns the Bakers presented in Chapters 2, 3 and 4. You should refer back to Illustrations 2.1, 3.1 and 4.1 in these chapters or look up the copies available in the **online workbook** as you work through this chapter.

Liquidity and the cash flow cycle

Liquidity refers to the ability of an entity to raise cash to pay off its liabilities as they become due for payment. Any company that is unable to generate this cash with which to meet its debts will be unable to survive and will file for bankruptcy; in this situation, an administrator is appointed to sell the company's assets and the cash raised from these asset sales is used to pay at least some of what is owed to the company's creditors. Insolvent companies have more liabilities than assets, so it is unlikely that the liabilities of such companies will be repaid in full as shown in Give me an example 7.1.

7

GIVE ME AN EXAMPLE 7.1   Insolvent companies failing to repay all their debts

Plymouth Argyle have moved a step closer to coming out of administration after creditors voted in favour of a deal to reduce the club's debt. Plymouth's proposed Company Voluntary Arrangement had offered creditors less than a penny in every pound owed…The League One outfit entered administration in March with debts of over £17m, divided between more than 240 unsecured creditors. By voting in favour of the CVA, the club's unsecured creditors stand to lose the vast majority of their money as just 0.77 pence of every pound owed will be returned.

Amongst the big losers are Plymouth City Council, who will get back just over £2,000 from the £285,000 due. Inscapes, the company who laid Argyle's brand new pitch last summer, will be handed £2,695 of the £350,000 worth of payments still outstanding.

Source: Reprinted with permission from BBC Sport: www.bbc.co.uk/sport/0/football/13313804

How do business entities generate cash from their operations? Some businesses sell their goods for cash so they immediately have money with which to pay suppliers and other parties (such as employees or banks) what they are owed. Other entities sell goods to customers on credit, allowing their customers time in which to pay. In this case, organisations will have to wait for payment, but the cash will be expected to flow in eventually to meet the demands of creditors as they become due. What effect do these two different approaches to selling goods have on the length of the cash flow cycle? The **cash flow cycle** for retailers and manufacturers is illustrated in Figure 7.1.

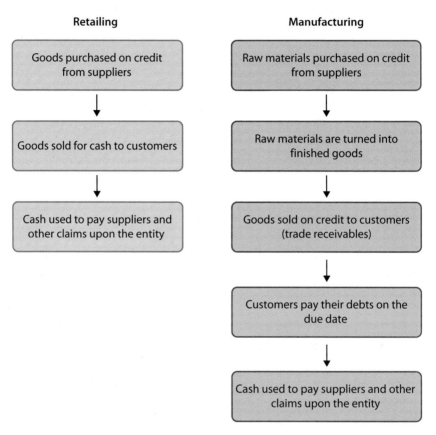

Figure 7.1 The cash flow cycle for retailers and manufacturers

Figure 7.1 shows that the retailing cycle is very short: goods are purchased, sold on for cash and paid for. The manufacturing cycle is much longer. Raw materials first have to be converted into finished goods inventory. This is then sold to customers, but they demand time in which to pay. When they do pay the cash can be used to pay suppliers. There are thus many delays in the manufacturing cash flow cycle, first in producing the goods and then in waiting for the cash from customers. We shall consider the effect these different business cycles have on our assessment of a business's liquidity when we look at working capital management. However, you should appreciate at this early stage how the cash flow cycle operates and how it is vital for entities to have cash available to meet liabilities as they fall due.

Liquidity ratios

Have a look at Bunns the Bakers' current assets (Illustration 2.1): there is inventory, trade and other receivables and cash. Now look at the current liabilities, which show the current portion of long-term liabilities, that part of borrowings that is due within one year, trade and other payables (the amounts due to suppliers and for other liabilities such as rent, business rates and electricity among others) and current tax liabilities. Along with the cash and cash equivalents already available, the other current assets are used to generate cash from sales of inventory and receipts from receivables to pay off the current liabilities. Short-term assets are thus used to meet short-term liabilities: this is the liquidity, the availability of cash in the near future, referred to in the IASB Framework document earlier. How is the ability of short-term assets to meet short-term liabilities assessed? Not surprisingly, the first step in this assessment will be through the calculation of ratios.

Current ratio

The first ratio that we will look at compares current assets to current liabilities in an attempt to determine whether an organisation has sufficient short-term assets from which to meet short-term liabilities. This ratio is called the current ratio and is calculated as follows:

$$\text{Current ratio} = \frac{\text{Current assets}}{\text{Current liabilities}}$$

This figure is expressed as a ratio and tells us how many £s of current assets there are for each £ of current liabilities. Calculating the current ratio for Bunns the Bakers at 31 March 2016 and 31 March 2015 gives us the following results:

$$2016:\text{Current ratio}:\frac{£334,000}{£840,000}=0.40:1$$

$$2015:\text{Current ratio}:\frac{£319,000}{£707,000}=0.45:1$$

What do these ratios mean? At 31 March 2016, Bunns the Bakers has 40 pence of current assets for each £1 of current liabilities, while at 31 March 2015 the company had 45 pence of current assets for each £1 of current liabilities. This might not sound very good as the company does not seem to have much in the way of current assets with which to meet liabilities as they fall due.

However, remember that the statement of financial position is just a snapshot of the financial position at one day in the year: the position will change tomorrow and the next day and the day after that as goods are produced, sales are made, cash flows in and liabilities are paid. The current ratio also ignores the timing of the receipt of cash and of the payment of liabilities.

How quickly is cash received by the business? If this is immediately at the point of sale then the entity will have a very positive cash inflow from which to meet its liabilities. If cash is received from trade receivables some time after the sales were made then a much more careful management of cash inflows and outflows will be required. The current ratio's logic assumes that all the liabilities will be due for payment on the day following the statement of financial position date; this is highly unlikely and we will investigate the likely payment pattern for liabilities later on in this chapter to show that, contrary to appearances, Bunns the Bakers is a very liquid, cash generative business indeed.

WHY IS THIS RELEVANT TO ME? Current ratio

To enable you as a business professional and user of accounting information to:

- Understand what the current ratio represents and how it is used in the assessment of short-term liquidity
- Calculate current ratios for organisations
- Appreciate the shortcomings of the current ratio as a key measure in short-term liquidity assessment

GO BACK OVER THIS AGAIN! Do you really understand what the current ratio is trying to do and what factors you have to take into account when using it? Go to the **online workbook** and have a go at Exercises 7.2 to check your understanding.

MULTIPLE CHOICE QUESTIONS Sure that you can calculate a current ratio from a given set of financial information? Go to the **online workbook** and have a go at Multiple choice questions 7.1 to test out your ability to calculate this ratio.

Quick (acid test) ratio

This ratio is a modification of the current ratio and ignores inventory in its assessment of an entity's ability to pay its short-term liabilities. Why is inventory taken out of the calculation? There is always a chance that inventory produced by an organisation will not be sold quickly, so that this inventory cannot be counted as convertible into cash in the near future. Therefore, the quick (acid test) ratio only takes account of current assets that are cash or that are readily realisable in cash: trade receivables are readily convertible into cash as the entity has a contractual right to receive the money due for sales already made to customers. The quick (acid test) ratio is calculated as follows:

$$\text{Quick (acid test) ratio} = \frac{\text{Current assets} - \text{Inventory}}{\text{Current liabilities}}$$

Using Bunns the Bakers' statement of financial position at 31 March 2016 and 31 March 2015 the following quick ratios can be calculated:

$$\text{2016: Quick ratio:} \quad \frac{(£334,000 - £60,000)}{£840,000} = 0.33:1$$

$$\text{2015: Quick ratio:} \quad \frac{(£319,000 - £55,000)}{£707,000} = 0.37:1$$

These ratios are inevitably lower than the current ratios calculated above as inventory is taken out of the current assets with no corresponding decrease in current liabilities. Again, this paints a very gloomy picture of Bunns the Bakers' short-term liquidity as the company only has 33 pence of readily realisable current assets per £1 of current liabilities at 31 March 2016, a figure that has fallen from 37 pence per £1 of current liabilities at 31 March 2015.

How realistic is the assumption that inventory will not sell quickly? It all depends upon the particular activity in which an entity is engaged. A moment's thought should convince you that the quick ratio is completely irrelevant to any assessment of Bunns the Bakers' short-term liquidity. The company sells freshly baked goods from their shops in towns. People usually get up too late to make their own sandwiches or snacks to take to work (or are too lazy to do so!) and will go out at lunch time to buy the company's products, which will sell quickly rather than being stockpiled for several weeks or months before they are sold. Therefore, what is produced today is sold today and cash is received immediately from cash paying customers at the till. Even if there are sandwiches, pies and pastries left towards the end of the day, shop staff will discount the prices in order to tempt customers to buy up the left over inventory so only very small amounts of the goods produced will be wasted.

The quick ratio may be much more relevant in a manufacturing situation. The swift pace of change in markets and products means that any advance production might result in such goods becoming obsolete or out of fashion so that entities are unable to sell them to recover the costs of producing or buying them. As a result of this risk, many companies today only produce to order rather than manufacturing goods in the hope that they will sell. Such an approach removes the risk of goods becoming obsolete and the losses that disposal of such goods will incur as, first, discounts are given on the original selling price and then goods have to be scrapped as interest in them finally runs out. It is particularly important only to produce goods to order in the high-tech sector; new developments are taking place every few minutes so that products are being improved all the time and earlier models quickly become outdated. As a result, high-tech goods such as laptops, tablets, mobile phones and other electronic devices are produced as orders come in to avoid the losses that would arise if several months' advance sales of such goods were produced all at once.

Consider Give me an example 7.2, which shows a sudden fall in demand resulting in obsolete goods that have to be discounted to entice customers to buy them.

GIVE ME AN EXAMPLE 7.2   Out of date goods that do not sell

S Africa faces reality after World Cup party
Global Insight: Richard Lapper in Johannesburg

Just ten days ago, Mary Muthui was doing a roaring trade in football scarves, beanie hats and vuvuzelas at her stall in the Rosebank Mall crafts centre in Johannesburg. But yesterday—less than two weeks after the end of South Africa's much acclaimed World Cup—the 28-year-old trader was struggling to unload anything at all and was offering the controversial plastic horn for a quarter of the R120 ($16, €12, £10) that football fans were paying last month. 'It's very, very slow,' she said. 'I have sold less than 50 vuvuzelas since the final.'

Financial Times, 22 July 2010, page 7

[Note: The 2010 World Cup final was held in Johannesburg on 11 July 2010]

Where entities are subject to this kind of unpredictable pattern of demand that can suddenly be turned off or interrupted by, for example, an economic downturn or a change in consumer tastes, your evaluation of liquidity will be much more cautious. If an organisation does not enjoy steady demand for its products then that organisation is at much higher risk of suffering liquidity problems and you would expect that entity to maintain much higher current and quick ratios as well as operating a very sophisticated forecasting system to stop production of its goods at the first sign of a decline in demand. In Bunns the Bakers' case, office workers will keep visiting their outlets at lunch time and shoppers will drop in throughout the day as they seek out the company's value for money products, so declines in demand will not be a problem for this organisation.

GO BACK OVER THIS AGAIN!   How well have you grasped what the quick ratio is trying to do and what factors you have to take into account when using it? Go to the **online workbook** and have a go at Exercises 7.3 to check your understanding.

SUMMARY OF KEY CONCEPTS   Can you remember the formulae for current ratio and quick ratio? Take a look at Summary of key concepts 7.1 and 7.2 to reinforce your understanding.

MULTIPLE CHOICE QUESTIONS   Are you totally confident that you can calculate a quick ratio from a given set of financial information? Go to the **online workbook** and have a go at Multiple choice questions 7.2 to test out your ability to calculate this ratio.

Current and quick ratios: the traditional view

Convention has it that a business entity needs a current ratio of 2:1, £2 of current assets for every £1 of current liabilities, and a quick ratio of 1:1, £1 of trade receivables and cash for every £1 of current liabilities, in order to be able to survive financially. On a conventional reading of the figures for Bunns the Bakers, then, the assessment would be that the company is heading into bankruptcy. Bunns the Bakers has nowhere near current and quick ratios of 2:1 and 1:1, so the question must be asked how the company manages to survive quite happily on much lower ratios than convention dictates.

Working capital

A much more effective way in which to assess liquidity is to look at the working capital cycle, the time it takes for an entity to turn raw materials into goods for sale, sell these goods, collect the cash and then pay suppliers for goods and raw materials supplied (Figure 7.2). We looked at the cash flow cycle at the start of this chapter for both

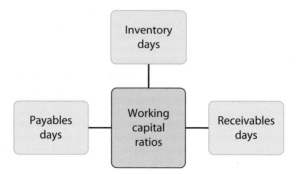

Figure 7.2 The three working capital ratios

retailing and manufacturing, but it is now time to look in more detail at the components of working capital and how to use these as a guide to the liquidity and cash flow generating ability of an organisation.

First, though, what is working capital? The basic definition of working capital is as follows:

Working capital = current assets − current liabilities

Working capital thus comprises:

- Inventories of raw materials for use in production, of finished goods ready for sale or of goods purchased for resale to customers.

- Trade receivables from customers of the business who have been provided with a credit facility by the entity.

- Cash in the bank or in hand that is held to meet day-to-day needs.

- Trade payables of the business which require settlement on a daily basis. For the purposes of the working capital calculation, amounts due to lenders and money due to settle tax liabilities would be ignored as these (as we shall see later in this chapter) do not require payment on a day-to-day basis, being settled on a monthly or three-monthly basis.

Working capital ratios

In order to evaluate the efficiency of working capital management, the ratios in Table 7.1 are used.

GO BACK OVER THIS AGAIN!   Certain you can distinguish between the three working capital ratios? Go to the **online workbook** and have a go at Exercises 7.4 to make sure you can make these distinctions.

Table 7.1 Working capital ratios, how they are calculated and what they tell users

Ratio	Calculation	What does this ratio tell us?
Inventory days or inventory turnover (also known as stock days or stock turnover)	$\dfrac{\text{Inventory}}{\text{Cost of sales}} \times 365$	• This ratio measures the average stockholding period, how long an entity holds goods in inventory before they are sold • The more quickly inventory turns over the better, as inventory is turned into sales (and hence into cash) much more quickly while obsolete inventories and the risk of deterioration (and hence loss of future cash inflows from the sale of this inventory) are minimised • However, when calculating their optimum level of inventory holding, businesses should consider future demand (no inventory, no sale), any future shortages or price rises, discounts available for buying in bulk, storage, insurance and any other costs involved in holding inventory
Receivables days (also known as debtor days)	$\dfrac{\text{Trade receivables}}{\text{Credit sales}^{1}} \times 365$	• This ratio indicates the average credit period taken by customers, the length of time it takes for credit customers to pay what they owe • Evaluates the efficiency of the credit control system and the speed with which credit sales are turned into cash • Where this ratio is increasing, steps can be taken to speed up payments (e.g. by offering early payment discounts) to minimise the funds tied up in receivables: it is better to have cash in our bank account than in our customers' bank account
Payables days (also known as creditor days)	$\dfrac{\text{Trade payables}}{\text{Cost of sales}^{2}} \times 365$	• This ratio measures how quickly the business is paying off its purchases made on credit • Ideally, the receivables days and payables days should be equal: as cash is received, it is used to pay off liabilities • Paying trade payables before trade receivables have paid usually has a negative impact upon cash flow: see the profit ≠ cash flow example for Start Up in Example 4.1 in Chapter 4

[1] Strictly this ratio should use only credit sales in the calculation of receivables days: sales made for cash have already been settled and thus no cash is outstanding from these transactions. Therefore, cash sales should be omitted in the determination of receivables days, the number of days of credit allowed to credit customers. However, in practice, companies do not disclose separate figures for their cash sales and their credit sales, so it is normal just to use total sales in this calculation.

[2]Again, while trade payables should be compared to purchases of goods on credit, entities do not publish details of their credit purchases, so cost of sales is used to approximate the cost of purchases. In reality, cost of sales may include the wages and salaries of production operatives in the manufacturing part of a business, which should not strictly be classified as purchases on credit, but the cost of sales is a useful substitute for the credit purchases of a business.

As long as you are consistent in your calculations (as noted in Chapter 6), the relationships and ratios produced should provide a suitable like-for-like basis on which to assess the working capital strengths or weaknesses of a business.

The working capital ratios for Bunns the Bakers are as follows:

$$2016: \text{Inventory days/inventory turnover: } \frac{£60,000}{£4,535,000} \times 365 = 4.83 \text{ days}$$

$$2015: \text{Inventory days/inventory turnover: } \frac{£55,000}{£4,596,000} \times 365 = 4.37 \text{ days}$$

Trade and other receivables for Bunns the Bakers at 31 March 2016 and 31 March 2015 from the statement of financial position are £62,000 and £75,000, respectively. By looking at the notes to the financial statements we can determine that the actual trade receivables, as distinct from other receivables and prepayments, are £25,000 at 31 March 2016 and £35,000 at 31 March 2015. This will give us the following receivables days for the two accounting periods:

$$2016: \text{Receivables days: } \frac{£25,000}{£10,078,000} \times 365 = 0.90 \text{ days}$$

$$2015: \text{Receivables days: } \frac{£35,000}{£9,575,000} \times 365 = 1.33 \text{ days}$$

This ratio is very low, but, as most sales will be made for an immediate cash payment from customers in the shops, this is not at all surprising. As we noted in Chapter 2, credit sales will be limited to a small number of credit customers such as supermarkets.

The rest of the sales will be made for cash to customers as they come into the shops and make their purchases, so a very low receivables days ratio would be expected in such a situation.

Trade and other payables for Bunns the Bakers at 31 March 2016 and 31 March 2015 from the statement of financial position are £390,000 and £281,000, respectively. By looking at the notes to the financial statements we can determine that the actual trade payables, as distinct from other payables, are £300,000 at 31 March 2016 and £220,000 at 31 March 2015. This will give us the following payables days for the two accounting periods:

$$2016: \text{Payables days: } \frac{£300,000}{£4,535,000} \times 365 = 24.15 \text{ days}$$

$$2015: \text{Payables days:} \ \frac{£220,000}{£4,596,000} \times 365 = 17.47 \text{ days}$$

WHY IS THIS RELEVANT TO ME?   Working capital ratios

As a business professional and user of accounting information you will be expected to:

- Understand what working capital ratios are and what they represent
- Be able to calculate working capital ratios for organisations

---

SUMMARY OF KEY CONCEPTS Do you remember the formulae for the three working capital ratios? Take a look at Summary of key concepts 7.3–7.5 to reinforce your understanding.

MULTIPLE CHOICE QUESTIONS Certain you can calculate working capital ratios from a given set of financial information? Go to the **online workbook** and have a go at Multiple choice questions 7.3 to test out your ability to calculate these ratios.

What do these figures tell us? First, that, in 2016, inventories are sold within 4.8 days, a very slight increase on the 4.4 days it took to sell inventory in 2015. Much of Bunns the Bakers' inventory will comprise raw materials ready for use in the production of bread, pies, pastries and other bakery goods. Finished goods themselves will probably represent only one day's production as goods are produced fresh and ready for delivery and sale the next day. Certain other inventories, such as soft drinks, which have a longer sell-by date, can be kept in storage for several weeks or months before they are out of date, but most of the company's raw materials will be delivered on a daily basis and turned into finished goods for sale on the same or the next day.

This is a very low inventory turnover ratio and indicates that stocks are turned into sales very quickly indeed. As most of these sales are for cash, the receivables days are also very low. However, trade payables are settled every 24 days in the year to 31 March 2016 (an increase on the previous year) so Bunns the Bakers is holding on to the cash received from customers before they pay this cash out to their suppliers. Money is received at the point of sale, but the company holds on to the cash until the time to pay their suppliers comes around.

The cash conversion cycle

The ratios shown in Figure 7.2 enable us to calculate the cash conversion cycle (sometimes referred to as the operating cycle or working capital cycle). The cash conversion cycle tells us how quickly inventory is turned into trade receivables

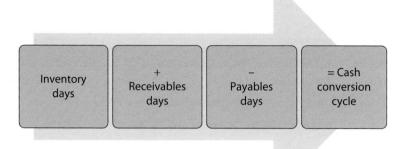

Figure 7.3 The cash conversion cycle

and how quickly trade receivables are turned into cash with which to pay trade payables (Figure 7.3). The shorter this cycle, the better the working capital is being managed and the more readily cash is available with which to meet liabilities. Conversely, the longer this process, the higher the investment required in working capital and the higher the emergency sources of cash will need to be (for example, financing by an agreed short-term overdraft from the bank) to pay liabilities as they fall due.

The cash conversion cycle is calculated in the following way:

Inventory days + receivables days – payables days

For Bunns the Bakers, the cash conversion cycle for the two years under consideration is as follows:

2016: Cash conversion cycle: 4.83 days + 0.90 days – 24.15 days = –18.42 days

2015: Cash conversion cycle: 4.37 days + 1.33 days – 17.47 days = –11.77 days

Figure 7.4 shows that the figures for both years are negative. This means that Bunns the Bakers are converting their sales into cash well before they have to pay their suppliers. The negative cash conversion cycles also mean that the company is holding onto this cash for several days before it is paid out and this will enable the company to use this cash to generate additional finance income (interest receivable) on their surplus bank deposits. This additional interest may not amount to much in total in the income statement, but it is an important extra source of income for the company and this spare cash is being used effectively to generate additional profits for the shareholders. From Bunns the Bakers' point of view, the increase in the cash conversion cycle this year means that they are taking an extra 6.65 days

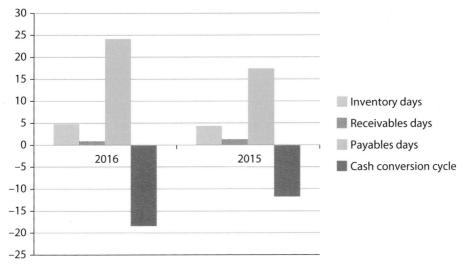

Figure 7.4 Bunns the Bakers' working capital ratios and cash conversion cycle

(18.42 days – 11.77 days) in which to pay their suppliers, indicating that they are holding onto their cash for longer. By using the credit facilities provided by their suppliers, Bunns the Bakers do not have to rely on a short-term bank overdraft to finance their working capital: this finance is in effect being provided by the company's suppliers.

WHY IS THIS RELEVANT TO ME?   **Working capital ratios and the cash conversion cycle**

To enable you as a business professional and user of accounting information to:

- Calculate additional ratios with which to evaluate short-term liquidity
- Calculate the length of the cash conversion cycle
- Appreciate how working capital ratios and the cash conversion cycle help to supplement the current and quick ratios in liquidity analysis

GO BACK OVER THIS AGAIN!   Quite sure that you understand what the cash conversion cycle is telling you? Go to the **online workbook** and have a go at Exercises 7.5 to check your understanding.

MULTIPLE CHOICE QUESTIONS   How easily can you calculate the cash conversion cycle from a given set of financial information? Go to the **online workbook** and have a go at Multiple choice questions 7.4 to test out your ability to undertake the required calculations.

Why is working capital so important?

Organisations need short-term finance to enable them to buy raw materials with which to produce goods to sell to customers. A firm's suppliers cannot wait for payment until the raw materials have been turned into finished goods, sold on credit and then paid for by that firm's customers. Such a period would be too lengthy and the supplier might well have gone bankrupt while waiting for payment. Therefore, manufacturers and their suppliers rely on short-term credit provided by banks in the form of overdrafts. These overdrafts are used to finance the purchase of materials and the payment of wages to workers to tide them over the short-term lack of funds that arises when waiting for products to be manufactured and sold and for customers to pay. Such short-term working capital allows organisations to build up momentum with this short-term finance being paid back when projects are up and running and cash inflows from customers are financing cash outflows to suppliers.

The importance of working capital is illustrated in Give me an example 7.3.

GIVE ME AN EXAMPLE 7.3   German companies scramble to adjust to suddenly overfilled order book

Industrialists do not usually complain when their business is thriving. But after several months in which orders have been more than double the level [of] a year before, Ulrich Reifenhäuser, owner of the eponymous German plastics machinery maker, says he is longing for growth rates to ease.

'I really hope that this will start to level off and that growth rates will come down again. I am hoping for a more moderate growth rate,' says the managing director of Reifenhäuser group, an engineering company employing 1,200 staff and based between Cologne and Bonn.

Mr Reifenhäuser is not alone. Orders in Germany's key export driven sectors such as machinery, cars and chemical goods are pouring in at such a speed that many companies are struggling to cope with the sudden demand boom.

Significant parts of the country's plants are running at full speed again, driven by a fast rise in demand from China and the US in particular. Some companies are already expanding capacity and many are rehiring contract workers.

'We are approaching a normal capacity utilisation in our sector,' said Manfred Wittenstein, president of VDMA, the German engineering association ...

But the upbeat mood in the sector is still damped by fears that the upswing could be blown off course by a lack of finance, as some companies struggle to obtain the large amounts of working capital that are suddenly needed to finance the new orders.

'There are more and more signs that banks refrain from giving loans to small companies,' Mr Wittenstein warns.

Research by Demica, a UK based working capital solutions provider, shows that 78 per cent of German companies are faced with difficulties in obtaining traditional bank credit. Some 59 per cent say they will be left with insufficient working capital to take advantage of the economic upswing.

'The credit crunch has come back to the fore in the past six weeks,' Mr Reifenhäuser says. 'Some of our customers are not able to receive project finance.'

Mr Heitmann of Lanxess says a full recovery of the financial system is crucial for a sustained economic upturn. 'The sooner we tidy up the financial system and get back to financial stability the faster we will reach pre-crisis levels,' he says.

Daniel Schäfer, *Financial Times*, 5 July 2010, page 20

WHY IS THIS RELEVANT TO ME?   Why is working capital so important?

To enable you as a business professional and user of accounting information to appreciate that:

- Entities need short-term finance with which to finance growth and to start up new projects
- That short-term finance has to come either from cash saved within the entity or from outside sources such as bank overdrafts
- Such short-term finance is not always readily available from outside sources

Current liabilities: the timing of payments

7

Our calculations in the Current ratio section earlier showed that at 31 March 2016 Bunns the Bakers has only 40 pence of current assets for each £1 of current liabilities. At that point we also noted that the current and quick ratios take no account of when liabilities are actually due for payment and make the assumption that all liabilities might call in the money owed to them at the statement of financial position date. Let us now think about how much of Bunns the Bakers' current liabilities might actually be due for payment on the day after the statement of financial position date so that we can assess how liquid the company really is and how easily it can afford to pay its debts from the current assets it already owns.

Bunns the Bakers' statement of financial position shows the following current liabilities at 31 March 2016:

Current liabilities at 31 March 2016	£000
Current portion of long-term borrowings	300
Trade and other payables	390
Current tax liabilities	150
	840

At 31 March 2016, Bunns the Bakers has £212,000 of cash with which to meet these current liabilities. This does not appear to be a good position to be in, as current liabilities exceed the cash available with which to pay them. However, by thinking about when these liabilities will actually fall due we will be able to see that the company can meet its liabilities very easily from the cash it has at the year end.

First, let us think about when the current portion of long-term borrowings will be payable. When an entity borrows money from a bank under a formal loan agreement, the entity and the bank sign a contract. This contract governs the loan terms, the terms of repayment and the interest that is payable on the loan. As long as the borrower does not breach the terms of the contract (e.g. by failing to pay either any interest due or a loan instalment by the agreed date), then the bank cannot demand its money back immediately and has to wait for the borrower to meet each repayment as it becomes due. The £300,000 due at 31 March 2016 probably represents 12 monthly payments of £25,000 each so that the most that could be due on 1 April 2016 would be £25,000. The other monthly repayments would be due one month after this, two months after this and so on. This is a very pessimistic assumption: most loan instalments are payable at the end of the month rather than at the beginning, giving the company up to 30 days to save up for the next payment. But for now we will assume that loan repayments are due on the first day of each month so that £25,000 is repayable on 1 April 2016.

While bank loans are covered by contracts in this way, bank overdrafts are not. Should the entity you are evaluating have an overdraft with its bank, do remember that overdrafts are repayable on demand so that all of the overdraft should be added in to the calculation of immediate liquidity on the day after the statement of financial position date.

Turning now to what is owed to suppliers, we saw above that trade payables amount to £300,000 and that this represents 24.15 days of purchases. We noted above that suppliers of raw materials will deliver to the company each day so that the ingredients going into the bread, sandwiches, pies and pastries are always fresh. Therefore, the total amount due to trade payables on 1 April 2016 would be £300,000/24.15 = £12,422, with £12,422 due on 2 April, £12,422 on 3 April and so on. In reality, these amounts will not be spread so evenly, but the £12,422 is a useful average to work with, based on the payables days we calculated earlier. The other payables of £90,000 (£390,000 − £300,000 trade payables) will probably be payable to a variety of different creditors at different times over the next two to three months. However, as we are cautious accountants, let us assume that one-quarter of this amount is due tomorrow, which represents £90,000/4 = £22,500 payable immediately.

Tax liabilities in the UK are payable in quarterly instalments three months, six months, nine months and twelve months after the statement of financial position date, so the earliest that any of the £150,000 tax is due would be 30 June 2016, three months after 31 March 2016. Therefore, none of the tax liabilities will be due on 1 April 2016.

Summarising our results below tells us that we have only a fraction of the total current liabilities at 31 March 2016 to pay on 1 April 2016. The figures below may be seriously overestimated as the long-term borrowings are probably repayable at the end of April 2016 rather than at the beginning of the month and it is unlikely that 25% of the other payables is actually due one day after the year end:

	£
Current portion of long-term borrowings	25,000
Trade payables	12,422
Other payables	22,500
Current tax liabilities	—
Total payable on 1 April 2016	59,922
Cash available at 31 March 2016	212,000
Surplus cash available on 1 April 2016 (£212,000 − £59,922)	152,078

Thus, when it comes to determining how liquid a company is and how easily it can meet its current liabilities when they fall due, timing is critical. In addition, we should not forget that cash will be coming into the business on 1 April 2016 as sales are made at the tills. How much will this be? Given that annual sales are £10,078,000 and that there are, say, 300 trading days a year, this would give daily sales of £33,593. As this cash will come into the business on every trading day of the year, there is always going to be plenty of cash available from which to meet debts as they become payable. Therefore, the current and quick ratio, while giving a good idea of how many £s of current assets are available to meet each £ of liabilities, should not be used as the final indicator of how easily a company can meet its liabilities as they fall due. You must think about the timing of receipts and payments of cash and the way in which an entity manages its cash inflows and outflows to make a full evaluation of an entity's short-term liquidity.

To illustrate the truth of this approach, just think about your own situation for a moment. If we all drew up our own personal statement of financial position at the end of each calendar year and included everything that we had to pay for the next twelve months and compared this to what cash we had available at the end of the year, we would all be in despair. However, we know that all our liabilities for the next twelve months are not due immediately on 1 January and that we have monthly inflows of cash from our salaries that will gradually pay what we owe throughout the year. Cash outflows are matched by cash inflows and, with a bit of luck, we will be able to save some cash towards a holiday or towards some other treat for ourselves. We do not worry that we do not have enough cash now to pay everything off and neither do businesses.

7

WHY IS THIS RELEVANT TO ME?   **The timing of payments and the shortcomings of the current and quick ratios**

To enable you as a business professional and user of accounting information to:

- Appreciate that an entity's current liabilities will never all be due for payment at the same time unless that entity is in liquidation

- Calculate the amounts due for payment on the day after the statement of financial position date as part of your assessment of an entity's liquidity

- Forecast monthly cash outgoings for the next year to determine whether entities can meet those monthly outgoings from current trading

- Appreciate how timing of payments analysis helps to overcome the shortcomings of the current and quick ratios in liquidity analysis

GO BACK OVER THIS AGAIN!   Sure you understand how the timing of payments is critical to an assessment of short-term liquidity? Go to the **online workbook** and look at Exercises 7.6 to enable you to appreciate that not all liabilities are due immediately and that the assumptions of the current and quick ratios are invalid when assessing an entity's ability to meet its short-term liabilities.

Capital structure ratios: long-term solvency assessment

Working capital, cash conversion cycle and current and quick ratios measure short-term liquidity and the ability of entities to pay their debts on a short-term (within the next 12 months), day-to-day basis. But just as there are ratios with which to measure short-term liquidity, there are also ratios to determine long-term solvency (Figure 7.5). As we saw in Chapter 5, companies have a choice of financing models through which to raise the capital required to finance their operations for the long term. They can

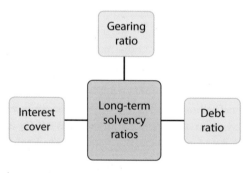

Figure 7.5 Long term solvency ratios

either raise the necessary funds through an issue of share capital or they can raise the money from borrowings from the bank or the money markets. Many companies combine both share capital and borrowings in their long-term financing. The combination of the two will have implications for our assessment of how easily entities will be able to repay those borrowings while still servicing that long-term capital from profits either through dividends on ordinary shares or interest on borrowings.

When assessing long-term solvency, the ratios in Table 7.2 are used.

Table 7.2 Long-term solvency ratios, how they are calculated and what they tell users

Ratio	What does this ratio tell us?
$$\text{Gearing} = \frac{\text{Long and short-term borrowings}}{\text{Equity}} \times 100\%$$	• The gearing percentage is often seen as a measure of risk: companies with higher borrowings are supposedly more risky than those with lower borrowings
$$\text{Debt ratio} = \frac{\text{Total liabilities}}{\text{Total assets}}$$	• This ratio measures the £s of liabilities per £1 of total assets • The lower the ratio, the more secure the entity
$$\text{Interest cover} = \frac{\text{Profit before interest and tax}}{\text{Interest}}$$	• Assesses how many times interest payable on borrowings is covered by operating profits (in the same way that dividend cover measures how many times the ordinary dividend is covered by profit for the year) • The higher the figure, the better, as a high figure indicates an ability to continue meeting interest payments from profits in the future

WHY IS THIS RELEVANT TO ME?   Capital structure ratios: long-term solvency assessment

As a business professional and user of accounting information you will be expected to:

• Understand what gearing, debt and interest cover ratios are telling you about an entity's long-term solvency

• Be able to calculate gearing, debt and interest cover ratios for organisations

• Evaluate the results of gearing, debt and interest cover ratio calculations to produce an assessment of an entity's long-term solvency position

Gearing ratio

Looking at the statement of financial position for Bunns the Bakers (Illustration 2.1), the company has borrowings of £300,000 in current liabilities and borrowings of £2,700,000 in non-current liabilities, giving a total borrowings figure of £3,000,000 at 31 March 2016. At 31 March 2015, the figures are £300,000 and £3,000,000 giving total borrowings of £3,300,000. Equity in the statement of financial position in Illustration 2.1 is £8,459,000 at 31 March 2016 and £7,767,000 at 31 March 2015. Using these figures we can calculate gearing percentages as follows:

$$2016: \text{Gearing \%:} \ \frac{£3,000,000}{£8,459,000} \times 100\% = 35.47\%$$

$$2015: \text{Gearing \%:} \ \frac{£3,300,000}{£7,767,000} \times 100\% = 42.49\%$$

Gearing has fallen this year as borrowings represent a lower proportion of equity than in previous years. This fall is partly due to the repayment of £300,000 during the year to 31 March 2016 and partly due to the increase in equity as a result of the issue of new share capital and the profits retained for the current year. The statement of cash flows (Illustration 4.1) shows us that the company has repaid £300,000 of their borrowings over each of the past two years, so this debt seems to be very manageable. The percentage of borrowings to equity is low and, given the consistency of the trade in which Bunns the Bakers are engaged and the constant demand that their products enjoy, it would be perfectly logical to draw the conclusion that the company's long-term financing strategy is very manageable and poses no solvency risk to the organisation.

MULTIPLE CHOICE QUESTIONS How easily can you calculate gearing from a given set of financial information? Go to the **online workbook** and have a go at Multiple choice questions 7.5 to test out your ability to calculate this ratio.

Debt ratio

Total assets and total liabilities just have to be read off the relevant lines of the statement of financial position (Illustration 2.1). The company has total assets of £12,199,000 at 31 March 2016 and total assets of £11,674,000 at 31 March 2015. Similarly, total liabilities at 31 March 2016 amount to £3,740,000 and £3,907,000 at

31 March 2015. Comparing the total liabilities with the total assets gives us the following results:

$$2016: \text{Debt ratio:} \quad \frac{£3,740,000}{£12,199,000} = 0.31{:}1$$

$$2015: \text{Debt ratio:} \quad \frac{£3,907,000}{£11,674,000} = 0.33{:}1$$

Bunns the Bakers has 31 pence of total liabilities for every £1 of total assets at 31 March 2016 compared to 33 pence of total liabilities for every £1 of total assets at 31 March 2015. This is not a high figure and it would be reasonable to conclude that the company is highly solvent.

MULTIPLE CHOICE QUESTIONS Quite confident you can calculate the debt ratio from a given set of financial information? Go to the **online workbook** and have a go at Multiple choice questions 7.6 to test out your ability to calculate this figure.

Interest cover

The gearing percentages and debt ratios are not high, but how easily can the company meet its interest obligations? To determine the interest cover, we will need to turn to the income statement in Illustration 3.1. This statement tells us that the finance expense (= interest payable) for the years to 31 March 2016 and 31 March 2015 was £150,000 and £165,000, respectively. This expense now needs matching to the operating profit (the profit before interest and tax) of £895,000 and £767,000 for the two years that concern us.

$$2016: \text{Interest cover:} \quad \frac{£895,000}{£150,000} = 5.97 \text{ times}$$

$$2015: \text{Interest cover:} \quad \frac{£767,000}{£165,000} = 4.65 \text{ times}$$

Increased profits and reduced finance expense in 2016 mean that this ratio has improved greatly this year. Given that interest is covered nearly six times by the operating profit, we can conclude that Bunns the Bakers is a very secure company indeed, with low gearing, low total liabilities to total assets and with a very strong interest cover ratio that indicates that the company will be able to keep servicing its long-term borrowings into the foreseeable future.

7

SUMMARY OF KEY CONCEPTS   Can you remember the formulae for the three long-term solvency ratios? Take a look at Summary of key concepts 7.6– 7.8 to reinforce your understanding.

MULTIPLE CHOICE QUESTIONS   Totally confident you can calculate interest cover from a given set of financial information? Go to the **online workbook** and have a go at Multiple choice questions 7.7 to test out your ability to calculate this ratio.

When are borrowings risky?

How much borrowing is too much? The answer to this question is, 'it all depends'. Provided that an organisation has sufficiently strong cash inflows from operations and can afford to keep paying the interest as well as saving money towards repayment of borrowings, then that organisation will be able to borrow as much as it likes. Profitability, remember, is not enough: we saw in Chapter 4 that, without the associated inflows of cash from operations, profit means nothing. Many profitable companies have gone out of business because they were unable to generate the necessary cash flows from which to repay borrowings they had taken on.

Let's illustrate these issues with Give me an example 7.4 and 7.5.

GIVE ME AN EXAMPLE 7.4   Next plc

At the end of January 2015, Next plc had borrowings of £841.0 million and equity of £321.9 million. The gearing ratio based on these figures is 261.26% (£841.0 m/£321.9 m x 100%). Looked at in isolation, this figure would suggest that Next plc has seriously over-borrowed and is in imminent danger of collapse. And yet, the company is still trading and lenders are falling over themselves to lend the company money: of the total borrowings of £841.0 million, £250.0 million was lent to the company during the financial year ended in January 2014. Clearly, lenders would not continue to provide this amount of funding unless they had cast iron confidence in Next's ability to repay this debt. Therefore, several additional factors must be taken into consideration before we can draw a conclusion on the long-term solvency position of Next plc.

Affordability

Is this debt affordable? Next plc had an operating profit of £812.1 million and interest payable of £30.6 million for the accounting year ended 25 January 2015, giving interest cover of 26.54 times (£812.1 m/£30.6 m). The interest is thus very affordable and sales and profits would have to collapse to very low levels before the interest on the borrowings could not be covered by profits from operations.

Repayment dates

When are the borrowings repayable? Of the total borrowings, only the bank overdraft of £2.8 million has to be repaid immediately. The remainder of the borrowings comprise bonds, of which £215.5 million is due in 2016, £337.4 million is repayable in 2021 and £285.3million is due for repayment in 2026, so the company has plenty of time in which to save up the necessary cash to meet these repayment dates. The

interest rates on the three bonds are fixed at 5.875%, 5.375% and 4.375% respectively, so the company will not suffer higher interest charges if there were to be a sudden increase in bank base rates.

Operating cash inflows

How easily can this debt be repaid? Cash inflows from operations amounted to £895.8 million for the financial year ended 24 January 2015. With cash inflows this strong, there is little doubt that the company has the operating cash inflows to meet these liabilities when they become due.

In reality, the group's bankers will probably offer the company new loans with which to

repay their existing loans when they are due for payment, fixing the interest rates on these new loans for a further five to ten years. Much public company borrowing is rolled over in this way: borrowings are not actually repaid, they are just swapped for new borrowings at rates of interest fixed at a suitable level given the prevailing rate of interest at the time the new borrowings are taken out.

Consistency of product demand

As a clothing retailer appealing to the 16–35 age group, Next has a consistency of demand for its goods ensuring a steady stream of profits and cash flows for the foreseeable future. There is nothing risky in its business and nothing to suggest that its products will suddenly go out of fashion. This would not be the case for a mobile

phone manufacturer, for example, whose products might suddenly become obsolete if a revolutionary new technology were to be introduced to the market by a competitor.

Source: Next report and accounts for the year ended 24 January 2015 www.next.co.uk

7

GIVE ME AN EXAMPLE 7.5   **The dangers of borrowing too much**

The private equity firm Terra Firma bought EMI plc in 2007 for £4.2 billion. Despite turning the ailing music business round and generating much improved profitability, with operating profit rising to nearly £300 million, by late 2010 it was clear that Terra Firma had paid far too much for EMI. Interest on the borrowings used to fund the acquisition could not be met from the improved operating cash inflows, resulting in Citigroup, Terra Firma's lender, taking control of EMI in February 2011. Organisations that do not keep within their

borrowing capacity will not survive, so it is important for entities to borrow only as much as they can afford to service through interest payments and to repay when the debt becomes due. Contrast Terra Firma's situation with that of Next, whose interest cover of 26.54 times and operating cash inflows of £896 million from which to meet annual interest payments of around £31 million indicate that their borrowings are highly affordable.

Source: *Guardian* news 5 February 2010; *Financial Times* news 14 February 2010

What lessons can we draw from Give me an example 7.4 and 7.5? First, as with the current and quick ratios, you should never jump to conclusions based on isolated figures. An apparently unhealthy gearing ratio turns out to be perfectly sound when all the facts are taken into consideration. When evaluating long-term solvency, you should look at:

- The interest cover to determine how affordable the borrowings are: does the business generate sufficiently high profits from which to meet interest payments?

- The dates on which repayments are to be made: the more distant the repayment date, the bigger the chance the business has of meeting repayments by that date.

- The strength of the operating cash inflows from the statement of cash flows: high operating cash inflows indicate that there will be sufficient cash on hand to repay borrowings when they become due for payment.

- The consistency of demand for a company's products: the more consistent the demand, the less likely the company will be to collapse in the future and be unable to meet its liabilities when they become due. You should also think about the likelihood of new products from different firms replacing the current market leader's products: the more likely this is, the riskier the business will be and the higher the possibility that they could eventually default on their borrowings.

WHY IS THIS RELEVANT TO ME?   When are borrowings risky?

To enable you as a business professional and user of accounting information to:

- Appreciate that apparently high levels of borrowings do not always indicate potential problems for an organisation in meeting repayments when these become due

- Evaluate the affordability of long-term borrowings and the ability of entities to repay those borrowings from current resources and cash inflows

- Consider the consistency of demand for a business's products and the impact that replacement products would have on a business's long-term solvency

NUMERICAL EXERCISES   Think you can calculate long- and short-term solvency ratios, working capital ratios, and evaluate the cash conversion cycle and timing of payments for a real company? Do you think that you can interpret these ratios in a meaningful way? Have a look at Numerical exercises 7.1 dealing with the financial statements of Greggs plc and then have a go at the various exercises linked to this example in the **online workbook**.

CHAPTER SUMMARY

You should now have learnt that:

- An entity's liquidity depends upon how quickly goods purchased are turned into cash

- Current and quick ratios express the relationship between current assets and current liabilities at an arbitrary point in time, the statement of financial position date

- Current and quick ratios make the misleading and unrealistic assumption that creditors will demand the payment of all monies owed on the same day
- Careful working capital management is vital to an organisation's short-term liquidity
- Working capital ratios are used to determine the speed of an entity's cash conversion cycle
- A full appreciation of the short-term liquidity of an organisation must be based upon an assessment of the timing of cash receipts and cash payments
- Long-term solvency depends upon an entity's ability to repay interest and borrowings from operating cash flows

QUICK REVISION   Test your knowledge with the online flashcards in Summary of key concepts and attempt the Multiple choice questions, all in the **online workbook**. www.oxfordtextbooks.co.uk/orc/scott/

END-OF-CHAPTER QUESTIONS

Solutions to these questions can be found at the back of the book from page 466.

> *Develop your understanding*

Question 7.1

Samoco plc operates a chain of in town grocery convenience stores and edge of town super-markets across the UK. The company is expanding rapidly and is adding new stores every year. Below are the income statements for the company for the years ended 31 May 2016 and 31 May 2015 together with statements of financial position at those dates.

Samoco plc: income statements for the years ended 31 May 2016 and 31 May 2015

	2016	2015
	£m	£m
Revenue	13,663	12,249
Cost of sales	12,570	11,330
Gross profit	1,093	919
Distribution and selling costs	121	108
Administration expenses	240	225
Operating profit	732	586
Finance income	20	15
Finance expense	104	84
Profit before tax	648	517
Income tax	162	129
Profit for the year	486	388

Samoco plc: statements of financial position at 31 May 2016 and 31 May 2015

	2016	2015
	£m	£m
Assets		
Non-current assets		
Property, plant and equipment	6,040	5,150
Current assets		
Inventories	485	500
Other receivables	45	40
Cash and cash equivalents	122	99
	652	639
Total assets	6,692	5,789
Liabilities		
Current liabilities		
Current portion of long term borrowings	240	216
Trade payables	830	790
Other payables	150	140
Dividends	200	180
Current tax	170	150
	1,590	1,476
Non-current liabilities		
Long term borrowings	2,230	2,024
Pension liabilities	756	524
	2,986	2,548
Total liabilities	4,576	4,024
Net assets	2,116	1,765
Equity		
Called up share capital	110	100
Share premium	145	140
Retained earnings	1,861	1,525
Total equity	2,116	1,765

7

Notes to the above financial statements:

- Samoco Plc's sales are made on an entirely cash basis, with no credit being allowed to customers at its convenience stores and supermarkets. Therefore, at 31 May 2016 and 31 May 2015 there were no monies owed by trade receivables.
- Finance expense is made up entirely of interest payable on the long-term borrowings.
- Samoco Plc's long-term borrowings are repayable over the next 10 years.

Required

(a) Using the financial statements for Samoco plc calculate for both years:

- Current ratio
- Quick ratio
- Inventory days
- Payables days
- The cash conversion cycle
- Gearing %
- Debt ratio
- Interest cover

(b) Using the ratios you have calculated and the financial statements above, evaluate the liquidity, working capital and long-term solvency of Samoco plc at 31 May 2016.

Question 7.2

A colleague who has just started studying accounting has read in another book that companies without current ratios of 2:1 and quick (acid test) ratios of 1:1 will find it difficult to meet their current liabilities as they fall due. She has just noticed your current and quick ratio calculations for Samoco plc in Question 7.1 and has concluded that the company is about to collapse. Using the information in Question 7.1, ratios that you have already calculated and details of when liabilities can be assumed to be due for payment below, calculate the maximum amount of the current liabilities of Samoco plc that could be due for repayment on the day after the statement of financial position date (1 June 2016 and 1 June 2015). Draw up arguments to put to your colleague to show her that a simple reliance on current and quick ratios as an indicator of short-term liquidity fails to address all the relevant issues.

For the purposes of this exercise you should assume that current liabilities are due for payment as follows:

- Bank loans: repayable in 12 monthly instalments
- Trade payables: repayable according to your payables days calculations in Question 7.1
- Current tax: due in four instalments: three months, six months, nine months and twelve months after the statement of financial position date
- Other payables: assume that 20% of this figure is payable immediately
- Dividends: due for payment in August 2016 and August 2015

You can assume that there are 360 days during the financial year on which Samoco plc's shops are open and trading.

» Take it further

Question 7.3

Listed below is information relating to four companies:

- Ted Baker is a global lifestyle brand that operates through three main distribution channels: retail, which includes e-commerce, wholesale and licensing, which includes territorial and product licences. The company offers a wide range of fashion and lifestyle collections.
- Nichols is a producer of still and carbonated soft drinks.
- Rolls Royce designs, develops, manufactures and services integrated power systems for use in the air, on land and at sea.
- National Express is a leading public transport operator with bus, coach and rail services in the UK, Continental Europe, North Africa, North America and the Middle East.

	Ted Baker	Nichols	Rolls Royce	National Express
Year ended	03/02/2015	31/12/2014	31/12/2014	31/12/2014
Income statement	£m	£m	£m	£m
Revenue	387.6	109.2	13,736	1,867.4
Cost of sales	152.4	59.0	10,533	1,084.0
Operating profit	49.8	25.6	1,390	193.1
Finance expense	1.2	—	70	52.2

	Ted Baker	Nichols	Rolls Royce	National Express
Year end date	03/02/2015	31/12/2014	31/12/2014	31/12/2014
Statement of financial position	£m	£m	£m	£m
Total assets	231.7	85.7	22,224	2,326.2
Total liabilities	91.1	27.6	15,837	1,490.0
Current assets				
Inventory	111.1	4.7	2,768	21.8
Trade receivables	25.8	21.9	4,215	105.6
Other receivables	15.3	1.6	1,343	96.8
Cash and cash equivalents	7.4	34.5	2,862	83.7
Current assets (total)	159.6	62.7	11,188	307.9

	Ted Baker	Nichols	Rolls Royce	National Express
Year end date	03/02/2015	31/12/2014	31/12/2014	31/12/2014
Current liabilities				
Bank overdrafts	26.2	—	—	—
Bank loans	—	—	68	55.9
Trade payables	32.2	5.7	1,348	144.2
Other current liabilities	32.7	15.6	6,269	365.9
Current liabilities (total)	**91.1**	**21.3**	**7,685**	**566.0**
Total equity	140.6	58.1	6,387	836.2
Total borrowings	26.2	—	2,261	797.7

Using the above financial information, calculate for all four companies:

- Current ratio
- Quick ratio
- Inventory days/inventory turnover
- Receivables days
- Payables days
- The cash conversion cycle
- Gearing percentage
- Debt ratio
- Interest cover

Question 7.4

Given the activities of each company, comment on how you would expect each company to generate its cash inflows together with an assessment of the liquidity and solvency of each company. Your answers should address the following issues, among others:

- The current and quick ratios of the four companies.
- The cash conversion cycles of the four companies.
- Why do the inventory, receivables and payables days vary so much in the four companies?
- The gearing levels in the four companies and whether these are manageable.

Part 2

Management accounting

Costing

LEARNING OUTCOMES

Once you have read this chapter and worked through the questions and examples in both this chapter and the online workbook, you should be able to:

- Define management accounting and explain its role in organisations
- Define costing
- Understand the importance of costing to business organisations in making pricing decisions
- Explain what is meant by the terms direct costs and indirect costs
- Explain the distinction between fixed costs and variable costs
- Construct simple costing statements to determine the total cost of products on an absorption (total) costing basis
- Draw simple graphs to illustrate fixed, variable and total cost behaviour in a business context
- Understand the limitations of absorption costing approaches in allocating overheads to products
- Apply activity-based costing to overhead allocation problems
- Discuss the assumptions on which costing is based

Introduction: management accounting v. financial accounting

In the first part of this book we have looked at financial accounting, how the three key financial accounting statements are put together, the information they contain and their usefulness in understanding a business's past performance. As we have seen, financial accounting reports summarise accounting data, usually on an annual basis, for presentation to interested parties. It is important to appreciate the historical aspect of these financial accounts, that they report on what has happened not on what might or is expected to happen in the future. They are thus not specifically designed to be used for planning purposes although users of these financial accounts might use them as a basis for making investment decisions, to buy, hold or sell shares in an entity. Financial accounts are prepared for parties outside the business and summarise all the transactions that have taken place, together with information relevant to a specific accounting period.

But accounting has other uses. If you worked out your expected income and what you expected to spend during your first year at university, you have already undertaken a management accounting exercise: you prepared a forecast to enable you to determine when you might need additional income to meet your spending plans or you will have reduced your planned expenditure to stay within your expected level of income. Comparing what you have actually spent with what you expected to spend will enable you to modify your income and expenditure plans to enable you to keep within your budget or to find ways in which to earn extra income to meet those plans.

In the same way, businesses use budgeting to model how they expect money to flow into and out of the business, to identify cash shortfalls or surpluses. They can then plan to borrow money from their bank or to invest surplus cash to earn interest for the organisation. At the simplest level of planning, organisations will calculate the expected costs of making or buying a product and the expected income from selling that product to other parties. Comparisons will be made between expectations and actual outcomes to enable the organisation to plan more effectively in the future and to provide more relevant information to management about how the organisation is performing and how it is expected to perform.

What does management accounting do?

Management accounting thus presents information to parties internal to the business and aims to provide data that is relevant to making business decisions now and in the future. The starting point of this information is not a summary of all transactions but a detailed analysis of individual cost components of products and services with a view to determining selling prices for those products and services. This detailed information can then be used to plan what the business will do and what decisions it will make to enable it to operate profitably in the future. For planning and control purposes, this detailed information will be summarised into budgets for a particular period of time and these budgets will be used to compare actual performance with budgeted performance as a way of controlling the operations of the business. Costing and its use in making decisions and how costing information is used in budgeting and planning will form the basis of the next four chapters of this book and of the exercises and presentations in the workbook.

Given the characteristics of management accounting outlined above, it is clear that management accounting information is forward looking, broken down initially into its smallest component parts and used by management to guide and control the business's internal operations. Such guiding and controlling is undertaken with a view to enabling the achievement of an entity's short- and long-term aims. Without a plan, no one, whether an individual or a business, will achieve anything. Without monitoring actual outcomes against the plan entities will be unable to determine whether their plans are reaching fulfilment or not.

WHY IS THIS RELEVANT TO ME?   **What does management accounting do?**

As a business professional and user of accounting information you should appreciate:

- The critical role that management accounting plays in the planning and evaluation of business activities
- That no matter what your particular business specialism, a knowledge of the techniques and practice of management accounting will be crucial to your success in that specialist role

8

GO BACK OVER THIS AGAIN!   How well have you understood the differences between financial and management accounting? Go to the **online workbook** and complete Exercises 8.1 to make sure you understand the distinction.

SUMMARY OF KEY CONCEPTS   Quite sure you understand what management accounting involves? Take a look at Summary of key concepts 8.1 and 8.2 to reinforce your understanding.

This first chapter will look at the basic building blocks of management accounting information: costs. We will consider what costing involves, what types of cost a business will incur in its operations and how this costing information is used to inform that most critical management decision, what prices to charge for products and services so that an organisation can make a profit.

Why is it important to know about costs?

Businesses exist to make a profit. Without knowing what costs a business will incur in producing goods for sale or in providing a service, it will not be possible for that business to set a selling price higher than the costs incurred. When selling price exceeds the costs, a profit is made. Should selling price be lower than the costs, then a loss will be made and the business will soon be in financial trouble. We saw in Chapter 3 that revenue (income, sales) − costs = profit. All businesses will be seeking to increase their profits over time. There are two paths an entity can take when it wishes to increase profits: either revenue has to increase or costs must decrease. Let's prove this in Example 8.1.

EXAMPLE 8.1

Henry buys T-shirts for £5 and sells them for £10 each. Currently he sells 1,000 T-shirts a year on his market stall. He wishes to increase his profits.

Given his current level of sales, Henry now has a profit of:

	£
Sales 1,000 × £10	10,000
Cost of sales 1,000 × £5	5,000
Profit	5,000

If Henry could buy 1,000 T-shirts for £4 while still selling them for £10 his profit would be:

	£
Sales 1,000 × £10	10,000
Cost of sales 1,000 × £4	4,000
Profit	6,000

Henry has reduced the cost of the goods he sells without reducing his selling price and so his profit has increased from £5,000 to £6,000.

However, by increasing his sales to 2,000 T-shirts, while still buying them at £5 each, his profit will be:

	£
Sales 2,000 × £10	20,000
Cost of sales 2,000 × £5	10,000
Profit	10,000

Reducing costs or increasing sales are thus the two ways in which businesses can increase their profits.

WHY IS THIS RELEVANT TO ME?   Costs and pricing °

- No matter what field of commercial or not for profit activity you are engaged in, as a business professional you must know about costs and income

- Knowing about your costs will enable you to determine a selling price to cover those costs and to generate a profit/surplus for your organisation

- Knowledge of an activity's costs will enable you as a business professional to devise strategies by which to increase profit, whether by reducing costs or increasing income

GO BACK OVER THIS AGAIN!   Happy that you understand the relationship between selling price, costs and profit? Go to the **online workbook** Exercises 8.2 to make sure you understand these relationships.

Give me an example 8.1 shows how cost reductions increase profits.

GIVE ME AN EXAMPLE 8.1   EasyJet on path to profit after fuel price fall

A lower fuel bill has set easyJet on a course to record an interim pre-tax profit for the first time in 13 years, Europe's second largest low-cost airline by revenue said yesterday. Carolyn McCall, easyJet chief executive, said yesterday the company expected its fuel bill to be £35m less in the six months to the end of March compared with the same period a year earlier – highlighting how airlines are benefiting from the 50 per cent plunge in oil prices since last summer.

Jane Wild

Financial Times, 27 March 2015, page 23

From the *Financial Times* © The Financial Times Limited 2015. All Rights Reserved.

8

Costs and costing

We have seen that costs are important to businesses, but what costs will a business consider in making its decisions? The type and number of costs will depend upon the complexity of each business. Very simple businesses will have very simple costing systems and very few costs, while more complex businesses will have many costs and very complex costing systems to inform management decisions. Consider Example 8.2.

EXAMPLE 8.2

Anna is a self-employed carpenter working at home producing handmade wooden dining chairs. During the month of June, she produced 30 chairs. What price should she sell her chairs for? She provides you with invoices showing the costs of the materials she used in June:

	£
Wood	540
Glue	18
Screws	30
Sandpaper	12

Totalling up the costs above, Anna has spent £600 on making 30 chairs. Dividing the costs by the 30 chairs made gives a cost of £20 per chair.

Setting a selling price

As long as Anna sells her chairs for more than £20 each, then she will make a profit on each sale. However, what other considerations should she bear in mind when setting her selling price? First, she will think about what a reasonable profit on each chair sold would be. If each chair takes her an hour to make, she would probably consider a profit of £30 to be a reasonable reward for the time and effort she has put into making each chair. The selling price for each chair would then be £50: £20 costs plus £30 profit. If each chair takes Anna five hours to make, then she would want significantly more profit and a significantly higher selling price to reflect the time spent on producing each chair.

While considering her own internal perspective, the profit she would like to make based on her time spent on making chairs, she will also need to consider the external market. She will thus take into account the prices her competitors are charging for the same type of chair; if she charges more than her competitors, she will not have many sales as buyers in the market like to buy goods as cheaply as possible. Alternatively, if she sets her selling price lower than her competitors, then she will expect to have a lot of orders from her customers, all of whom will want to buy her chairs at her lower price. However, can she fulfil all those orders? Does she have the time to produce as many chairs as her customers will demand?

Setting a selling price is thus a complex decision that needs to factor in many considerations. While cost is only one of those considerations it is now time to look in much more detail at the types of cost that organisations incur in their operations.

Direct costs, variable costs and marginal costs

In our example above, each one of Anna's costs can be attributed directly to each chair she produces. If she were to produce 31 chairs, we would expect her to incur costs of £600 ÷ 30 chairs × 31 chairs = £620. That is, for each additional chair she produces she will incur an additional £20 of materials cost. These costs are called the direct costs of production, the costs that are directly attributable to each unit of output. In Anna's case, these direct costs vary directly in line with each unit of output that is produced and are therefore her variable costs of production. Variable costs reflect the additional costs that are incurred by a business in producing one more unit of a product or service. Borrowing a term from economics, these variable costs are also known as the marginal cost of production, the costs that are incurred in producing one more unit of a product or service. However, as we shall see, not all direct costs of production are variable costs.

SUMMARY OF KEY CONCEPTS   Quite sure about what direct cost, variable cost and marginal cost mean? Go to the Summary of key concepts 8.3 to 8.5 to check your understanding.

Direct costs can be of three types. The first direct cost is materials. In Example 8.2 the wood, glue, screws and sandpaper are all materials used in the production of each chair. The second direct cost is labour, the amount paid to workers for making products. Direct labour may be paid to workers on the basis of an agreed amount for each unit of product produced so that the more the workforce produces, the more they are paid. In this case, direct labour is a variable cost or production. Where production workers are paid a fixed salary that does not depend upon the number of goods produced, this is still a direct cost of production, but it is not a variable cost as salary costs do not rise or fall in line with production. The final type of direct cost is direct expense, costs other than material and labour that can be traced directly to the production of each unit of product. An example of a direct expense would be the electricity required to power machinery to produce one unit of production: the total amount of electricity used by a piece of machinery can be measured precisely and the total cost of electricity divided by the number of units of production to determine a per unit expense for electricity.

8

EXAMPLE 8.3

To illustrate the three types of direct cost, material, labour and expense, let us consider the costs incurred in the bread making section of Bunns the Bakers' central bakery. Think about each cost and decide whether it is an example of direct material, direct labour or direct expense.

Cost:

- Flour
- Gas used to heat the ovens
- Bakers' wages paid on the basis of the number of loaves of bread produced
- Ingredient mixing costs

- Equipment cleaning costs after each batch of loaves is produced
- Bakers' productivity bonus
- Olive oil
- Packaging for loaves
- Water

Which of these costs are direct material, direct labour and direct expense? We can allocate these costs to each heading as shown in Table 8.1.

Table 8.1 Cost allocation

Cost	Direct material	Direct labour	Direct expense
Flour	✓		
Gas used to heat the ovens			✓
Bakers' wages paid on the basis of the number of loaves of bread produced		✓	
Ingredient mixing costs			✓
Equipment cleaning costs after each batch of loaves is produced			✓
Bakers' productivity bonus		✓	
Olive oil	✓		
Packaging for loaves	✓		
Water	✓		

Flour, olive oil, water and packaging are clearly materials used in each loaf, while the bakers' wages and productivity bonus are labour costs. The gas used to heat the ovens is a direct expense used in production of each loaf as, without the gas to heat the ovens to bake the loaves, there would be no product to sell. The gas is not a material as it is not part of the finished loaf. Similarly, the ingredient mixing costs (by machine rather than by hand) are expenses: the cost of mixing ingredients together is essential to the production of the loaves but is neither direct labour nor direct material. Cleaning the equipment after each batch of loaves is produced is another expense that has to be incurred in the production of bread. Each time a batch of loaves is produced, more cleaning costs are incurred so the cleaning costs are the direct result of production.

GO BACK OVER THIS AGAIN!   Can you distinguish between direct materials, direct labour and direct expenses? Go to the **online workbook** Exercises 8.3 to make sure you understand what types of cost fall into each category.

Variable cost behaviour: graphical presentation

In costing, the variable costs of production are assumed to behave in a linear fashion. This mathematical term just means that the variable costs of production rise precisely in line with the number of units produced. For each additional unit of production, the additional cost of producing that additional unit (the marginal cost) will be exactly the same as for all the previous units of production. In Example 8.2, the additional cost of producing one more chair is £20, which is exactly the same cost as all the other chairs Anna has produced.

The relationship between the variable costs of production and the number of units produced can be illustrated graphically as shown in Figure 8.1.

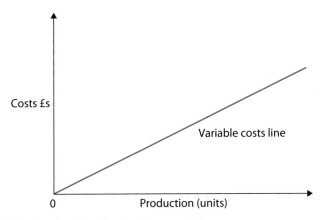

Figure 8.1 Graph showing the effect of production on variable costs

As production increases, variable costs rise in line with that production. Production of one chair costs Anna £20 in materials. Production of two chairs costs her £40 and so on. As each chair costs exactly the same to produce as the previous one, the total variable costs of production on the graph will rise in a straight line. If Anna produces no chairs, she will incur no variable costs and so the variable costs line starts at zero.

Fixed costs

However, not all costs incurred by a business are variable, marginal costs. There are also costs that are fixed, which do not vary in line with production. These costs are called fixed costs because, for a given period of time, they are assumed to remain the same whether zero units, 10 units or 1,000 units of product are produced. Fixed costs can be direct costs of production (such as the fixed salaries of production workers) or they may be general overheads incurred in the running of the business, costs that cannot be directly attributed to specific products or services. Fixed costs come in many forms, but let us start with the following simple example, Example 8.4.

EXAMPLE 8.4

Anna is so successful in her chair-making enterprise at home that she decides to expand and set up a workshop from which to produce her chairs. She starts renting a small workshop at an annual rental cost of £6,000. Business rates on the workshop amount to £1,000 per annum and the workshop heating and lighting bills amount to £800 for the year. In addition, she takes on two employees who are paid £25 for each chair that they make. Anna now concentrates on running the business rather than crafting chairs herself. How would you classify these additional costs? Which of these new costs do not vary directly in line with production and which will rise or fall precisely in line with the number of chairs produced?

Rent and business rates on the workshop are totally fixed as Anna has to pay these costs whether the employees make no chairs in the year or whether they make 10,000. Thus, her workshop can produce as few or as many chairs as she likes without incurring any additional rent or business rate costs. The rent and business rates are thus both fixed costs. They are also the indirect costs of production: the workshop is essential to the production of the chairs, but the rent and business rates cannot in any way be attributed directly to each chair produced.

By contrast, the employees are a direct cost of production as each additional chair that is made by each employee incurs a further cost of £25, this cost varying directly in line with production. Thus, £25 is a completely variable cost of production, the marginal labour cost of producing one more chair. This £25 will be added to the £20 material costs to give the total direct cost of one chair of £45.

The heating and lighting bills are a little trickier to classify. How much is paid for lighting will depend on how many days the workshop is open. If the workshop is closed, then the lights will not be turned on and no cost will be incurred. Similarly, if no one works in the workshop for the whole year, there will be no need to turn on the lights or the heating and the heating and lighting costs will be £nil. However, even if the workshop is open and the lights are turned on, there is no guarantee that a consistent level of production will be achieved each day. The two employees might be able to produce eight chairs in a day between them, but if either of them is unwell and absent from work, then only four chairs will be produced, assuming that they each make four chairs a day. However, the lighting cost would still be the same for four chairs as it was for eight chairs. If the weather is hot, then the employees will work more slowly and only six chairs a day might be produced. In the same way, more lighting will be used in winter than in summer and this variability is also true of the heating costs: a very cold winter will mean a higher heating bill than when the winter weather is milder. Given this difficulty in allocating the costs of heating and lighting to individual units of production, it is safer to treat these costs as a fixed cost for the year.

Can we illustrate the relationship between fixed costs and production as we did for variable costs in Figure 8.1? Yes we can and this relationship is shown in Figure 8.2.

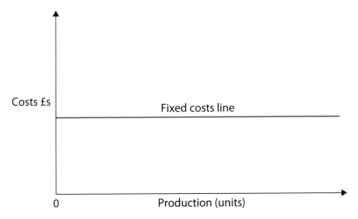

Figure 8.2 Graph showing the effect of production on fixed costs

The fixed costs line is a straight line just like the variable costs line. However, the fixed cost line shows that fixed costs are the same for all levels of production over a given period of time. As we noted earlier, the fixed costs are the same whether no chairs or 10,000 chairs are produced. Thus, the fixed cost line does not pass through zero but starts at the level of the fixed costs on the cost axis and continues as a straight line across the graph as there is no variation in the level of fixed costs. Even when no chairs are produced, the fixed costs are still incurred and have to be paid.

WHY IS THIS RELEVANT TO ME?   **Direct costs and indirect costs**

In your role as a business professional and user of accounting information you will need to:

- Identify those costs that are directly attributable to units of production or to services provided
- Identify those costs that vary in line with increased business activity
- Identify those costs that do not vary in line with increased business activity
- Possess the knowledge required to identify costs that are relevant in decision making (discussed further in Chapter 9)

GO BACK OVER THIS AGAIN!   Quite certain you appreciate the difference between fixed and variable costs? Go to the **online workbook** Exercises 8.4 to make sure you understand this distinction.

Variable costs, fixed costs and total costs

Total costs for an accounting period are the total variable costs incurred in producing goods or services plus the total fixed costs incurred in that same time period. This is illustrated graphically in Figure 8.3.

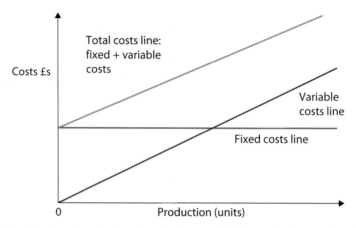

Figure 8.3 Graph showing the behaviour of production on variable costs, fixed costs and total costs

The variable cost and fixed cost lines are drawn on the graph as before in exactly the same positions. The total cost line adds together the variable and fixed costs for a period to give the total costs incurred by an organisation. At a zero level of production, variable costs are zero, so total costs are the same as fixed costs. However, as production takes place, variable costs are incurred and the total costs line rises as these variable costs are added to fixed costs. As production increases, the average total cost of each product produced will fall as the fixed costs are spread across more units of production. To prove that this is the case, consider Example 8.5.

EXAMPLE 8.5

Using the facts from Examples 8.2, 8.3 and 8.4, let's work out the average cost per unit for levels of production of Anna's chairs at 100 units, 200 units, 300 units and 400 units. Remember that variable costs are materials (£20) + labour (£25) = £45 per chair while the fixed costs of the workshop are £6,000 (rent) + £1,000 (business rates) + £800 (heating and lighting) = £7,800.

As Table 8.2 shows, the average total cost per chair falls as production increases and the fixed costs are gradually spread over an increasing number of chairs.

Table 8.2 Anna's average cost per chair at different levels of production

(a) Units of production	(b) Variable cost per unit	(c) = (a) × (b) Total variable costs	(d) Fixed costs	(e) = (c) + (d) Total costs	(f) = (e) ÷ (a) Average total cost per chair
100	45	4,500	7,800	12,300	123.00
200	45	9,000	7,800	16,800	84.00
300	45	13,500	7,800	21,300	71.00
400	45	18,000	7,800	25,800	64.50

NUMERICAL EXERCISES   How well have you appreciated that higher levels of production mean a smaller average total cost for each product produced? Go to the **online workbook** and complete Numerical exercises 8.1 to prove to yourself that this is still true for higher levels of production in Anna's workshop.

Allocating fixed overhead costs to products: absorption costing

We noted earlier in this chapter that organisations need to know the total cost of their products or services so that they can calculate a suitable selling price to enable them to make a profit on their activities. As we have seen, the costs involved are the direct and indirect costs of production and organisations will take both of these types of cost into account when setting their selling prices. Typically, a cost card will be drawn up for each product that shows the direct costs for one unit of production. Anna's cost card for one chair is shown in Example 8.6.

However, how should the indirect costs of production be allocated to products? Organisations have to take into account their indirect costs when setting a selling price for a product otherwise they might set the selling price too low and fail to cover their indirect as well as their direct costs. But different levels of production will result in different allocations of indirect costs to products and in different total costs for products. Anna has indirect costs of £7,800 for her rent, rates, heating and lighting. As we saw in Table 8.2, at different levels of production the average total cost for each product rises or falls depending on how many or how few products are produced. How can Anna set a selling price for her chairs if actual numbers of chairs produced are not known?

8

The answer to this problem is that entities will estimate the normal, expected level of production achievable within an accounting period and use this **normal level of production** as the basis for allocating indirect costs to products. Thus, an allocation of indirect costs is made to each unit of production on the basis of this expected production level so that the indirect costs are recovered with each unit of production sold. This technique is called **absorption costing**: indirect costs are absorbed into (allocated to) each unit of production to give a total cost for each product. At the same time, the indirect costs are recovered (essentially, paid for by the customer) as each unit of production is sold. Let us see how this will work in the case of Anna's chairs in Example 8.6.

EXAMPLE 8.6

Anna decides that her workshop will be capable of producing 1,000 chairs in the next year. She now needs to calculate the total cost for one chair based on the figures given in Examples 8.2, 8.3 and 8.4 so that she can decide upon her selling price. Her cost card for one dining chair is shown here.

Cost card: wooden dining chair	£
Direct production costs	
Wood £540 ÷ 30 (Example 8.2)	18.00
Glue £18 ÷ 30 (Example 8.2)	0.60
Screws £30 ÷ 30 (Example 8.2)	1.00
Sandpaper £12 ÷ 30 (Example 8.2)	0.40
Direct labour (Example 8.4)	25.00
Prime cost (total direct cost of production of one chair: direct material + direct labour + direct expenses)	45.00
Indirect production costs (overheads)	
Rent £6,000 ÷ 1,000 (Example 8.4)	6.00
Business rates £1,000 ÷ 1,000 (Example 8.4)	1.00
Heating and lighting £800 ÷ 1,000 (Example 8.4)	0.80
Total production cost of one chair	52.80

Figure 8.4 The components of prime cost

Figure 8.5 The total production cost of one unit of production

Direct costs of production are split into their component parts (direct material, direct labour and direct expense). The total direct production cost is called **prime cost** (Figure 8.4), the direct cost of producing one dining chair. Indirect (overhead) costs are then allocated to each item of production on the basis of what production is expected to be, the normal level of production. Thus, each element of indirect costs is divided by the total expected production of 1,000 units to give the overhead cost that should be allocated to each unit of production. Adding the indirect (overhead) costs per unit of production to the total direct cost (prime cost) gives the total production cost of one chair (Figure 8.5).

SUMMARY OF KEY CONCEPTS   Can you define prime cost and production cost? Go to the Summary of key concepts 8.6 to reinforce your understanding.

WHY IS THIS RELEVANT TO ME?   Prime cost and production cost

As a business professional and user of accounting information you should understand that:

- Setting a selling price to achieve a profit requires knowledge of all the costs incurred in the production of a good or service
- Indirect overhead costs as well as direct costs of production have to be taken into account when setting a selling price
- A suitable method of allocation of indirect overhead costs to products has to be found in order to build the indirect costs incurred into the cost of each product produced and sold

8

NUMERICAL EXERCISES   Quite sure you can allocate direct and indirect costs to a product or service? Go to the **online workbook** and complete Numerical exercises 8.2 to make sure you can apply this technique.

Setting the selling price

As management accounting is about forecasting and planning as well as costing, Anna will now consider what selling price she ought to charge for each chair and how much profit she will make.

EXAMPLE 8.7

Given that each chair is expected to incur a total production (absorption) cost of £52.80, Anna decides that a selling price of £85 is reasonable and will meet market expectations. How much profit will she make if she sells all of the 1,000 chairs produced? The detailed profit calculation is shown below.

	£	£
Sales 1,000 × £85		85,000
Direct costs		
Wood 1,000 × £18	18,000	
Glue 1,000 × £0.60	600	
Screws 1,000 × £1	1,000	
Sandpaper 1,000 × £0.40	400	
Direct labour 1,000 × £25	25,000	
Prime cost (total direct cost for 1,000 chairs)		45,000
Rent 1,000 × £6	6,000	
Business rates 1,000 × £1	1,000	
Heating and lighting 1,000 × £0.80	800	
Indirect production costs		7,800
Total expected profit for the year		32,200

Rather than drawing up the detailed costing statement shown above, you might have taken a short cut to determine Anna's expected profit for next year. You could have taken the selling price of one chair of £85 and deducted the total production cost of one chair of £52.80 to give you a profit per chair of £32.20 (£85.00 − £52.80). Multiplying this profit per chair of £32.20 by 1,000 chairs produced and sold would give you the same answer of £32,200.

NUMERICAL EXERCISES How well have you understood the calculation of profit from a given set of costing data? Go to the **online workbook** Numerical exercises 8.3 to make sure you can apply this technique.

Absorption costing and inventory valuation

At the end of each accounting period, most organisations will hold unsold items of production. The question that arises is how such inventory should be valued. In Chapter 3, Julia's retail business valued her inventory at the cost to the business, the costs charged by suppliers for goods sold to the business (Chapter 3, Closing inventory). This is an acceptable method of inventory valuation in a retail trading business as this is the cost of the inventory to the business. However, accounting standards allow organisations to value their inventory on an absorption costing basis, the direct production costs of a product plus a proportion of the indirect production overheads incurred in each product's manufacture. Therefore, it is important for organisations to be able to calculate the costs associated with each item of production both in terms of its direct costs and the proportion of indirect production overhead costs attributable to each unit of product.

In Anna's case, any unsold chairs at the end of the accounting period would be valued at £52.80 each, the direct costs of £45 per chair plus the attributable overheads of £7.80 allocated to each chair. These costs would be carried forward under the accruals basis of accounting (see Chapter 3, The accruals basis of accounting) to match against sales made in the following accounting period.

Give me an example 8.2 reproduces Rolls Royce Holdings plc's accounting policy on inventory valuation: note how direct materials, direct labour and overheads are included in the valuation of inventory.

> **GIVE ME AN EXAMPLE 8.2   Overheads included in inventory valuation**
>
> **Inventories**
>
> Inventories and work in progress are valued at the lower of cost and net realisable value on a first-in, first-out basis. Cost comprises direct materials and, where applicable, direct labour costs and those overheads, including depreciation of property, plant and equipment, that have been incurred in bringing the inventories to their present location and condition.
>
> Source: www.rolls-royce.com

NUMERICAL EXERCISES   Happy with how to calculate the value of inventory at the end of an accounting period? Go to the **online workbook** Numerical exercises 8.4 to make sure you can calculate an inventory valuation.

> **WHY IS THIS RELEVANT TO ME?   Inventory valuation**
>
> As a business professional and user of accounting information you should understand that:
> - Not all production will be sold by the end of an accounting period
> - This inventory has to be valued to determine the profit for the accounting period and to match costs to products actually sold
> - To comply with relevant accounting standards inventory should be valued at direct cost plus a proportion of the indirect production overheads incurred

Anna's business is simple, with just three indirect overhead costs to allocate to production units of one product. How would these indirect overhead costs be allocated in a more complex organisation in which more than one product is produced?

Absorption costing: overhead allocation

In reality, manufacturing and service organisations have many indirect production overhead costs and many different products and services. Entities will seek to allocate these overheads to departments and then to products on the most appropriate basis. This will enable organisations to absorb these overheads into products or services on the way to determining a selling price for each product or service. Commonly, each overhead is determined in total and it is then apportioned to departments. The overhead total for each department is then divided up into an hourly rate on the basis of the number of labour hours or the number of machine hours used in each department (Figure 8.6).

Where labour is the key input to a production process, overheads will be allocated on the basis of the number of labour hours worked in a year. Service industries such as car maintenance, delivery services or catering will allocate overheads on the basis of labour hours as the provision of the service is based on employees rather than on machines. Where a production process is highly mechanised, as is the case in most manufacturing industries, then machine hours will be used as the basis for overhead allocation.

How will the number of hours of labour or machine time be calculated? Businesses will first determine their operating capacity, the number of hours that production employees work or the number of hours that production machinery operates during a year. Once capacity has been determined, then overheads will be totalled up and divided by the number of hours of capacity to give an hourly overhead absorption rate.

As an example of this technique, suppose that a car maintenance operation has ten employees who each work a 40-hour week for 48 weeks of the year (allowing for four weeks of holidays for each employee). The labour hour capacity of the business in one

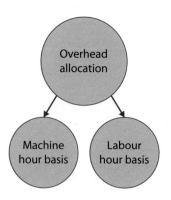

Figure 8.6 Overhead absorption bases

week is 10 employees × 40 hours = 400 hours. The labour hour capacity of the business for the year is then 400 hours in one week × 48 working weeks = 19,200 hours. Annual overheads incurred in the car maintenance operation will be totalled up and this total divided by the 19,200 available hours in the year to determine an overhead recovery rate for each job that the operation quotes for. If the total overheads of the business come to £288,000, then the hourly allocation rate will be £288,000 ÷ 19,200 labour hours = £15 per hour. If a job is expected to take five hours, then an overhead cost of £15 × 5 hours = £75 will be added to the direct cost estimate for that job when the customer is quoted a price. Remember that direct costs plus overhead costs give the total cost of providing a service and will be used as a basis on which to determine a selling price that will give a profit on each job.

The car maintenance operation is a simple example. In more complex situations, the stages in overhead allocation will be to:

1. Determine each overhead cost from invoices and payments.
2. Allocate overhead costs to departments on the most appropriate basis.
3. Total up overhead costs for each department.
4. Determine a labour hour or machine hour absorption rate for departmental overheads.
5. Allocate overheads to products or services on the basis of labour or machine hours used in the production of each product or provision of each service.

Think about how steps 1–5 are applied in the next example.

EXAMPLE 8.8

Information relating to the Picture Frame Company is presented in Table 8.3. You have been asked to allocate the costs to two departments, machining and finishing. The directors of the Picture Frame Company want to absorb overheads in each department into products on the basis of machine hours used in each department, as they consider that this basis will best reflect the way in which departmental overheads are incurred. The Picture Frame Company sells its products at absorption cost plus 20%.

Table 8.3 The Picture Frame Company's annual overhead costs and machine hours

Annual Costs	Total £	Machining	Finishing
Rent	100,000	Floor area: 1,800 square metres	Floor area: 1,200 square metres
Business rates	25,000		
Depreciation	40,000	Machinery value: £160,000	Machinery value: £240,000

→

Annual Costs	Total £	Machining	Finishing
Heating	15,000	Departmental volume: 10,000 cubic metres	Departmental volume: 5,000 cubic metres
Directors' salaries	80,000	Percentage of directors' time spent in department: 37.5%	Percentage of directors' time spent in department: 62.5%
Machining department manager	29,000		
Finishing department manager	34,000		
Employee salaries	270,000	Number of employees in department: 9	Numbers of employees in department: 6
Repairs: machining	19,000		
Repairs: finishing	35,000		
Water rates	20,000	Departmental water usage: 1,800,000 litres	Departmental water usage: 1,200,000 litres
Lighting	18,000	Number of lights in department: 3,600	Number of lights in department: 1,800
Service department	50,000	Departmental usage: 20% of service department	Departmental usage: 80% of service department
	Total hours	**Machining**	**Finishing**
Machine hours	195,000	75,000	120,000

This mass of information might look daunting, but the application of common sense to how these overheads should be allocated to machining and finishing should enable you to determine the total overheads for each department. When allocating overheads, you should use any systematic basis that will result in a fair and equitable allocation of overheads to each department. Taking rent as an example in Table 8.3, the total floor area for the two departments is 1,800 square metres in machining and 1,200 square metres in finishing, a total of 3,000 square metres. The total rent cost is £100,000 so £100,000 × 1,800/3,000 = £60,000 allocated to machining and 1,200/3000 × £100,000 = £40,000 allocated to finishing.

Using the additional information on departmental usage of each particular production overhead cost and department specific details on particular production costs, overheads can be allocated to the machining and finishing departments as shown in Table 8.4.

Table 8.4 The Picture Frame Company's annual costs allocated to machining and finishing

Annual costs	Total £	Machining £	Finishing £	Notes
Rent	100,000	60,000	40,000	Total floor area: 3,000 sq metres, split both rent and rate costs 1,800:1,200
Business rates	25,000	15,000	10,000	Split on the basis of total floor area 1,800:1,200
Depreciation	40,000	16,000	24,000	Split according to machinery value, 160,000:240,000
Heating	15,000	10,000	5,000	Split according to volume heated, 10,000:5,000
Directors' salaries	80,000	30,000	50,000	£80,000 split according to usage, 37.5%:62.5%
Machining department manager	29,000	29,000	—	Actual departmental cost
Finishing department manager	34,000	—	34,000	Actual departmental cost
Employee salaries	270,000	162,000	108,000	£270,000 split 9:6 on the basis of the number of employees in each department
Repairs: machining	19,000	19,000	—	Actual departmental cost
Repairs: finishing	35,000	—	35,000	Actual departmental cost
Water rates	20,000	12,000	8,000	Split according to water usage, 1,800:1,200
Lighting	18,000	12,000	6,000	Split according to number of lights, 3,600:1,800
Service department	50,000	10,000	40,000	Split according to usage, 20%:80%
Totals	735,000	375,000	360,000	

SHOW ME HOW TO DO IT Are you happy with how these allocations were calculated? View Video presentation 8.1 in the **online workbook** to see a practical demonstration to reinforce your understanding of how this overhead allocation between departments was carried out.

Now that overheads have been allocated to each department, we can work out an overhead absorption rate, the amount to be charged per hour of resource consumed within the department. As noted in Example 8.8, the directors have chosen to allocate overheads to products on the basis of machine hours as the most appropriate method of overhead allocation and absorption.

In the machining department, £5 will be allocated per machine hour (£375,000 ÷ 75,000 hours), while in finishing, £3 will be allocated per machine hour (£360,000 ÷ 120,000 hours).

Let us assume that the 50 × 60 centimetre gilt edged frame has a direct material, direct labour and direct expense cost of £56 and requires four hours of machining department time and eight hours of finishing department time. The total absorption cost for 50 × 60 centimetre gilt edged frames is as follows:

	£
Direct material, direct labour and direct expense cost	56
Machining department overhead absorbed: 4 hours at £5/hour	20
Finishing department overhead absorbed: 8 hours at £3/hour	24
50 × 60 centimetre gilt edged frame total absorption cost	100

Selling price for 50 × 60 centimetre gilt edged frames will be £100 absorption cost × 120% (100% cost + 20% of the absorption cost) = £120.

8

WHY IS THIS RELEVANT TO ME?   Overhead allocation, overhead allocation rates

As a business professional and user of accounting information you should understand how to:

- Allocate total overheads between different operating departments with a view to determining overhead allocation rates for each department

- Use overhead allocation rates to determine the overhead absorbed by particular products or services

- Set a selling price on the basis of the total absorption cost of a product or service

---

NUMERICAL EXERCISES   Quite convinced you could carry out this kind of overhead allocation exercise for yourself? Go to the **online workbook** Numerical exercises 8.5 to practise this technique.

Give me an example 8.3 illustrates the level of overhead allocation practices in businesses across the world.

GIVE ME AN EXAMPLE 8.3   The use of overhead allocation in business

The July 2009 CIMA report,

Management accounting tools for today and tomorrow, surveyed the current and intended usage by business of more than 100 management accounting and related tools based on a questionnaire completed by 439 respondents from across the globe. The 7th most commonly used technique in practice was overhead allocation. When used as an operational tool, overhead allocation was undertaken by 66% of respondents, the second most popular operational tool in use behind variance analysis on 73%. The survey discovered that the larger the organisation, the more likely it was that overhead allocation would be in use in determining product cost.

Source: www.cimaglobal.com

Allocating service department overheads

Service departments do not make sales to outside parties, but they are an essential support activity in many business operations. Service department costs are allocated to production departments on the basis of each department's usage of each service department. In this way, service department costs are allocated to products and thus built into product selling prices to enable all costs incurred to be recovered through sales of products and services. In the example of the Picture Frame Company, the service department's overheads were allocated on the basis of usage by the two departments, machining and finishing. But what happens in cases where one service department provides services to another service department? In situations such as this, costs are apportioned between production departments and service departments until all the overheads have been allocated. Consider how this approach works in the following example.

8

EXAMPLE 8.9

Alpha Manufacturing has three production departments, welding, sanding and painting, and three service departments, parts, set up and repairs. The costs and overheads of the six departments together with the usage made of each of the service departments by the production and service departments are given in Table 8.5.

Table 8.5 Alpha Manufacturing's production and service department costs and overheads and service department usage percentages

	Production departments			Service departments		
	Welding	Sanding	Painting	Parts	Set up	Repairs
Costs and overheads	£94,200	£86,200	£124,200	£40,000	£24,000	£26,400
Percentage usage of parts	25%	30%	25%		20%	
Percentage usage of set up	20%	40%	10%			30%
Percentage usage of repairs	40%	25%	35%			

You are required to reallocate the overheads for the three service departments to the welding, sanding and painting departments to determine the total costs and overheads for each of the three production departments.

Method

The parts department's overheads of £40,000 will be allocated to each of the three production departments in the proportions indicated in Table 8.5 (25% to welding, 30% to sanding and 25% to painting) and then 20% of the £40,000 overheads will be allocated to the set up department. This will now give overheads in the set up department of £24,000 + (£40,000 × 20%) = £32,000. The set up department's new overheads of £32,000 will now be allocated in the proportions given in the question to the production departments (20% to welding, 40% to sanding and 10% to painting) while 30% of the set up department's overheads will be allocated to the repairs department. The repairs department now has overheads of £26,400 + (£32,000 × 30%) = £36,000 to allocate to each of the three production departments in the proportions 40% to welding, 25% to sanding and 35% to painting.

These calculations are shown in Table 8.6.

All the service department costs and overheads have now been reallocated to production departments. The overhead recovery rates can thus be determined on the basis of labour or machine hours in those departments and overheads allocated to products produced in the welding, sanding and painting departments.

Table 8.6 Alpha Manufacturing's service department overheads reallocated to production departments

	Production departments			Service departments		
	Welding	Sanding	Painting	Parts	Set up	Repairs
	£	£	£	£	£	£
Costs and overheads	94,200	86,200	124,200	40,000	24,000	26,400
Parts costs reallocated	10,000	12,000	10,000	(40,000)	8,000	—
Set up costs reallocated	6,400	12,800	3,200	—	(32,000)	9,600
Repairs costs reallocated	14,400	9,000	12,600	—	—	(36,000)
Total costs and overheads	125,000	120,000	150,000	—	—	—

SHOW ME HOW TO DO IT   Quite sure you understand how service department overheads are reallocated to production departments? View Video presentation 8.2 in the **online workbook** to see a practical demonstration of how this reallocation between service and production departments is carried out.

WHY IS THIS RELEVANT TO ME?   Absorption costing: overhead allocation, allocating service department overheads

8

As a business professional and user of accounting information you should:

- Understand how costs relating to non-production departments are allocated to production departments
- Appreciate that this reallocation process is necessary to ensure that all costs are absorbed into products and services to provide a solid basis on which to determine selling prices

NUMERICAL EXERCISES   Quite convinced you could carry out this kind of overhead reallocation exercise for yourself? Go to the **online workbook** Numerical exercises 8.6 to practise this technique.

Administration overheads, marketing overheads and finance overheads: period costs

So far, we have considered the costs of production, direct and indirect, fixed and variable. However, all business entities incur overhead costs through administration activities, marketing activities and the costs of financing their operations.

It is possible that marketing activities will incur certain costs that vary in line with sales: such costs might be the commission paid to sales representatives to reward them for the sales they generate, as higher sales would incur higher commission. However, most marketing costs such as advertising, brochures, product catalogues, the salaries of marketing staff, the costs of running delivery vehicles and of running sales representatives' cars will all count as fixed costs.

Administration, marketing and financing fixed costs are known as period costs and they relate only to the period in which they are incurred. Therefore, while these costs are not taken into account in the valuation of inventory, it is still important to set the production levels and selling prices of products and services in order to cover these costs. Thus, these additional period costs will be built into the cost price of products in the same way as indirect production costs are allocated to products.

GO BACK OVER THIS AGAIN!   An example of a cost card for a product that includes all costs and the determination of a selling price is given in Exercises 8.5 in the **online workbook**.

Problems with absorption costing

Absorption costing seems like an easy and effective way in which to build costs into products to determine first the total cost of the product and then its selling price. However, absorption costing has come in for criticism in recent years. The technique was originally developed as a way to cost products during the early part of the twentieth century. Each factory would turn out products that were all alike for undiscerning customers. Production runs were long and it was easy to spread fixed overheads over many products using the traditional absorption costing technique.

But times have changed. Modern manufacturers are no longer suppliers of goods to a passive market that accepts mass produced products lacking any individual distinction. Today's producers work assiduously to meet and fulfil customer demands and expectations. Production runs are now very short and products are individualised and tailored to each customer's specific requirements. Markets are not easily satisfied: customers have very specific requirements and, if their regular supplier is unable to meet those requirements, there are plenty of other businesses that will.

Costs are thus no longer incurred in a steady, easy to allocate way. Lots of different organisational activities give rise to costs as businesses seek to fulfil each order's very specific requirements. As a result, the simplistic allocation of costs to particular products on an absorption costing basis may no longer be the most appropriate method. A different approach has to be found to allocate overheads to products so that a more accurate cost and a more competitive selling price for each product can be determined.

Commentators have criticised absorption costing on the following grounds:

- The allocation of costs to products on either a labour or machine hour basis is too simplistic and does not reflect the actual costs incurred in the provision of specific goods and services.

- Traditional absorption costing fails to recognise the demands made by particular products on an entity's resources.

- Overheads arise not in proportion to direct labour and machine hours but as a result of the range and complexity of products and services offered.

- Selling prices calculated on the basis of absorption costs may be wrong in one of two ways:

  – overhead is either underallocated to products that consume more activities resulting in underpricing of these products, or

  – overhead is overallocated to products consuming lower levels of activity and so overprices these products.

- As a result of these misallocations, some products are subsidised by others rather than making a profit in their own right.

WHY IS THIS RELEVANT TO ME?   Problems with absorption costing

To enable you as a business professional and user of accounting information to appreciate that traditional absorption costing:

- Is not the only way in which costs can be allocated to products
- May not provide accurate product prices
- May not be well suited to allocating overhead costs to products in modern manufacturing environments

8

GO BACK OVER THIS AGAIN!   Confident you understand the limitations of traditional absorption costing? Go to the **online workbook** Exercises 8.6 to make sure you appreciate these shortcomings.

SUMMARY OF KEY CONCEPTS   Quite sure that you can state the limitations of traditional absorption costing? Take a look at Summary of key concepts 8.7 to reinforce your knowledge.

Overhead allocation: activity-based costing

As we have seen, the aim of costing is to allocate costs to products and services to enable businesses to determine selling prices for those goods and services so that entities generate profits. Absorption costing works well in the case of mass produced, indistinguishable products, but modern manufacturing approaches require a more sophisticated cost allocation mechanism. Activity-based costing has been put forward as a way of providing this more sophisticated, more precise method of costing products and services to enable businesses to produce more accurate costs and hence more realistic selling prices.

How does activity-based costing work?

Traditional absorption costing adds together all the indirect production overheads incurred by a business and then allocates them across products on the basis of labour or machine hours. Activity-based costing recognises that activities cause costs: the more activity that is undertaken, the more cost is incurred. Under activity-based costing, costs are allocated to products on the basis of activities consumed: the more activities that are associated with a particular product, the more overhead is allocated to that product and so the higher its cost and selling price will be.

Activity-based costing allocates overheads to products in the following way.

Step 1: establish cost pools

- Rather than lumping all indirect production overheads into cost centres (departments), activity-based costs are allocated to cost pools.
- Cost pools reflect different activities incurred in the production of goods and services.
- Examples of cost pools might be set up costs, quality control costs, material ordering costs and production monitoring costs.
- The number of cost pools will depend upon the complexity or simplicity of an entity's operations: the more complex the operations, the more cost pools there will be.

Step 2: allocate costs to products and services

- Once cost pools have been established, a systematic basis on which to allocate those costs to products and services has to be found.

- The most logical method of allocating costs is on the basis of cost drivers: cost drivers reflect the level of activity associated with each cost pool.
- For example, if there were 50 machine set ups in a year, then the total cost in the machine set ups cost pool would be divided by 50 to give the cost per machine set up.
- Costs in the cost pools are then allocated to products on the basis of the activities consumed by those products. In our set up costs example, if a product used five machine set ups in the year, then the cost for five machine set ups would be allocated to that product.
- Where product costs turn out to be very high, management can take steps to reduce the activities consumed by those products as a way to lower costs and improve price competitiveness.

It is important to remember that activity-based costing is used to allocate overhead costs to products. Direct costs are still allocated to products in the usual way. Any costs directly linked to a product are still allocated to and form part of the prime cost of that product.

WHY IS THIS RELEVANT TO ME?   Activity-based costing

To enable you as a business professional and user of accounting information to:

- Understand how activity-based costing works
- Appreciate the terminology used in activity-based costing and what each term means

GO BACK OVER THIS AGAIN!   Do you really understand the differences between traditional absorption costing and activity-based costing? Go to the **online workbook** Exercises 8.7 to make sure you can distinguish between these two methods of overhead allocation.

SUMMARY OF KEY CONCEPTS   Think you can state the steps involved in activity-based costing? Take a look at Summary of key concepts 8.8 to reinforce your knowledge of these steps.

Having dealt with the theory and logic behind activity-based costing, let's look now at an example to see how overheads allocated under both the traditional absorption costing and activity-based costing methods produce different results.

EXAMPLE 8.10

Cookers Limited assembles microwave ovens and traditional electric cookers from parts produced by various suppliers. The following information relates to the costs and production of the two products:

	Microwave ovens	Electric cookers
Direct materials	£30	£52
Direct labour	£24	£48
Direct labour hours	3	7
Annual production	5,000	15,000
Annual number of set ups	15	30
Number of parts suppliers	14	6

Overheads	£
Output related overheads	160,000
Quality control	60,000
Set up related overheads	90,000
Supplier related overheads	50,000
Total overheads	360,000

The directors of Cookers Limited have traditionally allocated overhead costs to the two products on an absorption costing basis based on total labour hours. They have heard of activity-based costing and are wondering whether this would make a difference to the costing of their products. Selling prices for the company's two products are set at cost plus 25%, rounded to the nearest whole £.

Absorption costing

On an absorption costing basis, the first task will be to determine the total labour hours as the basis on which to allocate overheads: 5,000 microwaves each take three hours while 15,000 cookers each take seven hours of labour time to produce. Total labour hours are thus $3 \times 5,000 + 7 \times 15,000 = 120,000$ hours. The overhead absorption cost per labour hour is thus £360,000 ÷ 120,000 labour hours = £3 per labour hour.

Using this absorption cost rate gives us the following product costs on a traditional overhead absorption basis:

	Microwave ovens	Electric cookers
	£	£
Direct materials	30	52
Direct labour	24	48
Production overhead: $3 \times £3/7 \times £3$	9	21
Total cost	63	121
Selling price (cost + 25%, rounded)	79	151

Activity-based costing

In this question, our overhead costs have already been allocated to cost pools for output, quality control, set up and supplier related overheads. In order to allocate the costs in these cost pools to products, we now need to determine the cost drivers of each particular overhead cost pool.

Output related and quality control overhead costs will most logically be driven by the number of production units. The more of a particular product that is produced, the more that product drives those particular categories of overhead costs as more output is achieved and more quality control inspections take place.

Production units total up to 20,000 units (5,000 microwaves + 15,000 electric cookers) so the output related overhead per unit of production is £8 (£160,000 ÷ 20,000 units of production). Here, 15,000 × £8 = £120,000 output related overhead will be allocated to electric cookers and 5,000 × £8 = £40,000 will be allocated to microwaves.

Similarly, quality control costs are allocated over 20,000 units of production. The quality control overhead per unit of production is £3 (£60,000 ÷ 20,000 units of production). In this case £45,000 of quality control costs will be allocated to electric cookers (15,000 × £3) and £15,000 to microwaves (5,000 × £3).

The unit cost for set up overheads will be based upon the number of set ups consumed by each product. Microwaves have 15 set ups in the year and electric cookers have 30, so the total set up related overhead of £90,000 is divided by 45 (15 + 30) set ups to determine the cost per set up of £2,000. Thus, 15 × £2,000 = £30,000 set up related costs are allocated to microwaves and 30 × £2,000 = £60,000 set up costs are allocated to electric cookers.

In the same way, supplier related overheads will be driven by the number of suppliers for each product. The more suppliers or parts there are for a particular product, the more overhead cost will be incurred in ordering, handling and processing those parts from the different suppliers. There are 14 parts suppliers for microwaves and 6 for electric cookers, a total of 20 suppliers. The total supplier related overhead of £50,000 is divided by 20 to determine the cost per supplier of £2,500 and then 14 × £2,500 = £35,000 of supplier related costs allocated to microwaves and 6 × £2,500 = £15,000 supplier related costs allocated to electric cookers.

Summarising the above calculations, the total overhead cost allocated to each product is as follows:

Overhead	Allocation basis	Unit cost £	Microwave ovens £	Electric cookers £
Output related	Production	8	40,000	120,000
Quality control	Production	3	15,000	45,000
Set up related	Set ups	2,000	30,000	60,000
Supplier related	Number of parts suppliers	2,500	35,000	15,000
			120,000	240,000

These total overhead costs are now divided by the number of units of production and allocated to product costs to determine the total cost price of each product. The 5,000 microwaves drive £120,000 of related costs, so £24 is added to the cost of each microwave (£120,000 ÷ 5,000); £240,000 of overhead cost is driven by electric cookers, so £240,000 ÷ 15,000 = £16 is added as the unit overhead to the cost of electric cookers. These overhead allocation rates now give the following costs and selling prices.

	Microwave ovens £	Electric cookers £
Direct materials	30	52
Direct labour	24	48
Production overhead	24	16
Total cost	78	116
Selling price (cost + 25%, rounded)	98	145

As the above calculations demonstrate, overheads have been under allocated to microwaves and over allocated to electric cookers under the traditional absorption costing approach. Under activity-based costing, microwaves carry a much greater load of overhead cost compared with electric cookers and should sell for a much higher price. Once management are aware of this overhead cost burden attaching to microwaves, they can begin to think about reducing these costs. Most obviously, they should start by sourcing parts for microwaves from fewer suppliers to reduce the supplier related overheads allocated to this product and so lower the cost and selling price.

WHY IS THIS RELEVANT TO ME? Traditional absorption costing v. activity-based costing overhead allocation

To enable you as a business professional and user of accounting information to:

• Allocate overheads to products using both absorption costing and activity-based costing

• Make recommendations for ways in which product costs could be lowered to improve profitability and make product pricing more competitive

SHOW ME HOW TO DO IT Quite sure you understand how overheads are allocated to products using the activity-based costing methodology? View Video presentation 8.3 in the **online workbook** to see a practical demonstration of how this allocation of overheads was carried out.

NUMERICAL EXERCISES How well could you allocate overheads using the activity-based costing methodology? Go to the **online workbook** and complete Numerical exercises 8.7 to test out your ability to apply your knowledge to activity-based costing problems.

What advantages does activity-based costing bring in practice? Give me an example 8.4 provides a summary of a case study that illustrates the benefits of adopting an activity-based costing approach to product costing.

GIVE ME AN EXAMPLE 8.4   The practical benefits of implementing activity-based costing

Dr Lana Yan Jun Liu of the university of Newcastle University in the UK and Professor Fei Pan of the Shanghai University of Finance and Economics in China studied the implementation of activity based costing (ABC) at Xu Ji Electric Co. Ltd, a large Chinese manufacturing company (*Activity Based Costing in China: Research executive summary series*, vol. 7(13), 2011, CIMA). An ABC pilot was implemented in one of the main production divisions in December 2001, with two further attempts to expand the use of ABC in a subsidiary and in its sales functions in 2005 and 2008. The subsidiary ran trials with the system in 2009 and then in 2010 reported a record annual sales increase of 50% over 2009 together with a net profit margin increase of 13%. Following the introduction and roll out of the ABC system, management expressed confidence in the accuracy of the company's product costs while the marketing department was able to compete more quickly and more effectively in its market as quotes could now be given instantly. The cost information presented by the new system made staff much more aware of cost savings and the ways in which to achieve them while top management were able to use the ABC information to exercise informed control over sales expenses.

Source: www.cimaglobal.com

The limitations and assumptions of costing

So far, we have taken it for granted in this chapter that fixed and variable costs are easily identifiable and that they behave in exactly the way we have described. Thus, it has been stated that variable costs vary directly in line with production and that fixed costs for a period (usually one year) are fixed and do not vary at all in that period. However, as we shall see, these assumptions should be challenged and it is important to understand the limitations of costing analysis when you are considering what price to charge for a product or service.

Assumption 1: fixed costs are fixed

In all of our examples so far we have assumed that fixed costs will remain at the same level for all levels of production over that period. However, this might not be the case. Once a certain level of production is reached, additional fixed costs might have to be

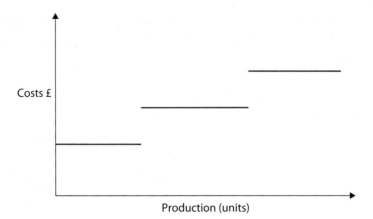

Costs £

Production (units)

Figure 8.7 Stepped fixed costs behaviour

incurred to cope with the increase in capacity. Thus, once Anna's production reaches, say, 2,000 chairs in a year, she might have to rent additional workshop space in which to increase production to more than 2,000 chairs. This would entail more rent, more business rates and more heating and lighting costs causing her fixed costs to jump when production reaches 2,001 units. This increased level of fixed costs would stay the same until production reached 4,000 chairs, at which point Anna would need to rent even more workshop space to produce 4,001 chairs or more. Fixed costs thus rise in steps, staying the same up to a certain level of production and then rising to a new level once the limit of production capacity is reached.

Fixed costs might thus behave in a stepped fashion as shown in Figure 8.7. In this figure, costs remain fixed for a given range of production and then they rise to a new level once the original range of production is exceeded, remaining steady over the next range of production. Once this increased range of production is exceeded, the fixed costs rise again. Thus, it might not be true to say that fixed costs remain fixed for a given period of time; they might only be fixed for a given range of production.

GO BACK OVER THIS AGAIN!   Totally confident you understand how fixed costs might rise in steps? Visit the **online workbook** and work through Exercises 8.8 to see how fixed costs will rise in steps as production increases.

Assumption 2: variable costs remain the same for all units of production

Our analysis in this chapter has been based on the assumption that variable costs remain the same for all units of production. A moment's thought should enable you to see that this assumption will probably not be true in the real world. Increased purchases of materials from suppliers will earn quantity or bulk discounts from those suppliers. The higher the level of direct material purchases, the bigger the discounts and so the lower the average price of those materials will become.

Similarly, we have assumed that the unit cost of labour for each item produced will remain constant. However, this assumption, too, will not hold in the real world as increased productivity will earn productivity bonuses for employees, thereby pushing up the average cost of each unit of production.

GO BACK OVER THIS AGAIN!   Reckon you understand how bulk discounts and productivity bonuses might affect the variable cost of materials and labour per unit of production? Try Exercises 8.9 in the **online workbook** to see how variable costs can change at different levels of production.

In situations in which production facilities use materials that fluctuate in price, such as metals and oil, the price of these direct materials can rise and fall during an accounting period. This makes forecasting very difficult but, again, it illustrates our point that variable costs will not necessarily remain the same for all units of production during an accounting period.

It is thus quite likely that the variable costs of production will not behave in the truly linear fashion we have assumed and that variable costs will not be represented by a sloping line of a perfectly even gradient as shown in Figures 8.1 and 8.3.

Assumption 3: costs can be determined with the required precision

An underlying assumption of all the discussions thus far has been that the costs of products and of activities in making those products can be determined with the necessary degree of accuracy in order to produce accurate selling prices. This is highly unlikely in practice as there are often under or over estimations of the time it will take to complete a given task, of the cost of materials used in the production of goods and of the amount of direct expenses used to make products. Material costs will vary in line with market prices or become cheaper or more expensive depending on the current supply of those materials to the market. Labour may become more expensive if the required skills are in short supply and so push up the direct labour cost of production.

In the same way, your estimate of how quickly you expected to work through this chapter and the online workbook may have proved completely wrong. Whatever your original estimate, it is likely to have been rather different from the actual time taken. Similarly, you may over or under estimate how much you will spend on a night out with your friends; again, though you have been out with them many times before, your expectations of what each evening out will cost will be very different from the costs in reality.

Cost accountants in industry may not achieve complete accuracy in their calculations and they may under or over estimate the cost of direct materials, the time that it will take direct labour to produce each unit of production and the overheads that will be incurred in a given period. Absolute accuracy is not going to be achieved and the best that can be done is a reasonably close estimate. As we shall see in Chapter 10, standard costing makes assumptions about what the costs of production should be and then uses variance analysis to explain the differences between what costs and income were expected to be and what they turned out to be.

WHY IS THIS RELEVANT TO ME?   The limitations and assumptions of costing

As a business professional and user of accounting information you should:

- Appreciate that product costing is not an exact science
- Understand the bases of product costing and how these give rise to its limitations
- Be equipped with the tools to critique solutions that are produced by product costing analysis in a real world context

---

CHAPTER SUMMARY

You should now have learnt that:

- Direct costs are those costs directly attributable to products or services
- Direct costs of production may be variable or fixed
- Variable costs are assumed to vary directly in line with levels of activity
- Fixed costs are assumed to be fixed for a given period of time
- Product and service costing is used by business organisations in making pricing decisions
- A cost card for a product is drawn up by splitting product costs into direct and indirect production costs
- Indirect production costs (overheads) are apportioned to departments to determine total overhead costs for each production department
- Overhead recovery rates for products are calculated on the basis of total departmental overheads and expected levels of production
- Service department overheads are reapportioned to production departments as part of each production department's total overheads
- Simple graphs can be drawn up to illustrate fixed, variable and total cost behaviour in a business context

- Using traditional absorption costing to allocate overhead costs to products may no longer be relevant in modern manufacturing environments and may result in the mispricing of products

- Activity-based costing allocates overhead costs to products on the basis of resources consumed by each product

- Costing is based on the assumptions that:

  - Fixed costs are and remain fixed for a given period of time or range of production

  - Variable costs remain the same for all units of production

  - Costs can be determined with the required precision

QUICK REVISION Test your knowledge with the online flashcards in Summary of key concepts and attempt the Multiple choice questions, all in the **online workbook**. www.oxfordtextbooks.co.uk/orc/scott/

END-OF-CHAPTER QUESTIONS

Solutions to these questions can be found at the back of the book from page 473.

> *Develop your understanding*

Question 8.1

Mantinea Limited manufactures various kitchenware products. The following direct costs are incurred in producing a batch of 2,000 food processors.

	£
Materials	22,500
Direct labour	16,500
Direct expenses	13,000

The factory overheads for the year are £3,000,000. Total machine hours for the year are 750,000 and each processor takes 4.5 hours of machine time to produce. The selling price of food processors is total absorption cost plus 50%.

Required

Calculate the total absorption cost of one food processor together with the selling price for each food processor produced by Mantinea Limited.

Question 8.2

Printers Limited has been asked by the local university press to quote for the printing of a new book. The print run will be for 2,000 books of 400 pages each. The costing records of Printers Limited contain the following information:

- Paper is bought from a local supplier. The local supplier provides paper at a price of 2,500 sheets for £9.
- Printing ink costs £57.50 per gallon, which is sufficient to print 20,000 pages.
- Covers for each book will be bought in at a cost of 66 pence for each book.
- Finishing costs per book are 50 pence.
- Production workers are paid an hourly rate of £12.50. The costing records show that a print run of 2,000 books would require 200 hours of production labour time.
- Printers' total overheads for the year are £500,000 and the normal production level of the business is 50 million pages per annum.
- Printers Limited's pricing policy is to set selling price at total absorption cost plus 25%.

Required

Calculate the price that Printers Limited should charge the local university press for the print run of 2,000 books.

» Take it further

Question 8.3

Applokia Limited is a manufacturer of smart phones. The company has the following costs for the month of September:

	£000
Factory rent	100
Factory manager's salary	38
Administration salaries	85
Marketing costs*	50
Plastic smart phone covers	250
Quality control staff salaries	75
Production line workers' salaries*	500
Chip assemblies for smart phones produced	1,498
Administration office rent	25
Marketing office rent	20
Factory rates	47
Power for production machinery	50
Factory lighting and heating	43
Administration lighting and heating	5
Marketing lighting and heating	4
Marketing department salaries	51
Batteries	242
Production machinery depreciation*	37

* These costs remain the same no matter how many or how few smart phones are produced and sold in the month.

Required

(a) For the above costs, state whether they are:

- Fixed or variable.
- Direct production costs, production overheads or period costs.

(b) Draw up a table that summarises the above costs into prime cost, production cost and total cost.

(c) If Applokia produces 130,000 smart phones in a month and selling price is total cost + 25%, calculate the selling price for each smart phone produced in September.

(d) If rival companies are selling similar products for £27, what margin will Applokia make on its costs per smart phone if it sells its smart phones at the same price as its rivals?

Question 8.4

Folly Limited produces novelty products. The products are produced on machines in the manufacturing department and they are then hand painted and finished in the finishing department. Folly Limited has forecast the following indirect production overheads for the year ended 31 January 2017:

	£000
Machinery maintenance staff salaries (manufacturing department)	100
Employees' salaries (painting and finishing department)	300
Employers' national insurance contributions for both departments	40
Rent and rates	60
Heating (the manufacturing department is not heated)	25
Lighting	25
Machinery depreciation	75
Canteen expenses*	56
Electricity for machinery	50
Insurance: machinery	25

* The canteen is in a separate building. The canteen rent, rates, heating, lighting, insurance and staff costs are all included in the figure for canteen expenses.

The manufacturing department has a capacity of 96,000 machine hours and 2,000 labour hours. The painting and finishing department has a capacity of 4,000 machine hours and 80,000 labour hours.

Additional information:

Recovery/absorption bases	Manufacturing	Painting and finishing
Area (square metres)	4,800	1,200
Value of machinery	£360,000	£15,000
Number of employees	5	15

Required

(a) Using the information provided, calculate the total production overheads to be allocated to the manufacturing and painting and finishing departments.

(b) Calculate the most appropriate overhead recovery/absorption rate for the manufacturing and painting and finishing departments and justify your choice of machine or labour hours as an absorption basis for the two departments.

(c) Using the rates you have calculated in (b), calculate the cost of the following job:

Novelty Christmas pixies: 5,000 units	
Direct materials and packaging	£10,000
Direct labour	£1,000
Machine time: manufacturing department	500 hours
Labour time: manufacturing department	5 hours
Machine time: painting and finishing department	10 hours
Labour time: painting and finishing department	1,000 hours

Question 8.5

Metal Bashers Limited produces steel fabrications for the construction industry. Steel girders and supports are cut to size and welded in the welding department and then painted in the paint shop before proceeding to the finishing department. Details of the overheads incurred by the three production departments are given below along with information on the two additional departments, the canteen and the service department. The canteen is used by all the employees of Metal Bashers Limited but the canteen staff are too busy to make use of the canteen facilities themselves. The service department repairs and cleans the machinery used in the three production departments. External catering equipment maintenance contractors service the canteen equipment.

	Welding	Painting	Finishing	Canteen	Service
Overheads	£100,000	£75,000	£43,000	£60,000	£42,000
Number of employees	15	5	6	2	4
Percentage usage of service department	40%	30%	30%		
Department labour hours	30,000	12,500	10,000		

Metal Bashers Limited is currently quoting for Job No 12359 which will require £1,500 of direct material, £2,000 of direct labour and £500 of direct expenses. It is estimated that job 12359 will use 120 hours of labour in the welding department, 50 hours in the painting department and 25 hours in the finishing department. Overheads are absorbed into jobs on the basis of direct labour hours in each department. The selling price for jobs is the total production cost of each job plus 40% of cost.

Required

(a) Calculate overhead recovery rates for the welding, painting and finishing departments.

(b) Calculate the production cost and selling price of job 12359.

Question 8.6

Playthings Limited produces two dolls houses, the standard and the deluxe. The direct costs and overhead information relating to these two dolls houses are listed below.

	Standard	Deluxe
Direct materials	£50	£76
Direct labour	£30	£42
Labour hours	5	7
Annual production	2,500	1,000
Direct materials orders	400	600
Employees	5	10
Machine hours	10,000	5,000
Annual number of set ups	15	35

Overheads

	£
Machining	45,000
Factory supervisor	30,000
Set up related overheads	50,000
Purchasing department costs	25,000
Total overheads	150,000

Playthings currently absorb their total overheads into their dolls houses on the basis of machine hours. The selling price of dolls houses is total cost plus 50%. The directors are concerned about a build up in the warehouse of standard dolls houses. Deluxe models are still selling well and the current price charged by Playthings is the most competitive in the market: their nearest rivals are selling the same type of dolls house for £300. Investigations have shown that competitors are selling comparable standard dolls houses for £165. You have been asked for your advice on the current costing system at Playthings and whether you can suggest a better way in which to allocate overheads to products together with any other suggestions you are able to provide.

Required

(a) Calculate the current total absorption cost and selling price for standard and deluxe dolls houses based on the absorption of total overheads on a machine hour basis.

(b) Determine suitable cost drivers for the four overhead cost pools

(c) Calculate the activity-based cost of standard and deluxe dolls houses and determine the selling price of each based on activity-based cost plus 50%.

(d) Given your results in (a), advise the directors on how they might reduce the cost of deluxe dolls houses in order to compete more effectively in the market.

Relevant costs, marginal costing and decision making

9

LEARNING OUTCOMES

Once you have read this chapter and worked through the questions and examples in both this chapter and the online workbook, you should be able to:

- Define contribution
- Use the distinction between fixed and variable costs to determine the costs that are relevant and those that are irrelevant in making short-term decisions
- Understand how analysis of contribution is used to make short-term decisions
- Undertake break-even analysis and determine the margin of safety
- Use marginal costing and contribution analysis to make a range of decisions aimed at maximising short-term profitability
- Understand the assumptions upon which marginal costing analysis is based

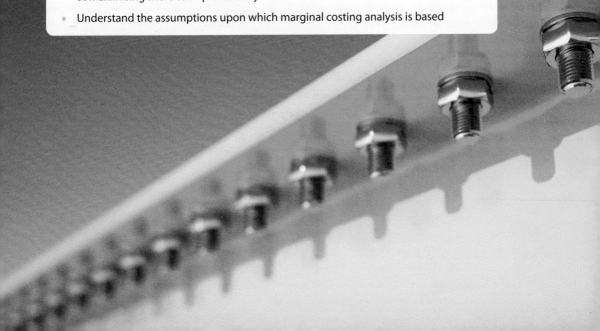

Introduction

The previous chapter discussed the various types of costs that organisations incur in their activities. These costs can be variable or fixed and can be categorised as direct costs of production, indirect costs of production and period costs. We also saw how fixed production overheads are absorbed into products to enable organisations to make pricing decisions to set the selling price at the right level so that an overall profit is generated from operations.

SUMMARY OF KEY CONCEPTS   Not quite sure about the terminology here? Revisit Summary of key concepts 8.3, 8.4 and 8.5 to revise direct, variable and marginal costs.

In this chapter, we will expand the analysis of costs to enable us to use this costing information in making decisions that will be valid in the short term (a period of one year or less). This analysis will be used to show which costs are relevant in short-term decision-making situations and which costs are not. In making these decisions, the profitability of the organisation will always be uppermost in our minds and we will be seeking to maximise the profits that can be made.

Decision making: not just selling price

Our focus in Chapter 8 was on determining a product's costs to make just one decision: what our selling price should be to enable us to cover all our expenses and make a profit. However, there are other decisions that entities need to make. For example:

- What minimum level of production and sales is required to ensure that all costs are covered and that losses are not incurred?
- What level of production would be required to make a certain target profit?
- How profitable will our business be if the economy takes a downturn and sales and profits fall?
- If we lowered our selling price as a marketing strategy, would we make more or less profit?
- Will orders from new customers be profitable if these customers are looking to buy our products at a price lower than our usual selling price?

- Is it more profitable to make components for our products ourselves or to buy those components in the open market?

- If there are several products that could be made, but there are only sufficient resources to make some of them, which product(s) should be made in order to maximise the short-term profits of the organisation?

The first step on the road to using costing to help us make these additional decisions is to look at the calculation and definition of **contribution**, the surplus that arises from the production and sale of one unit of product or service. As we shall see, contribution is a highly relevant consideration in the decision-making process and is a crucial step in determining those costs that are relevant and those costs that are irrelevant in a short-term decision-making context.

Contribution

We noted in the last chapter that fixed costs are assumed to be fixed over a given period of time and that variable costs vary with production or service delivery. Variable costs thus rise and fall directly in line with rises and falls in production as more or fewer goods or services are produced. However, no matter what the level of production is, fixed costs remain the same. Contribution for one unit of production and sales is the selling price less the variable costs of production (Figure 9.1).

Figure 9.1 Contribution

EXAMPLE 9.1

Taking the example of Anna from Chapter 8 (Example 8.6), the contribution from selling one dining chair is given as follows:

	£	£
Selling price for one dining chair		85.00
Materials (wood, glue, screws and sandpaper)	20.00	
Direct labour cost to produce one chair	25.00	
Total variable cost		45.00
Selling price – variable costs = contribution		40.00

So, with a selling price of £85 and a total variable cost of £45, Anna is making £40 contribution from each dining chair that she sells. Contribution is very similar to the gross profit that we considered in Chapter 3 (Different categories of profit), the selling price less the directly attributable costs of making that sale.

WHY IS THIS RELEVANT TO ME? Contribution

- To provide you as a business professional and user of accounting information with knowledge of the basic building blocks used in marginal cost decision making

- As a business professional, you will need to appreciate that contribution = selling price − the variable costs of production/service provision

---

SUMMARY OF KEY CONCEPTS   Use Summary of key concepts 9.1 to remind yourself of how contribution is calculated throughout your reading of this chapter.

Contribution v. absorption costing

But hold on, you might say. In Chapter 8, we used absorption costing and a production level of 1,000 dining chairs per annum to work out the total cost of one chair at £52.80, which would give a profit per chair of £85 − £52.80 = £32.20. This is different from the analysis undertaken above. Why is this?

The answer to this question lies in the distinction between fixed and variable costs. The variable costs rise and fall directly in line with production whereas the fixed costs do not. Remember that Anna set her production level at 1,000 chairs per annum and absorbed her fixed costs into each chair on this basis to enable her to set a selling price. However, the rate at which Anna absorbed her fixed costs into her production was based on a purely arbitrary assumption that production would be 1,000 chairs in a year. To illustrate the effect that this decision has had on the absorption cost of one chair, consider the following alternative scenarios in Example 9.2.

EXAMPLE 9.2

Anna's total fixed cost of £7,800 means that each of the 1,000 chairs was allocated a fixed cost element of £7,800 ÷ 1,000 chairs = £7.80. Anna could just as easily have set her production level at 2,000 dining chairs per annum and she would then have absorbed her fixed costs into production at the rate of £7,800 ÷ 2,000 chairs = £3.90 per chair. Alternatively, Anna might have been less optimistic about the level of production her workshop could achieve and set her expected production level at 500 chairs. In this case, her fixed costs would have been absorbed into production at the rate of £7,800 ÷ 500 chairs = £15.60 per chair.

The total fixed costs do not change, but the rate at which they can be absorbed into the cost of products does. This absorption rate is a decision for management and one that is arbitrary and completely dependent upon management's expectations of what represents a normal level of production over a given period of time.

Have a look now at Example 9.3. What are the differences between the two production and sales scenarios in this example? The fixed costs have not changed, but have remained the same for both the original and the increased levels of production and sales. Sales, however, have increased by the selling price of one additional dining chair (£85) and variable costs have increased by the cost of materials (£20) and the cost of direct labour (£25) for one additional dining chair. This has had the effect of both increasing contribution by £40 (selling price of £85 – materials cost of £20 – direct labour cost of £25) and increasing profit for the year by £40. Fixed costs have already been more than covered by the contribution generated by sales of 1,000 chairs per annum, so every additional unit of production and sales will add all of the contribution to the profit for the year.

EXAMPLE 9.3

While fixed costs in total are fixed, sales, variable costs and profits change with each additional unit of production and sales. To prove that this is true, consider what the profit would be if Anna produced 1,001 chairs rather than 1,000 chairs in a year.

	Selling 1,000 chairs in a year		Selling 1,001 chairs in a year	
	£	£	£	£
Sales: 1,000 × £85/1,001 × £85		85,000		85,085
Materials 1,000 × £20/1,001 × £20	20,000		20,020	
Direct labour 1,000 × £25/1,001 × £25	25,000		25,025	
Total variable costs		45,000		45,045
Selling price – variable costs = contribution		40,000		40,040
Fixed costs (rent, rates, heating and lighting)		7,800		7,800
Profit for the year		32,200		32,240

This approach, as we saw in Chapter 8, is called marginal costing: the costs and revenues of producing and selling one more or one fewer unit of product or service and the contribution that results from this increased or decreased activity at the margin. The contribution from each unit of production and sales contributes towards meeting the fixed costs of the organisation. The higher the sales, the higher the contribution and the more easily a business can generate a net profit (sales less all fixed and variable costs) by covering its fixed costs and providing a profit on top.

As a business professional and user of accounting information you need to be aware:

- That a product's absorption cost depends upon the production level used to absorb fixed costs into products or services
- That fixed costs do not change in line with production and sales
- That variable costs and contribution vary directly in line with production and sales
- Of the distinction between contribution and the absorption cost profit per unit of production and sales
- That, once fixed costs are covered, the contribution from every additional unit of production and sales is pure profit

GO BACK OVER THIS AGAIN!   Can you really distinguish between fixed and variable costs? Go to the **online workbook** and complete Exercises 9.1 to make sure you understand the distinction.

SUMMARY OF KEY CONCEPTS   Quite sure you understand contribution and marginal cost? Take a look at Summary of key concepts 9.1 and 9.2 to reinforce your understanding.

Relevant costs and sunk costs

Contribution analysis helps us to consider the short-term costs that are relevant and those that are irrelevant when a choice between two alternatives has to be made. Relevant costs are those costs that we will incur if we decide to follow a certain course of action. Relevant costs are the costs that influence our decision making.

As we have already seen, entities incur both fixed costs and variable costs in their activities. Fixed costs already incurred cannot influence future decision making as this money has already been spent and nothing you subsequently do will change those costs. Costs that have already been incurred and that do not influence future decisions are known as sunk costs. Sunk costs are past costs and have no further influence on decisions to be made for the future.

EXAMPLE 9.4

To illustrate this idea, let us consider an example. You are on holiday for a week in a seaside town. Your train fare has been paid and cost you £70 for a return ticket. Your hotel bill for the week is £500, which you have paid in advance. Now you have arrived you are free to decide what you want to do during your week. You have the option of going to the beach, going walking in the hills, visiting the local historical sites or travelling to another local town that is staging a sporting event you are keen to attend. You have £300 spending money for the week. What are the relevant costs and the sunk costs in this situation?

Your train fare and your hotel bill are now sunk costs, costs that have been paid and that have no further bearing on how you will spend your week. The only costs you will take into account now are the different costs of the four options in front of you and how much of your spending money each of these activities will use up. Going to the beach and going walking in the hills are likely to be less expensive alternatives compared with visiting the historical sites or attending the sporting event: both of the latter two options will require the purchase of entrance tickets whereas the former two options will not.

The past sunk costs will have no influence on your decisions about how to spend your time and money and so are disregarded when you consider your future options and actions. What counts now and what will influence your decisions are the costs and benefits that will be incurred enjoying any one of the four options available to you and the relative costs of each.

In the same way, fixed costs that an entity incurs, whether any activity takes place or not, are irrelevant to its short-term decision making. Costs relevant in short-term decision making are those costs that will be incurred as a result of making decisions and implementing a particular course of action. In Anna's case, the relevant costs are the variable costs of producing a larger or smaller number of dining chairs. The rent, rates and heating and lighting costs are all fixed and will be incurred regardless of the number of chairs produced and sold. All Anna has to do is to decide what level of production she needs to achieve in order to cover her fixed costs and what additional revenue she will generate and what additional costs she will incur in doing so.

WHY IS THIS RELEVANT TO ME? Relevant costs and sunk costs

As a business professional and user of accounting information, knowledge of relevant and sunk costs will enable you to:

- Distinguish between those costs that are relevant and irrelevant in a decision-making context
- Appreciate that costs that do not change as a result of a decision have no bearing on that decision
- Understand that fixed costs are irrelevant in short-term decision making

9

GO BACK OVER THIS AGAIN! Certain you can identify sunk costs and costs relevant to a decision? Go to the **online workbook** and complete Exercises 9.2 to reinforce your understanding of this distinction.

SUMMARY OF KEY CONCEPTS Confident you understand what relevant costs and sunk costs represent? Take a look at Summary of key concepts 9.3 and 9.4 to reinforce your understanding.

Relevant costs: opportunity cost

Another relevant cost that has to be taken into account is opportunity cost. This is the loss that is incurred by choosing one alternative course of action over another. Opportunity cost only applies when resources are limited: when there is no shortage of a resource, then there is no opportunity cost. This might seem like an academic exercise, but a moment's reflection will enable you to see that opportunity cost is involved in many everyday choices. See how the idea of opportunity cost works in Examples 9.5 and 9.6.

EXAMPLE 9.5

Before you started your university course, you were faced with a choice. You could spend three years gaining your degree or you could start work immediately and earn money straight away. Choosing to study for your degree involves the loss of income from employment for three years and the loss of being able to spend that money on whatever you wanted. However, by deciding to start work immediately, you faced the loss of three years studying a subject you enjoy and the improved personal and career prospects that such study would have brought to you. Time is limited and you can only make one of the two choices, so making either choice for your time involves an opportunity cost.

EXAMPLE 9.6

In a decision-making context in business, opportunity cost will be the next best alternative use for a resource. In a manufacturing business, raw materials can either be used for one project or another. That piece of steel that cost £100 could be used to produce a new steel fabrication to sell to a customer for £5,000 or it could be scrapped for £20. The opportunity cost of using the steel in the new fabrication is the next best alternative to using it, which is scrapping it. Therefore, the opportunity cost of using the steel in the fabrication is £20. The £100 purchase cost is irrelevant as this is a past cost, a sunk cost and a cost that has no further bearing on your decision. Your choice lies in using the steel in the fabrication to sell to a customer or scrapping it and receiving £20.

WHY IS THIS RELEVANT TO ME?   Relevant costs: opportunity costs

As a business professional and user of accounting information:

- You should appreciate that the opportunity cost of a decision is the next best alternative use for the resource used in that decision

- You need to be able to identify the opportunity cost of a resource as a relevant cost in a decision-making context

GO BACK OVER THIS AGAIN!   Opportunity cost sounds like a difficult concept, doesn't it? Go to the **online workbook** and complete Exercises 9.3 to see if you can decide what the opportunity costs of various decisions are.

SUMMARY OF KEY CONCEPTS   Sure you understand what opportunity cost represents? Take a look at Summary of key concepts 9.5 to reinforce your understanding.

As we have discovered earlier, relevant costs are those costs that affect short-term decision making. Let us now see how marginal costing and relevant costs are used in decision making by businesses.

Contribution analysis and decision making

Break-even point

Anna's first concern when setting up her business was to determine the selling price of her dining chairs. Her second concern (and the concern of many new businesses when they start up) is to calculate the number of units of production she will need to sell to cover all her costs, both fixed and variable. The point at which the revenue from sales = the total costs (Figure 9.2) is known as the break-even point, the level of sales that produces neither a profit nor a loss. Contribution analysis is relevant in determining break-even point. As we have seen, each additional unit of production and sales adds contribution towards the fixed costs so each sale is a further step towards covering those fixed costs. This is very similar to walking up a hill: the hill does not move (fixed costs) and each step you take (contribution) brings you closer to the top of the hill. Just as all your steps take you to the top, so the contribution from each sale takes an entity closer and closer to the break-even point.

This knowledge enables us to calculate the break-even point as:

$$\frac{\text{Total fixed costs}}{\text{Contribution per unit of sales}} = \text{Break-even point in sales units}$$

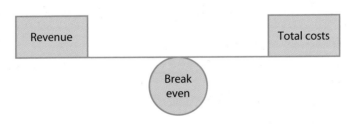

Figure 9.2 Break-even point: revenue = total costs

EXAMPLE 9.7

How many dining chairs does Anna need to sell to break even? We know from our calculations in Example 9.1 that the contribution from the sale of one chair is £40. We also know from our examples in Chapter 8 that Anna's annual fixed costs for her workshop are £7,800 (annual rent of £6,000, annual business rates of £1,000 and heating and lighting costs of £800, see Example 8.4).

Using the break-even formula given above, Anna's break-even point is thus:

$$\frac{£7,800}{£40} = 195 \text{ Dining chairs}$$

Anna needs to sell 195 chairs in order to break even. Using this figure, let's prove that she does in fact break even if she sells 195 chairs in the year.

	£	£
Sales of 195 dining chairs at £85 each		16,575
Materials cost for 195 dining chairs at £20 each	3,900	
Direct labour cost for 195 dining chairs at £25 each	4,875	
Total variable cost		8,775
Selling price – variable costs = contribution		7,800
Fixed costs (rent, rates, heating and lighting)		7,800
Profit/loss for the year		—

The above calculations prove that our formula for break-even point works and gives us the correct answer. For Anna, at the break-even point, her sales of £16,575 are exactly equal to her variable costs for the break-even level of sales (£8,775) plus the fixed costs that she is incurring during the year (£7,800). She makes neither a profit nor a loss at this point. Once she sells 196 chairs, the additional £40 of contribution is pure profit as there are no further fixed costs that must be covered before a profit can be made.

9

WHY IS THIS RELEVANT TO ME?   Break-even point

As a business professional and user of accounting information, knowledge of break-even point analysis will enable you to:

• Appreciate that a business breaks even when all of its costs, both fixed and variable, are exactly covered by the revenue from sales

• Calculate the break-even point in sales units and sales value in £s for different products and services

• Determine break-even points for new products or services that your company intends to introduce

SUMMARY OF KEY CONCEPTS Can you state the break-even formula and what break-even represents? Take a look at Summary of key concepts 9.6 to test your knowledge.

MULTIPLE CHOICE QUESTIONS Confident that you can calculate a break-even point from a given set of data? Go to the **online workbook** and have a go at Multiple choice questions 9.1 to try out your new knowledge.

Graphical illustration

Just as we drew graphs to illustrate the behaviour of fixed, variable and total costs in Chapter 8, so, too, can we draw a graph to show the break-even point. Break-even charts require three lines to be drawn: the line representing sales, the line representing fixed costs and the line representing total costs. Fixed costs remain the same throughout the period under review just as we saw in Chapter 8, but sales and total costs both rise directly in line with the level of sales and production activity. The point at which the sales line and total costs line intersect is the break-even point as shown in Figure 9.3. Beneath the break-even point losses will be made while above the break-even point profits are made.

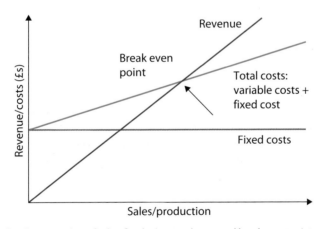

Figure 9.3 Graphical presentation of sales, fixed costs, total costs and break-even point

The margin of safety

As we have seen, the break-even point in sales tells us how many units of production we have to sell in order to cover all our fixed costs and make neither a profit nor a loss. However, it also tells us how far our projected sales could fall before we reach a break-even position. In Anna's case earlier, we found that she needs to sell 195 chairs before she breaks even. As her projected sales are 1,000 units for the year, she has a margin of safety

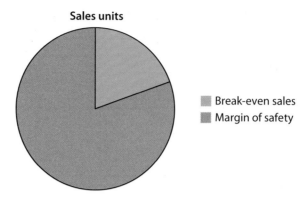

Sales units

- Break-even sales
- Margin of safety

Figure 9.4 Anna's break-even sales units and margin of safety

of 1,000 − 195 = 805 chairs (Figure 9.4). This means that her projected sales could fall by 805 chairs before she reaches her break-even point. The higher the margin of safety, the less an organisation is exposed to the risk of a fall in sales that could result in a loss-making situation. In Anna's case, even if her projected sales fell to 500 units, she will still make a profit as sales of 500 chairs are still well above the break-even point of 195 chairs.

WHY IS THIS RELEVANT TO ME? Margin of safety

To enable you as a business professional and user of accounting information to:

- Calculate the margin of safety for a product or service
- Appreciate that the larger the margin of safety, the less likely it is that a business will make a loss

---

SUMMARY OF KEY CONCEPTS Can you say what the margin of safety represents? Take a look at Summary of key concepts 9.7 to test your knowledge.

MULTIPLE CHOICE QUESTIONS Happy you can calculate break-even point and the margin of safety? Complete Multiple choice questions 9.2 in the **online workbook** to reinforce your learning.

Sensitivity analysis

Knowledge of the break-even point enables us to determine the profit or loss from any given level of sales.

EXAMPLE 9.8

Anna knows that selling her chairs at £85 each will give her a contribution per chair of £40. Her break-even point is 195 chairs, so what will be her profit or loss if she sells 180 chairs or 300 chairs?

We could calculate individual profit and loss accounts for sales of 180 chairs and 300 chairs to determine profit or loss at the two sales levels. However, as we know that the break-even point is 195 chairs, we can calculate Anna's profit or loss by subtracting the break-even point from the projected sales units and then multiplying the difference by the contribution per unit of sales.

Thus, using our calculations above, the loss at sales of 180 chairs will be $(180 - 195) \times £40 = £600$. Is this right? Contribution of £40 per chair will result in total contribution from sales of 180 chairs of $180 \times £40 = £7,200$. After deducting the fixed costs of £7,800, Anna's loss will be $£7,200 - £7,800 = £600$ so our calculation using the number of chairs from the break-even point is correct.

Similarly, at sales of 300 chairs, Anna's profit will be $(300 - 195) \times £40 = £4,200$. Proof: $300 \times £40 =$ a total contribution of £12,000. Deducting fixed costs of £7,800 gives a profit of £12,000 − £7,800 = £4,200.

WHY IS THIS RELEVANT TO ME?   **Break-even point and sensitivity analysis**

As a business professional and user of accounting information, knowledge of break-even point and sensitivity analysis will:

- Enable you to calculate quickly the profit or loss at a given level of sales

- Show you that the profit or loss depends on how far the level of sales differs from the break-even point

- Provide you with a useful analysis tool when evaluating the profit or loss from different levels of sales of products or services

---

SUMMARY OF KEY CONCEPTS   Certain you can state the relationship between break-even point and the profit or loss at a given level of sales? Take a look at Summary of key concepts 9.8 to test your knowledge.

MULTIPLE CHOICE QUESTIONS   How well can you use break-even analysis to determine profits and losses at a given level of production? Complete Multiple choice questions 9.3 in the **online workbook** to reinforce your learning.

Target profit

EXAMPLE 9.9

If Anna sells 1,000 chairs she will make a profit of £32,200 (Chapter 8, Example 8.7). However, she might consider that this profit does not compensate her sufficiently for the time and effort she has put into the business. She might decide that a profit of £40,000 is much more acceptable. How many chairs would she need to sell to achieve this target profit?

Break-even analysis will enable us to calculate the number of sales units required to achieve this target profit. Anna makes a contribution per chair sold of £40. Sales of her first 195 chairs will cover her fixed costs and enable her to break even. Therefore, she will need to sell a further $£40,000 \div £40 = 1,000$ chairs to make a net profit of £40,000. Adding these two figures together means that Anna will have to sell $1,000 + 195 = 1,195$ chairs to make a profit of £40,000.

Is this right? Let's check. 1,195 chairs produce a total contribution of 1,195 × £40 = £47,800. Deducting the fixed costs of £7,800 gives a net profit for the year of £47,800 − £7,800 = £40,000, so our calculations above are correct.

WHY IS THIS RELEVANT TO ME?   Break-even point and target profit

As a business professional and user of accounting information knowledge of break-even analysis will:

• Enable you to calculate a target profit

• Provide you with the technique to calculate the number of units of sales required to achieve a target profit

---

SUMMARY OF KEY CONCEPTS   Can you state the relationship between break-even point and the target profit? Take a look at Summary of key concepts 9.9 to test your knowledge.

MULTIPLE CHOICE QUESTIONS   Certain you can use break-even analysis to determine a target profit? Complete Multiple choice questions 9.4 in the **online workbook** to reinforce your learning.

Cost-volume-profit analysis

The techniques we have considered so far in this chapter are examples of cost-volume-profit (**CVP**) analysis. CVP analysis studies the relationship between costs, both fixed and variable, the level of activity, in terms of sales, and the profit generated. Do entities actually use these techniques in practice? Give me an example 9.1 describes the findings of a CIMA sponsored survey into the use of management accounting practices in small and medium sized entities in the UK.

GIVE ME AN EXAMPLE 9.1   Break-even point and cost-volume-profit analysis

Management Accounting Practices of UK Small-Medium-Sized Enterprises published in July 2013 investigated the management accounting techniques and practices used by a sample of small and medium sized enterprises in the UK. All of the small and medium sized enterprises used break-even analysis with managers having a rough idea of their fixed costs and the level of sales revenue required to cover these. However, while all of the medium sized entities surveyed used cost-volume-profit analysis, this technique was only used by a few of the small organisations in the survey: the view was taken that, as small entities are unable to exercise much control over the selling price that they can charge or the variable costs that they pay for inputs, respondents considered that they would gain little benefit from trying to evaluate alternative scenarios based on selling and cost prices.

Source: www.cimaglobal.com

9

High and low fixed costs

Anna has very low fixed costs and, consequently, a high margin of safety given that she aims to make sales of 1,000 units in a year. However, many businesses have very high fixed costs with very low levels of variable costs. Such businesses will have a very high break-even point and, as a result, a very low margin of safety. Such businesses are thus very vulnerable during a downturn in the economy and, if they do not collapse, they will incur very large losses before the recovery enables them to reach their break-even level of sales.

EXAMPLE 9.10

Premier League football clubs are an example of businesses with very high fixed costs. Players' wages are a very high proportion of each club's total costs. These wages are fixed and do not vary in line with the number of paying customers who support the team each week. Therefore, Premier League clubs need to fill their stadia for every match in order to cover these fixed costs and still make some sort of profit. Thus, their margin of safety is very low and they have made regular losses in recent seasons. However, changes in the rules imposed by football's governing body have forced clubs into cutting costs in order to make a profit, as shown in Give me an example 9.2.

GIVE ME AN EXAMPLE 9.2   English football's top flight back in profit after 15 years

English top-flight football has long been a sink-hole for cash. In the past decade, the Premier League's 20 clubs have racked up £2.6bn in losses, with the proceeds of lucrative television rights largely being spent on ever higher salaries for players.

Last season marked the start of a turnaround. On Thursday, Deloitte, the accounting firm, released figures showing the Premier League clubs made a collective pre-tax profit last season for the first time in 15 years. The £190m in pre-tax profit in 2013–14 was almost four times higher than the previous record of £49m in 1997–98

The figures, compiled from clubs' financial statements, showed that wage growth had slowed following the introduction of rules designed to curb the spending of owners with deep pockets.

Wages increased just 6 per cent to £1.9bn, although the season included the first year of the lucrative £3bn television rights deal signed in 2012. Wage costs as a proportion of revenue fell to their lowest level since the 1998–99 season.

According to Dan Jones, a partner at Deloitte's sports business group, the 'transformational' shift was due to new financial fair play rules, which required clubs to break-even.

Kadhim Shubber

Financial Times, 28 March 2015, page 14

9

Relevant costs and decision making

Marketing and selling price

EXAMPLE 9.11

Anna is currently selling her chairs at £85 each. A friend who is in marketing and who knows the market well has looked at her chairs and has suggested that she should reduce the selling price to £70. Her friend estimates that this reduction in selling price will enable her to increase sales by 50%. As the workshop has spare capacity, there would be no need to take on any additional workshop space and so fixed costs will not increase as a result of this decision. Similarly, the costs of materials and labour will not increase and will remain the same at £20 and £25 per chair, respectively. Anna is now trying to decide whether this marketing strategy will increase her profits or not.

To help her make this decision, we can draw up two costing statements as follows to assess the profits produced by the two different strategies, one for the original level of sales of 1,000 chairs at £85 and one for the expected level of sales of 1,500 chairs (1,000 × 150%) at £70.

	Selling 1,000 chairs at £85 each		Selling 1,500 chairs at £70 each	
	£	£	£	£
Sales 1,000 × £85/1,500 × £70		85,000		105,000
Materials 1,000 × £20/1,500 × £20	20,000		30,000	
Direct labour 1,000 × £25/1,500 × £25	25,000		37,500	
Total variable costs		45,000		67,500
Selling price − variable costs = contribution		40,000		37,500
Fixed costs (rent, rates, heating and lighting)		7,800		7,800
Profit for the year		32,200		29,700

However, if you have been following the argument so far, you will have realised that you could have used contribution analysis to solve this problem much more quickly. A selling price of £70 and a variable cost per chair of £45 gives a revised contribution of £70 − £45 = £25. Selling 1,500 chairs at £70 each would give a total contribution of 1,500 × £25 = £37,500. Fixed costs will not change, so the profit for the year after deducting fixed costs will be £37,500 − £7,800 = £29,700, lower than the current strategy of selling 1,000 chairs at £85.

How many chairs would Anna need to sell to make the new strategy as profitable as the current strategy? Again, contribution analysis will help us to determine the answer to this question. Current contribution from selling 1,000 chairs at £85 each is £40,000. The contribution per unit in the new strategy will be £70 − £45 = £25. To produce a total contribution of £40,000 from selling the chairs at £70 each would thus require sales of £40,000 ÷ £25 = 1,600 chairs. This is a large increase on current sales and Anna might well decide that she is quite happy selling 1,000 chairs at £85 each rather than taking the risk of trying to increase production by 60% for no increase in the profit generated.

WHY IS THIS RELEVANT TO ME? Relevant costs and evaluating the profitability of different marketing strategies

- As a business professional and user of accounting information you will be involved in pricing decisions for products
- Knowledge of relevant costs and contribution will enable you to evaluate different strategies in terms of their relative profitability and to choose the profit maximising pricing strategy

---

GO BACK OVER THIS AGAIN! Happy you can use contribution analysis to determine the profit that will arise from different marketing strategies? Have a go at Exercises 9.4 in the **online workbook** to make sure you can use contribution analysis in analysing such decisions.

Special orders

Thus far, we have assumed that selling prices will remain the same for all customers and for all of an organisation's output. In reality, this is rather unrealistic and most organisations will have different selling prices for different customers. When a new customer approaches an entity with a price they would be willing to pay for goods or services, the organisation has to decide whether to accept the new order or not at the customer's offered price. Again, contribution analysis will enable us to determine whether the new order is worth taking and whether it will add to our profit or not. An example will illustrate the techniques involved in decisions such as these.

9

EXAMPLE 9.12

Anna receives an enquiry from a charity that wishes to place an order for 50 dining chairs. They have seen examples of Anna's chairs and are very impressed by the quality of the workmanship and the sturdiness of the chairs, but they have been put off by the £85 selling price. They can only afford to pay £50 for each dining chair and have asked Anna whether she would be willing to sell the chairs at this price or not. Anna looks at her cost card for one chair (see Chapter 8, Example 8.6) and discovers that her absorption cost price per chair is £52.80. Her first thoughts are that if she sells the chairs at £50 each, she will be making a loss of £2.80 per chair. The workshop has spare capacity and the order could be accommodated without incurring any additional costs other than the variable costs of producing each chair. This additional order will not affect Anna's current production of 1,000 chairs. As the price offered by the charity is £2.80 less than the absorption cost per chair, Anna is considering refusing the order. Is she right to do so?

Let's see what Anna's total profit will be if she accepts the new order for 50 chairs at £50 each.

	£	£
Current sales: 1,000 chairs at £85 each		85,000
Additional sales: 50 chairs at £50 each		2,500
Total sales		87,500
Variable costs of production		
Materials: 1,050 chairs at £20 each	21,000	
Direct labour: 1,050 chairs at £25 each	26,250	
Total variable costs		47,250
Total contribution		40,250
Fixed costs (rent, rates, lighting and heating)		7,800
Profit for the year		32,450

Anna's original production level of 1,000 chairs produced a profit of £32,200. Accepting the new order alongside the current production of 1,000 chairs increases profit by £250 to £32,450. Anna expected to make a loss of £2.80 per chair (£50.00 selling price – £52.80 absorption cost per chair) so why is her profit not lower if she accepts the new order?

The answer again lies in the fact that the fixed costs are irrelevant to this decision; fixed costs are fixed for a given period of time and do not change with increased levels of activity. The only relevant costs are those that do change with the increase in the level of activity. These are the variable costs relating to production and the selling price for each additional chair produced. The selling price of £50 is £5 higher than the variable costs of production which are £45. Each additional chair in the new order adds £5 of contribution (and a total additional contribution and profit of £5 × 50 chairs = £250), the selling price less the variable costs, so, as the new order generates more profit for Anna, she should accept.

9

EXAMPLE 9.13

The decision above was made on the basis that Anna has spare capacity in her workshop and can easily add the new order to her existing level of production. Would your advice have been different if the additional order for 50 dining chairs had meant giving up 50 chairs of current production? Again, let's look at the effects of this decision and consider the relevant costs of making this decision to decide whether accepting the new order would be worthwhile in terms of the overall effect on profit.

If the new order were to be accepted and 950 full price chairs and 50 special price chairs produced, Anna's profit for the year would be as follows.

	£	£
Full price sales: 950 chairs at £85 each		80,750
Discounted sales: 50 chairs at £50 each		2,500
Total sales		83,250
Variable costs of production		
Materials: 1,000 chairs at £20 each	20,000	
Direct labour: 1,000 chairs at £25 each	25,000	
Total variable costs		45,000
Total contribution		38,250
Fixed costs (rent, rates, lighting and heating)		7,800
Profit for the year		30,450

As we can see, the decision now would be to reject the new order as profits fall by £1,750 from £32,200 for 1,000 full price chairs to £30,450 for 950 full price chairs and 50 special price chairs. How has this fall occurred? Our 50 special price chairs generate a contribution of £5 each, but to generate this contribution of £5, a contribution of £40 has been given up on each of the 50 full price chairs that this order has replaced. This has led to the fall in profit of £1,750 as follows: (£40 (contribution per chair given up) − £5 (contribution per reduced price chair gained)) × 50 chairs = £1,750. Thus, from a profitability point of view, no additional contribution is generated and so the order should be declined. More profitable production would have to be given up to take in a less profitable order so the charity would be turned away if there were no spare capacity in the business.

WHY IS THIS RELEVANT TO ME?   Relevant costs and special orders

To enable you as a business professional and user of accounting information to:

- Use contribution analysis to evaluate the profitability of new orders with a selling price lower than the normal selling price
- Appreciate that new orders should be accepted if they give rise to higher total contribution, add to total profits and make use of spare capacity
- Understand that where more profitable production is given up, orders at a special price should not be accepted

SUMMARY OF KEY CONCEPTS   Not sure whether to accept a special order or not? Take a look at Summary of key concepts 9.10 to review the criteria you should apply when evaluating such decisions.

NUMERICAL EXERCISES   Think you can use contribution analysis to determine whether a special order should be accepted? Have a go at Numerical exercises 9.1 in the **online workbook** to test your grasp of the principles.

Additional considerations

Other than additional income and costs and the effects on overall profit, what other considerations should be taken into account when making these special order decisions? First, as we have seen, entities faced with this choice should have spare capacity with which to fulfil orders at a lower selling price. Entities operating at full capacity have no idle resources with which to meet new orders at lower selling prices and so will not accept them. To do so would be to replace production generating higher contribution with production generating lower contribution. As a result, profits after fixed costs will fall.

Second, entities must also consider how easily information about a special price for a new customer could leak into the market. If existing customers found out that dining chairs are being supplied to a charity at £50 when they are paying £85, they are likely to demand a similar discount and this would have a very severe effect on Anna's profitability in the long run. Where information is likely to be available in the wider market, special orders should thus be declined as long-run profits will suffer as all customers will demand special prices.

In order to avoid rejected orders and hence lost profits, organisations can adopt a product differentiation strategy. Rather than producing and selling all their production under one label, producers have a quality label and an economy label to enable them to overcome the problem of all customers demanding the same reduced price. In the same way, supermarkets sell branded products from recognised manufacturers and they also sell goods with the supermarkets' own label at lower prices. Both quality and economy products might have been manufactured in the same production facility, but they are marketed in different ways.

On the positive side, should Anna accept the order from the charity, she might well receive some welcome publicity for her dining chairs as the charity recommends her business by word of mouth. This would amount to free advertising in return for her cutting the selling price for this special order and, in her attempts to expand her business, she might consider this short-term reduction in profits to be a worthwhile sacrifice for the longer-term growth of the business as a whole.

In such special order situations, after taking into account the additional considerations, the short-term decision will always be to accept the new order when this increases contribution and to reject the order when this results in a reduction in contribution.

WHY IS THIS RELEVANT TO ME?   Relevant costs and special orders: additional considerations

To enable you as a business professional and user of accounting information to:

- Appreciate that additional profit is not the only consideration in deciding whether to accept a special order or not

- Understand the non-accounting, business related considerations involved in making special order decisions

- Discuss and evaluate the non-accounting aspects relating to special order decisions

Outsourcing (make or buy decisions)

Relevant costs can also be used in making decisions on whether it is more economical to buy goods and services from external parties or whether it will be more profitable to produce or provide these goods and services in-house. Again, when making this decision, only those costs that change with the level of activity will be considered. Think about this in the following example.

EXAMPLE 9.14

Anna is expanding rapidly and has more orders for dining chairs than she can currently fulfil with two employees in her workshop. She has annual orders now for 1,500 dining chairs at a selling price of £85 each. She is considering whether to take on a third employee to help with these additional orders. Taking on this third employee will not increase her fixed costs as she has spare capacity in her workshop to accommodate another two workers and the new employee will be paid at the same rate for producing chairs as the existing employees. Another dining chair producer, Wooden Wonders, has offered to make the additional 500 dining chairs for Anna and to sell them to her at a cost of £49 each. Anna is delighted as this £49 cost is lower than her absorption cost per chair of £52.80, so she is expecting to make an additional profit of £1,900 (500 × (£52.80 −£49.00)) by buying in the chairs. She is ready to accept Wooden Wonders' offer, but, knowing how your advice has proved invaluable in the past, she has asked you whether it will be more profitable to take on the new employee or to contract out the manufacture of the dining chairs to Wooden Wonders.

Let us solve this problem in both a long and short way to show that both approaches give us the same answer and to provide you with a quick method of calculating the alternatives where profit maximisation is the objective. First, let us look at a comparison of Anna's sales, costs and profits if she either makes all of her production in-house or if she makes 1,000 chairs in her workshop and contracts out the additional 500 chairs to Wooden Wonders.

	Making and selling 1,500 chairs at £85 each		Making 1,000 chairs, buying in 500 chairs and selling 1,500 chairs at £85 each	
	£	£	£	£
Sales 1,500 × £85		127,500		127,500
Materials 1,500 × £20/1,000 × £20	30,000		20,000	
Direct labour 1,500 × £25/1,000 × £25	37,500		25,000	
Buying in 500 chairs at £49 each	—		24,500	
Total variable costs		67,500		69,500
Selling price − variable costs = contribution		60,000		58,000
Fixed costs (rent, rates, heating and lighting)		7,800		7,800
Profit for the year		52,200		50,200

Anna's expectation was of £1,900 more profit, gained by buying in 500 chairs at £49 each along-side the in-house production of 1,000 chairs. However, this option results in a profit for the year that is lower by £2,000 in comparison with making all the chairs in-house. How does this difference arise?

Using marginal costing and contribution analysis, you could have solved this problem much more quickly. Contribution from in-house production is £40 (£85 selling price less the £20 material costs less the £25 labour cost) whereas contribution from the bought in chairs is £36 (£85 selling price less the £49 purchase cost from Wooden Wonders). The difference in contribu-tion per chair of £4 (£40 – £36) multiplied by the 500 chairs that are bought in from Wooden Wonders gives the £2,000 lower profit if the second alternative course of action is chosen.

Fixed costs are again irrelevant in making this decision as these do not change with the level of production: only those costs that change with the decision should be taken into account alongside the contribution that will be gained from each alternative. Anna had forgotten that the fixed costs had already been covered by the production of 1,000 chairs and that the only relevant costs in this decision were the additional variable costs that she would incur. These would either be £45 if she produces the chairs in her own workshop or £49 if she buys them in from an outside supplier. Given that the outside supplier charges more for the chairs than Anna's employees can make them for, Anna will engage the third employee in the workshop as this is the more profit-able solution to her production problem.

WHY IS THIS RELEVANT TO ME?   Relevant costs and outsourcing (make or buy) decisions

To enable you as a business professional and user of accounting information to:

- Use contribution analysis and relevant costs to determine whether outsourcing decisions are more or less profitable than in-house production

- Appreciate that where profit maximisation is the only consideration, products should be bought in when additional contribution is generated by outsourcing production

---

SUMMARY OF KEY CONCEPTS   Quite sure you understand the relevant costs in making outsourcing decisions? Take a look at Summary of key concepts 9.11 to review the criteria you should apply when evaluating such decisions.

NUMERICAL EXERCISES   Convinced you can use contribution analysis and relevant costs to determine whether production should be outsourced or not? Have a go at Numerical ques-tions 9.2 in the **online workbook** to test your grasp of the principles.

Additional considerations

While profit maximisation is a valid aim for many organisations, costs saved and ad-ditional profit will be only one of the considerations in a make or buy or outsourcing situation. There are also various qualitative factors that have to be taken into account when making decisions of this nature as shown in Figure 9.5.

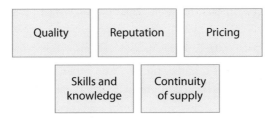

Figure 9.5 Factors to consider in outsourcing (make or buy) decisions

First, we will need to consider the products or services that the external provider will be offering us. Will these products or services meet our quality standards? Will the product or service be of the same quality or at the same level as our own in-house employees provide? Should the level of quality be lower, then further costs will arise. Products that use lower quality outsourced parts will break down more often and require more maintenance visits or refunds to dissatisfied customers. Services such as cleaning might not be carried out to the same exacting standards as the organisation sets for its own staff, leading to an increase in complaints and a loss of customers as they go to other product or service providers who are providing the quality that customers demand.

While the product or service might look cheaper to buy in now, there are longer-term hidden costs that have to be considered. These longer-term costs might be much more damaging for the organisation in terms of loss of reputation and they will often outweigh the benefit of saving a few pounds at the present time. In Anna's case, she would need to determine whether the chairs bought in from Wooden Wonders will be made to the same standards and with the same care and attention as that given by her own employees. Where the chairs are not made to the same standards, Anna will want to ensure that her own reputation for quality chairs is maintained by producing all her chairs in-house.

Second, the price might be cheaper now, but will it always be cheaper? Once our new supplier has captured our custom and we have closed down our own production facility, will the price rise and wipe out all the previous savings? Contracts for the supply of goods and services have to be drawn up very carefully to ensure that a short-term advantage is not suddenly eroded by a change in price.

Organisations will also need to consider their willingness to be reliant upon another entity. In this case, one organisation relies upon the other to maintain continuity of supply and continuity of quality. This may not always happen and disruptions at a supplier very soon affect production and sales to customers. Where components are produced in-house, there is a much greater level of control over production and, hence, sales. Organisations might prefer to maintain their self-reliance rather than handing over responsibility for their parts, sales and production to other businesses.

Similarly, handing over production to another organisation will lead to a loss of skills within the business and an inability to reintroduce production at a later date should

9

the current supply contract prove inadequate. Entities will lack in-house knowledge of how their products work and be unable to provide customers with advice on these products. When an organisation closes down part of its production facility and makes workers redundant, there is a knock-on effect on other workers. Job losses weaken employee morale, job satisfaction and productivity. These knock-on effects also have an effect on profitability as the current workforce becomes demoralised and more concerned about their own job security than completing the work in hand. Anna's two employees might become concerned about the continuity of their employment with Anna if production is outsourced. Concerned employees are distracted employees and they will not be concentrating on the quality of what they are producing but on whether they will still be employed in a year's time.

Give me an example 9.3 shows how Toyota overcomes the potential difficulties of outsourcing through very close relationships with its suppliers.

GIVE ME AN EXAMPLE 9.3   Outsourcing at Toyota

The Japanese car company, Toyota, prizes high quality at a low price. However, the company outsources 70% of the components for its cars to suppliers and produces just 30% of the components in its own production facilities. In order to ensure the quality of the products produced by its suppliers, Toyota adopts a policy of strong relationships and collaboration with its suppliers through the Toyota Production System. Toyota's high quality has been achieved as a result of the collaborative advantage it enjoys with its suppliers. Toyota regularly evaluates its suppliers' performance and provides suggestions on how they could improve their operations. However, this is not a one way relationship: the company also invites its suppliers to evaluate Toyota and to provide their suggestions for operational improvement. This continuous improvement approach enables the Toyota Production System to deliver the high quality products demanded by both Toyota and its customers despite the fact that most of its car parts are not manufactured in-house.

Source: www.scribd.com/doc/53016595/Vertical-Integration-or-Outsourcing-Nokia-Ford-Toyota-IBM-Intel-Toshiba-Matsushita#scribd

---

WHY IS THIS RELEVANT TO ME?   Relevant costs and outsourcing (make or buy) decisions: additional considerations

As a business professional and user of accounting information you should:

- Appreciate the additional strategic factors that must be taken into account when an outsourcing decision is being made
- Understand that cost reduction and profit are not the only grounds on which to base make or buy/outsourcing decisions
- Be able to discuss and evaluate non-accounting, business related considerations when undertaking make or buy/outsourcing decisions

Limiting factor (key factor) analysis

Contribution analysis can also be used in making decisions to maximise short-term profits where organisations are facing a shortage of direct material or direct labour. In this situation, contribution analysis can be used to determine which products generate the highest contribution per unit of material or labour input in order to maximise profits. Those products that generate the highest contribution per unit of limiting factor will be produced, while those that produce a lower contribution per unit of limiting factor will be discontinued in the short term. Limiting factor analysis is only relevant where two or more products are produced. If only one product is produced, then there is no decision that has to be made, manufacturers will just produce their one product up to the maximum number that they can based upon the limitations imposed by the shortage of direct materials or direct labour. Let us consider an example of how this would work and the steps that would be undertaken to determine which products produce the highest level of contribution per unit of limiting factor.

EXAMPLE 9.15

Anna's business has grown and is now a very successful producer of wooden dining chairs, small wooden coffee tables and wooden kitchen cabinets. However, a new government has come to power in the country from which she sources her supplies of wood. This new government has introduced restrictions on the export of timber as new environmental policies are put in place to preserve rather than exploit the local forests. Anna is thus currently facing a shortage of wood from her suppliers because of these restrictions. While she investigates new production methods to enable her to use wood from other sources, Anna is looking to maximise her short-term profit and needs help in deciding which products she should make to achieve this.

The selling price and variable costs for her three products are as follows.

	Dining chairs	Coffee tables	Kitchen cabinets
	£	£	£
Selling price	85.00	50.00	80.00
Materials: wood	(18.00)	(12.60)	(10.80)
Materials: other	(2.00)	(5.40)	(9.20)
Direct labour	(25.00)	(18.00)	(30.00)
Contribution	40.00	14.00	30.00

All three products use the same type of wood at a cost of £1.80 per kg. The new government in the country of her supplier has allocated Anna a maximum of 12,600 kg of wood for the next three months. Anna has thought about the figures above and is considering diverting all her production into dining chairs as these provide the highest total contribution of the three products and she thinks that producing just chairs will maximise her profit for the period. Is Anna right? If she is not right, which (or which combination) of the three products should she produce to maximise her profits in the next three months?

In problems of this nature you should work through the following three steps.

Step 1: calculate the quantity of limiting factor used in the production of each product

In order to maximise contribution when there is a limiting factor, the first step is to determine the usage that each unit of production makes of that limiting factor. Given that wood costs £1.80 per kg and using the product costing details above, each of the three products uses the following amounts of material:

Dining chairs: material usage: £18.00 ÷ £1.80 = 10 kilograms

Coffee tables: material usage: £12.60 ÷ £1.80 = 7 kilograms

Kitchen cabinets: material usage: £10.80 ÷ £1.80 = 6 kilograms

Step 2: calculate the contribution per unit of limiting factor delivered by each product

The next step is to determine how much contribution each product generates per unit of limiting factor. This calculation divides the total contribution for each product by the number of units of limiting factor used in the production of each product. The products are then given a ranking: the highest contribution per unit of limiting factor is placed first and the lowest contribution per unit of limiting factor comes last.

Using the information about Anna and our calculations in Step 1, the three products generate the following contributions per unit of limiting factor:

	Contribution per unit of limiting factor	**Ranking**
Dining chairs	£40/10 kg per unit = £4 of contribution per unit of material used	2
Coffee tables	£14/7 kg per unit = £2 of contribution per unit of material used	3
Kitchen cabinets	£30/6 kg per unit = £5 of contribution per unit of material used	1

As the above calculations show, the highest contribution per unit of limiting factor is delivered by kitchen cabinets. These use 6 kg of material in each finished unit and deliver a total contribution of £30 per product. Dining chairs are ranked second with the second highest contribution per unit of limiting factor, while coffee tables are ranked last out of the three products, with a contribution per unit of limiting factor of only £2.

Step 3: calculate the contribution maximising production schedule

If Anna wishes to maximise her contribution and profit, she will now need to determine how much of the limiting factor is available to use and the most profitable products to produce. In Anna's business, if demand for each product is not limited, then she would just produce kitchen cabinets as each kitchen cabinet delivers £5 per unit of limiting factor used. A more likely scenario would be that demand for each product would be limited and so the contribution maximising production schedule will involve producing all of the product delivering the highest contribution per unit of limiting factor first, then producing the product delivering the second highest contribution per unit of limiting factor next and so on until all of the limiting factor is used up.

Anna estimates that demand for each product for the next three months will be as follows: What will the profit maximising production schedule be?

Dining chairs:	580 units
Coffee tables:	500 units
Kitchen cabinets:	900 units

As we have seen, she should produce as many kitchen cabinets as she can, as this product gives her the highest contribution per unit of limiting factor. She should then produce as many dining chairs as possible and finally produce coffee tables up to the total amount of material available, the limiting factor. Her production schedule and contribution will look like this:

	(a)	(b)	(c)	(d)	(e)	(f)
			((a) × (b))	(12,600 − (c))		((b) × (e))
Product	Kg of material per unit	Quantity produced	Kg of material used	Kg of material remaining	Contribution per unit	Total contribution
	kg	units	kg	kg	£	£
Cabinets	6	900	5,400	7,200	30	27,000
Chairs	10	580	5,800	1,400	40	23,200
Tables	7	200	1,400	—	14	2,800
Total material used (kg)			12,600		Total contribution	53,000

The above production schedule shows that demand for kitchen cabinets and chairs can be met in full as there is sufficient material to make the 900 kitchen cabinets and 580 chairs that customers require. However, there is only sufficient material remaining to produce 200 of the 500 coffee tables that customers are looking to buy, so production of these will be limited if Anna adopts a profit maximising strategy. This strategy will produce a total contribution of £53,000.

SHOW ME HOW TO DO IT!   Are you sure that you understand how the above allocation of limiting factor was made to the three products? View Video presentation 9.1 in the **online workbook** to see a practical demonstration of how this allocation between the three products is carried out.

What of Anna's intention to produce only chairs? How much contribution would this production scheme have produced? As there are 10 kg of wood in each chair, 12,600 kg of wood would have produced 1,260 chairs. The contribution from one chair is £40, so 1,260 chairs would produce a total contribution of 1,260 × £40 = £50,400. This is a good contribution, but it is not as high as the contribution produced by using the

9

contribution per unit of limiting factor calculated above. Given that demand for dining chairs is only 580 units, Anna will have a lot of chairs in stock at the end of the three months and these unsold chairs, too, will limit her profit for the three-month period.

The above production schedule shows what the maximum profit could be, given the limiting factor and the current maximum demand. However, in reality, it would be very difficult for Anna to stick to this schedule as her customers will be ordering her products in the expectation that she will fulfil all those orders. It would not be easy to refuse an order for coffee tables from a current customer on the grounds that she could not produce those products as they were not profitable enough. Such an excuse would lead to the loss of that customer, who would then source coffee tables from another supplier. In the longer term, the loss of customers could lead to a loss of reputation with all the attendant effects that this would have on sales and profits. Therefore, while the profit maximising schedule is a useful technique to determine what maximum profit could be in times of shortage, considerations other than cost and profit will tend to determine what is produced to meet customers' expectations of the organisation.

WHY IS THIS RELEVANT TO ME?   Relevant costs and limiting factor analysis

To enable you as a business professional and user of accounting information to:

- Use contribution analysis and relevant costs to devise contribution and profit maximising strategies when resources are scarce
- Understand that this technique has certain limitations in the real world

SUMMARY OF KEY CONCEPTS   Do you remember the steps to follow when calculating profit maximising strategies in a limiting factor situation? Take a look at Summary of key concepts 9.12 to review the steps you should follow when making such decisions.

NUMERICAL EXERCISES   Can you use contribution analysis and relevant costs to determine which products should be produced to maximise contribution when resources are scarce? Have a go at Numerical exercises 9.3 in the **online workbook** to test whether you have fully grasped the techniques involved.

Relevant costs, marginal costing and decision making: assumptions

The decisions discussed and illustrated above all seem to be very straightforward and easy to apply. However, in practice, difficulties will be encountered. This is because of the assumptions upon which marginal costing analysis is based. These assumptions can be summarised as follows:

- First, it has been assumed that the variable costs of a product can be identified by a business with the required level of precision to enable accurate calculations to be made.

- Second, fixed costs for a period are assumed to be completely predictable and unchanging.

- Variable costs are assumed to be linear, that is, variable costs vary directly in line with production. In reality, the purchase of more materials will result in bulk discounts causing the average cost of materials used in each product to fall (see Chapter 8, Assumption 2: variable costs remain the same for all units of production). Similarly, additional units of production might well entail the payment of overtime premiums or bonuses to existing staff, causing the direct labour cost to jump when higher levels of production are reached.

- Prices have been assumed to be stable whereas, in reality, prices of materials change all the time depending on whether there is a shortage or an oversupply of those materials in the market. For example, in a delivery business, the price of fuel to run delivery vans changes on a daily basis.

- In break-even analysis, it is assumed that only one product is produced. Once two or more products are produced, the techniques behind break-even analysis are invalidated by the presence of two sets of variable costs and two contributions, making it impossible to determine the break-even point for one set of fixed costs.

Nevertheless, despite these limitations, relevant cost analysis does have some application in practice, as illustrated in Give me an example 9.4.

GIVE ME AN EXAMPLE 9.4   Relevant costing for decisions in practice

The July 2009 CIMA report,

Management accounting tools for today and tomorrow, surveyed the current and intended usage by business of more than 100 management accounting and related tools based on a questionnaire completed by 439 respondents from across the globe. The findings indicated that relevant costing for decisions was used by small (43%), medium (48%), large (50%) and very large (44%) companies worldwide. However, product/service profitability analysis was the preferred profitability analysis tool across all companies surveyed. Of those intending to introduce relevant costing for decisions in the coming year, only a small % of UK respondents aimed to adopt this technique while much higher %s of respondents across all regions were planning to introduce product/service profitability analysis.

Source: www.cimaglobal.com

WHY IS THIS RELEVANT TO ME?   Relevant costs, marginal costing and decision making: assumptions

To enable you as a business professional and user of accounting information to:

• Appreciate the assumptions upon which marginal costing and decision-making analysis are based

• Develop an insight into the limitations posed by these assumptions

CHAPTER SUMMARY

You should now have learnt that:

• Contribution = sales − variable costs

• The concept of opportunity cost is used to determine the benefits lost by using a resource in one application rather than in another

• Fixed costs are not relevant when making short-term decisions as these costs do not vary with changes in the level of activity in the short term

• The only costs relevant in short-term decision making are those that change in line with levels of activity

• The break-even point is calculated by dividing fixed costs by the contribution per unit

• The margin of safety is the number of units of sales above the break-even point: the higher this number, the higher the margin of safety

• Knowledge of the break-even point enables entities to calculate the profit or loss from any given level of sales

• Contribution analysis enables entities to determine the effect of different pricing strategies on short-term profits

• Special orders should be accepted when they increase contribution

• Make or buy decisions can be made on the basis of the marginal costing technique

• Calculation of the contribution per unit of resource enables entities to devise profit maximising strategies when resources are limited

• Users of the costing techniques discussed in this chapter have to be aware of the advantages and limitations of marginal costing

QUICK REVISION   Test your knowledge with the online flashcards in Summary of key concepts and attempt the Multiple choice questions, all in the **online workbook**. www.oxfordtextbooks.co.uk/orc/scott/

END-OF-CHAPTER QUESTIONS

Solutions to these questions can be found at the back of the book from page 483.

> *Develop your understanding*

Question 9.1

Define the following terms

(a) Contribution

(b) Relevant costs

(c) Irrelevant costs

(d) Sunk costs

(e) Opportunity cost

(f) Break-even point

(g) Margin of safety

(h) Target profit

Question 9.2

Podcaster University Press is a small publishing company producing a range of introductory text books on a range of academic subjects for first year undergraduate students. The company's marketing department is considering reducing the selling price of text books to generate further sales and profit. The company's text books currently retail at £30 each. Variable production costs are £10 per book and Podcaster University Press has annual fixed costs of £3,000,000. Current sales of text books are 200,000 per annum. The marketing department has forecast that a £5 reduction in the selling price of each text book will boost annual sales to 275,000 books whereas decreasing the selling price to £21 would increase annual sales to 360,000 books.

Required

Using contribution analysis, evaluate the proposals of the marketing department and advise the company on whether the two proposals would be financially beneficial or not.

> *Take it further*

Question 9.3

Big Bucks University is planning to offer a series of professional accounting course classes. The fee payable for this professional accounting course is £400 per student per module. The university has already allocated lecturers currently employed at the university to each class and has determined that lecturers are being paid £60 per hour for the 60 hours required to deliver each module. The lecturers will be paid whether any students are enrolled on each module or not and they can be diverted to other classes if the professional accounting course modules do not run. Books and handouts are provided to each student at a cost of £100 per student per module. The university allocates £1,200 of central overhead costs for the year to the room used in the provision of each module. The university has asked for your help in deciding on the number of students that should be recruited to each module.

Required

(a) State which costs are relevant to the decision as to how many students to recruit to each module.

(b) Determine how many students the university should recruit to each module to ensure that each module breaks even.

(c) What is the margin of safety if the university recruits 25 students to each module?

(d) Calculate the profit or loss the university will make on each module if 14 students or 30 students are recruited to each module.

(e) What will the break-even point be if the university decides to charge £340 per module instead of £400?

Question 9.4

Gurjit Limited produces and sells ink jet printers. The selling price and cost card for each printer are as follows:

	£	£
Selling price		40.00
Direct materials	9.50	
Direct labour	11.25	
Direct expenses	3.65	
Fixed overhead	5.60	
Total cost of one ink jet printer		30.00
Profit per ink jet printer sold		10.00

Currently, production and sales are running at 5,000 printers per annum. The fixed overhead allocated to each printer has been based on production and sales of 5,000 units. However, because of the popularity of the product and a strong advertising campaign, the directors of Gurjit Limited are expecting sales to rise to 10,000 units. The directors are currently reviewing the costs and profits made by printers along with their expectations of future profits from the increased sales. One option open to Gurjit Limited is to outsource production of their printers to another company. It is estimated that any outsourcing of production would lead to an increase in total fixed overheads of £40,000 to enable Gurjit Limited to ensure the quality of printers produced outside the company. The directors have a quote from Anand Limited to produce all 10,000 ink jet printers for £200,000. The directors of Gurjit Limited are considering whether to accept this offer and have asked for your advice.

In order to advise the directors of Gurjit Limited on whether to accept the offer from Anand Limited, you should:

(a) Calculate the current profit made at a level of sales and production of 5,000 ink jet printers per annum.

(b) Calculate the profit that will be made if sales and production rise to 10,000 printers per annum.

(c) Calculate the profit that will be made if sales and production rise to 10,000 printers and production of printers is outsourced to Anand Limited.

(d) Advise the directors of Gurjit Limited whether to outsource production to Anand Limited and what additional factors they should take into account in this decision other than costs and profit.

Question 9.5

Diddle Limited produces ornamental statues for gardens whose selling price, costs and contribution per unit are as follows:

	Clio	Diana	Athena
	£	£	£
Selling price	81	58	115
Materials (clay)	(30)	(12)	(42)
Direct labour	(15)	(27)	(30)
Variable overheads	(6)	(3)	(8)
Contribution	30	16	35

The same specialised clay is used in all three statues and costs £6 per kg. The company faces a shortage of this clay, with only 3,000 kg available in the next month. The board of directors is therefore considering which statues should be produced in order to maximise contribution in the coming month. The sales director has suggested that production should concentrate on Athena as this statue has the highest contribution of the three products. Is the sales director right?

Maximum predicted demand for the three products for the coming month is as follows:

Clio: 198 units

Diana: 900 units

Athena: 200 units

9

10 Standard costing and variance analysis

LEARNING OUTCOMES

Once you have read this chapter and worked through the questions and examples in both this chapter and the online workbook, you should be able to:

- Appreciate that a standard cost is an expected cost rather than an actual cost
- Understand how a standard cost is calculated
- Calculate direct material total, price and usage variances
- Calculate direct labour total, efficiency and rate variances
- Calculate sales volume and price variances
- Calculate fixed overhead expenditure variance
- Calculate variable overhead total, expenditure and efficiency variances
- Understand the function of standard costing as an accounting control device
- Understand that variances are merely an indication of a problem that requires further management investigation to establish and rectify the causes

Introduction

In the last two chapters we have looked at the different types of cost that organisations incur in their operations and how the distinction between fixed and variable costs can be used to make decisions that aim to maximise the short-term profitability of an organisation. It is now time to turn to the second function of management accounting: planning. Initially, this involves the use of accounting data to make predictions and forecasts for the future. Once actual outcomes are known, then comparison of actual results with these forecasts is used as a means to control an organisation's operations. The next chapter will consider budgeting in much greater detail and look at how the use of budgets and the comparison of outcomes with expectations enable an entity to control its operations, to enhance positive trends and to take action to correct problems as they arise. In this chapter we will consider the use of the related technique of standard costing and how the analysis of divergences from the standard can be used to identify problems requiring management's attention.

What is standard costing?

The last two chapters have considered product costing. As we have seen, this process takes up a lot of time as information is gathered about the inputs of direct material, direct labour, direct expenses and indirect production overheads and as costs are allocated to products and services. This information is then used to determine selling prices for products so that a profit is made. However, prices of inputs change rapidly. The cost of materials rises and falls as users demand more or less of a particular raw material, wages rise each year, electricity and gas prices go up and down as the weather warms or cools. To change all these prices on a daily or weekly basis would be time consuming in the extreme and the task would eventually overwhelm the individuals performing this role. What is needed is an efficient, predictive tool that provides a reasonably accurate estimate of what the cost of a product or service should be over a given period of time. Variations from this estimate can then be analysed to determine whether the estimate needs revising or not. This reasonably accurate estimate can be provided by standard costing.

A standard cost card will include all the direct materials, direct labour, direct expenses, variable overheads and an allocation of fixed overheads that go into a product or service. These standard costs are the expected costs of that product and the standard cost card will also include the expected selling price for each product, along with the standard profit. Standard costs are derived from numerous observations of an activity over time and represent an expectation of costs incurred by and income generated from mass produced products and services. As the number of observations

10

increases, so the standard is revised and the accuracy of the estimate becomes much closer to the actual cost of each product.

Standard costs recognise that goods are made up of a fixed set of inputs, whether materials, labour or overheads. These inputs are measured and costed and then summarised to present the total costs of producing one item of output. As an example, consider this book. Variable costs will include the paper, the ink, the covers, the binding, the power to drive the printing machinery and the handling of each book as it comes off the press. Fixed costs to be allocated across each print run will include typesetting, editing, development, website construction and maintenance and advertising and marketing. All these costs can be readily determined as a result of Oxford University Press's vast experience of printing books and the staff's detailed knowledge of the costs of book production. All the costs involved can be summarised to calculate the cost of one book and this is then the standard cost of that book. Management will set an expected selling price based on the costs incurred and the anticipated market for the book, and this becomes the standard selling price.

WHY IS THIS RELEVANT TO ME?   Standard costing

To provide you as a business professional and user of accounting information with:

- A basic understanding of what standard costing involves and how it works

- A predictive accounting tool you can use in the future to forecast the costs and profits of mass produced products and services

---

GO BACK OVER THIS AGAIN!   Confident you can say what standard costing is? Go to the **online workbook** and complete Exercises 10.1 to make sure you understand the aims and objectives of standard costing.

Variance analysis

Standard costs just represent expectations, the expected costs and revenues from each book produced and sold. What happens when the reality turns out to be different from the expectation? When the actual costs and revenues are known, then a comparison of the standard expected results and the actual results is undertaken. The differences between the standard costs and revenues and the actual figures are known as variances. These variances are calculated and then used to explain the difference between anticipated and actual outcomes. In the case of book production, the cost of materials might be more than expected as a shortage of the expected quality of paper might have resulted in more expensive paper being used. Ink prices might have been higher or lower than forecast, a rise or fall in power costs might have resulted in changes to the anticipated printing cost, the selling price might have been set higher to cover these additional costs and so on. Explanations for variances will be sought as a means of controlling operations. Where actual costs are significantly different from the standard, the standard can be updated to produce more accurate information in the future.

What use do organisations across the world make of variance analysis? Give me an example 10.1 describes the findings of a 2009 CIMA survey.

GIVE ME AN EXAMPLE 10.1   Variance analysis

The July 2009 CIMA report,

Management accounting tools for today and tomorrow, surveyed the current and intended usage by business of more than 100 management accounting and related tools based on a questionnaire completed by 439 respondents from across the globe. The 4th most commonly used technique in practice was variance analysis. When used as a costing tool, variance analysis was undertaken by 73% of respondents, the most popular costing tool in use. Over 60% of small companies in the survey used variance analysis while more than 80% of large companies employed this technique.

Source: www.cimaglobal.com

WHY IS THIS RELEVANT TO ME?   Variance analysis

To enable you as a business professional and user of accounting information to:

- Understand how expected and actual costs and revenues are compared to explain deviations from forecast performance

- Appreciate that variances between expected and actual costs and revenues can lead to improvements in standards

- Give you an initial appreciation of the roles that standard costing and variance analysis perform in the control of business operations

---

GO BACK OVER THIS AGAIN!   How well have you grasped what variance analysis is? Go to the **online workbook** and complete Exercises 10.2 to make sure you understand how variance analysis works and what it aims to achieve.

10

Different standards

The different types of standards are shown in Figure 10.1. Setting standards requires thought about expectations and what you want to achieve through the use of standards. You might hope that your favourite sports team will win all its matches, win all the trophies for which they are competing and play perfectly in

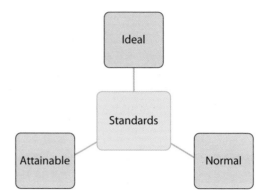

Figure 10.1 Different standards

every match. This would be an **ideal standard**, the best that can be achieved. However, ideal standards are unrealistic and unachievable as they would only ever be attained in a perfect world. In the real world, your team will lose some matches and draw others, play poorly yet win and play well but still lose. Therefore, a degree of realism is required in setting standards. **Attainable standards** are those standards that can be achieved with effort and you might set your team the attainable standard of winning one trophy during the coming season: it can be done, but winning that trophy will require focus, concentration and special effort. Alternatively, you might just set a **normal standard**, which is what a business usually achieves. Your team might finish in the middle of the table each year, avoiding relegation yet not playing particularly well or winning any trophies and you might settle for this as this is what is normally achieved. Anything beyond this is a bonus!

In the same way, businesses will set standards based on what they consider to be achievable under normal circumstances, with anything beyond this basic level of achievement being seen as a bonus for the business. Alternatively, directors can set performance targets to encourage staff to put in more effort to generate higher levels of productivity. Staff will be incentivised with the prospect of additional rewards to work towards these attainable standards.

10

WHY IS THIS RELEVANT TO ME?   Different standards

To give you as a business professional an appreciation of the different performance standards that can be set by businesses and what these different performance standards involve

GO BACK OVER THIS AGAIN!   Sure you can summarise what ideal, attainable and normal standards are? Go to the **online workbook** and complete Exercises 10.3 to make sure you understand the different standards of performance that can be set.

Setting the standard

We have already considered Anna's cost card, the revenue and costs for one dining chair. This is reproduced below. This cost card can be seen as an example of a standard cost card, the expected costs of each input into each chair along with the revenue that each chair is expected to generate.

Standard cost card: wooden dining chair	£
Variable costs	
Wood	18.00
Glue	0.60
Screws	1.00
Sandpaper	0.40
Direct labour	25.00
Prime cost (total variable cost)	45.00
Rent	6.00
Business rates	1.00
Heating and lighting	0.80
Total production cost of one chair	52.80
Standard selling price	85.00
Standard profit per dining chair	32.20

The standard cost card shows the direct inputs into a product, together with an allocation of fixed overhead to each product. Anna will use this standard cost card to measure actual outcomes and to analyse variances from her expectations. These variances could be positive (favourable variances) resulting in lower costs or more revenue than expected, or negative (unfavourable variances) arising from higher costs or lower revenue than anticipated. Unfavourable variances are sometimes called adverse variances but we will stick with the term unfavourable in this book.

To illustrate how standard costing and variance analysis work, let us consider a comprehensive example.

10

EXAMPLE 10.1

Anna has completed her first year of dining chair production. Things have gone well and her workshop has made and sold 1,100 chairs over the first 12 months of operations. While happy with her success, Anna is puzzled. She has used her original standard cost card to produce a forecast of the profit she should have made based on production and sales of 1,100 chairs. This calculation is shown in Illustration 10.1. However, her actual results are somewhat different from this forecast and these actual results are shown in Illustration 10.2.

Illustration 10.1 Anna: expected sales income, costs and profit for the first year of trading based on the standard cost card for sales and production of 1,100 dining chairs

	£	£
Sales 1,100 chairs at £85		93,500
Direct materials: wood 1,100 chairs at £18	19,800	
Direct materials: other 1,100 chairs at £2	2,200	
Direct labour 1,100 chairs at £25	27,500	
Total variable costs		49,500
Total contribution (sales – variable costs)		44,000
Fixed costs		
Rent	6,000	
Rates	1,000	
Heating and lighting	800	
Total fixed costs		7,800
Expected profit for the year		36,200

Illustration 10.2 Anna: actual sales income, costs and profit for the first year of trading from the production and sale of 1,100 dining chairs

	£	£
Sales		92,400
Direct materials: wood	19,720	
Direct materials: other	2,200	
Direct labour	28,644	
Total variable costs		50,564
Total contribution (sales – variable costs)		41,836
Fixed costs		
Rent	6,000	
Rates	1,000	
Heating and lighting	600	
Total fixed costs		7,600
Actual profit for the year		34,236

Given that her calculations show that she should have made a profit of £36,200 from the sale of 1,100 dining chairs, Anna is disappointed that her actual income and sales statement above shows a profit of only £34,236, a difference of £1,964. She has asked you to investigate how this difference has arisen.

A comparison of the two statements will enable us to determine where the differences between expected and actual profit lie. A comparison table can be drawn up as shown in Illustration 10.3.

Illustration 10.3 Anna: comparison of actual and expected sales, expenses and profit for the first year of trading from the production and sale of 1,100 dining chairs

	Actual for 1,100 chairs	Expected for 1,100 chairs	Total variance
	£	£	£
Sales	92,400	93,500	(1,100)
Less:			
Direct materials: wood	19,720	19,800	80
Direct materials: other	2,200	2,200	—
Direct labour	28,644	27,500	(1,144)
Rent	6,000	6,000	—
Rates	1,000	1,000	—
Heating and lighting	600	800	200
Profit for the year	34,236	36,200	(1,964)

What is this comparison telling us? We can summarise our conclusions as follows:

- Sales revenue from the sale of the 1,100 chairs is £1,100 lower than it should have been had Anna sold all her output at £85 per chair.

- The wood for chairs cost £80 less than it should have done based on a wood cost per chair of £18.

- Direct labour cost Anna £1,144 more than it should have done for the production of 1,100 chairs.

- Heating and lighting cost £200 less than expected.

- All other expenses (direct materials: other, rent and rates) cost exactly what Anna had expected them to.

- The positive reductions in spending on wood and heat and light are deducted from the lower sales income and the overspend on direct labour to give the net difference between the two profits of £1,964.

WHY IS THIS RELEVANT TO ME? Expected costs v. actual costs and calculation of total variances

As a business professional and user of accounting information you will be expected to understand:

- How standard costs can be used to calculate a statement of expected revenue and costs at any given level of production and sales
- How to compare actual revenue and costs with expected revenue and costs
- How to produce a variance statement comparing actual and expected outcomes
- That each total variance is the difference between the expected revenue and costs of actual production and sales and the actual revenue and costs of actual production and sales

10

NUMERICAL EXERCISES   Quite happy that you could use a standard cost card to:

- Produce a statement of expected costs and revenue

- Compare this to a statement of actual costs and revenue and

- Calculate total variances from this comparison?

Go to the online workbook and attempt Numerical exercises 10.1 to make sure you can undertake these tasks.

You explain these differences to Anna, but she is still not satisfied. Why has sales revenue fallen from what she expected it to be and why has so much more been spent on labour than she expected? You ask Anna for her accounting records for the year in order to investigate these differences. Once you have undertaken your investigations, you make the following discoveries:

- The average selling price for each dining chair was not £85, but £84.

- The wood was bought in at a cost of £1.70 per kg instead of the expected cost of £1.80 per kg (Chapter 9, Example 9.15).

- The expected usage of wood for 1,100 chairs should have been 10 kg per chair (Chapter 9, Example 9.15 Step 2) × 1,100 chairs = 11,000 kg whereas actual usage was 11,600 kg.

- Anna expected each chair to take two hours to make and she expected to pay her employees £25 for each chair produced. In fact, she decided to pay her employees an hourly rate of £12.40 instead of a payment for each chair produced.

- The 1,100 chairs should have taken 2,200 hours to produce (1,100 × 2), but her wages records show that her two employees were paid for a total of 2,310 hours.

- Because of the autumn and winter weather being milder than anticipated, the heating costs came in at £200 lower than expected.

How can this information be used to explain the differences between the actual results and the expected results based on the increased levels of production and sales?

Direct materials price and usage variances

We saw above that the wood for 1,100 chairs cost £19,720 against an expected cost of £19,800 (1,100 × £18 per chair in Anna's original estimates). This gave a total variance of £80. This is a favourable variance as Anna spent £80 less on the wood used in production of her dining chairs. However, our additional investigations revealed two facts relating to the wood used in the chairs. First, the purchase price of wood was £1.70

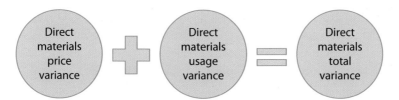

Figure 10.2 Direct materials variances

per kg instead of the expected £1.80 and 11,600 kg of wood were used instead of the expected 11,000 kg. So the material was cheaper than expected but the usage was more than expected. Do these two differences explain the total variance of £80?

Standard costing calls these two differences the direct material price variance and the direct material usage variance (Figure 10.2). The price variance shows how much of the difference is due to a higher or lower cost for direct materials while the usage variance shows how much of the difference is due to the quantity of material used varying from what the standard says should have been used.

The direct material price variance is calculated in the following way:

	£
11,600 kg of wood should have cost (11,600 × £1.80)	20,880
11,600 kg of material actually cost	19,720
Direct material price variance	1,160

Does this make sense? The standard cost for wood is £1.80 per kg, whereas Anna paid £1.70 per kg, a difference of £0.10 per kg. Anna's employees used 11,600 kg of wood, so 11,600 × £0.10 = £1,160, the same answer as above.

Is this variance favourable or unfavourable? To answer this question you should ask whether the cost is higher or lower than the standard cost says it should be. In this case, the actual quantity of material used cost less than the standard cost says it should have done, so this is a favourable variance. Anna has spent less on wood for her chairs than the standard says she should have done.

However, while Anna has spent less on wood for her chairs than her standard says she should have spent, her craftsmen have used more material than anticipated in the standard. Each chair should use 10 kg of wood and so 1,100 chairs should have used 11,000 kg in total. As actual usage was 11,600 kg, Anna's employees have used 600 kg more than expected. The usage variance is calculated as follows:

	Kg
1,100 chairs should have used 10 kg of wood × 1,100 chairs	11,000
1,100 chairs actually used	11,600
Direct material usage variance in kg	600

	£
Direct material usage variance in kg × standard price per kg 600 × £1.80	1,080

10

Again, we can ask whether this variance is favourable or unfavourable. More material has been used than the standard says should have been used, so this variance is unfavourable. Anna's craftsmen have used more wood than they should have done and this has meant that her profit has been reduced as a result of this over usage.

Direct material total variance

How do the price and usage variances relate to the total variance that we calculated earlier? This total variance was a favourable variance of £80 (£19,720 actual cost of the wood compared to £19,800 expected cost of wood for 1,100 chairs). Summarising our two variances above will give us this £80 total variance thus:

	£	Favourable/ (Unfavourable)
Direct materials price variance	1,160	Favourable
Direct materials usage variance	(1,080)	(Unfavourable)
Direct materials total variance	80	Favourable

WHY IS THIS RELEVANT TO ME? Direct material price variance, direct material usage variance and direct material total variance

To enable you as a business professional and user of accounting information to:

- Appreciate that variations in both the price and the usage of material should be used to explain the total direct materials variance
- Calculate the direct materials price variance and direct materials usage variance
- Demonstrate that the total direct materials variance is the sum of the direct materials price variance and the direct materials usage variance

10

SUMMARY OF KEY CONCEPTS Can you state the formulae for the direct materials variance and the two sub-variances, direct materials price variance and direct materials usage variance? Revise these variances with Summary of key concepts 10.1.

MULTIPLE CHOICE QUESTIONS Confident that you can calculate the direct materials variance and the sub-variances, direct materials price variance and direct materials usage variance? Go to the **online workbook** and have a go at Multiple choice questions 10.1 to test out your ability to calculate these figures.

Direct materials variances: information and control

We have calculated our variances, but what do they tell Anna and what use can she make of them? Our investigations and calculations show that cheaper material has been purchased and that this has saved Anna money on the material acquired. However, this money seems to have been saved at a cost. While the material is cheaper, more has been used than should have been and this suggests that the wood may not have been of the expected quality. Lower quality materials tend to lead to more wastage as they require more work to shape and fit them into the final product. This additional working has resulted in a higher usage as material was lost in the production process. Anna now needs to conduct further investigations to determine whether this lower cost material really is of lower quality. If so, she should in future demand only material of the requisite quality to minimise wastage.

Alternatively, Anna's employees might just have been careless in the way they handled the wood. More careful handling and more thoughtful workmanship might have resulted in less wastage and bigger savings from using this cheaper material. If this is the case, then her workers may need additional advice or training on how to make the best use of the material they are provided with so that wastage is reduced and profits increased. Price and usage variances thus point the way towards the areas that require further investigation to determine the reasons behind these variances and the means to resolve the problems arising.

WHY IS THIS RELEVANT TO ME?   Direct material variances: information and control

To enable you as a business professional and user of accounting information to appreciate that:

- Unfavourable materials variances are only indicators of problems that require management investigation, intervention and action to correct them

- Management must consider possible reasons for the variances that have arisen, along with potential solutions to ensure that unfavourable materials variances do not persist

10

GO BACK OVER THIS AGAIN!   Do you think you can identify reasons for changes in the direct material price and usage variances? Go to the **online workbook** and complete Exercises 10.4 to test your skill in this area.

Direct labour rate and efficiency variances

Figure 10.3 Direct labour variances

Our summary table of expected and actual costs in Illustration 10.3 shows that direct labour cost £28,644 against an expected cost to produce 1,100 chairs of £27,500. This is an unfavourable variance as Anna has incurred £1,144 more in direct labour costs than she expected to. Let's look first at the additional information uncovered by our investigations. Anna's employees were paid not for the dining chairs that they produced but at a fixed rate per hour. This hourly rate was £12.40 instead of the expected £12.50 and the actual hours used in producing 1,100 chairs were 2,310 against an expected 2,200. Again, can these two differences explain the total variance of £1,144?

Just as for direct materials, we can also calculate sub-variances for direct labour (Figure 10.3). The direct labour rate variance performs the same function as the direct materials price variance by taking into account the unit cost of each hour paid for production. The direct labour efficiency variance looks at the time taken to make the actual goods and compares this with the hours that were expected to be used for that level of production. Where the hours taken are lower than they should have been, workers have been more efficient in producing goods. However, where more hours have been used to make the production than were expected, this will mean that labour has been less efficient. In just the same way, the standard time to work through this chapter might be set at ten hours, but different students will have very different experiences of how long studying this chapter will take them!

	£
2,310 labour hours should have cost (2,310 × £12.50)	28,875
2,310 labour hours actually cost	28,644
Direct labour rate variance	231

Direct labour rate variance is calculated in the following way:
Direct labour cost is lower than the standard cost says it should be for the hours actually worked, so this variance is favourable. This would be expected as the actual rate at which labour is paid is £12.40 per hour compared to the standard rate of £12.50 per hour. Thus you could have calculated this variance by taking the difference between the

two hourly rates of £0.10 (£12.50 – £12.40) and multiplied this by 2,310 hours to give you the same answer of £231 less than 2,310 standard hours should have cost.

Again, while Anna has spent less on labour for her chairs than her standard says she should have done, her craftsmen have also used more hours than they should have spent in making the actual production. Each chair should use two hours of direct labour and so 1,100 chairs should have used 2,200 labour hours. As actual labour hours were 2,310, Anna's employees have taken 110 hours more than they should have done to make the actual production. The direct labour efficiency variance is calculated as follows:

	Hours
1,100 chairs should have used 1,100 × 2 hours	2,200
1,100 chairs actually used	2,310
Direct labour efficiency variance in hours	110
	£
Direct labour efficiency variance in hours × standard rate/hour 110 × £12.50	1,375

This variance is unfavourable as more labour hours have been used than the standard says should have been used in the production of 1,100 chairs. This means that Anna has incurred more cost and made a lower profit as a result of this increased usage.

Direct labour total variance

The sum of the direct labour rate and direct labour efficiency variances should equal the total variance that we calculated in Illustration 10.3. This total variance was £1,144 (£28,644 actual cost of direct labour compared to a £27,500 expected direct labour cost for 1,100 chairs). Summarising our two variances above will give us this £1,144 total variance thus:

	£	Favourable/Unfavourable
Direct labour rate variance	231	Favourable
Direct labour efficiency variance	(1,375)	(Unfavourable)
Direct labour total variance	(1,144)	(Unfavourable)

10

WHY IS THIS RELEVANT TO ME? Direct labour rate variance, direct labour efficiency variance and direct labour total variance

To enable you as a business professional and user of accounting information to:

- Appreciate that variations in both the rate at which labour is paid and the speed at which employees work should be used to explain the total direct labour variance
- Calculate the direct labour rate variance and the direct labour efficiency variance
- Realise that the total direct labour variance is the sum of the direct labour rate variance and the direct labour efficiency variance

Direct labour variances: information and control

Again, merely calculating the variances is not enough: these variances have to be investigated and the causes, once identified, used to improve operations with a view to improving efficiency and making additional profit.

It seems that Anna can employ craftsmen at a slightly lower hourly rate than she had expected. This is helpful as a small amount shaved off the labour rate means additional profit for the business. Unfortunately, her craftsmen have taken rather longer than they should have done to make the 1,100 chairs over the course of the year. Why might this be? Under our analysis of the direct material variance, we suggested that the wood used in the chairs might be of lower quality and hence require more working and shaping before it could be incorporated into the finished chairs. If this were the case, then the additional hours taken in the production of the chairs could be accounted for by this additional working and shaping. Anna should therefore discuss this issue with her employees to find out why these additional hours were worked and whether there is a problem with the wood that is being used. A lower price for direct materials is always welcome, but if this lower price is causing additional costs to be incurred elsewhere in the production cycle, then higher quality materials at a higher price should be acquired. In this way, the higher quality materials will pay for themselves as less labour cost will be incurred in making goods and more profit will be generated. Alternatively, Anna's craftsmen might just have worked more slowly to increase the number of hours they worked, thereby increasing their pay. To avoid this problem, Anna needs to think about incentivising her staff to work to the standard while still producing goods of the expected quality.

10

WHY IS THIS RELEVANT TO ME? Direct labour variances: information and control

As a business professional and user of accounting information you should understand:

- That direct labour rate and efficiency variances are only indicators of problems that require management investigation, intervention and action

- How to suggest possible reasons for the labour variances that have arisen, along with potential solutions to ensure that unfavourable variances do not persist

GO BACK OVER THIS AGAIN!   How easily can you identify reasons for changes in the direct labour rate and efficiency variances? Go to the **online workbook** and complete Exercises 10.5 to test your skill in this area.

Variable overhead variances

Anna does not incur any variable overheads in her business. If she did incur such overheads, the variances between standard and actual would be calculated in exactly the same way as for direct material and direct labour. First, there would be the variable overhead total variance, the total cost of variable overheads for actual production compared to the standard cost of variable overheads for actual production. This total variance would then be split down into the variable overhead expenditure variance and the variable overhead efficiency variance. To avoid disrupting the flow of our comparison and analysis of Anna's actual and expected profit, further discussion and an example of variable overhead variances is given at the end of this chapter (Appendix: variable overhead variances).

Fixed overhead variance

Figure 10.4 Fixed overhead variance

Fixed overheads are, of course, fixed. Therefore, the only relevant consideration in analysing this variance is the expected expenditure compared to the actual expenditure (Figure 10.4). In Anna's case, she expected her fixed costs to be £7,800 (rent: £6,000, rates: £1,000, heating and lighting: £800) whereas the actual outcome was £7,600 (rent: £6,000, rates: £1,000, heating and lighting: £600). As we discovered from our investigations into Anna's accounting records, £200 less was spent on heating and lighting during the year as a result of milder than expected winter weather. This £200 fixed overhead expenditure variance is favourable as less was spent on fixed costs than was expected.

SUMMARY OF KEY CONCEPTS   Reckon you can calculate the fixed overhead variance? Check your understanding of how these variances are calculated with Summary of key concepts 10.4.

Fixed overhead variance: information and control

As fixed overheads are fixed, businesses usually experience only small variations between expected and actual fixed costs. Organisations will not usually investigate fixed overhead variances in depth. There is little that can be done to reduce fixed costs that are mostly imposed from outside the business. On the other hand, since materials, labour and variable overheads are driven directly by internal business activity, time will be spent on investigating these variances as much more can be done to reduce unfavourable variances arising from operations under the direct control of management.

WHY IS THIS RELEVANT TO ME?   Fixed overhead variances

As a business professional and user of accounting information you should appreciate that:

- Fixed overhead variance is the difference between total forecast fixed overheads and actual fixed overhead expenditure
- Fixed overheads are largely outside the control of businesses
- Management time and effort will therefore focus upon investigating unfavourable material, labour and variable overhead variances as businesses can take action to control and eliminate these variances

Sales variances

Our final variances relate to income, the sales variances.

Sales price variance

The first of these is the sales price variance (Figure 10.5). Anna's expectation was that she would sell her dining chairs for £85 each. However, further investigation revealed that her average selling price was only £84, a reduction of £1 per chair sold. Anna sold 1,100 chairs, so her **sales price variance** was 1,100 × £1 = £1,100. This is unfavourable as she received less income per chair than budgeted.

Figure 10.5 Sales price variance

Sales volume variance

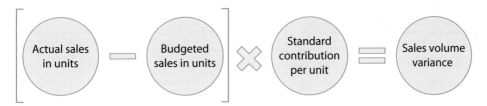

Figure 10.6 Sales volume variance

We have now explained all the variances between Anna's expected and actual profit from the sale of 1,100 chairs as shown in Illustration 10.3, but there is one more variance we need to consider. Anna's original expectation was that she would sell 1,000 chairs and make a profit of £32,200. Her actual results show that she sold 1,100 chairs and made a profit of £34,236. The additional sales of 100 chairs give rise to another variance, the **sales volume variance** (Figure 10.6). This variance takes the additional standard contribution from each sale and multiplies this by the additional number of units sold to reflect the increased contribution arising from higher sales. This is logical as each additional sale will increase revenue by the selling price of one unit, but will also increase variable costs by the standard cost of direct material, direct labour and variable overhead for each additional unit of production and sales. Therefore, the contribution, the selling price less the variable costs, is used in this calculation. This variance is calculated as follows:

	Units
Actual units sold	1,100
Budgeted sales in units	1,000
Sales volume variance	100
	£
Sales volume variance at standard contribution 100 × £40	4,000

Is this variance favourable or unfavourable? As more sales have been made and more contribution earned, this is a favourable variance.

Anna will want to know why she is selling more chairs than budgeted and so she will investigate this increase with a view to selling even more. Similarly, she will also be keen to find out why her selling price is lower than budgeted and what factors in the market are pushing her selling price down.

Variances: summary

We can now summarise all our variances and reconcile Anna's forecast to her actual profit as follows. Anna's original expectation was that she would sell 1,000 dining chairs at £85 each and generate a profit of £32,200 so our starting point is this original expected profit.

	Unfavourable £	Favourable £	Profit £
Expected profit from selling 1,000 chairs at £85			32,200
Sales price variance	(1,100)		
Sales volume variance		4,000	
Direct materials price variance		1,160	
Direct materials usage variance	(1,080)		
Direct labour rate variance		231	
Direct labour efficiency variance	(1,375)		
Fixed overhead expenditure variance		200	
Total variances	(3,555)	5,591	
Add: favourable variances			5,591
Deduct: unfavourable variances			(3,555)
Actual profit for the year			34,236

WHY IS THIS RELEVANT TO ME? **Summary of variances and reconciliation of expected to actual profit**

To enable you as a business professional and user of accounting information to:

- Present all your variances in summary form to explain the difference between expected and actual profit

---

NUMERICAL EXERCISES How confident do you feel handling extensive variance analysis questions? Go to the **online workbook** and have a go at Numerical exercises 10.2 to see how effectively you have absorbed the lessons of this chapter and how well you understand standard costing and variance analysis.

SHOW ME HOW TO DO IT This chapter has involved a lot of tricky calculations and ideas. View Video presentation 10.1 in the **online workbook** to reinforce your knowledge of how standard costing and variance analysis is undertaken.

Standard costing: limitations

Standard costing is a useful technique in comparing expected with actual financial performance. Where variances arise, these can be investigated to determine their causes and to identify ways in which unfavourable variances can be reduced and favourable variances maintained or enhanced. While setting standards encourages improvement and change for the better over time, standard costing also suffers from the following limitations:

- You will agree, I am sure, that this is a very complicated system and that this complexity can be discouraging when you first come across standard costing and variance analysis.
- It is also a time consuming system: a great deal of time will be needed to gather information from which to set the standards, to collect data from which to monitor standards against actual performance and to produce and evaluate variances.
- Time will also be needed to update standards for changes in costs owing to rising or falling material costs, wage costs, changes in overheads and selling prices.
- The information produced by variance analysis can be extensive and management may be overwhelmed by the volume of data presented to them.
- Standard costing systems tend to be rigid and inflexible: lack of flexibility should be avoided in the modern, ever changing business environment.
- However, modern computer systems should be able to assist management with the production of standard costs and variance analysis and in highlighting those

10

variances that indicate that operations are out of control rather than within set tolerance limits. Profitability improvement depends upon careful cost control and such cost control is one of the key functions of business managers.

Given these limitations, it is probably not surprising to find that small and medium sized companies make no use of standard costing variance analysis. Give me an example 10.2 describes this failure to adopt this approach.

GIVE ME AN EXAMPLE 10.2   Adoption of standard costing variance analysis by small and medium sized companies in the UK

Management Accounting Practices of UK Small-Medium-Sized Enterprises published in July 2013 investigated the management accounting techniques and practices used by small and medium sized enterprises. While all the organisations surveyed undertook product costing, break even analysis and working capital measures, none of the respondents engaged in standard cost variance analysis. However, the researchers considered that the failure to use this technique was appropriate for small and medium sized enterprises on cost benefit grounds as the costs of obtaining the information were substantial while the benefits gained were very limited.

Source: www.cimaglobal.com

Appendix: variable overhead variances

Figure 10.7 Variable overhead variances

Variable overheads are absorbed into products on the basis of the number of hours of activity incurred to produce one unit of production. The standard cost for variable overheads will estimate the number of hours products take to produce on either a labour or machine hour basis (see Chapter 8, Absorption costing: overhead allocation, to refresh your memory on how absorption cost bases work) and then allocate the variable overhead to each product on the basis of the standard number of hours required to produce one unit multiplied by the standard variable overhead cost per hour.

Variable overhead variance calculations divide the total variance into variable overhead expenditure and variable overhead efficiency variances (Figure 10.7), in much the same way that the total direct labour variance is divided into labour rate and labour efficiency variances. The expenditure variance measures the difference between the variable overhead that should have been incurred for the level of production achieved and the actual expenditure paid. The variable overhead efficiency variance compares the difference between the actual hours taken to produce the actual production and the standard hours that actual production would have been expected to take. Think about how these variances are calculated in Example 10.1.

EXAMPLE 10.1

The Ultimate Chef Company manufactures food processors. Variable overhead incurred in the production of each food processor is set at 2½ hours at £6 per hour. During September, 1,000 food processors were produced. The employees of the Ultimate Chef Company were paid for 2,450 hours. The variable overhead cost for September was £14,540. Calculate:

- The variable overhead total variance
- The variable overhead expenditure variance
- The variable overhead efficiency variance

State whether each variance is favourable or unfavourable.

Variable overhead total variance

This is what the actual production should have cost and what it did cost.

	£
1,000 food processors should have cost 1,000 × 2½ hours × £6	15,000
1,000 food processors actually cost	14,540
Variable overhead total variance	460

The variable overhead total variance is favourable as the actual variable overhead cost is lower than the expected cost for the given level of production.

Variable overhead expenditure variance

This is what the variable overhead should have cost compared with what it did cost for the actual hours worked.

	£
2,450 hours should have cost (2,450 × £6.00)	14,700
2,450 hours actually cost	14,540
Variable overhead expenditure variance	160

The variable overhead expenditure variance is favourable as less cost was incurred than expected for the actual number of hours used in production.

Variable overhead efficiency variance

This is how many hours should have been worked and how many were actually worked for the actual level of production.

	Hours
1,000 food processors should have used 1,000 × 2½ hours	2,500
1,000 food processors actually used	2,450
Variable overhead efficiency variance in hours	50
	£
Variable overhead efficiency variance in hours × standard rate/hour 50 × £6.00	300

The efficiency variance is favourable as fewer hours were used than expected for the level of production achieved.

The variable overhead expenditure variance and the variable overhead efficiency variance can be summarised as follows to give the variable overhead total variance:

	£	Favourable/Unfavourable
Variable overhead expenditure variance	160	Favourable
Variable overhead efficiency variance	300	Favourable
Variable overhead total variance	460	Favourable

WHY IS THIS RELEVANT TO ME?   Variable overhead expenditure variance, variable overhead efficiency variance and variable overhead total variance

As a business professional and user of accounting information you should now:

- Appreciate that variations in both the variable overhead expenditure and the speed of working should be used to explain the variable overhead total variance
- Be able to calculate the variable overhead total variance, variable overhead expenditure variance and variable overhead efficiency variance
- Understand that the variable overhead total variance is the sum of the variable overhead expenditure variance and the variable overhead efficiency variance

SUMMARY OF KEY CONCEPTS   Are you sure you know how to calculate the variable overhead total variance and the associated sub-variances, variable overhead expenditure variance and variable overhead efficiency variance? Check your understanding of how these variances are calculated with Summary of key concepts 10.3.

Happy that you can calculate the variable overhead total variance and its associated variances, variable overhead expenditure and variable overhead efficiency variances? Go to the **online workbook** and attempt Multiple choice questions 10.4 to check your ability to calculate these figures.

CHAPTER SUMMARY

You should now have learnt that:

- Selling price, materials, labour, direct expenses, variable overhead and fixed overhead are the components that make up a standard cost

- Standard cost is an expected rather than an actual cost

- Standard costs are used in the planning and evaluation of operations

- Total variances between what should have been achieved and what was achieved explain the difference between actual and expected profits

- Variance analysis splits total variances into their constituent sub-variances arising from:

  - Price (material), rate (labour) and expenditure (variable overhead) and

  - Usage (material) and efficiency (labour and variable overhead)

- Sales variances are split into sales price and sales volume variances

- Variances help identify problems requiring further investigation and analysis to assist in the control of operations

Test your knowledge with the online flashcards in Summary of key concepts and attempt the Multiple choice questions, all in the **online workbook**. www.oxfordtextbooks.co.uk/orc/scott/

END-OF-CHAPTER QUESTIONS

10

Solutions to these questions can be found at the back of the book from page 488.

> *Develop your understanding*

Question 10.1

There are 30 apple trees in the orchard attached to Bill's farm. Bill reckons that each tree will be given five doses of fertiliser each year at a cost of £4 per tree and that 10 hours of labour per tree will be required to pick the apples and prune the trees. Workers are paid £7.50 per hour.

At the end of the apple picking season, Bill calculates that the 30 trees only received four doses of fertiliser, although these cost £4.50 for each tree, and that the picking and pruning was undertaken at a cost of £8 per hour for 270 hours of labour.

Required

Calculate:

(a) The total expected costs of the orchard for the past year.

(b) The actual total costs of the orchard for the past year.

(c) Material total, price and usage variances.

(d) Labour total, rate and efficiency variances.

State whether the variances are favourable or unfavourable.

Question 10.2

Fred bakes cakes. His budget indicates that he will produce and sell 1,000 cakes during March at a selling price of £15 each. At the end of March he calculates that his selling price was £15.50 for each cake produced and sold and that he has generated £14,725 in sales. His standard cost card for each cake shows that his variable cost of production is £6 per cake.

Required

Calculate for Fred for March:

(a) The sales price variance.

(b) The sales volume variance.

State whether the variances are favourable or unfavourable. Assuming that Fred's actual production costs are £6 per cake, prove that the sales price and sales volume variances explain fully his additional contribution for March.

» *Take it further*

Question 10.3

Sanguinary Services carries out blood tests for local hospitals, surgeries and doctors. The standard cost card for each blood test is given below.

	£
Chemicals used in blood tests: 10 millilitres at 50 pence/ml	5.00
Laboratory worker: 15 minutes at £16 per hour	4.00
Fixed overhead of the testing centre	2.00
Total cost	11.00
Charge for each blood test	15.00
Standard profit per blood test	4.00

The centre has fixed overheads of £72,000 per annum and plans to carry out 36,000 blood tests every year at the rate of 3,000 tests per month.

In April, the following results were recorded:

	Number
Blood tests carried out	3,600

	£
Chemicals used in blood tests: 33,750 millilitres at 48 pence/ml	16,200
Laboratory workers: 925 hours at £16.20 per hour	14,985
Fixed overhead of the testing centre	7,500
Total cost	38,685
Charge for each blood test 3,600 at £15.50	55,800
Profit for April	17,115

Required

(a) Calculate the profit that the centre expected to make in April, based on the original forecast of 3,000 blood tests in the month.

(b) Calculate the following:

- Sales volume variance
- Sales price variance
- Direct materials total variance
- Direct materials price variance
- Direct materials usage variance
- Direct labour total variance
- Direct labour rate variance
- Direct labour efficiency variance
- Fixed overhead expenditure variance

Stating whether each variance is favourable or unfavourable.

(c) Prepare a statement reconciling the expected profit to the actual profit for April.

Question 10.4

Smashers Tennis Club runs coaching courses for its junior members. Each course lasts for ten weeks and is priced at £70 for each junior member. Smashers expects each course to attract 12 junior members. Each course is allocated 20 tennis balls for each participating junior at an expected cost of £10 for 20 balls. A professionally qualified tennis coach undertakes each hour-long coaching session over the ten weeks at a cost of £30 per hour.

The club administrator is reviewing the costs and income for the latest junior coaching course and she is trying to understand why the surplus from the course is £438 instead of £420. She tells you that the course actually attracted 16 juniors instead of the 12 expected and that a total of 400 balls had been allocated to and used by juniors on the course. Balls for the latest coaching course had cost 60 pence each. The coach had received an increase in her hourly rate to £33 per hour. The price for each course had been reduced by 10% on the original price in order to attract additional participants.

Required

(a) Calculate the original expected surplus from the coaching course.

(b) Calculate the expected surplus from the coaching course given that 16 juniors were enrolled.

(c) Calculate the actual income and costs for the course.

(d) Calculate variances for income and expenditure and present these in tabular form to reconcile the original expected surplus to the actual surplus.

Question 10.5

Vijay Manufacturing produces garden gnomes. The standard cost card for garden gnomes is as follows:

	£
Plastic: 2 kg at £2.25 per kg	4.50
Labour: 0.5 hours at £8 per hour	4.00
Variable overhead: 4 machine hours at £0.75 per hour	3.00
Fixed overhead	1.00
Total cost	12.50
Selling price to Plastic Gnome Painters Limited	15.00
Standard profit per garden gnome	2.50

Fixed overheads total £24,000 and are allocated to production on the basis that 24,000 gnomes will be produced each year, 2,000 each month.

Vijay is reviewing the actual production and sales for the month of June. The weather has been wet and garden gnome sales have fallen from their normal levels. Consequently, the company has had to reduce the selling price in June to £14 per gnome in order to keep production and sales moving. Production and sales for the month were 1,800 gnomes. The input price per kg of plastic was £2.50 as a result of a sharp rise in the oil price but, because of reduced wastage and careful material handling, only 3,500 kg of plastic were used in June. Owing to the high level of unemployment in the area, Vijay has been able to pay his employees at the rate of £7.50 per hour. Total labour hours for the month were 950. Total machine hours for the month were 7,000 and the fixed and variable overheads totalled £1,600 and £5,500 respectively. Vijay has been trying to understand why his profit has fallen from its expected level for the month and has asked for your help. You are meeting him later on today to discuss his figures and to show him how his expected profit has fallen to the actual profit for the month.

Required

Draft figures for your meeting later on today with Vijay. Your figures should include:

(a) Calculations to show the profit Vijay expected to make from the production and sale of 2,000 garden gnomes in the month of June.

(b) Calculations to show the profit Vijay might have expected to make from the production and sale of 1,800 garden gnomes for the month of June.

(c) Calculations to show the profit Vijay actually did make for the month of June.

(d) A reconciliation statement showing all the necessary favourable and unfavourable variances to explain the difference between the expected profit for June calculated in (a) and the actual profit calculated in (c).

11 Budgeting

LEARNING OUTCOMES

Once you have read this chapter and worked through the questions and examples in both this chapter and the online workbook, you should be able to:

- Understand how budgets perform planning, communicating, coordinating, motivating and control functions

- Prepare budgeted monthly income statements for an entity

- Determine the timing of cash inflows and outflows from budgeted income and expenditure

- Prepare a budgeted month-by-month cash flow forecast for an entity

- Draw up a forecast statement of financial position at the end of a budgeted accounting period

- Undertake comparisons between budgeted and actual income and expenditure to highlight variances in expected and actual financial performance

- Undertake sensitivity analysis upon budgeted forecasts to assess the effect that any changes in budget assumptions will have

Introduction

The word **budget** is all around us, every day. There are constant reminders of the national budget, individuals' budgets and business budgets. You yourself may have made a budget for what you expected to spend during your first year at university. This budget might have been quite basic to start with, but, as you thought more about the costs you would be likely to incur, your budget would have been refined and become a more realistic means of forecasting your anticipated expenditure and its timing. However, **budgeting** can occur at a much simpler level. When you go out for the evening, the amount of money you take with you is your budget for that evening. In both cases, actual expenditure is likely to be very different from your original plan due to unforeseen costs—an expensive book or field trip for your course or a taxi home when you missed the last bus. This does not mean that the exercise was not worthwhile: planning ahead is important for both individuals and business organisations. Experience helps us to refine our future budgets so that the actual outcomes gradually become closer to our forecast expectations.

What is budgeting?

For business people, a budget is the expression of a plan in money terms. That plan is a prediction or a forecast of future income, expenditure, cash inflows and cash outflows. Once each stage of the plan is completed, then the actual results can be compared to expectations to determine whether actual outcomes are better, worse or the same as anticipated. As we saw in Chapter 10 on standard costing, such comparisons are a means of controlling an organisation's operations and taking action to reduce or eliminate unfavourable divergences from the plan while finding out how better than expected performance can be maintained and built upon.

WHY IS THIS RELEVANT TO ME? What is budgeting?

As a business professional and user of accounting information:

- You need to appreciate that all businesses undertake budgeting
- You will be expected to take part in the annual budgeting process no matter what your particular business speciality is
- Having an awareness of what budgeting is, what it involves and how to budget in practice will be essential business knowledge

11

SUMMARY OF KEY CONCEPTS Can you define budgeting? Revise the definition with Summary of key concepts 11.1.

Give me an example 11.1 highlights the importance accorded to budgeting and forecasting by the business community.

The July 2009 CIMA report,

Management accounting tools for today and tomorrow, surveyed the current and intended usage by business of more than 100 management accounting and related tools based on a questionnaire completed by 439 respondents from across the globe. The most commonly used technique in practice was financial year forecasting with 86% of respondents engaging in this activity. The third most popular technique was cash forecasting which was used by 78% of those businesses surveyed. These two activities were the most popular budgeting tools across every size of company in the survey from small to very large. These findings indicate the very high priority that is accorded to budgeting and forecasting in the business community.

Source: www.cimaglobal.com

Budget objectives and the budgeting process

Everyone has objectives, both individuals and organisations. It is not enough to have a vague hope that everything will work out and that objectives will be achieved without any planning or positive actions and a great deal of hard work being undertaken. Thus, individuals and organisations have to decide how they will achieve their objectives through careful planning on a step-by-step basis. A well-known phrase among university tutors is 'failing to plan is planning to fail'. This is just as true when you are writing an essay as it is when making projections of what a business will achieve in the next 12 months.

Budgets and the budgeting process thus assist organisations to focus upon achieving and the means to achieve their objectives in the ways shown in Table 11.1.

WHY IS THIS RELEVANT TO ME?   Budgeting objectives and the budgeting process

As a business professional and user of accounting information you need to be aware of:

- What the objectives of the budgeting process are
- The roles budgeting plays in setting and achieving organisational goals
- What the budgeting process will expect of you

Table 11.1 The objectives of the budgeting process

Planning	Budgeting forces entities to look ahead and plan. Planning helps organisations think about the future and what they want to achieve, as well as helping them anticipate problems to determine how these will be overcome.
Communication	The directors will have plans to achieve certain objectives. However, if they do not tell everyone else involved in the organisation about those objectives, then they will not be achieved. Budgets communicate information to those persons and departments involved in achieving objectives to tell them what level of performance they have to attain to fulfil their part in reaching the desired goal.
Coordination and integration	Different departments have to work together to achieve objectives. The directors have to tell marketing what level of sales they need to achieve to reach the profit goal. Marketing then have to liaise with production to make sure that production can produce this number of goods and to the required timescale. Production has to make sure that purchasing is buying in the necessary raw materials to enable production to take place on schedule while personnel have to recruit the necessary workers to make the goods. Budgets thus coordinate and integrate business activities to give the organisation the best chance of achieving its goals.
Control	Budgeting enables an organisation to control its activities and check its progress towards achieving objectives by regularly comparing actual results with budgeted outcomes. Differences can then be investigated and action taken either to bring operations back on track or to exploit favourable trends further.
Responsibility	Responsibility for different parts of the budget is delegated to individual managers. One person alone cannot achieve everything on their own, so various managers work as part of a team, each with their own responsibility for hitting the targets assigned to them in the budget. These managers are then assessed and rewarded on the basis of their ability to meet their agreed objectives. Breaking down one big task into various smaller tasks and then making several managers responsible for achieving each of these smaller targets is a very good way to get things done.
Motivation	Budgets are used as motivating devices. Something too easy is not motivating and managers need to be challenged to achieve more. In the same way, your degree is challenging so that achieving your qualification motivates you and makes it worthwhile. As an incentive to achieve challenging budget targets, managers will be rewarded with bonuses. However, it is important to make sure that the targets are not completely unrealistic as impossible targets will result in managers giving up before they have even started.

11

Budgeting: comprehensive example

Now that we have defined a budget and considered what the organisational objectives in preparing budgets are, let's look in detail at the process of actually setting a budget through a practical example. This process involves several steps, which we will look at one by one.

Anna is considering the expansion of her business. She is planning to move her operations to a bigger workshop and has asked her bank for a loan with which to finance this expansion. In connection with her application for the loan, the bank has asked Anna to produce a budget covering sales, costs and cash flows for the next 12 months, together with a budgeted statement of financial position at the end of those 12 months. Anna has made a start on her forecasts and has produced information for the first three months of the next financial year. However, she is finding budgeting difficult and has asked for your assistance in helping her to complete the remainder of the forecasts.

Step 1: setting the strategy and deciding on selling prices

Anna first has to decide what she wants to achieve and whether there are any obstacles she must overcome or which will stand in the way of her achieving her goals. She wants to expand, but she feels that the lack of finance is holding her back. However, her products are selling well and her customers are pleased with the quality of her output. Will she be able to finance her proposed expansion from current operations if the bank is not willing to help her? Budgeting will help her to answer this question and Figure 11.1 illustrates the first step in the budgeting process.

Figure 11.1 Budgeting step 1: set the strategy and the selling prices

Her first decision will be to set her selling prices. Should she raise these, leave them at the same level or reduce the selling prices of each product? She has gone back to the costings for her three products that she presented in Chapter 9. These are reproduced in Illustration 11.1. Can she justify raising her selling prices? This will first depend on whether her costs are rising.

Illustration 11.1 Anna: selling prices and variable costs for dining chairs, coffee tables and kitchen cabinets

	Dining chairs	Coffee tables	Kitchen cabinets
	£	£	£
Selling price	85.00	50.00	80.00
Materials: wood	(18.00)	(12.60)	(10.80)
Materials: other	(2.00)	(5.40)	(9.20)
Direct labour	(25.00)	(18.00)	(30.00)
Contribution	40.00	14.00	30.00

Anna tells you that she has discussed the price of wood and other materials with her suppliers. They have reassured her that there are no price rises or material shortages anticipated in the next 12 months. This tells Anna that there will be no supply difficulties which will need to be planned for over the course of the coming year. At the same time she now knows that there are no expected increases in the cost of inputs to her products which would need to be built into her selling prices to pass on these cost increases to her customers.

Her workforce is loyal and they have stated that they have no intention of leaving in the next 12 months. Anna has looked into the current rates she is paying her workers and these are in line with market rates. The furniture makers' trade association informs her that labour costs are likely to remain steady over the course of the next year. Again, Anna now knows that she should not encounter any shortages of labour or pay rises which she would have to build into her budget for the coming year.

As her direct costs should remain unchanged for the next 12 months, it will be difficult for Anna to change her selling prices. She is happy with the levels of profit her sales are currently generating and, as she does not want to lose her customers through pitching her selling prices too high, she decides to leave the selling prices of each of her three products at the same level for the next 12 months.

11

Step 2: the sales budget

Now that the pricing decision and the supply of materials and labour are clear, Anna's next thoughts will focus on her sales. Once decisions on strategy and prices have been made, this is exactly the right place to start the budgeting process as so many other costs and cash flows depend upon the volume of sales achieved. As we discovered in Chapters 8 and 9, Anna's direct costs for wood, other materials and labour will depend directly upon the number of products she sells: the more products she makes and sells, the more direct materials and direct labour cost she will incur. However, she will be unable to produce her material and labour budgets until she has set her sales budget in terms of units sold. Figure 11.2 outlines this process.

Figure 11.2 Budgeting step 2: setting the sales budget

Illustration 11.2 Anna: budgeted sales in units of product for January, February and March

	January number	February number	March number	Total number
Dining chairs	150	200	350	700
Coffee tables	100	250	300	650
Kitchen cabinets	300	350	400	1,050

Anna has been talking to her customers to see how many of her products they propose buying in the near future. She has managed to determine that orders from customers for the first three months of the year are likely to be as shown in Illustration 11.2.

From these budgeted units of sales, Anna can now produce a sales budget in £s. This sales budget is presented in Illustration 11.3.

Illustration 11.3 Anna: budgeted sales in £s for January, February and March

	January	February	March	Total
	£	£	£	£
Dining chairs	12,750	17,000	29,750	59,500
Coffee tables	5,000	12,500	15,000	32,500
Kitchen cabinets	24,000	28,000	32,000	84,000
Total sales for month	41,750	57,500	76,750	176,000

How did Anna arrive at the above figures? Monthly sales of each product are calculated by multiplying the monthly expected sales in units in Illustration 11.2 by the selling price for each product in Illustration 11.1. Thus, Anna expects to sell 150 dining chairs in January at a selling price of £85. This gives her a sales figure of $150 \times £85 = £12,750$ for this product line in January.

WHY IS THIS RELEVANT TO ME? The sales budget

To enable you as a business professional and user of accounting information to understand:

- How a sales budget is prepared
- The influence of projected sales on the direct costs of making and selling products and providing services

---

NUMERICAL EXERCISES Totally confident you can produce a sales budget? Work your way through the above example again to confirm your understanding of how the monthly sales figures for each product were calculated and then go to the **online workbook** and attempt Numerical exercises 11.1 to make sure you can produce a sales budget from monthly budgeted sales units and budgeted selling prices.

Step 3: calculate the direct costs of budgeted sales

Now that the sales budget has been set, the direct costs associated with those sales can be calculated. As already noted, direct costs are dependent upon the level of sales. In Anna's case, the more of each product her workshop makes, the more wood will be used, the more other materials will be consumed and the more direct labour will be needed. Figure 11.3 outlines this process.

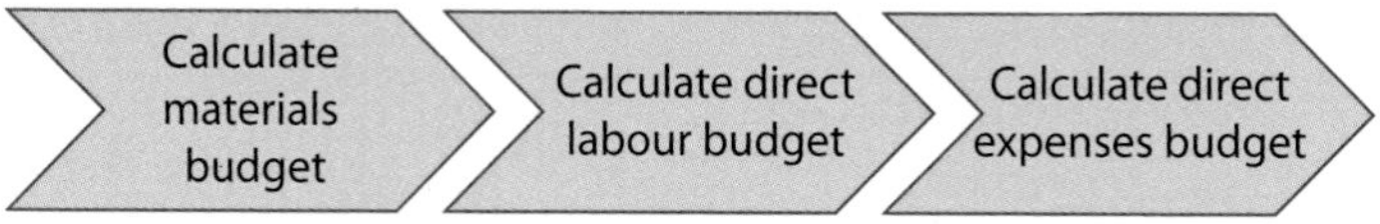

Figure 11.3 Budgeting step 3: setting the direct costs budget

Budgeted sales income for each month was calculated by multiplying the selling price by the number of units sold. In the same way, budgeted direct costs are found by multiplying the direct materials and direct labour by the number of units of sales. This gives the material costs for wood shown in Illustration 11.4.

Illustration 11.4 Anna: budgeted costs for wood in January, February and March

	January	February	March	Total
Direct materials: wood	£	£	£	£
Dining chairs	2,700	3,600	6,300	12,600
Coffee tables	1,260	3,150	3,780	8,190
Kitchen cabinets	3,240	3,780	4,320	11,340
Total direct materials (wood) for month	7,200	10,530	14,400	32,130

Illustration 11.2 tells us that Anna expects to sell 150 dining chairs in the month of January, while Illustration 11.1 shows us that the wood for each chair costs £18.00; 150 chairs × £18.00 gives a total cost of wood for dining chairs in January of £2,700. Using the budgeted sales in Illustration 11.2 for each product and the product costs for wood in Illustration 11.1, check the calculation of the other materials costs for wood in Illustration 11.4 to reinforce your understanding of how we arrived at these costs.

In the same way and using the information in Illustrations 11.1 and 11.2, the costs for other materials and direct labour for each product for each month have been calculated in Illustrations 11.5 and 11.6. Other materials used in dining chairs amount to £2 per chair. Multiplying this cost of £2 per chair by the 150 chairs Anna expects to sell in January gives us a cost for other materials of £300 in that month. Similarly, labour costs of £25 per dining chair are multiplied by the 150 chairs budgeted for January to give a total labour cost for dining chairs in that month of £3,750.

Illustration 11.5 Anna: budgeted costs for other materials in January, February and March

	January	February	March	Total
Direct materials: other	£	£	£	£
Dining chairs	300	400	700	1,400
Coffee tables	540	1,350	1,620	3,510
Kitchen cabinets	2,760	3,220	3,680	9,660
Total direct materials (other) for month	3,600	4,970	6,000	14,570

Illustration 11.6 Anna: budgeted costs for direct labour in January, February and March

Direct labour	January £	February £	March £	Total £
Dining chairs	3,750	5,000	8,750	17,500
Coffee tables	1,800	4,500	5,400	11,700
Kitchen cabinets	9,000	10,500	12,000	31,500
Total direct labour for month	14,550	20,000	26,150	60,700

WHY IS THIS RELEVANT TO ME? **The direct costs of budgeted sales**

To provide you as a business professional and user of accounting information with the knowledge and techniques to:

• Prepare budgets for direct costs based on budgeted sales

• Understand how direct cost budgets are compiled

NUMERICAL EXERCISES Think you can produce a direct costs budget for materials and labour? Work your way through the above example again to confirm your understanding of how we arrived at the materials and labour cost figures for each product and then go to the **online workbook** and attempt Numerical exercises 11.2 to see if you can produce a direct materials and direct labour budget from monthly budgeted sales units and budgeted cost prices per unit.

Step 4: set the budget for fixed costs

The fixed costs budget will be different for every organisation and will depend upon what sort of resources are consumed by each entity as shown in Figure 11.4.

Anna expects her fixed costs and her capital expenditure for the next three months to be as follows:

• Rent on the new workshop of £3,000 will be paid in January to cover the months of January, February and March.

• New machinery and tools will cost £15,000 and will be delivered and paid for in January. These new non-current assets will have an expected useful life of five years and will be depreciated on the straight line basis.

• Anna anticipates that she will receive and pay an electricity bill in March covering the period 1 January to 15 March. She expects that this bill will be for around £1,500. Anna estimates that the new workshop will use a further £300 of electricity between 16 and 31 March. Each month of operation should be allocated an equal amount of electricity cost.

11

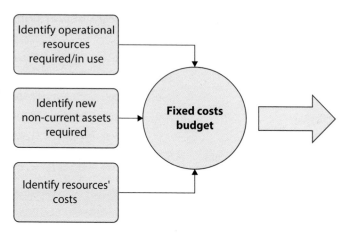

Figure 11.4 Budgeting step 4: setting the fixed costs budget

- An invoice for business rates of £1,200 on the new workshop will be received and paid on 15 February. These rates will cover the six-month period to 30 June.
- The insurance company requires a payment of £1,500 on 1 January to cover all insurance costs for the whole year to 31 December.

Step 5: draw up the monthly income statement

Anna can now draw up her monthly income statement from the information gathered together in steps 1–4 (Figure 11.5). This income statement is presented in Illustration 11.7.

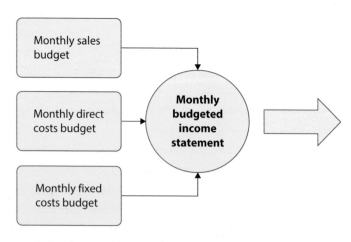

Figure 11.5 Budgeting step 5: draw up the monthly income statement

Illustration 11.7 Anna: budgeted income statement for January, February and March

	January	February	March	Total	Note
	£	£	£	£	
Sales	41,750	57,500	76,750	176,000	1
Cost of sales					
Direct material: wood	7,200	10,530	14,400	32,130	2
Direct material: other	3,600	4,970	6,000	14,570	3
Direct labour	14,550	20,000	26,150	60,700	4
Cost of sales	25,350	35,500	46,550	107,400	
Gross profit (sales – cost of sales)	16,400	22,000	30,200	68,600	
Expenses					
Rent	1,000	1,000	1,000	3,000	5
Rates	200	200	200	600	6
Machinery and tools depreciation	250	250	250	750	7
Electricity	600	600	600	1,800	8
Insurance	125	125	125	375	9
Net profit (gross profit – expenses)	14,225	19,825	28,025	62,075	

How did Anna calculate the budgeted results in Illustration 11.7? The following notes will help you understand how she determined the numbers in her budgeted income statement:

1. The monthly sales are derived from Illustration 11.3.
2. Similarly, the direct materials for wood are given in Illustration 11.4.
3. Figures for other direct materials are given in Illustration 11.5.
4. Direct labour costs were calculated in Illustration 11.6. Check back to Illustrations 11.3–11.6 to make sure that the numbers in the income statement have been correctly transferred from these workings.
5. While the rent of £3,000 was paid in January, this payment relates to three months, so the total expense is spread equally over the three months to which it relates. If you are unsure of why this expense is presented in this way, you should revise this allocation of costs in the accruals basis of accounting in Chapter 3.
6. In the same way, the rates payment relates to the six months from January to June. The total cost of £1,200 is therefore divided by six months and £200 allocated as the rates cost to each month. The total cost for rates for the three months amounts to £600. How is the remaining £600 (£1,200 paid – £600 charged to the income statement) classified in the accounts? Chapter 3 Prepayments and accruals covers the subject of prepayments—expenses paid in advance that belong to a future accounting period.

11

7. Depreciation was another expense we tackled in Chapter 3 (Depreciation). The total cost of £15,000 is divided by five years, giving an annual depreciation charge on these new assets of £3,000. As there are 12 months in a year, a monthly depreciation charge of £3,000 ÷ 12 = £250 is allocated to each of the three months considered here.

8. The total electricity charge for the three months will be the £1,500 bill received and paid in the middle of March plus the £300 that has been used in the last two weeks of March. This £300 will be treated as an accrual (see Chapter 3, Prepayments and accruals), a cost incurred up to the end of an accounting period that has not been paid for by that period end date. The total electricity expense for the three months is thus £1,800. Dividing this figure by three gives us an expense of £600 for each month of the budgeted income statement.

9. While the total insurance payment is £1,500, this cost covers the whole 12-month period. Therefore, the monthly charge for insurance in our budgeted income statement will be £1,500 ÷ 12 = £125 per month, the remaining £1,125 (£1,500 − £375) being treated as a prepayment at the end of March.

WHY IS THIS RELEVANT TO ME? The budgeted monthly income statement

To enable you as a business professional and user of accounting information to understand how:

• Budgeted income statements you will be presented with have been drawn up

• To prepare your own budgeted monthly income statements

NUMERICAL EXERCISES Perfectly happy you could put together a budgeted income statement for a given time period using budgeted sales, materials, labour and fixed overheads? Work through the above example again to confirm your understanding of how we arrived at the figures in the budgeted income statement and then go to the **online workbook** and attempt Numerical exercises 11.3 to make sure you can produce a budgeted income statement from the sales, materials, labour and fixed overhead budgets.

SHOW ME HOW TO DO IT Did you really understand how this budgeted income statement in Illustration 11.7 was put together? View Video presentation 11.1 in the **online workbook** to see a practical demonstration.

Step 6: calculating cash receipts from sales

The budgeted income statement for the first three months of the year in Illustration 11.7 shows that Anna expects to make a healthy profit of £62,075. However, as we have already seen in this book, profit does not equal cash (Chapter 4, Profit ≠ cash). The

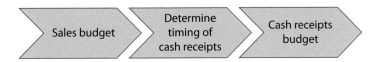

Figure 11.6 Budgeting step 6: cash receipts from sales budget

main concern of both entities and their banks will always be the cash flowing in and the cash flowing out, so it is important in any budgeting exercise to prepare the cash flow forecast alongside the budgeted income statement (Figure 11.6).

As we saw in Chapter 3 (Determining the amount of income or expense), sales are recognised as sales in the months in which they occur, but cash from those sales will not necessarily be received in those same months. Where goods are purchased on credit, there is a time lag between the date of the sale and the day on which cash from that sale is received.

Based on her past experience and knowledge, Anna expects 30% of her customers to pay in the month of sale and the remaining 70% to pay in the following month. These expected monthly cash receipts from sales are shown in Illustration 11.8.

Illustration 11.8 Anna: budgeted cash receipts from sales in January, February and March

	January	February	March	Total
	£	£	£	£
30% of sales received in month	12,525	17,250	23,025	52,800
70% of sales received next month	—	29,225	40,250	69,475
Total cash receipts per month	12,525	46,475	63,275	122,275

How were these cash receipts calculated? Anna expects to make total sales in January of £41,750 (Illustration 11.3); 30% of £41,750 is £12,525 received in January, the month of sale. Cash from the remaining 70% of January's sales will be received in the following month, February. This amounts to £29,225. You could calculate this number as 70% of £41,750 or just deduct the £12,525 already received from £41,750 to give you the same result. Work through the other sales and cash receipts in Illustrations 11.3 and 11.8 to ensure that you understand how the cash inflows from sales were calculated on the basis of Anna's expectations of when her customers will pay for the goods they have received.

Anna expects to make sales of £176,000 in the three months to the end of March (Illustrations 11.3 and 11.7). However, she has only collected £122,275 in cash (Illustration 11.8), a difference of £53,725. What does this difference represent and where should it be recorded in the budgeted accounts? Remember that this figure represents trade receivables due to the company, a current asset, which will be posted to Anna's forecast statement of financial position at 31 March.

11

WHY IS THIS RELEVANT TO ME?   Calculating cash receipts from sales

To enable you as a business professional and user of accounting information to understand:

- That, unless an entity sells for cash, sales do not equal cash receipts in the months in which the sales are recognised

- How to prepare budgets for receipts of cash from sales made to customers on credit terms

---

NUMERICAL EXERCISES   Totally convinced you could produce a statement of budgeted cash inflows from sales? Work through the above example again to confirm your understanding of how we arrived at the receipts from sales and then go to the **online workbook** and attempt Numerical exercises 11.4 to make sure you can produce a statement of budgeted cash inflows from sales.

Step 7: calculating cash payments to direct materials suppliers and direct labour

Just as Anna's customers do not pay for their goods immediately, so Anna, as a customer of her materials suppliers, does not pay for all her direct materials in the month she receives them. Therefore, cash payments to suppliers have to be worked out in the same way as cash receipts from customers (Figure 11.7).

Anna expects to pay for her purchases of wood as follows:

- 50% of the wood used in each month will be paid for in the actual month of use

- 30% of the wood used each month will be paid for one month after the actual month of use

- 20% of the wood used each month will be paid for two months after the actual month of use

Illustration 11.9 shows Anna's cash payments for wood.

Illustration 11.9 Anna: budgeted cash payments for wood for January, February and March

	January	February	March	Total
	£	£	£	£
50% of wood used in month	3,600	5,265	7,200	16,065
30% of wood used one month ago	—	2,160	3,159	5,319
20% of wood used two months ago	—	—	1,440	1,440
Total cash payments per month	3,600	7,425	11,799	22,824

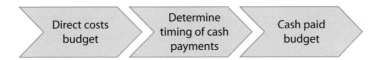

Figure 11.7 Budgeting step 7: cash payments from direct costs budget

How were these cash payments for wood calculated? Anna's direct materials budget (Illustrations 11.4 and 11.7) shows that she expects to use wood costing £7,200 in January. This will be paid for as follows:

- 50% in month of use (January): £7,200 × 50% = £3,600
- 30% one month after the month of use: £7,200 × 30% = £2,160
- 20% two months after the month of use: £7,200 × 20% = £1,440
- Check: £3,600 + £2,160 + £1,440 = £7,200

On top of these payments for January's wood made in February and March are payments for wood used in those months, as well as March's payment for the wood used in February.

Illustration 11.9 shows that Anna will be paying £22,824 in cash for her wood purchases in the three months to 31 March, while her income statement (Illustration 11.7) shows that she is incurring total direct materials costs for wood of £32,130. She therefore still has £9,306 to pay (£32,130 − £22,824), made up of £2,106 (20% of February's usage (£10,530 × 20%)) and £7,200 (50% of March's usage (£14,400 × 50%)). This figure of £9,306 represents a liability incurred and due to be paid to her suppliers. This amount will be recorded as a trade payable in Anna's forecast statement of financial position at 31 March.

As well as her suppliers of wood, Anna also buys in other direct materials for use in producing her furniture. She intends to pay the suppliers of these other materials in the month in which these materials are used in production. Similarly, she will be paying her employees in the month in which production and sales are made. The cash outflows for other direct materials and direct labour in her monthly cash flow forecast will be the same as the expenses already presented in Illustrations 11.5, 11.6 and 11.7.

WHY IS THIS RELEVANT TO ME? Calculating cash payments for direct materials and direct labour

To enable you as a business professional and user of accounting information to understand:

- That, unless an entity pays cash for all its direct materials and other purchases, direct materials do not equal cash payments in the months in which the costs are recorded
- How to prepare budgets for payments of cash to suppliers of direct materials and other purchases where these goods are purchased on credit terms

11

Quite confident you could put together a budgeted statement of cash outflows for direct materials and direct labour? Work through the above example again to confirm your understanding of how we calculated the cash outflow figures for direct materials and direct labour and then go to the **online workbook** and attempt Numerical exercises 11.5 to see how accurately you can produce a budgeted statement of cash outflows for direct materials and direct labour.

Step 8: draw up the monthly cash flow forecast

Anna now has all the information from which to draw up her month-by-month cash flow forecast. To do this she will look at the timing of her cash inflows from sales, the timing of her cash payments for direct materials and labour, together with any other payments or inflows of cash, as shown in Figure 11.8. Details of other outflows of cash were given in step 4, the budget for fixed costs. In addition, Anna decides that she will be paying £10,000 of her own money into her business bank account on 1 January and that she will be drawing out £2,000 a month for her personal expenses.

Her monthly cash flow forecast for January, February and March is presented in Illustration 11.10.

Illustration 11.10 Anna: budgeted cash inflows and outflows for January, February and March

	January £	February £	March £	Total £	Note
Cash received					
Sales	12,525	46,475	63,275	122,275	1
Capital introduced	10,000	—	—	10,000	2
Total cash receipts	22,525	46,475	63,275	132,275	
Cash paid					
Direct material: wood	3,600	7,425	11,799	22,824	3
Direct material: other	3,600	4,970	6,000	14,570	4
Direct labour	14,550	20,000	26,150	60,700	5
Rent	3,000	—	—	3,000	6
Machinery and tools	15,000	—	—	15,000	7
Electricity	—	—	1,500	1,500	8
Rates	—	1,200	—	1,200	9
Insurance	1,500	—	—	1,500	10
Drawings: personal expenditure	2,000	2,000	2,000	6,000	11
Total cash payments	43,250	35,595	47,449	126,294	

→

	January	February	March	Total	Note
	£	£	£	£	
Cash receipts – cash payments	(20,725)	10,880	15,826	5,981	12
Cash at the start of the month	—	(20,725)	(9,845)		13
Cash at the end of the month	(20,725)	(9,845)	5,981		14

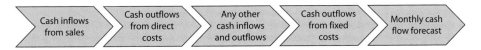

Figure 11.8 Budgeting step 8: drawing up the monthly cash flow forecast

How did Anna produce her monthly cash flow forecast for January, February and March? The following notes explain the numbers in each line of the cash flow forecast.

1. The budgeted cash receipts from sales were calculated in Illustration 11.8.

2. Anna is paying in £10,000 of her own money on 1 January as noted.

3. The budgeted cash payments to suppliers of wood were presented in Illustration 11.9.

4. Anna is paying her suppliers of other direct materials in the month in which the other direct materials are used, so the cash payments to these suppliers are the same as the budgeted costs in Illustrations 11.5 and 11.7.

5. Likewise, direct labour is paid in the month in which production and sales take place so these cash payments are the same as the costs given in Illustrations 11.6 and 11.7.

6. Step 4 tells us that the rent is paid on 1 January. Although the cost of this rent is spread across the three months to which it relates in the income statement (Illustration 11.7), the actual cash payment is budgeted to take place in January, so the whole £3,000 is recognised in the January cash payments.

7. In the same way, the cash outflow to buy the machinery and tools occurs in January so the whole of the £15,000 cash payment is recognised in January. Remember that depreciation is not a cash flow, just an accounting adjustment (Chapter 4, The indirect method, and Table 4.1) that spreads the cost of non-current assets over the periods benefiting from their use, so depreciation does not appear in a cash flow forecast. The actual outflow of cash to pay for the machinery and tools is £15,000 and this occurs in January so, just like the rent, this is the month in which this cash payment for these non-current assets is recognised.

11

8. Step 4 explains that the electricity bill received in March will be for £1,500 and that this electricity bill is paid in that month. Thus, £1,500 is the amount of cash that leaves the bank. The additional £300 accrual in the income statement will be paid in a later period so no cash outflow is recognised in these three months for this amount which has not yet been paid.

9. Step 4 notes that the rates bill is paid in February and the full £1,200 payment is recognised in the cash flow forecast as this is the actual amount paid in February regardless of the amounts that are allocated to each month in the forecast income statement.

10. Similarly, the insurance for the year is paid in January, so the whole cash outflow of £1,500 is shown in January's column even though the cost in the income statement is spread over the next 12 months.

11. Anna pays herself £2,000 a month from which to meet her personal expenditure so she recognises this as a cash outflow each month.

12. After totalling up the cash receipts (inflows) and the cash payments (outflows), the receipts – payments line is presented. For January, total receipts in Illustration 11.10 are £22,525 while payments total £43,250. Thus, £22,525 – £43,250 = –£20,725, which means that there is a shortfall of cash in January and Anna's bank account will be overdrawn. January thus shows greater payments than receipts of cash, while both February and March show a net inflow of cash, receipts in both months being greater than payments.

13. Cash at the start of the month is the cash balance at the end of the previous month. In the first month of a new business venture, as in Anna's case, this will be £nil. In continuing businesses, this will be the forecast or actual figure at the end of the last financial period.

14. The cash at the end of the month is the net cash inflow or outflow for the month plus or minus the cash or overdraft at the start of the month. In January, the net outflow for the month is £20,725 while the cash at the start of January is £nil so (£20,725) +/– £nil = (£20,725). At the end of February, there is a net cash inflow of £10,880 (total cash inflows of £46,475 – total cash outflows of £35,595). Adding this positive inflow of £10,880 to the negative balance at the start of the month (£20,725) gives us a lower overdraft at the end of February (£9,845), which then forms the balance at the start of March.

11

WHY IS THIS RELEVANT TO ME?　The budgeted monthly cash flow forecast

To enable you as a business professional and user of accounting information to understand:

- How budgeted cash flow forecasts you will be presented with have been drawn up
- How to prepare your own monthly budgeted cash flow forecasts

NUMERICAL EXERCISES   Reckon you could draw up a budgeted cash flow forecast? Work through the above example again to confirm your understanding of how the cash flow forecast was constructed and then go to the **online workbook** and attempt Numerical exercises 11.6 to make sure you can produce these budgeted statements.

SHOW ME HOW TO DO IT   How easily did you follow the preparation of Anna's budgeted monthly cash flow forecast? View Video presentation 11.2 in the **online workbook** to see a practical demonstration of how the budgeted monthly cash flow forecast in Illustration 11.10 was put together.

The importance of cash flow forecasts

The cash flow forecast is the most important budgeted statement that you will ever produce. We have already seen in this book that cash generation is the critical task for businesses as, without adequate cash inflows, a business will be unable to meet its liabilities as they fall due and will collapse. Give me an example 11.2, from the Entrepreneur column in the *Financial Times*, emphasises how business professionals must continue to produce cash flow forecasts no matter how high up an organisation they climb. If they do not, they are risking the very survival of their organisations.

GIVE ME AN EXAMPLE 11.2   Custodians of finance make the difference

The weak link in many failed companies is the finance director. Better custody of borrowed or invested money by them would so often have prevented disaster. In most cases their words betray them as much as the numbers. I am indebted to John Dewhirst of Vincere, the turnaround specialists, for collecting some of the classic lines I discuss below.

'I don't do cash forecasts. I've never found them useful.'

A lack of focus on cash is perhaps the greatest sin. A finance professional who does not prepare reasonably accurate projections of liquidity on a rolling basis is guilty of dereliction of duty. Often FDs drop such nitty gritty as they ascend the ranks, while some have historically enjoyed a cash cushion and never felt the pressure. They are the ones exposed when conditions deteriorate.

Luke Johnson, *The Entrepreneur*, Business Life, 19 January 2011, page 14

From the *Financial Times* © The Financial Times Limited 2011. All Rights Reserved.

WHY IS THIS RELEVANT TO ME?   The importance of cash flow forecasts

To emphasise to you as a business professional and user of accounting information:

- The critical importance of forecasting cash flows on a regular basis
- The risks you run if you do not undertake regular cash flow forecasting

Step 9: draw up the budgeted statement of financial position

The final step in the budgeting process is to draw up the budgeted statement of financial position at the end of the budgeted period, as shown in Figure 11.9. As we saw in Chapter 2, this statement summarises the assets and liabilities of an entity at the end of an accounting period, whether actual or budgeted. We have already looked at all the numbers that will go into Anna's statement of financial position when we prepared the budgeted income statement and budgeted cash flow forecast. Anna's budgeted statement of financial position is presented in Illustration 11.11, together with notes reminding you of the sources of the figures.

Illustration 11.11 Anna: budgeted statement of financial position at 31 March

	£	Note
Non-current assets		
Machinery and tools	14,250	1
Current assets		
Trade receivables	53,725	2
Insurance prepayment	1,125	3
Rates prepayment	600	4
Cash at bank	5,981	5
Total current assets	61,431	
Total assets	75,681	
Current liabilities		
Trade payables for wood	9,306	6
Electricity accrual	300	7
Total current liabilities	9,616	
Net assets: total assets – total liabilities	66,075	
(£75,681 – £9,616)		
Capital account		
Capital introduced	10,000	8
Net profit for the three months	62,075	9
Drawings	(6,000)	10
	66,075	

Notes to Anna's statement of financial position

1. Machinery and tools cost £15,000. Depreciation of £750 has been charged to the income statement for the three months to the end of March (Illustration 11.7), so the net book value (cost – depreciation) of these assets is £15,000 – £750 = £14,250.

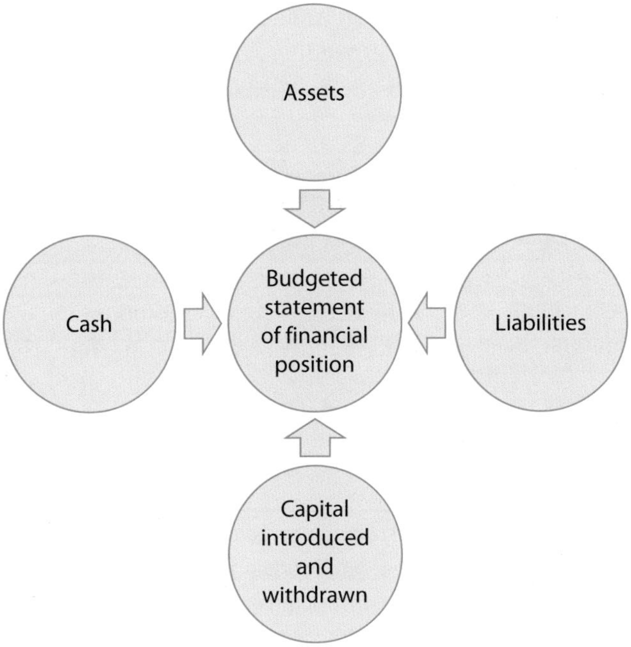

Figure 11.9 Budgeting step 9: drawing up the budgeted statement of financial position at the period end

2. The cash not collected from customers by the end of March. We calculated this figure in Step 6.

3. The payment of £1,500 covers 12 months of insurance; £375 has been charged against profits as the insurance cost for the three months in the budgeted income statement to the end of March (Illustration 11.7), so there is an insurance prepayment of nine months. Therefore, the insurance prepayment is £1,500 × 9/12 = £1,125.

4. Similarly, the payment of £1,200 covers six months of rates expenditure. At 31 March only three of the six months paid for have been used up and charged as an expense in the budgeted income statement (Illustration 11.7), so there is a prepayment at 31 March of £1,200 × 3/6 = £600. This £600 represents the rates cost to be charged as an expense in the income statements for April, May and June.

5. The cash at bank must equal the closing cash figure in the cash flow forecast (Illustration 11.10).

6. This trade payables figure was calculated in Step 7.

7. The electricity accrual is the expense incurred but not yet paid.

8. Anna introduced £10,000 to the business on 1 January in the cash flow forecast.

9. Net profit for the three months is read off the forecast income statement in Illustration 11.7.

10. Drawings are the total amount that Anna has withdrawn from the business bank account for her own personal expenditure over the course of the three months. This figure appears in the cash flow forecast in Illustration 11.10.

WHY IS THIS RELEVANT TO ME?   The budgeted statement of financial position

To enable you as a business professional and user of accounting information to understand how:

• The budgeted statement of financial position is compiled from the budgeted income statement and cash flow forecast

• To prepare your own budgeted statements of financial position

---

NUMERICAL EXERCISES   Quite certain you can draw up a budgeted statement of financial position? Work through the above example again to confirm your understanding of how the statement of financial position was constructed and then go to the **online workbook** and attempt Numerical exercises 11.7 to make sure you can produce this statement.

SHOW ME HOW TO DO IT   How well did you understand how Anna's budgeted statement of financial position was put together? View Video presentation 11.3 in the **online workbook** to see a practical demonstration of how this statement was prepared.

Conclusions: financing expansion

What has Anna learnt from her budgeting exercise? At the start of the process, she had approached the bank for finance to start her new workshop. The bank asked her to undertake a budgeting exercise. By producing her budgets she now knows that, if everything goes exactly to plan, she will need to borrow a maximum £20,725 (Illustration 11.10) from the bank as a result of her expansion. Happily, her cash flow forecast also shows that this maximum borrowing of £20,725 will be paid off by the end of March, so any financing she needs will be very short term. A short-term overdraft with the bank would be the most appropriate form of financing for Anna.

Budgeting flowchart summary

We have now looked in detail at the budgeting process, the steps that are followed and the order in which those steps proceed. We can summarise the budgeting process in a flow chart. This flow chart is shown in Figure 11.10. Look back at the earlier sections of this chapter and relate each step to what you have learnt during our study of the budgeting process so far.

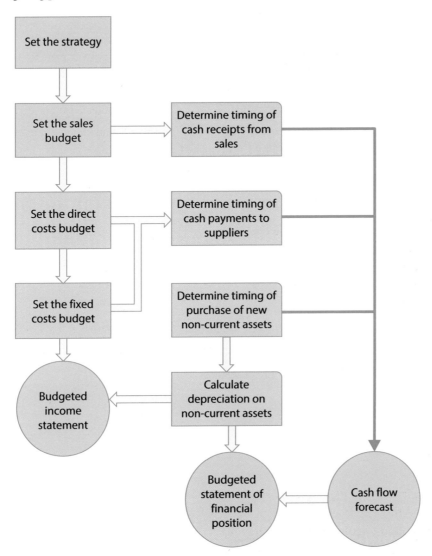

Figure 11.10 The budgeting process

11

GO BACK OVER THIS AGAIN! Think you could reproduce the above flowchart with all the steps in the right order? Go to the **online workbook** and have a go at Exercises 11.3 to see if you can.

GO BACK OVER THIS AGAIN! A copy of this budgeting flowchart summary (Figure 11.10) is available in the **online workbook**: you might like to keep this on screen or print off a copy for easy reference while you revise the material in this chapter to provide you with a route map through the budgeting process.

Budgetary control: income statement

Figure 11.11 The budgetary control process

As we noted earlier in this chapter, budgets are used for control purposes. Once each month of actual activity is complete, comparisons are made between what was budgeted to occur and what actually happened. Figure 11.11 illustrates this process. It is important to undertake this comparison activity every month so that variances from the budget can be determined and their causes investigated. It would be pointless waiting to complete a whole year of activity before any comparisons were made. By then it would be too late to undertake the necessary action to correct budget deviations. In the same way, you do not wait until the end of the academic year to review feedback on your coursework, but instead look at the feedback on each assignment as it is returned so that you can make the necessary improvements in your next piece of assessment.

Monthly comparisons are an example of relevant accounting information (Chapter 1, What qualities should accounting information possess?). Monthly data is provided on a timely basis with a view to influencing managers' economic decisions in terms of, for example, what products to continue selling, whether to discount products that are not selling or to seek out cheaper sources of material if direct material prices from the current supplier are now too high. Comparisons are also confirmatory as well as predictive. The closer budgeted figures are to actual results in a month, the more likely budgeted figures for future months are to predict future outcomes accurately.

As an example, let's look at Anna's budgeted and actual results for January. These are shown in Illustration 11.12.

Illustration 11.12 Anna: budgeted v. actual income statements for January

	January budget £	January actual £	January variances £
Sales	41,750	43,000	1,250
Cost of sales			
Direct material: wood	7,200	8,000	(800)
Direct material: other	3,600	3,550	50
Direct labour	14,550	14,500	50
Cost of sales	25,350	26,050	(700)
Gross profit (sales – cost of sales)	16,400	16,950	550
Expenses			
Rent	1,000	1,000	—
Rates	200	200	—
Machinery and tools depreciation	250	300	(50)
Electricity	600	600	—
Insurance	125	125	—
Net profit (gross profit – expenses)	14,225	14,725	500

In Illustration 11.12, numbers in brackets in the January variances column are classified as unfavourable, those variances that have reduced the budgeted profit, whereas figures without brackets are favourable, those variances that have increased the budgeted profit.

Now that we have produced our budget v. actual comparison, we can make the following observations.

Higher sales

- Sales are higher than budgeted. This suggests that the original estimates of product sales were a little lower than they should have been. If more products have been sold, Anna should find out why this has occurred and determine whether she can continue to exploit this favourable trend to make higher sales in the future.

- Alternatively, selling prices might have been higher than budgeted because of increased demand pushing prices up. Anna should do her best to maintain any higher selling prices as she will make more profit as a result.

- As there are two possible explanations for this sales variance, Anna will have to conduct further investigations to determine which of the two options is correct or whether it is a combination of both. The sales variance tells her to investigate further, but does not tell her the cause of this variance.

Direct costs

- The cost of wood used in production of goods sold rose in January. This, in itself, is not a surprise as higher production and sales will require more raw material input. However, Anna will need to investigate whether the price of wood has increased or more wood than expected was used in production.

- Other direct material cost less than expected, suggesting lower prices than budgeted or more efficient usage by the workforce.

- Similarly, the cost of labour was lower despite the increased production and sales, suggesting that the workforce has been more productive than budgeted.

- Anna should try to encourage more efficient working as this will increase productivity and lower the costs per unit of production, resulting in the generation of higher profits.

- To encourage this higher productivity, Anna might introduce a bonus scheme for her workers to give them a share in any increased profits. However, she will need to make sure that the bonus scheme does not encourage the workforce to work with less care and attention to detail so that the finished production, while taking less time to produce, is of lower quality.

Fixed costs

- Rent and insurance overheads should be as budgeted as these costs should be easily predictable in advance.

- The rates and electricity budget and actual figures are currently the same as we do not have any actual bills to work from. Remember that the rates bill is expected in February and the electricity bill will arrive in March. Once the actual bills are received Anna will be able to determine whether these costs are higher or lower than budgeted.

- The higher than budgeted depreciation figure suggests that the machinery and tools cost Anna more than anticipated, resulting in a higher monthly depreciation charge. Anna will need to check the actual payment for machinery and tools.

Net profit

- Overall, actual profits for January were higher than budgeted by £500.
- Based upon her investigations of the causes of the variances in January, Anna will aim to correct any unfavourable variances in the cost and usage of wood, while attempting to exploit the favourable variances in the sales to sell more goods or to sell goods at a higher price.

WHY IS THIS RELEVANT TO ME? Budgetary control: actual v. budget comparisons: income statement

As a business professional and user of accounting information, you will be expected to:

- Take on responsibility for your departmental budget and explain variations between budgeted and actual results
- Produce actual v. budget comparisons on a monthly basis
- Ask relevant questions when evaluating actual v. budget comparisons

GO BACK OVER THIS AGAIN! Could you suggest reasons for changes in budgeted v. actual sales and costs? Go to the **online workbook** and have a go at Exercises 11.4.

Budgetary control: cash flow forecast

As well as comparing her budgeted and actual income statements, Anna will also undertake a comparison of her budgeted and actual cash flows. As we noted at the start of this chapter, Anna needs additional finance from the bank to expand her business and move into the larger workshop. Her initial forecasts suggested that she would only need to borrow a maximum of £20,725. Because of the critical nature of cash inflows and outflows in her business operations, both Anna and her bank will be watching her cash position very closely to make sure that she does not exceed her borrowing capacity or her borrowing limits.

11

Anna produces her forecast and actual cash flow comparisons for January in Illustration 11.13.

Illustration 11.13 Anna: budgeted v. actual cash inflows and outflows for January

	January budget £	January actual £	January variances £
Cash received			
Sales	12,525	13,760	1,235
Capital introduced	10,000	10,000	—
Total cash receipts	22,525	23,760	1,235
Cash paid			
Direct material: wood	3,600	4,000	(400)
Direct material: other	3,600	3,550	50
Direct labour	14,550	14,500	50
Rent	3,000	3,000	—
Machinery and tools	15,000	18,000	(3,000)
Electricity	—	—	—
Rates	—	—	—
Insurance	1,500	1,500	—
Drawings – personal expenditure	2,000	2,000	—
Total cash payments	43,250	46,550	(3,300)
Cash receipts – cash payments	(20,725)	(22,790)	(2,065)
Cash at the start of the month	—	—	—
Cash at the end of the month	(20,725)	(22,790)	(2,065)

What does this forecast v. actual cash flow comparison tell Anna? She can draw the following conclusions:

- Her customers are paying more quickly than she expected. While she anticipated that 30% of her customers would pay in the month of sale, 32% of actual sales have paid in January (£13,760 ÷ £43,000 (actual sales from the income statement in Illustration 11.12) × 100%). Anna should try to persuade her customers to continue paying more quickly as this will improve her cash inflows and thereby reduce her borrowings more rapidly.

- While £400 more has been paid out for wood, this is consistent with Anna's forecast that she would pay for 50% of the wood she used in the month of usage. As her actual usage was £8,000 (Illustration 11.12), she has paid half this amount in January.

- Payments for both other materials and labour are £50 less than expected, but these are the actual amounts used in January according to the forecast v. actual income statement (Illustration 11.12). Cash payments are thus in line with Anna's policy of paying in full for labour and other materials in the month in which they were used.

- Machinery and tools were forecast to cost £15,000 but in fact cost £18,000. This is consistent with the increase in depreciation shown in the income statement in Illustration 11.12. The machinery and tools are expected to have a five-year life, which gives an annual depreciation charge of £3,600 per annum (£18,000 ÷ 5) which equates to £300 per month (£3,600 ÷ 12). Anna tells you that the machinery and tools had been imported from Germany and that the increased cost was because of a fall in the value of the pound against the euro at the time the machinery and tools were paid for.

- All other inflows and outflows of cash were as forecast.

- As a result of the above differences in her expected cash inflow and outflows, Anna has borrowed an additional £2,065 from the bank in January. The sole cause of this problem was the payment for her machinery and tools. Her aim now will be to pay off this additional borrowing as quickly as possible by encouraging her customers to pay more promptly or trying to sell more products each month to increase her cash inflows while keeping outflows of cash as low as possible.

WHY IS THIS RELEVANT TO ME?   Budgetary control: actual v. budget comparisons: cash flow

As a business professional and user of accounting information you must appreciate that:

- Cash is the lifeblood of business and without it businesses will run out of money and collapse

- Monitoring forecast v. actual cash is thus just as (if not more) important than comparing forecast v. actual profits

NUMERICAL EXERCISES   Positive you could produce a comparison of forecast v. actual cash flows? Go to the **online workbook** and have a go at Numerical exercises 11.8.

Sensitivity analysis

Anna has produced her forecasts for the first three months of operations and predicted her maximum borrowings from the bank. However, what if her forecasts don't turn out as she expects? How will this affect her profits and her cash flows? Given questions such as these, it is usual when budgeting to conduct sensitivity analysis to assess how profits and cash flows would turn out if certain expectations are changed. Thus, for example, a reduction in forecast sales units might be applied, or an increase in direct costs of 10% or a fall in selling price of 10%. Spreadsheets make these 'what if?' calculations easy to undertake.

As an example, let's see what would happen to profits and cash flows if forecast unit sales of Anna's products fell by 10% while keeping selling prices the same. We will adopt various short-cuts in producing our figures here, but all the calculations will be available in the online workbook.

First, let's look at the income statement showing a 10% fall in numbers of products sold compared with Anna's original expectations. This is shown in Illustration 11.14.

Illustration 11.14 Anna: budgeted income statement for January, February and March assuming a 10% fall in the number of products sold while keeping selling prices the same

	January £	February £	March £	Total £	Note
Sales	37,575	51,750	69,075	158,400	1
Cost of sales	22,815	31,950	41,895	96,660	2
Gross profit (sales – cost of sales)	14,760	19,800	27,180	61,740	
Expenses					
Fixed costs	2,175	2,175	2,175	6,525	3
Net profit (gross profit – expenses)	12,585	17,625	25,005	55,215	

Notes on the above forecast income statement:

1. Sales volumes reduce by 10%, which results in sales 10% lower than those shown in Illustrations 11.3 and 11.7.

2. As sales volumes fall by 10%, cost of sales (direct costs) also fall by 10% as Anna's direct costs in producing 10% fewer goods will be 10% lower.

3. Budgeted fixed costs are made up of £1,000 (rent) + £200 (rates) + £250 (depreciation) + £600 (electricity) + £125 insurance to give total budgeted fixed costs per month of £2,175. These are the same costs that we used in Illustration 11.7. Remember that fixed costs do not change with different levels of sales and production, so these costs are the same for the original budgeted sales and the revised budgeted sales volumes of 10% lower than originally forecast.

Anna's original budgeted profit of £62,075 in Illustration 11.7 has now fallen to £55,215 given a 10% fall in sales volumes.

However, Anna's main concern was with finance and how much she would need to borrow from the bank. Surely the effect of this fall of 10% in sales volumes will increase the size of her projected overdraft? The effect of the 10% fall in sales volumes on the cash flow forecast is shown in Illustration 11.15.

Illustration 11.15 Anna: budgeted cash inflows and outflows for January, February and March assuming a 10% fall in the number of products sold while keeping selling prices the same

	January £	February £	March £	Total £
Cash received				
Sales	11,273	41,827	56,947	110,047
Capital introduced	10,000	—	—	10,000
Total cash receipts	21,273	41,827	56,947	120,047
Cash paid				
Direct material: wood	3,240	6,683	10,619	20,542
Direct material: other	3,240	4,473	5,400	13,113
Direct labour	13,095	18,000	23,535	54,630
Rent	3,000	—	—	3,000
Machinery and tools	15,000	—	—	15,000
Electricity	—	—	1,500	1,500
Rates	—	1,200	—	1,200
Insurance	1,500	—	—	1,500
Drawings: personal expenditure	2,000	2,000	2,000	6,000
Total cash payments	41,075	32,356	43,054	116,485
Cash receipts – cash payments	(19,802)	9,471	13,893	3,562
Cash at the start of the month	—	(19,802)	(10,331)	
Cash at the end of the month	(19,802)	(10,331)	3,562	

Forecast payments for rent, machinery and tools, electricity, rates, insurance and drawings across the three months under review do not change, so these stay the same in both Illustrations 11.10 and 11.15. Receipts from sales fall, but forecast payments for wood, other materials and direct labour fall by more than the reduction in sales receipts. This has the effect of actually reducing the expected borrowings at the end of January from £20,725 to £19,802, so, even with lower sales volumes, Anna is borrowing less. Her cash balance at the end of three months is lower at £3,562 compared to the £5,981 shown in Illustration 11.10, but she still pays off the borrowings by the end of March as in her original forecast.

The assumptions on which Anna's original budgets were based can be relaxed further to see what effect these changes will have on her budgeted income statement, cash flow forecasts and projected statement of financial position and you can have a go at some of these in the online workbook.

11

The following extract, in Give me an example 11.3, from the Audit Committee's report in the annual report and accounts of Greggs Plc, shows how sensitivity analysis is used in practice to test the assumptions on which forecasts and financial plans are based and to determine whether these forecasts and plans are realistic and achievable.

GIVE ME AN EXAMPLE 11.3   Sensitivity analysis

The significant areas of judgement considered by the Committee in relation to the financial statements for the 52 weeks ended 28 December 2013 are set out below. These significant areas of judgement are principally borne out of the strategic review which took place during the year, the results of which were announced in August 2013. The strategic review took place as a response to declining like-for-like sales and reduced profitability. The impact of the suggested measures was reflected in a five-year financial plan and liquidity forecasts which were presented to the Board along with sensitivities for each scenario. The assumptions underlying each scenario were challenged robustly by the Committee which concluded that they represented an appropriate and prudent position.

Source: Greggs Plc Annual Report and Accounts for the year ended 28 December 2013, page 44

WHY IS THIS RELEVANT TO ME?   Sensitivity analysis

To enable you as a business professional and user of accounting information to:

- Appreciate that original budgets will be subjected to sensitivity analysis to determine the effect of changes in budgeted numbers on forecast profits and cash flows

- Undertake sensitivity analysis on budgeted information

GO BACK OVER THIS AGAIN!   How readily did you understand how the figures for Anna were calculated for the reduction in sales volumes of 10%? Visit the **online workbook** Exercises 11.5 to view all the calculations involved in this exercise.

NUMERICAL EXERCISES   Quite convinced you could undertake sensitivity analysis on a set of budgeted figures? Go to the **online workbook** and have a go at Numerical exercises 11.9 to see what effect various changes would have on Anna's budgeted income statement and cash flow forecast for January, February and March.

CHAPTER SUMMARY

You should now have learnt that:

- Budgets perform planning, communicating, coordinating, motivating and control functions within organisations

- The sales budget is the starting point for all other budgeted figures and statements

- Entities prepare budgeted income statements and budgeted statements of cash inflows and outflows on a monthly basis

- Monthly comparisons are made between budgeted income and expenditure and budgeted cash inflows and outflows to ensure that operations are under control

- Businesses undertake comparisons between budgeted and actual income and expenditure to highlight variances in expected and actual financial performance

- Sensitivity analysis is applied to assumptions made in budgeted financial statements and forecasts to determine how easily an entity could make a loss or require overdraft financing

---

QUICK REVISION   Test your knowledge with the online flashcards in Summary of key concepts and attempt the Multiple choice questions, all in the **online workbook**. www.oxfordtextbooks.co.uk/orc/scott/

END-OF-CHAPTER QUESTIONS

Solutions to these questions can be found at the back of the book from page 500.

› *Develop your understanding*

Question 11.1

Dave is planning to start up in business selling ice cream from a van around his local neighbourhood from April to September. He wants to open a business bank account, but the bank manager has insisted that he provides a cash flow forecast together with a budgeted income statement and budgeted statement of financial position for his first six months of trading. Dave is unsure how to put this information together, but he has provided you with the following details of his expected income and expenditure:

- Dave will pay in £5,000 of his own money on 1 April to get the business started.

- He expects to make all his sales for cash and anticipates that he will make sales of £3,500 in April, £5,500 in May, £7,500 in each of the next three months and £2,500 in September.

- He will buy his ice cream from a local supplier and expects the cost of this to be 50% of selling price. Dave has agreed with his supplier that he will start paying for his ice cream in May rather than in the month of purchase.

- Dave intends to sell all his ice cream by the end of September and to have no inventory at the end of this trading period.

- Ice cream vans can be hired a cost of £1,500 for three months. The £1,500 hire charge is payable at the start of each three-month period.

- Van running costs are estimated to be £250 per month.

- Business insurance payable on 1 April will cost £500 for six months.

- Dave will draw £1,000 per month out of the business bank account to meet personal expenses.

11

Required

Provide Dave with:

- A cash flow forecast for the first six months of trading.
- A budgeted income statement for the first six months of trading.
- A budgeted statement of financial position at 30 September.

Question 11.2

Hena plc has a branch that manufactures and sells solar panels. Demand for solar panels has picked up recently and the company is looking to increase its output. Hena plc's branch currently manufactures 600,000 solar panels annually and is looking to double this capacity. A new factory has become available at an annual rent of £600,000 per annum payable quarterly in advance. New plant and machinery would cost £1.8 million, payable immediately on delivery on 1 January. This new plant and machinery would have a useful life of ten years and would be depreciated on a straight line basis with £nil residual value. The directors of Hena plc are now wondering whether they should go ahead with the new solar panel factory. They have produced the following projections upon which to base their forecasts.

Hena plc sells each solar panel for £150. Demand for the increased output is expected to be as follows:

- January: 20,000 panels
- February and March: 30,000 panels per month
- April: 40,000 panels
- May to August: 80,000 panels per month
- September: 60,000 panels
- October and November: 40,000 panels per month
- December: 20,000 panels
- All panels are sold to credit customers, 10% of whom pay in the month of sale, 60% in the month after and the remaining 30% two months after the month of sale.

Details of production costs are as follows:

- Materials cost is 30% of the selling price of the panels. Materials suppliers are paid in the month after production and sales have taken place.
- Production labour is 20% of the selling price; 70% of this amount is payable in the month of sale and the remainder, representing deductions from production wages for tax and national insurance, is paid to HM Revenue and Customs one month after production and sales have taken place.
- Other variable production costs of 10% of selling price are paid in the month of sale.

Fixed costs are estimated to be £50,000 per month and are to be treated as paid in the month in which they were incurred. Hena plc manufactures to order and sells all its production and has no inventories of solar panels at the end of the year.

Required

Using a spreadsheet of your choice, prepare the following statements for the next 12 months:

- A sales budget.
- A production costs budget.
- A monthly cash flow forecast.
- A monthly budgeted income statement.
- A statement of financial position at the end of the 12 months.

Advise the directors of Hena plc whether they should go ahead with the proposed expansion or not.

Question 11.3

The directors of Hena plc are impressed with your spreadsheet and your recommendation. However, they have new information that they would like you to build into your projections. The directors now expect that the selling price of panels will fall to £120 in the near future because of new competitors entering the market. Production materials, due to high levels of demand, will rise to 58% of the new selling price, while employees will have to be given a 5% pay rise based on production labour costs originally calculated in Question 11.2 to encourage them to stay. Other variable production costs will now fall to 10% of the new selling price. All other expectations in Question 11.2 will remain the same. The directors are now wondering if your recommendation would be the same once you have incorporated the above changes into your budget and forecast projections.

Required

Using the spreadsheet you have prepared for Question 11.2, prepare the following statements for the next 12 months on the basis of the directors' new expectations:

- A sales budget.
- A production costs budget.
- A monthly cash flow forecast.
- A monthly budgeted income statement.
- A statement of financial position at the end of the 12 months.

Advise the directors of Hena plc whether they should go ahead with the proposed expansion or not given the new information that has come to hand.

» *Take it further*

Question 11.4

It is now August 2017. You have been asked by your head of department to prepare the monthly budgeted income statement, the monthly cash flow forecast and the budgeted statement of financial position for the 12 months ending 31 December 2018. You have been provided with the following details to help you in this task:

(a) Positive cash balances at the end of each month will earn interest at the rate of 0.5% of the month end balance and this interest will be receivable in the following month.

(b) Negative cash balances at the end of each month will be charged interest at the rate of 2% of the month end balance and this interest will be payable in the following month.

(c) Cash of £30,000 will be spent in March 2018 on new plant and equipment. The new plant and equipment will be brought into use in the business in the month of purchase.

(d) Your company produces three products: shirts, dresses and skirts. The cost cards for each product are as follows:

	Shirts	Dresses	Skirts
	£	£	£
Direct materials	10.00	12.00	6.00
Direct labour	12.00	15.00	7.50
Variable overhead	3.00	5.00	1.50
Total variable cost	25.00	30.00	15.00

(e) Selling prices are 140% of total variable cost. Payments for direct labour are made in accordance with note (i) below. 60% of the cost of materials is paid for one month after the month in which the materials were used in production, with the other 40% of materials being paid for two months after the month in which they were used in production. Where purchases of direct materials are greater than £20,000 in any one month, a 2½% discount is given on all purchases of direct materials in that month. When purchases of direct materials are greater than £25,000 in any one month, a 3½% discount is given on all purchases of direct materials in that month.

(f) The marketing department has estimated that sales of each product for the year will be as follows:

	Shirts	Dresses	Skirts
2018	Number	Number	Number
January	500	300	800
February	600	350	900
March	750	400	700
April	900	700	650
May	1,000	800	500
June	1,000	1,200	400
July	800	1,000	350
August	700	600	200
September	950	400	500
October	650	300	600
November	850	450	750
December	1,100	600	850
Total	9,800	7,100	7,200

Your company sells its products directly to retailers. Retailers pay for the goods purchased as follows: 10% on delivery, 25% one month after delivery, 50% two months after delivery and the remaining 15% three months after delivery. All goods produced in the month are sold in the month and there are no inventories of finished goods or raw materials at the start or end of each month.

(g) The company rents its factory and offices and currently pays a total of £30,000 a year in rent. A rent review in March 2018 is expected to increase the annual factory rent to £36,000 from 1 August 2018. Quarterly rental payments in advance will be made on 1 February, 1 May, 1 August and 1 November 2018.

(h) Business rates for the six months to March 2018 will be paid on 1 October 2017 and the prepayment relating to January, February and March is shown in the forecast statement of financial position at 1 January 2018 below in note (k). Business rates of £7,500 per half year will be payable on 1 April 2018 and 1 October 2018. These business rates will cover the year from 1 April 2018 to 31 March 2019.

(i) Administrative and supervisory staff salaries are expected to total up to £9,000 a month. 68% of staff salaries and direct labour costs are payable in the month in which they are incurred with the remaining 32% representing deductions for tax and national insurance being paid to HM Revenue and Customs in the following month.

(j) An insurance premium of £6,000 is payable on 1 May 2018 covering all the insurance costs of the business for the year to 30 April 2019.

(k) The forecast statement of financial position at 1 January 2018 is as follows:

	£
Non-current assets	
Plant, equipment and fittings: cost	120,000
Plant, equipment and fittings: accumulated depreciation	(36,000)
	84,000
Current assets	
Trade receivables (owed by customers)	122,000
Rent prepayment	2,500
Rates prepayment	3,600
Insurance prepayment	1,800
Bank interest receivable	17
Cash at bank	3,395
	133,312
Total assets	217,312
Current liabilities	
Trade payables (materials)	29,400
Trade payables (variable overhead)	7,200
Tax and national insurance (direct labour)	8,570
Tax and national insurance (admin and supervisory salaries)	2,752
Corporation tax payable	3,200
Dividend payable	5,000
Total liabilities	56,122
Net assets	161,190

→

	£
Equity	
Share capital	50,000
Retained earnings	111,190
	161,190

Notes to the forecast statement of financial position at 1 January 2018:

(i) Plant, equipment and fittings have a useful economic life of five years. Depreciation on these assets is charged monthly on the straight line basis.

(ii) Sales for October, November and December 2017 are budgeted to be £60,000, £70,000 and £75,000 respectively.

(iii) Purchases of materials totalled £20,000 in November 2017 and £21,400 (net of the 2% discount) in December 2017.

(iv) The dividend payable is scheduled for payment in April 2018 and the corporation tax is due for payment on 1 October 2018.

Required

Prepare the budgeted income statement and cash flow forecast for your company for the 12 months ended 31 December 2018 together with a budgeted statement of financial position at 31 December 2018.

Question 11.5

Your friend is proposing to make a bid for a manufacturing business that has come onto the market. The business makes white plastic patio chairs. The purchase price for this business is £240,000. This purchase price is made up of plant, equipment and fittings (£180,000) with a useful life of five years, a stock of raw materials (£20,000) and finished goods (£40,000). A delivery van will be purchased for £24,000 as soon as the business purchase is completed. The delivery van will be paid for in full in the second month of operations.

The following forecasts have been made for the business following purchase:

(a) Sales (before discounts) of plastic patio chairs, at a mark up of 60% on production cost (see (b) below), will be:

Month	January	February	March	April	May	June	July
Forecast sales (units)	10,000	12,000	14,000	20,000	24,000	22,000	18,000

30% of sales will be for cash. The remaining sales will be on credit with 60% of credit sales being paid in the following month and the remaining 40% paying what is owed two months after the month of sale. A discount of 10% will be given to selected credit customers, who represent 25% of gross sales.

(b) Production cost is estimated at £5.00 per unit. The estimated production cost is made up of:

- Raw materials: £4.00
- Direct labour: £1.00

Production will be arranged so that closing stock of finished goods at the end of every month is sufficient to meet 60% of sales requirements in the following month. The valuation of finished goods purchased with the business is based upon the forecast of production cost per unit given in (a) above.

(c) The single raw material used in production will be purchased so that stock at the end of each month is sufficient to meet half of the following month's production requirements. Raw material stock acquired on purchase of the business is valued at the forecast cost per unit as given in (b) above. Raw materials will be purchased on one month's credit.

(d) Costs of direct labour will be paid for as they are incurred in production.

(e) Fixed overheads are as follows: annual rent: £21,000, annual business rates: £8,100, annual heating and lighting: £7,500 and annual insurance: £1,500. Rent is payable quarterly in advance from 1 January. The business rates bill for January to March has been estimated at £1,800 and will be payable on 15 February while the rates bill from April to September has been estimated at £4,200 and will be payable by monthly instalments from 1 April. Heating and lighting will be payable quarterly in arrears at the end of each three-month period. Annual insurance will be payable on 1 January.

(f) Selling and administration overheads are all fixed, and will be £114,000 in the first year. These overheads include depreciation of the delivery van at 25% per annum on a straight line basis.

(g) Selling and administration overheads will be the same each month and will be paid in the month in which they are incurred.

Required

Prepare a monthly cash budget and a monthly income statement for the first six months of operations together with a statement of financial position at the end of June. As part of your budget, you should also produce a monthly production budget to calculate raw material purchases and a monthly sales budget to calculate both monthly sales and monthly cash receipts from sales.

12 Capital investment appraisal

LEARNING OUTCOMES

Once you have read this chapter and worked through the questions and examples in both this chapter and the online workbook, you should be able to:

- Understand what is meant by the term capital investment
- Understand why businesses undertake capital investment appraisal when making long-term investment decisions
- Explain how the four main capital investment appraisal techniques work
- Apply the four main capital investment appraisal techniques to capital investment decisions
- Explain the advantages and limitations of each of the four main capital investment appraisal techniques
- Understand the idea of the time value of money

Introduction

In the last few chapters we have looked at various short-term decision-making techniques as well as considering the management of short-term working capital in Chapter 7. These short-term decision-making techniques and working capital management aim to maximise contribution and profits over periods of a few weeks or months. What techniques should be applied if we want to maximise our value over the long term? This question arises when businesses want to make long-term investment decisions. What contribution and profits will new investments make to the business? Will the new investments be valuable in the long run rather than just being profitable over short periods? Will the contribution and profits be higher than the returns we could generate simply by putting the money into an interest paying bank account? These are important questions to ask when businesses are considering the investment of considerable sums of money in new plant and machinery or new buildings. Businesses want to know if the contribution generated by these new investments will return their original cost and more. If a long-term investment in non-current assets fails to return the money originally invested, there would be little point undertaking the project in the first place.

What is capital investment?

In Chapter 2 we considered the distinction between non-current assets and current assets. As we discovered, current assets are short-term assets (inventory, receivables and cash). In Chapter 7 we looked at how the cash arising from sales of inventory and the cash received from trade receivables is used to fund a business's short-term working capital requirements. Inflows of cash from inventory and trade receivables pay for the day-to-day expenditure that arises in running a business, such as payments for wages, rent, rates, electricity and heating bills as well as paying short-term liabilities as they become due.

However, non-current assets also require funding in order to maintain or expand a business's operations. Assets wear out or become outdated. Failure to replace and renew assets means that businesses are operating less efficiently and less profitably than they should. Without investment in new assets and new projects, businesses will not survive over the long term. When new investment is undertaken, this gives rise to new non-current assets that will be used to generate revenues, profits and cash over several years. Expenditure on these new non-current assets is termed capital expenditure, spending money now to benefit the future through the acquisition of these long-lasting, long-term assets.

12

If you were in charge of a haulage business, every few years you would need to invest in a new fleet of lorries. This fleet of lorries would then be used to generate revenue for several years before they themselves were replaced with a new fleet. Paying for these new vehicles would require long-term investment today. If the company did not currently have the cash on hand with which to pay for these new assets, these long-term funds would be provided by lenders in the form of loans (non-current liabilities, as we saw in Chapter 2) or by shareholders in the form of new share capital subscribed by the shareholders (considered in Chapter 5).

Businesses undertake **capital investment appraisal** to determine whether new investments will be worthwhile and whether they will generate more cash than they originally cost.

WHY IS THIS RELEVANT TO ME?   **Capital investment**

To enable you as a business professional and user of financial information to:

- Appreciate the need for businesses to invest continually in new long-term assets from which to generate increased revenue, profits and cash

- Reinforce your ability to distinguish between short-term working capital management and long-term capital investment

---

GO BACK OVER THIS AGAIN!   Can you distinguish between short- and long-term investment decisions? Go to the **online workbook** Exercises 12.1 to make sure you can make these distinctions.

Why is capital investment appraisal important?

Capital investment appraisal is essential when considering investments in new projects or in new assets. Without this appraisal, we will not be able to decide whether our investment is likely to be worthwhile in financial terms.

When choosing the university at which you wanted to study, you might have weighed up the benefits and drawbacks from your current course compared with the benefits and drawbacks of choosing another programme at another university. Your thoughts will have centred not just on financial considerations: you might have reflected on the nightlife, the sporting facilities and the academic reputation of your chosen university. But at some point you will have taken into account the costs of studying at a particular college compared with the costs of studying elsewhere and the likely career and salary opportunities that would be open to you upon completion of your chosen course.

In the same way, businesses will want to know whether proposed investments are likely to represent a valuable addition to current operations and whether a positive return will be generated for shareholders. If not, there is no point in undertaking the project. Businesses will want to take on all projects that capital investment appraisal techniques suggest will make a positive return. However, cash for investment purposes, like many other resources, is often in short supply. Therefore, entities will undertake capital investment appraisal to determine which one of the several options competing for funds is the most valuable project in which to invest, given the levels of risk involved.

EXAMPLE 12.3

If you have spare cash to invest, there are many banks, building societies and other investments competing for your money. You will weigh up each of the available options on the basis of which investment will give you the highest rate of interest, but also consider which investment is likely to be the safest home for your savings. It would be pointless putting your cash into an investment paying a high rate of interest if you were likely to lose all your money when the investment collapsed into liquidation.

Finally, the future is uncertain. What might seem like a good investment now might not look like such a good idea two years down the line. Therefore, managers have to exercise due care and attention when investing money into projects in the expectation that they will produce the best outcomes for investors and other stakeholders. Capital investment appraisal is a further example of managers exercising control over an entity's operations.

GIVE ME AN EXAMPLE 12.1   Capital investment appraisal

The following extract from the published report of Rio Tinto plc illustrates the rigorous approach adopted by company management to evaluating new investment opportunities.

We have strengthened our investment assessment criteria, our levels of independent review of opportunities and our investment approval processes. We approve investment only in opportunities that, after prudent assessment, offer attractive returns that are well above our cost of capital.

Rio Tinto plc Annual Report and Accounts 2014, Strategic Report, page 11.

Source: www.riotinto.com

12

WHY IS THIS RELEVANT TO ME?   Capital investment appraisal

As a business professional and user of financial information you will be expected to:

- Understand the importance of evaluating long-term investment projects and what they will contribute to your organisation

- Be involved in capital investment decisions and appraise both the financial and non-financial aspects of these decisions

- Undertake the necessary capital investment appraisal of long-term projects you are proposing yourself

---

GO BACK OVER THIS AGAIN!   Confident you can describe capital investment appraisal and explain why it's needed? Go to the **online workbook** Exercises 12.2 to make sure you appreciate what capital investment appraisal involves.

What financial information will I need to undertake capital investment appraisal?

Capital investment appraisal relates to future events, so a substantial amount of estimation is required when undertaking this technique, as shown in Figure 12.1. All costs and revenues associated with a proposed project are expressed in terms of cash inflows and cash outflows.

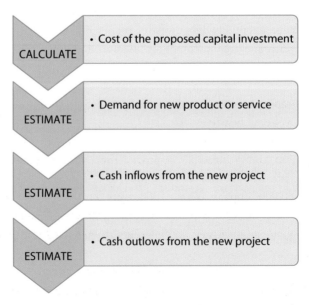

CALCULATE
- Cost of the proposed capital investment

ESTIMATE
- Demand for new product or service

ESTIMATE
- Cash inflows from the new project

ESTIMATE
- Cash outlows from the new project

Figure 12.1 Financial information and steps required in capital investment appraisal

The first piece of information required will be the cost of the new capital investment in £s. This is easily acquired as this cost will be readily available from the supplier of the new assets. In our haulage business example (Example 12.1), the capital investment will be the cost of the new lorries. This could be the list price or the list price less a discount for the purchase of several vehicles, but it is a readily ascertainable cost. If the capital investment involves the construction of a new building, then cost will be the cost of acquiring the land plus the construction costs. Again, the cost of the land will be a verifiable fact from the price the seller requires for the land, while the cost of the building will be determined by the engineers and designers at the construction company chosen to complete the project.

More difficult will be the estimates of revenue and costs arising from the new investment in each year of the proposed project's life. Demand for the new product or service will have to be determined along with the associated costs of providing the service or producing the product. Current demand and current revenue arising from that demand can be calculated quite easily, but future demand and future revenue will depend upon many uncertainties. Demand might fall to zero very quickly as a result of superior services and products from competitors or it might rise very rapidly as the business becomes the leading provider in the sector. Technology might reduce costs very quickly or costs might rise as a result of demand for particular raw materials that are in short supply. Whatever the revenues and costs, they will be subject to a high degree of estimation and in many ways will just represent a best guess.

Capital investment appraisal techniques: comprehensive example

To illustrate the capital investment appraisal techniques that are used in practice we will now turn to a comprehensive example.

Anna is looking to expand by diversifying into different areas of business. She currently has £500,000 to invest in acquiring the assets of an existing business from its owners. She has identified a stonemason, a furniture workshop and a garden design and build company as possible targets for her new investment. Market research and costings indicate that the net cash inflows (revenue – expenditure) into the three businesses over the next five years are expected to be those shown in Illustration 12.1.

All three businesses require the same initial investment, but produce differing total cash inflows after deducting the cost of the original investment. One business is expected

12

Illustration 12.1 Anna: cash flows from the three possible capital investment projects

	Stonemason	Furniture workshop	Garden design and build
	£000	£000	£000
Investment cost (an outflow of cash)	(500)	(500)	(500)
Net cash inflows in year 1	160	190	50
Net cash inflows in year 2	160	180	100
Net cash inflows in year 3	160	170	150
Net cash inflows in year 4	160	160	250
Net cash inflows in year 5	160	150	350
Cash inflow from sale of the investment at the end of year 5	200	100	300
Total net cash inflows	1,000	950	1,200
Total net cash inflows – investment cost	500	450	700

to provide a steady income throughout the five years, one produces high initial cash inflows, but these then decline, while the final opportunity starts with very low net cash inflows, which then grow rapidly. How will Anna choose the business in which she should invest? Initially, it would appear that Anna will choose the garden design and build business for her investment as this produces the highest net cash inflow over the five years along with a higher resale value for the assets. However, the majority of the cash inflows from the garden design and build operation occur towards the end of the five years. Later cash inflows are much less certain (and hence riskier) than cash inflows that occur earlier in the other projects' lives. The following capital investment appraisal techniques can be used to help Anna make her decision.

Capital investment appraisal techniques

There are four commonly used techniques when undertaking capital investment appraisal. These are:

- Payback
- Accounting rate of return (ARR)
- Net present value (NPV)
- Internal rate of return (IRR)

We will look at each of the above techniques in detail to show how each of them works and what each of them tells us about the positive or negative financial returns from each project.

Payback

This method calculates the number of years it will take for the cash inflows from the project to pay back the original cost of the investment. An investment of £1,000 into a deposit account that pays 5% interest per annum would provide you with annual interest of £50 (£1,000 × 5%). To repay your initial investment of £1,000 would take 20 years (£1,000 ÷ £50). In the same way, businesses assess how long the cash inflows from a project would take to repay the initial investment into the project.

GO BACK OVER THIS AGAIN! Convinced you can calculate a simple payback period? Go to the **online workbook** and have a go at Exercises 12.3 to make sure you can undertake these calculations successfully.

Looking at Anna's investment opportunities, let's consider the payback from the first option, the stonemason. To calculate the payback period, a payback table is drawn up to show how long the project will take to pay back the original investment. The first column of the table (see Table 12.1) lists the annual cash inflows and outflows, while the second column presents the initial investment outflow less the cash inflows received each year.

Table 12.1 Anna: payback table for the investment in the stonemason business

	Cash flows	Cumulative
	£000	£000
Initial investment year 0	(500)	(500)
Net cash inflows year 1	160	(340)
Net cash inflows year 2	160	(180)
Net cash inflows year 3	160	(20)
Net cash inflows year 4	160	140
Net cash inflows year 5	160	300
Cash inflow from sale of the investment at the end of year 5	200	500

In Table 12.1 the investment of £500,000 is made at the present time and so is shown as the initial outflow of cash from the project. Investments made at the start of a project, the present time, are conventionally referred to as being made in year 0 or at time 0. As cash flows into the project, so the initial investment is paid back and the investment in the project not yet paid back falls.

At the end of year 1, after deducting the first year's cash inflows of £160,000, there is £500,000 − £160,000 = £340,000 still to be recovered from the project before the full £500,000 is paid back. In year 2, the project generates another £160,000, so at the end of year 2 there is still £340,000 − £160,000 = £180,000 required from the project before the initial investment is repaid in full. This process is repeated until the cumulative cash flows show £nil or a positive number. At this point, the initial investment has been paid back by cash inflows into the project.

Table 12.1 shows that the stonemason project would repay the initial investment of £500,000 at some time between the end of years 3 and 4 as the cumulative cash flows (original investment − net cash inflows) turn positive by the end of year 4.

However, we can be more precise. Only £20,000 out of the £160,000 cash inflow in year 4 is required to repay the investment in the project that has not yet been repaid by the cash inflows in years 1, 2 and 3. Therefore, the exact payback period for an investment in the stonemason business would be:

$$3 \text{ years} + \frac{£20,000}{£160,000} = 3.125 \text{ years}$$

As 0.125 years is roughly equivalent to 1½ months (12 × 0.125), the initial investment of £500,000 at time 0 is fully repaid after 3 years and 1½ months.

NUMERICAL EXERCISES   Think you can calculate a payback period for a project? Work your way through the above example again to confirm your understanding of how we arrived at the payback period for the stonemason project and then go to the **online workbook** and attempt Numerical exercises 12.1 and 12.2 to make sure you can apply this investment appraisal technique to the other two investments that Anna is considering.

Payback: the decision criteria

When using the payback method of capital investment appraisal, the project chosen is always the investment that pays back its initial cash outlay most quickly. In Anna's case, on the basis of payback, she would choose to invest in the furniture workshop as this repays the initial outlay of £500,000 in less than three years while the other two projects repay the same initial investment in more than three years, as shown in Figure 12.2.

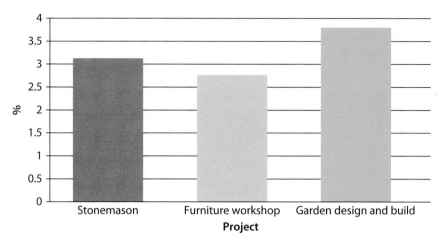

Figure 12.2 Payback periods in years of the three investment opportunities available to Anna

Would this be a good decision? If Anna is concerned with just the speed of her cash recovery, then the furniture workshop would be the correct choice as her initial investment is returned to her in the shortest possible time. The payback calculation is easy to make and easy to understand, but it does not consider the time value of money (see this Chapter, The time value of money). It also ignores the cash flows after the payback period is complete. In the case of the furniture workshop, a further £450,000 is generated from this project after the initial investment is paid back, whereas the garden design and build project yields a further £700,000 after payback, £250,000 more than the cash inflows from the preferred investment on the basis of the payback period.

Should the payback period be the sole criterion upon which to base an investment decision? The answer to this question is 'no'. Payback will be just one of the criteria upon which any investment decision is based. Further decisions have to be made about the long-term revenue generation prospects of the investment. You probably noticed that the cash inflows from the furniture workshop are reducing year by year and that the resale value of the assets of this business is significantly lower than the resale value of the assets in the other two projects under consideration. Any further investment in this business after the five-year period will probably generate lower cash inflows than the other two options, so, from a longer-term point of view, an investment in the furniture workshop is probably not the best use of Anna's money if she wants to maximise the potential returns on her investment.

Looking at the other investment options, the garden design and build, while presenting the longest payback period, shows rising cash inflows each year that accelerate towards the end of the five-year period. Therefore, this might well be a better investment for the longer term as demand for this business's services seems to be rising sharply and might be expected to increase even further after the end of year 5.

12

The stonemason business shows steady inflows of cash each year, but no increase or decrease in demand. This would seem to be the safest investment, but it is not one that will perform beyond expectations.

WHY IS THIS RELEVANT TO ME?   Payback method of capital investment appraisal

To enable you as a business professional and user of financial information to:

- Calculate a payback period for a proposed investment
- Understand the criteria on which to take an investment decision based on payback
- Understand the advantages and limitations of the payback method
- Appreciate that capital investment decisions have to be based on not just one but several criteria

---

SUMMARY OF KEY CONCEPTS   Totally happy you understand how payback works and what its advantages and limitations are? Revise payback with Summary of key concepts 12.1.

Accounting rate of return

This investment appraisal method averages the projections of accounting profit to calculate the expected rate of return on the average capital invested, as summarised in Figure 12.3. Accounting profit is represented by the net cash inflows of the project over its life, less the total depreciation (remember that depreciation is not a cash flow—refer back to Chapter 4, The indirect method, to revise this point). The total accounting profit projections are divided by the number of years the project will last to give the average profit over the life of the investment. This is then divided by the average capital employed over the life of the project to determine the ARR.

Let's see how the ARR would be calculated for the stonemason business and then you can practise this technique on the other two potential investment opportunities.

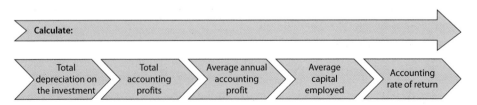

Figure 12.3 Steps in calculating the accounting rate of return (ARR) on an investment

ARR Step 1 Calculate the total depreciation on the investment

First, we will need to calculate the total depreciation on the investment in the stonemason project. Remember that the total depreciation provided on non-current assets is given by the assets' cost – the residual value of those assets (Chapter 3, Residual value and the annual depreciation charge).

From Illustration 12.1:

- The cost of the assets is £500,000
- The residual value is the cash inflow from the sale of the investment at the end of year 5 of £200,000

Therefore, total depreciation over the five years of the project's life is:

£500,000 (cost) – £200,000 (residual value) = £300,000

ARR Step 2 Calculate the total accounting profits

Total accounting profits are the total net cash inflows – the total depreciation. Total net cash inflows into the stonemason project are £160,000 for five years, a total of £800,000. The resale value of the assets is not included in the net cash inflows as this figure is used to calculate both the total depreciation on the project's assets and the average capital investment over the project's life.

Total accounting profits are thus £800,000 (net cash inflows) – £300,000 (depreciation) = £500,000.

ARR Step 3 Calculate the average annual accounting profit

The average annual accounting profit is then £500,000 ÷ 5 years = £100,000 per annum.

ARR Step 4 Calculate the average capital employed

The average capital employed in the stonemason project is found by adding together the original cost of the investment and the resale value of the assets at the end of the project and dividing this total figure by 2.

From Illustration 12.1:

- The cost of the assets is £500,000
- The residual value is the cash inflow from the sale of the investment at the end of year 5 of £200,000

12

Therefore, average capital employed in the stonemason business over the five years is:

$$(\text{£}500{,}000 \text{ (cost)} + \text{£}200{,}000 \text{ (residual value)}) \div 2 = \text{£}350{,}000$$

ARR Step 5 Calculate the accounting rate of return

The ARR is then the average annual accounting profit divided by the average capital employed in the project:

$$\frac{\text{£}100{,}000 \text{ (average annual profit)}}{\text{£}350{,}000 \text{ (average capital employed over the five years)}} \times 100\% = 28.57\%$$

NUMERICAL EXERCISES How confident are you that you can calculate an accounting rate of return for a project? Work your way through the above example again to confirm your understanding of how we arrived at the accounting rate of return for the stonemason project and then go to the **online workbook** and attempt Numerical exercises 12.3 and 12.4 to make sure you can apply this investment appraisal technique to the other two investments that Anna is considering.

Accounting rate of return: the decision criteria

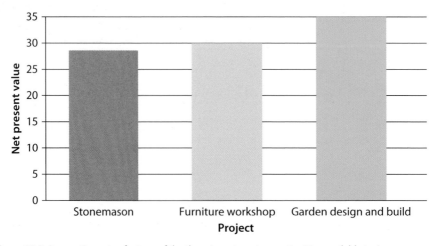

Figure 12.4 Accounting rate of return of the three investment opportunities available to Anna

The investment decision based on the ARR requires us to choose the proposed investment with the highest ARR, provided that this meets or exceeds the required ARR of the business. Assuming that the ARR meets Anna's target rate of return, the project that she will choose will be the garden design and build project as it produces an accounting rate of return of 35% compared with the furniture workshop, which has an accounting rate of return of 30%, as shown in Figure 12.4. This approach produces a quite different decision when compared to the payback method of investment appraisal.

While the ARR is easy to calculate and is based on accounting profits, it does suffer from some serious limitations:

- As with the payback method of investment appraisal, the ARR ignores the time value of money.

- The ARR is a percentage rather than the total profits generated by an investment, so projects with the same ARR could have hugely different cash flows, one with very low net cash inflows and one with very large net cash inflows. Managers will always prefer larger cash flows to smaller ones, but reliance on the relative measure of ARR might lead to the selection of a project with a higher rate of return but lower net cash inflows. In Anna's case the projects with the highest accounting rate of return and the highest accounting profits are the same, but this may not always be the case.

- ARR does not differentiate between projects (as payback does) that have the majority of the net cash inflows in the early stages of the project's life. As we have already noted, early cash inflows can be predicted with more accuracy and so are preferred by businesses as the money is in the bank rather than just being a potential future inflow of cash.

WHY IS THIS RELEVANT TO ME?   Accounting rate of return method of capital investment appraisal

To enable you as a business professional and user of financial information to:
- Calculate the ARR for a proposed investment
- Appreciate the criteria on which to make an investment decision based on the ARR
- Understand the advantages and limitations of the ARR method of capital investment appraisal

---

SUMMARY OF KEY CONCEPTS   Can you remember how the accounting rate of return is calculated and what its advantages and limitations are? Check your knowledge with Summary of key concepts 12.2.

12

GIVE ME AN EXAMPLE 12.2   Companies' use of payback and accounting measures in evaluating investment opportunities

Do companies use payback and accounting based measures in practice to evaluate investment opportunities? The following extracts from Next plc's Annual Report and Accounts for the financial year ended 25 January 2014 shows that they do.

Profitability of stores opened in the last 12 months is forecast to average 22% and payback on the net capital invested is expected to be 19 months. Both figures are within

Company investment hurdles of 15% store profitability and 24 months capital payback.

New store appraisals must meet demanding financial criteria before the investment is made, and success is measured by achieved profit contribution and return on capital against appraised targets.

Source: Next plc Annual Report and Accounts 2014, pages 7 and 18.

The time value of money

Before we consider the other two investment appraisal techniques, net present value (NPV) and the internal rate of return (IRR), we need to think about the time value of money. We noted above that both the payback and ARR methods of capital investment appraisal ignore this aspect of the investment decision. So why is the time value of money so important? And what do we mean when we talk about the time value of money? This approach to investment appraisal recognises that £1 received today is worth more than £1 received tomorrow. Why is today's money more valuable than tomorrow's?

Inflation will reduce the value of our cash: £1 will buy more today than it will buy this time next year. For example, if a litre of petrol costs £1.40 today, we can buy 30 litres of petrol for £42 (30 × £1.40 = £42). However, if the inflation rate is 5% per annum, this means that in one year's time, one litre of petrol will cost £1.47 (£1.40 × 1.05). Our £42 will now only buy us 28.57 litres of petrol (£42 ÷ £1.47), as the purchasing power of our £42 has fallen as a result of inflation. Therefore, given that inflation reduces the value of our money and what we can buy with it, it makes sense to receive cash today rather than receiving cash tomorrow.

We can combat the effects of inflation by investing our money to generate interest to maintain our purchasing power. £1 invested today at an annual interest rate of 5% will give us £1.05 in a year's time, our original £1 plus 5% interest. If the inflation rate over the same period has been 5%, we will be no worse off and our purchasing power will have remained the same. In our example above, £42 today invested at a rate of 5% would give us £44.10 (£42 × 1.05) in one year's time. With this £44.10 we could buy £44.10 ÷ £1.47 = 30 litres of petrol so the purchasing power of our money has been maintained.

However, if we can invest our £1 for a year at an interest rate of 5% while inflation is only 3%, at the end of the year we would need our original £1 plus a further 3p to buy the same goods in a year's time that £1 will buy today. We will thus be 2p better off as our £1.05 is more than the £1.03 we need for consumption in one year's time.

Finally, money that we will receive in the future is more risky than money we receive today because of the uncertainty that surrounds future income. Investing money carries the risk that we will not receive any interest as well as the risk that our original investment will not be repaid in full. Therefore, investors require a particular level of return to compensate them for the risk they are taking by investing their money. In the same way, businesses require a rate of return to compensate them for risking their capital in a particular venture. The riskier the venture is, the higher the rate of return that will be required to invest in that venture.

GIVE ME AN EXAMPLE 12.3   Higher risk = higher return

Two bailout packages totalling €240 billion were advanced to the Greek government in May 2010 and October 2011. In April 2015 growing fears that Greece would fail to repay what it owed to its international creditors, thereby forcing the country out of the European single currency, caused the value of Greek bonds to fall dramatically. As a result, anyone investing their money in Greek two-year bonds on 15 April 2015 would have seen the returns on these bonds rise to 27%. This very high return is due to the risk that the Greek government will be unable either to pay the interest or to repay the capital value of those bonds. Clearly, the higher the risk, the higher the return that investors will demand for taking on that risk. By contrast, the price that investors were paying for German 10-year government bonds (which are considered an ultra-safe investment) on the same day meant that their returns from their investment in these bonds are close to zero.

Source: www.wsj.com/articles/greek-government-bonds-plunge-on-ratings-downgrade-1429180492

WHY IS THIS RELEVANT TO ME?   The time value of money

To enable you as a business professional and user of financial information to:

• Understand that inflation erodes the value of today's money and reduces its future purchasing power

• Appreciate that money received today has more purchasing power than money received tomorrow

• Appreciate that cash expected in the future is less certain and so riskier

• Understand that investors will require a certain rate of return on money invested in order to compensate them for the risks they are taking in investing their money

---

GO BACK OVER THIS AGAIN!   Certain you have grasped the concept of the time value of money? Go to the **online workbook** and have a look at Exercises 12.4 to make sure you understand this concept and then have a go at Exercises 12.5 to check your grasp of this subject.

MULTIPLE CHOICE QUESTIONS   Totally happy you understand the time value of money? Go to the **online workbook** and have a go at Multiple choice questions 12.1 to test your understanding.

12

Business investment and the time value of money

In the same way, businesses invest money with the expectation that their investments will earn them a return in the future. Businesses will determine what they consider an acceptable level of return to be and use this level of return to discount expected future cash inflows and outflows to a present value. Present value expresses expected future inflows and outflows of cash in terms of today's monetary values. Discounting to present value thus expresses all cash inflows and outflows in the common currency of today, thereby facilitating a fair comparison of projected cash inflows and outflows for different investment proposals.

The acceptable level of return is referred to as the business's cost of capital and is sometimes known as the hurdle rate of return. If an investment clears the hurdle—that is, the NPV is greater than or equal to £nil—then it means that the project will deliver a positive return and generate more profit for the business over time than has to be invested at the beginning of the project.

Net present value

Anna estimates that her expected rate of return is 15%. This is the rate of return that she feels will compensate her for the risk she is taking in investing in a new business of which she has no experience. Applying this rate of return to the stonemason project produces the NPV results shown in Illustration 12.2.

Illustration 12.2 Anna: net present value of the investment in the stonemason business discounted at a rate of 15%

	Cash flows ×	Discount factor =	Net present value
	£000	15%	£000
Cash outflow year 0	(500)	1.0000	(500.00)
Net cash inflows year 1	160	0.8696	139.14
Net cash inflows year 2	160	0.7561	120.98
Net cash inflows year 3	160	0.6575	105.20
Net cash inflows year 4	160	0.5718	91.49
Net cash inflows year 5	160	0.4972	79.55
Cash inflow from sale of the investment at the end of year 5	200	0.4972	99.44
Stonemason investment: net present value of the project discounted at a rate of 15%			135.80

12

How did we arrive at these figures?

The initial investment is always made at the start of the project and so is already expressed in terms of today's money. Therefore, there is no need to discount this figure to present value as today's money is already stated at its present value. This figure is thus multiplied by a discount rate of 1.0000.

All cash inflows are assumed to be received at the end of each year of the project and so are discounted to present value as though they are received at the end of year 1, at the end of year 2, at the end of year 3 and so on, right up to the last expected cash inflow or outflow associated with the project. This is an important convention of the NPV and IRR capital investment appraisal techniques, but is obviously unrealistic as, in reality, cash will flow into and out of projects throughout the year. However, it is an assumption you need to be aware of and this assumption is made to keep the models as simple as possible.

Discount factors are presented in Table 1 in the Appendix. Check that the figures given earlier are the discount rates for time intervals 1, 2, 3, 4 and 5 for a 15% discount rate. If you ever need to derive your own discount rates, you would divide 1 by $(1 + \text{the interest rate being used})^n$ where n is the number of years into the project. In Anna's case, this is 1 divided by $(1 + 0.15)$ for year 1, 1 divided by $(1 + 0.15)^2$ for year 2, 1 divided by $(1 + 0.15)^3$ for year 3 and so on. Check that these calculations do give you the discount factors shown in Illustration 12.2 by working out these figures on your calculator now. Keep Table 1 in the Appendix handy for the remaining examples in this chapter and when you attempt the various activities in the online workbook.

Just as we saw with statements of cash flows in Chapter 4, cash outflows are shown in brackets while cash inflows are shown without brackets. This convention is also applied when calculating NPVs. Thus the initial investment, which is an outflow of cash, is shown in brackets while the inflows of cash are shown without brackets. Totalling up the NPV of the outflow and the NPVs of all the inflows gives us a positive NPV of £135,800 for the stonemason project.

NUMERICAL EXERCISES Confident you can calculate a net present value for a project? Work your way through the above example again to confirm your understanding of how we arrived at the net present value for the stonemason project and then go to the **online workbook** and attempt Numerical exercises 12.5 and 12.6 to make sure you can apply this investment appraisal technique to the other two investments that Anna is considering.

SHOW ME HOW TO DO IT How well did you understand the calculation of a proposed project's net present value? View Video presentation 12.1 in the **online workbook** to see a practical demonstration of how the net present value calculation is carried out.

12

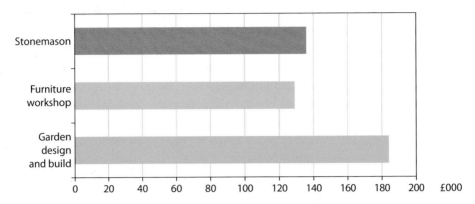

Figure 12.5   Net present value of the three investment opportunities available to Anna

Net present value: the decision criteria

Projects discounted at the business's cost of capital resulting in either a NPV of £nil or a positive NPV are accepted. If a company has several projects under consideration, then all projects with a positive or £nil NPV are taken on. Where more than one project is competing for investment capital, then the project with the highest NPV is accepted first. If investment capital is available to undertake a further project, then the project with the second highest NPV is accepted and so on until all the available capital for investment has been allocated to projects. Proposed projects with a negative NPV are rejected and are not developed beyond the evaluation stage.

In Anna's case, she can only invest in one of the three projects as her capital for investment is limited to £500,000. Figure 12.5 shows that the garden design and build project gives the highest NPV of £183,850, well above the project with the second highest NPV, the stonemason business. The furniture workshop, which was ranked first on the basis of payback and second on the basis of ARR, is now the worst performing project on the basis of NPV. Therefore, Anna will accept the garden design and build project on the basis of the evaluation provided by the NPV method of investment appraisal.

Net present value: advantages

The NPV technique has the following advantages:

- Unlike the payback and ARR investment appraisal techniques, NPV does take into account the time value of money. This makes it a superior method of evaluating and differentiating between several projects.

- NPV discounts all cash inflows and outflows from a project into today's money to enable a fair comparison between projects to be made.

- NPV accounts for all the cash inflows and outflows from a project.

- Cash inflows that arise later in the project's life are riskier than cash inflows that arise earlier. The use of discount factors enables users of this technique to reflect this increased risk arising from later cash inflows as these cash inflows are worth less in current money terms.

- The NPV technique can be used in conjunction with the payback approach to determine when NPVs become positive. The further into the future this happens, the riskier the project is.

Net present value: limitations

However, as with all investment appraisal techniques, the NPV approach also suffers from the following disadvantages:

- This method is more difficult to understand than the simpler payback method.

- The technique makes the very large assumption that cash inflows and outflows and discount rates can be predicted accurately.

WHY IS THIS RELEVANT TO ME?   Net present value method of capital investment appraisal

To enable you as a business professional and user of financial information to:

- Calculate a net present value for a proposed investment project

- Appreciate the criteria on which to make an investment decision based on the net present value method

- Understand the advantages and limitations of the net present value method

SUMMARY OF KEY CONCEPTS   Can you remember how net present value is calculated and what its advantages and limitations are? Revise these with Summary of key concepts 12.3.

Internal rate of return

The IRR is linked to the NPV technique, but is the discount rate at which the NPV of the project is £nil. The IRR is thus the discount rate at which a project breaks even, the discount rate at which the present value of the cash outflows is equal to the present value of the cash inflows.

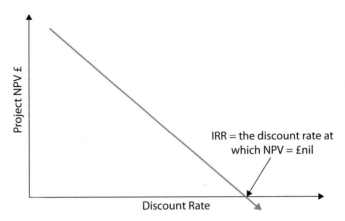

Figure 12.6 Graphical presentation showing the internal rate of return, the point at which the NPV of a project is £nil

To calculate the IRR, a process of trial and error is used. Project cash flows are discounted at successively higher rates until a negative NPV is given for that project. The IRR is then estimated using a mathematical technique called interpolation. This technique is illustrated below.

Figure 12.6 illustrates the IRR, the discount rate which gives a NPV of £nil. The NPV of a project at various discount rates is determined and plotted on the graph. As the discount rate increases, the NPV of the project falls. The point at which the NPV line crosses the x axis on the graph is the point at which the NPV is £nil and this is the IRR.

All this may sound very complicated, so let's see how the IRR is calculated using the proposed investment in the stonemason business. We saw in Illustration 12.2 that a discount rate of 15% gave a positive NPV of £135,800 for this project. Using a discount rate of 26% to discount the stonemason project will give us the NPV shown in Illustration 12.3.

Illustration12.3 Anna: net present value of the investment in the stonemason business discounted at a rate of 26%

	Cash flows ×	Discount factor =	Net present value
	£000	**26%**	**£000**
Cash outflow year 0	(500)	1.0000	(500.00)
Net cash inflows year 1	160	0.7937	126.99
Net cash inflows year 2	160	0.6299	100.78
Net cash inflows year 3	160	0.4999	79.98
Net cash inflows year 4	160	0.3968	63.49
Net cash inflows year 5	160	0.3149	50.38
Cash inflow from sale of the investment at the end of year 5	200	0.3149	62.98
Stonemason investment: net present value of the project discounted at a rate of 26%			(15.40)

We now know the following facts:

- A discount rate of 15% gives us a positive NPV of £135,800 (Illustration 12.2).
- A discount rate of 26% gives us a negative NPV of £15,400 (Illustration 12.3).
- Therefore, the discount rate that will give us a £nil NPV lies somewhere between 15% and 26%.

Calculating the internal rate of return

This discount rate is given by the following calculation:

$$15\% + \frac{135.80}{(135.80 + 15.40)} \times (26\% - 15\%) = 24.88\%$$

How did we arrive at this IRR of 24.88%?

- We know that a discount rate of 15% gives a positive return, so this will be our starting point.
- What we don't know is where the NPV line crosses the x axis on the graph, the point at which the NPV of the project is equal to £nil (Figure 12.6).
- Therefore, we have to estimate the discount rate at which the NPV is £nil.
- Our NPV has to fall by £135,800 before we reach the discount rate that gives a NPV of £nil.
- The total difference between the two results is £135,800 + £15,400 = £151,200 whereas we only need our NPV to fall by £135,800 before a net present value of £nil is reached.
- Therefore, if we divide £135,800 by £151,200 and then multiply this fraction by the difference between the positive (15%) and negative (26%) discount rates, this will tell us how far along the line between 15% and 26% the IRR is.
- Adding the 15% to this result gives us an IRR of 24.88%.

NUMERICAL EXERCISES Totally confident you can calculate an internal rate of return for a project? Work your way through the above example again to confirm your understanding of how internal rates of return are calculated and then go to the **online workbook** and attempt Numerical exercises 12.7 and 12.8 to make sure you can apply this investment appraisal technique to the other two investments that Anna is considering.

SHOW ME HOW TO DO IT How easily did you follow the calculation of a proposed project's internal rate of return? View Video presentation 12.2 in the **online workbook** to see a practical demonstration of how the internal rate of return calculation is carried out.

12

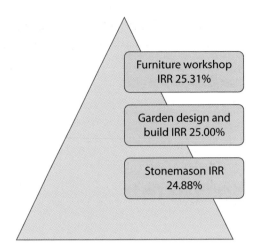

Figure 12.7 Internal rate of return of the three investment opportunities available to Anna

Internal rate of return: the decision criteria

Where a project has an IRR higher than an entity's required rate of return on invest-ment projects, then the project should be accepted. Where projects are competing for resources, then the project with the highest IRR would be selected for implementation. In Anna's case, Figure 12.7 shows that the furniture workshop now comes out on top again with an internal rate of return of 25.31% compared with the garden design and build's IRR of 25.00% and 24.88% on the investment in the stonemason. However, the IRR evaluation requires the project originally selected under the net present value technique to be preferred where the decision under the IRR investment appraisal tech-nique differs from the original NPV outcome. This makes sense as the NPV of the garden design and build investment discounted at a rate of 15% was £183,850 com-pared with a NPV of £128,890 for the furniture workshop investment discounted at the same rate. As we noted earlier, managers will always prefer a higher cash inflow to a lower one.

Internal rate of return: advantages

The IRR has the following advantages:

- As with the NPV technique, the time value of money is taken into account. This gives the IRR the same advantages as the NPV technique when compared with the ARR and payback investment appraisal methods.

- In the same way as NPV, the IRR method accounts for all the cash inflows and outflows from a project and discounts all these figures into today's money.

- Similarly, cash inflows that arise later in the project are riskier than cash inflows that arise earlier in the project. The use of discount factors enables users of this technique to reflect this increased risk arising from later cash inflows as these cash inflows are worth less in current money terms.

- The IRR technique is an absolute value and tells us what the percentage discount rate is that will give a NPV of £nil, the break-even NPV for a project. Thus, the technique does not require entities to specify in advance what their cost of capital is, but allows users to determine whether the rate of return is acceptable or not.

- The IRR provides more information than the NPV technique in that it tells users which project gives the highest rate of return where all projects have a positive NPV when discounted at the entity's cost of capital.

Internal rate of return: limitations

- Just as you found with the NPV technique, the IRR is difficult to understand! However, with practice and thought you will become familiar with this technique and be able to apply it in practice.

- The IRR cannot be used if cash flows are irregular. Where cash flows turn from being inflows to outflows and back again, a project will have two or more internal rates of return as the NPV line will cross the x axis in two or more places (illustration of this is beyond the scope of the present book).

WHY IS THIS RELEVANT TO ME?   Internal rate of return method of capital investment appraisal

To enable you as a business professional and user of financial information to:

- Calculate an IRR for an investment project
- Appreciate the criteria on which to make an investment decision based on the IRR
- Understand the advantages and limitations of the IRR method

SUMMARY OF KEY CONCEPTS   Confident you understand how internal rate of return is calculated and what its advantages and limitations are? Revise these with Summary of key concepts 12.4.

The following extracts from the annual report of GlaxoSmithKline plc illustrate the use of both the NPV and IRR methods of investment appraisal used in evaluating investment opportunities. (R&D = Research and Development)

"In 2010, we calculated that our estimated R&D internal rate of return (IRR) was 11% and stated a long-term aim of increasing this to 14%. We continue to improve the financial efficiency of our R&D and in February 2014 announced an estimated IRR of 13%. We continue to target 14% on a longer-term basis. Our estimated IRR is an important measure of our financial discipline and our strategic progress to improve the economics of R&D. It also underpins our strategy to create more flexibility around the pricing of our new medicines."

Source: GlaxoSmithKline plc, Annual Report 2014, page 27

"We have a formal process for assessing potential investment proposals in order to ensure decisions are aligned with our overall strategy. This process includes an assessment of the cash flow return on investment (CFROI), as well as its net present value (NPV) and internal rate of return (IRR) where the timeline for the project is very long term. We also consider the impact on earnings and credit profile where relevant."

Source: GlaxoSmithKline plc, Annual Report 2014, page 68

Making a final decision

Which project should Anna choose to invest in? Based on our earlier results and the results from the Numerical exercises, we can draw up a table to show us the rankings of the projects based on the results of each of the four capital investment appraisal techniques we have applied to the three proposals. These results are shown in Table 12.2.

Table 12.2 Anna: summary of rankings based on the results of each of the four capital investment appraisal techniques applied to the three proposed investments

Capital investment appraisal technique	Stonemason	Furniture workshop	Garden design and build
	Ranking	Ranking	Ranking
Payback	2	1	3
Accounting rate of return	3	2	1
Net present value	2	3	1
Internal rate of return	3	1	2

12

The investment in the stonemason fails to come out on top on any of the investment appraisal criteria. Therefore, on purely financial grounds, investment in this project would be rejected. The other two projects are ranked first on the basis of two techniques, second once and third once. However, as already noted under Internal rate of return, where the IRR technique gives a different result from the NPV technique, then the original choice under the NPV technique should be the project selected. In this case, the garden design and build will be accepted by Anna on the basis of the capital investment appraisal techniques applied to the three proposals. The garden design and build has the highest NPV and the highest ARR, as well as seeming to offer the highest net cash inflows and the highest growth potential among the projects on offer.

Sensitivity analysis

In Chapter 11 sensitivity analysis was applied to budgets to determine the extent to which the outcome would change if the assumptions on which the budget was based were relaxed. In the same way, capital investment appraisal can be subjected to sensitivity analysis to see what the result would be if the cash inflows were reduced or increased by 10% or 20%, if the cost of the investment were increased by 10% or 20% and if the cost of capital were increased or decreased. By undertaking these additional calculations, a more informed investment decision can be made.

CHAPTER SUMMARY

You should now have learnt that:

• Capital investment involves the acquisition of new non-current assets with the aim of increasing sales, profits and cash flows to the long-term benefit of a business.

• Capital investment appraisal is undertaken to evaluate the long-term cash generating capacity of investment projects.

• Capital investment appraisal of new projects is important in assisting decision makers in allocating scarce investment capital resources to projects that will maximise the profits of the entity in the long run.

• Payback, accounting rate of return, net present value and internal rate of return calculations assist in the appraisal of capital investment projects.

• All four capital investment appraisal techniques offer both advantages and limitations when used in capital investment decisions.

• Money received tomorrow is less valuable than money received today.

12

QUICK REVISION   Test your knowledge with the online flashcards in Summary of key concepts and attempt the Multiple choice questions, all in the **online workbook**. www. oxfordtextbooks.co.uk/orc/scott/

END-OF-CHAPTER QUESTIONS

Solutions to these questions can be found at the back of the book from page 503.

› *Develop your understanding*

Note to Questions 12.1–12.5: don't forget to use Table 1 in the Appendix when calculating the NPV and IRR of an investment project.

Question 12.1

Podcaster University Press is evaluating two book proposals, one in accounting and one in economics. The directors are keen on both books but have funding for only one and they cannot decide which book to publish. Details of the two books are as follows:

Accounting book

The accounting book requires an investment of £450,000 to be made immediately. The book will produce net cash inflows of £160,000 in years 1 to 3 and £100,000 in years 4 and 5. The non-current assets involved in the book's production are expected to have a resale value of £50,000 after five years. It is the directors' intention to sell the non-current assets from this project at the end of year 5 to realise the £50,000 cash inflow.

Economics book

The economics book requires an immediate investment of £600,000. The book will produce net cash inflows of £240,000 in year 1, £200,000 in year 2, £160,000 in year 3 and £105,000 in years 4 and 5. The non-current assets bought to print this book are expected to have a resale value of £100,000 at the end of the project. It is the directors' intention to sell the non-current assets from this project at the end of year 5 to realise the £100,000 cash inflow.

Podcaster University Press has a cost of capital of 10%.

You should use a discount rate of 20% when calculating the IRR of the two book projects.

Required

Evaluate the two book projects using the payback, ARR, NPV and IRR methods of investment appraisal. Which project will you recommend and why will you recommend this project?

Question 12.2

Zippo Drinks Limited is considering an investment into its computerised supply chain with a view to generating cash savings from using the benefits of currently available technology. Two options are under consideration. Option 1 will cost £200,000 and operate for five years, while Option 2 will cost £245,000 and remain operational for seven years. Given the longer implementation period, Option 2 will not realise any cash savings until the end of year 2. Neither investment will have any resale value at the end of its life. Because of the scarcity of investment capital, Zippo Drinks Limited can only undertake one of the supply chain projects. The directors of the company are asking for your help in evaluating the two proposals. The cash savings from any new investment in the years of operation are expected to be as follows:

	Option 1	Option 2
	£000	£000
Year 1	50	–
Year 2	70	80
Year 3	80	85
Year 4	70	86
Year 5	60	101
Year 6	–	81
Year 7	–	71

Zippo Drinks Limited has a cost of capital of 15%.

For your IRR calculations, you should discount the two projects using a 19% discount rate.

Required

Calculate the payback periods, ARRs, NPVs and IRRs of the two supply chain investment proposals. On the basis of your calculations, advise the directors which of the two investments they should undertake. You should also advise them of any additional considerations they should take into account when deciding which project to adopt.

Question 12.3

You are considering a five-year lease on a small restaurant serving light meals, snacks and drinks. The five-year lease will cost £80,000 and the lease will have no value at the end of the five years. The costs of fitting out the restaurant will be £30,000. After five years, you expect the restaurant fittings to have a scrap value of £2,000. You anticipate that net cash inflows from the restaurant will be £35,000 in the first year, £45,000 in the second year, £60,000 in the third year, £65,000 in the fourth year and £55,000 in the final year of operation. You have been approached by a fellow entrepreneur who is also very interested in the restaurant. She has proposed that you pay the £80,000 to take on the lease while she will fit out the restaurant at her own expense and pay you £40,000 per annum as rent and profit share. You expect a return of 12% per annum on any capital that you invest.

You are now uncertain whether you should fit out and run the restaurant yourself or sub-let the restaurant to your fellow entrepreneur. Running the restaurant yourself results in an IRR of 33.84% while allowing your fellow entrepreneur to run the restaurant and pay you rent and a share of the profits generates an IRR of 41.10%.

Required

Evaluate the above alternatives using the payback, ARR and NPV capital investment appraisal techniques. Which of the two options will you choose? In making your decision, you should also consider any other factors that you would take into account in addition to the purely financial considerations.

＞ Take it further

Question 12.4

Ambulators Limited makes prams and pushchairs. The company is currently evaluating two projects that are competing for investment funds.

The first project is the introduction to the market of a new pram. The new pram will require an initial investment of £3,300,000 in marketing and enhanced production facilities and each new pram will sell for £450 over the life of the product. Market research has shown that demand for the new pram is expected to be 5,000 units in the first year of production, with demand rising by 20% per annum on the previous year's sales in years 2 to 5. At the end of year 5, a new improved pram will have entered production and the investment in the new pram will have a residual value of £nil.

The second project is a new pushchair. This will require an initial outlay on marketing and enhanced production facilities of £2,200,000. Each new pushchair will sell initially in the first year of production and sales for £220, but the directors expect the price to rise by £10 each year in each of years 2 to 5. Market research has projected that initial demand will be for 6,000 pushchairs in year 1 and that demand will rise by 10% per annum on the previous year's sales in years 2 to 5. At the end of year 5, the production facilities will be used to produce a new pushchair and will be transferred to the new project at a valuation of £500,000.

Both projects are competing for the same capital resources and only one of the projects can be undertaken by the company.

The cost card for the new pram and the new pushchair are as follows:

	Pram £	Pushchair £
Direct materials	150.00	80.00
Direct labour	75.00	40.00
Variable overhead	25.00	10.00
Fixed overhead	50.00	20.00
Total cost	300.00	150.00

Fixed production overhead allocated to the cost of each product is based on 5,000 units of production for prams and 6,000 units of production for pushchairs.

Ambulators Limited has a cost of capital of 11%.

Required

For the proposed investment in the new pram or pushchair, calculate for each project:

- The payback period.
- The ARR.
- The NPV.
- The IRR.

You should round your sales projections to the nearest whole unit of sales.

The directors would like to hear your views on which project they should accept. Your advice should take into account both the financial aspects of the decision and any other factors that the directors of Ambulators Limited should consider when deciding which project to invest in.

Question 12.5

Chillers plc manufactures fridges and freezers. The company is considering the production of a new deluxe fridge-freezer. The fridge-freezer will sell for £600 and the company's marketing department has produced a forecast for sales for the next seven years as follows:

Year	Units sold
2016	3,500
2017	4,000
2018	4,500
2019	5,250
2020	5,750
2021	5,500
2022	5,250

Variable costs are budgeted to be 40% of selling price. Fixed costs arising from the sale and production of the new deluxe fridge-freezer are expected to be £1,200,000 per annum.

As a result of the introduction of the new deluxe fridge-freezer, the company expects to lose sales of 2,000 standard fridge-freezers each year over the next seven years. These standard fridge-freezers sell for £350 each with variable costs of 35% of selling price. The reduction in sales of standard fridge-freezers will save fixed costs of £395,000 per annum.

The initial expenditure on the production line for the new deluxe fridge-freezer has been estimated at £2,000,000. At the end of seven years, this production line will have a scrap value of £100,000.

Chillers plc has a required rate of return on new investment of 13%.

Required

For the proposed investment in the new deluxe fridge-freezer, calculate:

- The payback period.
- The ARR.
- The NPV.
- The IRR.

Advise the directors of Chillers plc whether the project should go ahead or not.

Answers to end-of-chapter questions

Chapter 1

Question 1.1

Your answers should have included the following points, among others. You may well have been able to think of more points than are given here. In all four cases, figures should be compared with previous years' figures to determine whether current year figures are higher or lower than in the past.

Information required by the trustees of a charity:

- Donations received
- Legacies received
- Money received from fund-raising campaigns
- Ability of the charity to continue to attract financial support
- Expenditure on charitable purposes
- Expenditure on administration
- Expenditure on administration as a percentage of total expenditure/income
- Number of beneficiaries assisted
- Whether the charity made a surplus this year or whether a deficit arose from expenditure being higher than income
- Spare funds to use in an emergency or in the case of a natural disaster

Information required by the managers of a secondary school:

- Number of pupils on roll
- Number of teachers

- Pupils per teacher
- GCSE and A level results
- Average GCSE and A level points per pupil
- Number of applications received for new entrants into year 7 next year
- Whether numbers of pupils are rising or falling
- Reputation of the school among parents, pupils and local residents
- Whether the secondary school is staying within its budget or not
- Pupil and parent satisfaction with the educational experience delivered

Information required by the managers of a university:

- Number of applications per course
- Number of offers per course
- Number of students enrolling each year
- Average A level points of students enrolling on courses
- Degree classifications gained by students at the end of their course
- Starting salaries of students entering employment at the end of their course
- Employment rate of students at the end of their course as a percentage of those graduating
- Graduating students still unemployed six months after the end of their course
- Satisfaction ratings from employers with graduates of the university
- Student satisfaction ratings for each course
- Staff/student ratios
- Drop-out rates
- Completion rates
- Surplus or loss generated each year
- Research papers published by staff
- Research grants awarded to staff
- The value of research grants awarded to staff
- Research awards gained by staff

Information required by the managers of a manufacturing business:

- Profit or loss for the year
- Number of products produced and sold in the year
- Selling prices for products whether these are rising or falling
- Demand for products whether this is rising or falling
- Investment in new machinery/facilities
- Number of new/improved products developed this year
- Productivity of employees, products produced per employee

- Number of customer complaints about products
- Health and safety record, number of employees injured while at work
- Financial stability of the business
- Whether the budget for the year was met or not

Question 1.2

Your chart should include the following details (though you may have thought of more points than are given here):

1. Costs

- Transfer fee demanded by potential targets' current clubs
- Weekly wages that new striker is likely to demand
- Signing on fee for new striker
- Agent's fees for handling the transfer
- Length of proposed contract in years

2. On-pitch performance

- Number of career goals
- Number of goals in the last 12 months (to determine current scoring record)
- Goals per game
- Number of yellow and red cards received over career
- Number of yellow and red cards received in the last 12 months (to determine current disciplinary record)
- Number of games missed through suspension in the last 12 months
- Number of minor injuries suffered in the last 12 months
- Number of serious injuries suffered over career
- Number of games missed through injury in the last 12 months

3. Off-pitch performance

- Number of charitable activities undertaken in the last 12 months
- Number of clubs played for during career (to gauge loyalty to past clubs)
- Diet
- Alcohol consumption
- Age (to assess the number of playing years left)
- Fitness levels
- Number of non-football related stories in the press about the player in the last 12 months (to gauge the likelihood that the player will get into trouble and damage the reputation of the club)
- Reputation among fellow professionals (scores out of 10)

Chapter 2

Question 2.1

Resources that are assets

Apply the four criteria to show why the resources in the question are assets of entities and so are recognised on the statement of financial position.

(a) Motor vehicles purchased by an entity

- Does the entity control the resource? Yes, by virtue of purchasing the motor vehicles and registering them in the company's name at the DVLA.
- Is there a past event giving rise to control of that resource by the entity? Yes, the purchase of the vehicles.
- Will future economic benefits flow to the entity from that resource? Yes, the motor vehicles can be used to deliver goods to customers, be used by sales reps to visit customers to generate more sales or for any other business purpose that will result in increasing profits, cash and the inflow of economic benefits.
- Can the cost of the asset be measured reliably in monetary terms? Yes, the cost of the motor vehicles can be readily determined from the purchase documents and the cash paid from the bank.

(b) Inventory received from suppliers

- Does the entity control the resource? Yes, by virtue of the contract signed or verbal agreement with suppliers for the supply of goods to the entity.
- Is there a past event giving rise to control of that resource by the entity? Yes, the delivery of the inventory by suppliers and the receipt of that inventory by the entity (legally, title to the goods passes on receipt by the customer).
- Will future economic benefits flow to the entity from that resource? Yes, the inventory can be used in production to produce more goods for sale or, in the case of retail businesses, the inventory can be sold at a higher price to customers and so produce economic benefits in the form of cash flow and profit.
- Can the cost of the asset be measured reliably in monetary terms? Yes, the cost of the inventory can be readily determined from the invoices from the suppliers and by the cash paid from the bank to suppliers for the goods delivered.

(c) Cash and cash equivalents

- Does the entity control the resource? Yes, the entity controls the cash through the presence of the cash on company premises or as a result of the cash being deposited into the entity's bank account.
- Is there a past event giving rise to control of that resource by the entity? Yes, the receipt of cash in exchange for goods or services sold and deposited in the bank.

- Will future economic benefits flow to the entity from that resource? Yes, the cash can be used to purchase more goods for use in production or for resale or to repay liabilities upon which interest is being charged thereby saving interest and increasing cash resources in the future still further.

- Can the cost of the asset be measured reliably in monetary terms? Yes, cash can be measured in terms of the amount of physical cash on the business's premises or by reference to the bank statements if the cash is in the bank.

Resources that are NOT assets

Applying the four criteria to show why the resources in the question are NOT assets of an entity and why they are no longer/not recognised on the statement of financial position of entities.

(a) Redundant plant and machinery

- Does the entity control the resource? Yes, by virtue of purchasing the plant and machinery in the past and using it in the business in the past to produce goods for sale.

- Is there a past event giving rise to control of that resource by the entity? Yes, the purchase of the plant and machinery in the past.

- Will future economic benefits flow to the entity from that resource? No, the plant and machinery is now redundant and will not produce any more goods or result in a cash receipt when it is sold or scrapped, so there are no more economic benefits associated with this piece of plant and machinery. If there are disposal costs for this plant and machinery, you might even be able to make out a case that a liability now exists in relation to this plant and machinery. There would then be an outflow of economic benefits and the obligation to pay these disposal costs exists and is unavoidable.

- Can the cost of the asset be measured reliably in monetary terms? Yes, the cost of the plant and machinery can be readily determined from the purchase documents and the cash paid from the bank.

Result: while the resource meets three of the four criteria, it fails on the third criterion (no future economic benefits) and so the asset, which would have been previously recognised by the entity on its statement of financial position, is now derecognised and is removed from property, plant and equipment.

(b) Trade receivable that will not be recovered

- Does the entity control the resource? Yes, by virtue of delivering goods/providing services to the customer and the customer taking delivery of those goods/services and assuming the obligation to pay for them.

- Is there a past event giving rise to control of that resource by the entity? Yes, the delivery of the goods/services to the customer.

- Will future economic benefits flow to the entity from that resource? No, the customer will not pay the invoice because of its bankruptcy and so no future economic benefits will flow to the entity from this trade receivable.

- Can the cost of the asset be measured reliably in monetary terms? Yes, the sales invoice from the entity to the customer can be used to measure the value of the trade receivable reliably.

Result: while the resource meets three of the four criteria, it fails on the third criterion (no future economic benefits) and so the asset, which would have been previously recognised by the entity on its statement of financial position is now derecognised and is removed from trade receivables.

(c) A highly skilled workforce

- Does the entity control the resource? Yes, to the extent that the entity controls the workforce while they are working for the organisation, but the entity is powerless to stop any individual worker leaving and joining another company, taking all their skills and knowledge with them.
- Is there a past event giving rise to control of that resource by the entity? Yes, each member of the workforce signed their contract.
- Will future economic benefits flow to the entity from that resource? Yes, the highly skilled workforce will produce goods/services and hence sales and profits for the company into the future.
- Can the cost of the asset be measured reliably in monetary terms? No: it is not possible to measure the cost of an employee to the business reliably.

Result: while the resource meets two of the four criteria, it fails on the other two criteria (lack of control and no reliable monetary measure) and so the asset, which would never have been previously recognised by the entity on its statement of financial position, still cannot be recognised.

Question 2.2

Oxford Academicals Football Club Limited

This is a further application of the criteria to determine whether entities can recognise assets on their statement of financial position or not. Looking at the four criteria:

- The football club controls the resources, the players, through the contracts that they signed.
- As the club holds the players' registrations and has contracts with the players that they will play exclusively for Oxford Academicals, other football clubs can legally be prevented from employing the club's players in their teams.
- There is a past event, the signing of the contracts by the players and, in the case of those players whose contracts were bought from other clubs, cash paid.
- All the players should produce future economic benefits for the club as spectators will pay to watch the team play, there will be monetary rewards for end of season league position and trophies won and, when the players become surplus to requirements, lose form or fall out with the manager, their contracts can be sold to other clubs for a transfer fee or used in player for player swaps.

- In the case of the players whose contracts have been bought, there is a reliable measurement of their cost, the transfer fees of £25 million. In the case of players developed by the club, there is no reliable measure of their cost or value.

Result: the contracts of the bought in players meet all the criteria for asset recognition, so they can be recognised on the statement of financial position at a cost of £25 million. The internally developed players cannot be recognised as assets on the statement of financial position as they only meet three out of the four criteria. This may seem unfair and even illogical, but this is how the accounting rules work.

The player registrations that can be recognised on the statement of financial position will be classed as intangible non-current assets. The players will normally be signed on contracts that exceed 12 months (once a player has one year or less to run on their contract, then these registrations should become intangible current assets as the assets will be used up within one year).

As accounting information is meant to be useful and to help users of accounts make economic decisions, it is quite likely that there will be a note in the accounts explaining that not all player registrations are recognised on the statement of financial position but that the current value of the players not so recognised is estimated by the directors to be so many £million. In this way, an additional disclosure will help users understand all the player resources controlled by Oxford Academicals Football Club.

Question 2.3

Alma Limited: statement of financial position at 30 April 2016

ASSETS	£000	Note
Non-current assets		
Intangible assets	—	1
Property, plant and equipment	6,500	2
	6,500	
Current assets		
Inventories	1,000	
Trade receivables	1,750	
Cash and cash equivalents	10	
	2,760	
Total assets	9,260	3

LIABILITIES	£000	Note
Current liabilities		
Short-term borrowings	1,000	4
Trade payables	1,450	
Taxation payable	540	
	2,990	
Non-current liabilities		
Long-term borrowings	1,000	5
Total liabilities	3,990	6
Net assets	5,270	7
EQUITY		
Called up share capital	1,000	
Share premium	1,500	
Retained earnings	2,770	
Total equity	5,270	8

Notes

1. There are no intangible assets in Alma so the total here is zero.

2. (Plant and machinery) £2,000 + (land and buildings) £4,500 = £6,500.

3. Total assets = non-current assets + current assets, so £6,500 + £2,760 = £9,260.

4. (Bank loan due within 12 months) £200 + (bank overdraft: overdrafts are repayable on demand, so due within the next 12 months) £800 = £1,000.

5. Long-term borrowings: the bank loan due seven years after the statement of financial position date on 30 April 2023.

6. Total liabilities = current liabilities + non-current liabilities, so £2,990 + £1,000 = £3,990.

7. Net assets: total assets – total liabilities = £9,260 – £3,990 = £5,270.

8. Total equity: share capital + share premium + retained earnings = £1,000 + £1,500 + £2,770 = £5,270.

Bella Limited: statement of financial position at 30 April 2016

ASSETS	£000	Note
Non-current assets		
Intangible assets	—	1
Property, plant and equipment	28,100	2
	28,100	
Current assets		
Inventories	700	
Trade receivables	3,000	
Cash and cash equivalents	825	3
	4,525	
Total assets	32,625	4
LIABILITIES		
Current liabilities		
Short-term borrowings	400	5
Trade payables	4,000	
Taxation payable	1,100	
	5,500	
Non-current liabilities		
Long-term borrowings	10,000	6
Total liabilities	15,500	7
Net assets	17,125	8
EQUITY		
Called up share capital	5,000	
Share premium	7,500	
Retained earnings	4,625	
Total equity	17,125	9

Notes

1. There are no intangible assets in Bella Limited so the total here is zero.

2. (Plant and machinery) £9,500 + (land and buildings) £17,100 + (motor vehicles) £1,500 = £28,100.

3. (Cash at bank) £800 + (cash in hand) £25 = £825.

4. Total assets = non-current assets + current assets, so £28,100 + £4,525 = £32,625.

5. Bank loan due within 12 months of the statement of financial position date.

6. Long-term borrowings: the bank loan due seven years after the statement of financial position date on 30 April 2023.

7. Total liabilities = current liabilities + non-current liabilities, so £5,500 + £10,000 = £15,500.

8. Net assets: total assets – total liabilities = £32,625 – £15,500 = £17,125.

9. Total equity: share capital + share premium + retained earnings = £5,000 + £7,500 + £4,625 = £17,125.

Carla Limited: statement of financial position at 30 April 2016

ASSETS	£000	Note
Non-current assets		
Intangible assets	600	1
Property, plant and equipment	15,900	2
	16,500	
Current assets		
Inventories	800	
Trade receivables	2,750	
Cash and cash equivalents	15	
	3,565	
Total assets	20,065	3
LIABILITIES		
Current liabilities		
Short-term borrowings	1,550	4
Trade payables	1,750	
Taxation payable	800	
	4,100	
Non-current liabilities		
Long-term borrowings	1,500	5
Total liabilities	5,600	6
Net assets	14,465	7
EQUITY		
Called up share capital	2,500	
Share premium	4,500	
Retained earnings	7,465	
Total equity	14,465	8

Notes

1. (Goodwill) £400 + (trademarks) £200 = £600.

2. (Plant and machinery) £3,750 + (land and buildings) £10,200 + (motor vehicles) £1,950 = £15,900.

3. Total assets = non-current assets + current assets, so £16,500 + £3,565 = £20,065.

4. (Bank loan due within 12 months) £300 + (bank overdraft: overdrafts are repayable on demand, so due within the next twelve months) £1,250 = £1,550.

5. Long-term borrowings: the bank loan due seven years after the statement of financial position date on 30 April 2023.

6. Total liabilities = current liabilities + non-current liabilities, so £4,100 + £1,500 = £5,600.

7. Net assets: total assets − total liabilities = £20,065 − £5,600 = £14,465.

8. Total equity: share capital + share premium + retained earnings = £2,500 + £4,500 + £7,465 = £14,465.

Deborah Limited: statement of financial position at 30 April 2016

ASSETS	£000	Note
Non-current assets		
Intangible assets	350	1
Property, plant and equipment	14,250	2
	14,600	
Current assets		
Inventories	750	
Trade and other receivables	3,200	3
Cash and cash equivalents	558	4
	4,508	
Total assets	19,108	5
LIABILITIES		
Current liabilities		
Short-term borrowings	—	6
Trade payables	5,600	
Taxation payable	—	7
	5,600	
Non-current liabilities		
Long-term borrowings	—	6
Total liabilities	5,600	8
Net assets	13,508	9

EQUITY

Called up share capital	3,000	
Share premium	5,000	
Retained earnings	5,508	
Total equity	13,508	10

Notes

1. (Goodwill) £250 + (trademarks) £100 = £350.

2. (Plant and machinery) £4,250 + (land and buildings) £8,750 + (motor vehicles) £1,250 = £14,250.

3. (Trade receivables) £2,950 + (tax repayable: cash will be coming into the business so this is a receivable, hence the title of this total is now trade *and other* receivables) £250 = £3,200.

4. (Cash at bank) £550 + (cash in hand) £8 = £558.

5. Total assets = non-current assets + current assets, so £14,600 + £4,508 = £19,108.

6. There are no short or long-term borrowings in Deborah, so a zero figure is recorded against these headings.

7. Taxation payable: this year there is a tax repayment due so this is recorded as a receivable rather than a payable, so there is zero taxation payable.

8. Total liabilities = current liabilities + non-current liabilities, so £5,600 + £nil = £5,600.

9. Net assets: total assets – total liabilities = £19,108 – £5,600 = £13,508.

10. Total equity: share capital + share premium + retained earnings = £3,000 + £5,000 + £5,508 = £13,508.

Eloise Limited: statement of financial position at 30 April 2016

ASSETS	£000	Note
Non-current assets		
Intangible assets	950	1
Property, plant and equipment	21,600	2
	22,550	
Current assets		
Inventories	900	
Trade and other receivables	3,900	3
Cash and cash equivalents	212	4
	5,012	
Total assets	27,562	5

LIABILITIES	£000	Note
Current liabilities		
Short-term borrowings	—	6
Trade payables	5,800	
Taxation payable	—	7
	5,800	
Non-current liabilities		
Long-term borrowings	—	6
Total liabilities	5,800	8
Net assets	21,762	9
EQUITY		
Called up share capital	4,500	
Share premium	9,000	
Retained earnings	8,262	
Total equity	21,762	10

Notes

1. (Goodwill) £500 + (trademarks) £450 = £950.
2. (Plant and machinery) £5,000 + (land and buildings) £15,000 + (motor vehicles) £1,600 = £21,600.
3. (Trade receivables) £3,100 + (tax repayable: cash will be coming into the business so this is a receivable, hence the title of this total is now trade *and other* receivables) £800 = £3,900.
4. (Cash at bank) £200 + (cash in hand) £12 = £212.
5. Total assets = non-current assets + current assets, so £22,550 + £5,012 = £27,562.
6. There are no short or long-term borrowings in Eloise Limited, so a zero figure is recorded against these headings.
7. Taxation payable: this year there is a tax repayment due, so this is recorded as a receivable rather than a payable so there is zero taxation payable.
8. Total liabilities = current liabilities + non-current liabilities, so £5,800 + £nil = £5,800.
9. Net assets: total assets − total liabilities = £27,562 − £5,800 = £21,762.
10. Total equity: share capital + share premium + retained earnings = £4,500 + £9,000 + £8,262 = £21,762.

Question 2.4

Maria: statement of financial position at 31 October 2016 and 7 November 2016

	Statement of Financial Position at 31 October 2016	Increase	Decrease	Statement of Financial Position at 7 November 2016
	£	£	£	£
Non-current assets				
Property, plant and equipment	15,000			15,000
Current assets				
Inventory	20,000	2,500[4]	1,200[3]	21,300
Other receivables	3,000			3,000
Cash and cash equivalents	500	2,000[3]	300[5]	2,200
	23,500			26,500
Total assets	38,500			41,500
Current liabilities				
Bank overdraft	7,000	3,500[1]	10,000[2]	500
Trade and other payables	8,000	2,500[4]	3,500[1]	7,000
Taxation	3,000			3,000
Total liabilities	18,000			10,500
Net assets	20,500			31,000
Capital account				
Balance at 31 October 2016	20,500	10,000[2]	300[5]	31,000
		800[3]		

Notes

1. Paying trade payables from the bank account will increase the overdraft by £3,500. Money has been paid out of the bank account thereby increasing the amount owed to the bank while reducing the amounts owed to trade payables by the same amount.

2. £10,000 paid into the bank account by Maria will increase the balance in her capital account by £10,000 (this is the owner's own money introduced into the business) and reduce the bank overdraft by £10,000. Less money is owed to the bank but more money is now owed to Maria.

3. Cash goes up by £2,000 as this is money flowing into the business. As inventory has been sold in the first week of November, the inventory will decrease by £1,200. This leaves a difference of £800 which is profit on the sales made (sales made – the cost of making those sales). Profit is added to the capital account. Any profit retained in the business during the year is added to the capital account as this profit belongs to and is owed to the business's owner.

4. New inventory purchased by the business means that the value of inventory will increase by £2,500. As the inventory was purchased on credit from suppliers (trade payables), trade payables will also increase by £2,500 as more money is now owed to them.

5. The £300 taken out of the business represents a repayment of money owed by the business to the owner. Therefore, the capital account is reduced by £300: the business owes Maria £300 less than it did before this transaction. The £300 was taken out in cash, so cash reduces by £300.

Question 2.5

Andy Limited: statement of financial position at 30 June 2016 and 7 July 2016

ASSETS	£	Increase	Decrease	£
Non-current assets		£	£	
Property, plant and equipment	320,000	$20,000^2$		340,000
Current assets				
Inventories	50,000	$15,000^5$	$2,500^4$ $7,500^3$	55,000
Trade receivables	75,000	$10,000^3$	$3,000^1$	82,000
Cash and cash equivalents	20,000	$3,000^1$ $3,250^4$	$2,500^1$ $10,000^6$	13,750
	145,000			150,750
Total assets	465,000			490,750
LIABILITIES				
Current liabilities				
Trade payables	80,000	$15,000^5$	$7,000^6$ $2,500^1$	85,500
Taxation	20,000		$3,000^6$	17,000
	100,000			102,500
Non-current liabilities				
Bank loan (long-term borrowings)	250,000	$20,000^2$		270,000
Total liabilities	350,000			372,500
Net assets	115,000			118,250
EQUITY				
Called up share capital	20,000			20,000
Retained earnings	95,000	$2,500^3$ 750^4		98,250
Total equity	115,000			118,250

Notes

- 1 July 2016: the payment of the trade payable reduces both trade payables and cash and cash equivalents by £2,500.

- 1 July 2016: the receipt of a cheque from a trade receivable reduces trade receivables by £3,000, but increases the cash and cash equivalents balance by the same amount.

- 2 July 2016: both the bank loan and the property, plant and equipment will increase by £20,000. There are £20,000 more assets and £20,000 more liabilities.

- 4 July 2016: inventory of £7,500 has been sold, so inventory decreases by this amount. The buyer has agreed to buy the goods for £10,000 and pay in August, so trade receivables increase by £10,000. The profit on the transaction of £2,500 (£10,000 − £7,500) will increase retained earnings.

- 5 July 2016: similarly, inventory of £2,500 has been sold, so inventory decreases by this amount. The buyer paid cash of £3,250 for the goods and so cash increases by £3,250. The profit on the transaction of £750 (£3,250 − £2,500) increases retained earnings.

- 6 July 2016: both inventory and trade payables increase by £15,000 as there are more goods in stock and there is a bigger liability due to trade payables for goods supplied.

- 7 July 2016: taxation payable reduces by £3,000 and trade payables decreases by £7,000 as these two amounts have now been paid and are no longer obligations of Andy Limited. The total payment of £10,000 reduces the balance in the bank account by this amount.

Question 2.6

(a) Frankie Limited: statement of financial position at 31 December 2016

ASSETS	£000	Note
Non-current assets		
Intangible assets	1,000	1
Property, plant and equipment	27,800	2
	28,800	
Current assets		
Inventories	2,500	
Trade receivables	4,910	
Cash and cash equivalents	605	3
	8,015	
Total assets	36,815	4

LIABILITIES	£000	Note
Current liabilities		
Short-term borrowings	850	5
Trade payables	6,720	
Taxation payable	1,380	6
	8,950	
Non-current liabilities		
Long-term borrowings	8,500	7
Total liabilities	17,450	8
Net assets	19,365	9
EQUITY		
Share capital	2,000	
Share premium	4,000	
Retained earnings	13,365	
Total equity	19,365	10

Notes

1. Goodwill is an intangible asset, so £1,000,000 is recorded as a non-current asset under this heading.

2. (Land and buildings) £15,500,000 + (fixtures and fittings) £1,670,000 + (plant and machinery) £10,630,000 = £27,800,000.

3. (Cash at bank) £600,000 + (cash in hand) £5,000 = £605,000.

4. Total assets = non-current assets + current assets, so £28,800,000 + £8,015,000 = £36,815,000.

5. Short-term, current borrowings are the borrowings due for repayment within one year of the statement of financial position date, i.e. due for repayment by 31 December 2017, so these borrowings are recorded as current liabilities.

6. Taxation payable is a short-term, current liability.

7. Long-term, non-current borrowings are those due for repayment after more than one year from the statement of financial position date. As 31 December 2025 is nine years after the current statement of financial position date, the £8,500,000 is classified as a non-current liability.

8. Total liabilities = current liabilities + non-current liabilities, so £8,950,000 + £8,500,000 = £17,450,000.

9. Net assets: total assets − total liabilities = £36,815,000 − £17,450,000 = £19,365,000.

10. Total equity: share capital + share premium + retained earnings = £2,000,000 + £4,000,000 + £13,365,000 = £19,365,000.

(b) Frankie Limited: statement of financial position at 31 December 2016 and 31 January 2017

	Statement of Financial Position at 31 December 2016	Increase	Decrease	Statement of Financial Position at 31 January 2017
ASSETS	£000	£000	£000	£000
Non-current assets				
Intangible assets	1,000			1,000
Property, plant and equipment	27,800	$2,500^3$	$2,000^8$	28,300
	28,800			29,300
Current assets				
Inventory	2,500	$12,200^1$	$11,450^2$	3,250
Trade receivables	4,910	$15,500^2$	$6,450^6$	13,960
Cash and cash equivalents	605	$1,500^4$	690^5	1,955
		$6,450^6$	$8,210^7$	
		$2,500^8$	200^9	
	8,015			19,165
Total assets	36,815			48,465
LIABILITIES				
Current liabilities				
Short-term borrowings	850		200^9	650
Trade payables	6,720	$12,200^1$	$8,210^7$	10,710
Taxation payable	1,380		690^5	690
	8,950			12,050
Non-current liabilities				
Long-term borrowings	8,500	$2,500^3$		11,000
Total liabilities	17,450			23,050
Net assets	19,365			25,415
EQUITY				
Share capital	2,000	500^4		2,500
Share premium	4,000	$1,000^4$		5,000
Retained earnings	13,365	$4,050^2$		17,915
		500^8		
Total equity	19,365			25,415

Notes

1. Inventory has been acquired, so the value of inventory increases by £12,200,000. As the inventory has not yet been paid for, trade payables (= suppliers) will also increase by £12,200,000 as they are now owed this additional amount for the inventory supplied on credit.

2. Sales have been made on credit to trade receivables (= customers), so trade receivables now owe a further £15,500,000 to Frankie Limited and so increase by this amount. The cost of the goods sold by the company was £11,450,000. As this inventory has now been sold, inventory decreases by £11,450,000 to derecognise the asset that is no longer represented on Frankie Limited's statement of financial position. The difference between the selling price of £15,500,000 and the cost of the inventory sold of £11,450,000 is £4,050,000, which represents the profit on the sales transactions. This profit is added to retained earnings.

3. New plant and machinery has been acquired, so property, plant and equipment increases by £2,500,000. The money used to acquire these new non-current assets has been borrowed, so borrowings must also rise by the same amount. The new borrowings are due for repayment in December 2021, which is more than one year after the end of January 2017, so these new borrowings are added to non-current liabilities.

4. Cash has been raised from the share issue, so cash increases by £1,500,000, the total proceeds of the share issue. As £500,000 of the cash raised relates to the share capital, this balance also increases by £500,000. The remaining £1,000,000 of the cash raised relates to share premium, so this balance increases by this amount.

5. Cash has been paid to the tax authorities, so cash must decrease by £690,000. Now that this liability has been discharged, taxation payable also falls by £690,000 as the obligation has been settled and economic benefits in the form of cash have flowed out of the company to settle the obligation.

6. Trade receivables have paid £6,450,000 of the amounts owed to Frankie, so trade receivables now decrease by this amount to reflect the realisation of this asset through the receipt of cash. Cash will also increase by the same amount as these amounts owed by the trade receivables have now turned into cash.

7. Frankie has discharged obligations owed to trade payables of £8,210,000, so trade payables fall by this amount as the liability has now been paid. As the amounts owed were paid in cash, cash also falls by the same amount to reflect the transfer of economic benefits to settle the obligations to trade payables.

8. The sale of the non-current asset results in the derecognition of the land as the resource is no longer owned or controlled by Frankie. As a result of the sale of the land, property, plant and equipment fall by the original historic cost of the land of £2,000,000. Cash has now been received of £2,500,000, so cash increases by this amount. The difference between the original cost of the land of £2,000,000 and the selling price of £2,500,000 represents a profit on the sale so this £500,000 profit on the transaction is reflected as an increase in retained earnings.

9. The transfer of cash to settle the obligation to short-term borrowings results in a decrease in short-term borrowings of £200,000 to reflect the settlement of the obligation. As the amounts owed were paid in cash, cash also falls by the same amount to reflect the transfer of economic benefits to settle the obligations to short-term borrowings.

Chapter 3

Question 3.1

1. Abi's capital account balance at 1 September 2015

   Remember that assets – liabilities = capital

	£
Assets	
Inventory	2,382
Cash and cash equivalents (= bank balance)	7,342
Total assets	9,724
Liabilities	
Trade payables	3,445
Assets – liabilities = capital	6,279

2. Abi's bank account for the year to 31 August 2016

	Cash in	Cash out
	£	£
Bank balance at 1 September 2015	7,342	
Rent for the year		6,000
Sales for the year	157,689	
Refunds given to customers during the year		3,789
Trade payable at 1 September 2015 paid		3,445
Cash paid for purchases		116,328
Wages paid to assistant 50 weeks paid × £100		5,000
Display stands		600
Drawings 12 months × £1,500		18,000
Bank balance at 31 August 2016 (total receipts – total payments)		11,869
	165,031	165,031

3. Income statement for the year ended 31 August 2016 and a statement of financial position at that date

Abi: income statement for the year ended 31 August 2016

	£	£	Note
Revenue: £157, 689 – £3,789 + £650		154,550	1
Cost of sales			
Opening inventory	2,382		2
Purchases	120,465		3
Closing inventory	(4,638)		4
Cost of sales		118,209	5
Gross profit		36,341	6
Expenses			
Rent	6,000		7
Assistant £5,000 + £200	5,200		8
Depreciation of display stands	190		9
Total expenses		11,390	10
Net profit for the year		24,951	11

Abi: statement of financial position at 31 August 2016

	£	Note
Non-current assets		
Display stands (£600 cost – £190 accumulated depreciation)	410	9
Current assets		
Inventory	4,638	4
Bank balance at 31 August 2016	11,869	
Cash in hand at the year end = unbanked sales	650	1
	17,157	
Total assets (£410 non-current assets + £17,157 current assets)	17,567	
Current liabilities		
Trade payables (£120,465 total purchases – £116,328 cash paid)	4,137	3
Assistant's wages accrual (£5,200 charge for year – £5,000 paid)	200	8
Total liabilities	4,337	
Net assets (£17,567 total assets – £4,337 total liabilities)	13,230	

Equity (capital account)

Capital account at 1 September 2015 calculated above in 1	6,279
Add: net profit for the year from the income statement	24,951
Less: drawings (personal expenses) paid from bank	(18,000)
Capital account at 31 August 2016	13,230

Notes

1. Revenue is made up of the cash receipts from sales to customers of £157,689 less the refunds to customers for goods returned of £3,789 (= sales returns, the cancellation of a sale) + £650 cash at 31 August 2016 representing sales that had not yet been banked. This £650 cash is added on to sales and is recorded as a cash asset on the statement of financial position at 31 August 2016. This cash represents sales that had taken place during the accounting year and a cash asset at the end of the financial year.

2. Opening inventory is the inventory of £2,382 that Abi held at 1 September 2015.

3. The cost of purchases is the total cost of goods purchased of £120,465, even though Abi has only paid out £116,328. Remember that, under the accruals basis of accounting, transactions are recorded in the accounting period in which they occurred, not in the accounting period in which cash is received or paid. Therefore, as the total cost of purchases for the year was £120,465, this is the amount recognised in the income statement for the year to 31 August 2016. While the cost of purchases is £120,465, only £116,328 of this amount has been paid, so there is a liability at the year-end of £120,465 − £116,328 = £4,137. This figure represents the obligation to pay for goods purchased during the year so that a purchase of goods and a trade payable are both recognised for this amount at the end of the financial year.

4. Closing inventory is a deduction from cost of sales and an asset in the statement of financial position. The cost of closing inventory is carried forward to the next accounting period to match against the sales revenue generated from the sale of these goods in the year to 31 August 2017.

5. Cost of sales = opening inventory + purchases − closing inventory.

6. Gross profit = revenue − cost of sales.

7. Rent is the annual cost of the rent paid from the bank account. As Abi has paid all the rent due for the year there is no prepayment or accrual of rent to recognise at the accounting year end.

8. The assistant has been paid for 50 weeks of the year, so £5,000 has been paid out of the bank account. As the assistant has carried out her work for the last two weeks of August, Abi has an obligation at 31 August 2016 to pay for two more weeks of work, so an additional £200 is recognised as a cost incurred in the financial year in the income statement and as an accrual in the statement of financial position.

9. Depreciation on the display stands is calculated by deducting the scrap value (= residual value) of the stands from the cost (£600 − £30 = £570) and then dividing £570 by the three years that the display stands are expected to last. £570 ÷ 3 = £190 depreciation for each of

the three years that the display stands will be in use in Abi's business. As the display stands have been in use for a whole year in the business (from 1 September 2015 to 31 August 2016) a whole year's depreciation is recognised in the income statement. The net book value of the display stands at the end of the financial year is £410: £600 cost – the accumulated depreciation at 31 August 2016 of £190 = £410.

10. Total expenses are given by adding £6,000 (rent) + £5,200 (assistant) + £190 (depreciation for the year) to give total expenses of £11,390.

11. Net profit for the year is given by deducting total expenses for the year of £11,390 from the gross profit of £36,341 to give a net profit figure of £24,951.

Question 3.2

Alison: income statement for the year ended 31 December 2016

	£	£	Note
Sales 439,429 (sales) – 17,682 (sales returns)		421,747	1
Opening inventory	27,647		2
Purchases 225,368 (goods purchased) – 5,724 (purchase returns) – 2,324 (discounts received)	217,320		3
Closing inventory	(22,600)		4
Cost of sales		222,367	5
Gross profit		199,380	6
Expenses			
Administration expenses	15,265		
Telephone expenses	5,622		
Discounts allowed	1,439		7
Rent on warehouse and office unit 15,000 – 3,000	12,000		8
Business rates 9,325 – 1,865	7,460		9
Delivery costs	36,970		
Electricity and gas	8,736		
Insurance	3,250		
Depreciation charge for the year on non-current assets	13,255		
Accountancy costs	1,250		10
Increase in doubtful debt provision in the year 2,740 – 0	2,740		11
Total expenses		107,987	12
Net profit for the year		91,393	13

Alison: statement of financial position at 31 December 2016

	£	Note
Non-current assets		
Racks, shelving and office furniture 33,600 cost – 14,650 accumulated depreciation	18,950	14
Computer equipment 20,775 cost –13,850 accumulated depreciation	6,925	15
	25,875	
Current Assets		
Inventory	22,600	4
Trade receivables 27,400 – 2,740 (provision for doubtful debts)	24,660	11
Rent prepayment	3,000	8
Rates prepayment	1,865	9
Cash and cash equivalents	52,315	
	104,440	
Total assets (non-current assets £25,875 + current assets £104,440)	130,315	
Current liabilities		
Trade payables	24,962	
Accountancy accrual	1,250	10
Total liabilities	26,212	
Net assets (total assets £130,315 – total liabilities £26,212)	104,103	
Equity (capital account)		
Capital account at 1 January 2016	52,710	
Profit for the year	91,393	13
Drawings	(40,000)	
Capital account at 31 December 2016	104,103	

Notes

Figures that do not change from the list of balances in the question are not discussed further in these notes. Check that you classified these balances correctly as assets, expenses, income or liabilities in the answer given above.

1. Sales are reduced by the sales returns. These returns are treated as a deduction from sales, as the return of goods amounts to the cancellation of a sale.
2. Inventory on the first day of the accounting year, 1 January 2016, is opening inventory. The closing inventory at 31 December 2016 is given in the additional information.

3. Purchases are the purchase of goods for resale, the goods bought in that are sold on to customers. Purchase returns are deducted from this figure as these represent cancelled purchases. Likewise, the discounts received are also deducted from the purchases figure as these discounts received represent a reduction in the cost of purchases made.

4. Closing inventory in the income statement is also a current asset in the statement of financial position as the cost of these unsold goods is carried forward to match against sales of these goods in the next accounting period.

5. Cost of sales is calculated as £27,647 (opening inventory) + £217,320 (purchases net of purchase returns and discounts received) – £22,600 (closing inventory) = £222,367.

6. Gross profit = £421,747 (sales) – £222,367 (cost of sales) = £199,380.

7. Remember that discounts allowed are an administrative expense and that this expense is not deducted from sales.

8. As £3,000 of the rent is prepaid, £3,000 is deducted from the rent expense for the year and recognised as a current asset in the statement of financial position.

9. Similarly, as £1,865 of rates have been paid in advance, this figure is deducted from the rates expense for the year and recognised as a current asset in the statement of financial position.

10. Accountancy costs have not been taken into account; as they have been incurred in the year, but not yet paid for, they must be recognised as both an expense in the income statement and as an accrual, a current liability at the financial year end, in the statement of financial position.

11. The provision for doubtful debts is calculated as 10% of year end trade receivables. Year end trade receivables stand at £27,400, so 10% of this figure is £2,740. £2,740 is deducted from trade receivables and charged as an expense in the income statement. As there was no provision for doubtful debts at the end of the previous accounting year, the change in the provision for doubtful debts is the provision now of £2,740 – the provision at the end of last year of £Nil = £2,740. Trade receivables in the statement of financial position are stated net of the doubtful debt provision at a figure of £27,400 – £2,740 = £24,660.

12. £107,987 is the total of all the expenses from administration expenses down to the increase in the provision for doubtful debts.

13. Net profit for the year is calculated by deducting total expenses of £107,987 from the gross profit of £199,380. This net profit for the year belongs to Alison, so this figure is added to the capital account balance on the statement of financial position.

14. The net book value of the racks, shelving and office furniture is calculated by deducting the accumulated depreciation of £14,650 at the end of the current accounting period, 31 December 2016, from the cost of the racks, shelving and office furniture of £33,600.

15. Similarly, the net book value of the computer equipment is calculated by deducting the accumulated depreciation of £13,850 at the end of the current accounting period, 31 December 2016, from the cost of the computer equipment of £20,775.

Question 3.3

Volumes Limited: income statement for the year ended 30 September 2016

	£000
Revenue (= sales)	4,750
Cost of sales (see working)	(3,550)
Gross profit	1,200
Distribution and selling costs	(200)
Administration expenses	(300)
Operating profit	700
Finance income	25
Finance expense	(100)
Profit before tax	625
Income tax	(250)
Profit for the year	375

Cost of sales working

	£000
Production costs	2,600
Opening inventory at 1 October 2015	100
Production wages	1,000
Closing inventory at 30 September 2016	(150)
Cost of sales	3,550

Cost of sales = opening inventory + production costs − closing inventory. Production wages are also added in to cost of sales in this example as these costs are directly incurred in the production of goods for sale. See the explanation of how cost of sales is made up in Chapter 3, Cost of sales.

Volumes Limited: statement of financial position at 30 September 2016

ASSETS	£000
Non-current assets	
Property, plant and equipment 2,000 (cost) – 800 (depreciation)	1,200
Current assets	
Inventory (= closing inventory in the income statement)	150
Trade receivables	430
Cash and cash equivalents	175
	755
Total assets 1,200 (non-current assets) + 755 (current assets)	1,955
LIABILITIES	
Current liabilities	
Trade payables	300
Taxation payable (= income tax charged in the income statement)	250
	550
Non-current liabilities	
Borrowings	500
Total liabilities 550 (current liabilities) + 500 (non-current liabilities)	1,050
Net assets: total assets – total liabilities 1,955 – 1,050	905
EQUITY	
Called up share capital	250
Share premium	125
Retained earnings 155 (at 30 September 2016) + 375 (profit for the year)	530
	905

Question 3.4

Textiles Limited: income statement for the year ended 30 June 2016

	£000
Revenue 7,750 (sales) – 150 (sales returns)	7,600
Cost of sales 4,550 (cost of sales) – 80 (purchase returns) – 125 (discounts received) + 600 (plant and machinery depreciation)	(4,945)
Gross profit (revenue – cost of sales)	2,655
Distribution and selling costs 1,000 + 100 (motor vehicle depreciation)	(1,100)
Administration expenses 700 + 200 (discounts allowed) + 10 (accountancy and audit fees for year) –15 (prepaid insurance) + 50 (known bad debt) – 20 (reduction in provision for doubtful debts)	(925)
Operating profit (gross profit – distribution and selling – administration)	630
Finance expense	(110)
Profit before tax	520
Income tax 520 (profit before tax) × 25%	(130)
Profit for the year	390

Textiles Limited: statement of financial position at 30 June 2016

ASSETS	£000
Non-current assets	
Plant and machinery 3,000 (cost) – 1,200 (depreciation to 30 June 2015) – 600 (depreciation for the year to 30 June 2016)	1,200
Motor vehicles 800 (cost) – 400 (depreciation to 30 June 2015) – 100 (depreciation for the year to 30 June 2016)	300
	1,500
Current assets	
Inventory	300
Trade receivables 1,050 – 60 (provision for doubtful debts at 30 June 2015) – 50 (known bad debt) + 20 (reduction in doubtful debt provision in year)	960
Insurance prepayment	15
	1,275
Total assets 1,500 (non-current assets) + 1,275 (current assets)	2,775
LIABILITIES	
Current liabilities	
Bank overdraft	200
Trade payables	300
Accruals 10 (audit and accountancy fees for the year)	10
Taxation payable (from the income statement: £520 (profit before tax) × 25%)	130
	640
Non-current liabilities	
Borrowings	1,000
Total liabilities 640 (current liabilities) + 1,000 (non-current liabilities)	1,640
Total assets – total liabilities 2,775 – 1,640	1,135
EQUITY	
Called up share capital	200
Retained earnings 545 (at 30 June 2015) + 390 (profit for the year)	935
	1,135

Workings and notes

- The audit and accountancy fees for the year have not been taken into account, so these represent an accrual at the end of the year, adding an expense incurred during the year to costs and liabilities. Administration expenses are increased by £10,000 and a current liability of £10,000 is recognised to reflect the obligation due at the year end.

- The insurance premium represents an expense for part of the year to 30 June 2016 and a prepaid expense for the financial year to 30 June 2017. Six months have been prepaid (July to December 2016), so £30,000 × 6/12 = £15,000 is deducted from administration expenses and added to current assets as a prepayment.

- £50,000 represents a known bad debt that must be charged as an expense (to administration expenses, not as a deduction from sales) and deducted from trade receivables.

- Trade receivables at the year end now stand at £1,000,000 (£1,050,000 (trade receivables at 30 June 2016) − £50,000 (known bad debt)); 4% of £1,000,000 = £40,000. The provision for doubtful debts at 30 June 2015 was £60,000, so there is a reduction in this provision of £20,000. This reduction in provision is added to trade receivables to give a net doubtful debt provision at 30 June 2016 of £40,000 (£60,000 at 30 June 2015 − £20,000 reduction in the provision in the year). The reduction in the provision of £20,000 is also deducted from administration expenses to reflect the reduction in the doubtful debts cost during the year to 30 June 2016. Essentially, this reduction in the doubtful debts provision is income that reduces expenditure in the current year.

- Depreciation on plant and machinery is to be calculated on the straight line basis. This means that the depreciation charge for the year is based upon the cost of the assets. Plant and machinery cost is £3,000,000, so 20% of this cost is £600,000; £600,000 is deducted from plant and machinery and added to cost of sales. The net book value of the plant and machinery is now:

	£000
Cost	3,000
Accumulated depreciation to 30 June 2015	(1,200)
Depreciation charge for the year ended 30 June 2016	(600)
Net book value at 30 June 2016	1,200

- Motor vehicle depreciation is to be charged on the reducing balance basis. As this is not the first year of ownership of the motor vehicles, depreciation cannot be based on cost but must be based on net book value, the cost − accumulated depreciation at the end of the preceding financial year. The net book value at the start of the year is £800,000 − £400,000 = £400,000; 25% of the net book value of £400,000 = £100,000. Thus, £100,000 is deducted from the net book value of the motor vehicles at 30 June 2016 and added to selling and distribution expenses. The net book value of motor vehicles is now:

	£000
Cost	800
Accumulated depreciation to 30 June 2015	(400)
Depreciation charge for the year ended 30 June 2016	(100)
Net book value at 30 June 2016	300

- The taxation charge is based upon the profit before tax for the year. Profit before tax totals up to £520,000; 25% of £520,000 = £130,000. Thus, £130,000 is deducted from profit before tax to give a profit for the year of £390,000. As the tax has not yet been paid, a current liability for taxation payable of £130,000 is also recognised on the statement of financial position as a liability due for payment. The profit for the year of £390,000 is now added to retained earnings in the statement of financial position.

Question 3.5

1. Laura's bank account

	Receipts £	Payments £
Cash paid in by Laura	50,000	
Receipts from cash sales	112,000	
Receipts from credit sales	36,000	
Payments for construction materials		38,000
Payment for van		6,000
Payment for construction equipment		5,000
Van running expenses		4,000
Wages paid to part time employees		9,600
Insurance		1,800
Bank charges		400
Bank interest paid		200
Interest received	250	
Drawings 12 months × £2,500		30,000
Drawings: mortgage repayment		90,000
Balance in bank at 31 August 2016		13,250
	198,250	198,250

Remember that the bank account just includes cash receipts and cash payments. If any of your figures are different from the above, check back to the information in Question 3.5 to make sure you have correctly identified the cash receipts and payments rather than cash that had not been received and payments that had not been made by 31 August 2016. The notes at the end of the statement of financial position below also provide further explanations of these figures.

2.   Laura: income statement for the year ended 31 August 2016

	£	£
Sales: 112,000 (cash sales) + 36,000 (credit sales cash received) + £12,000 (credit sales made but cash not yet received)		160,000
Opening inventory: nil as this is the first year of trading	—	
Purchases: 38,000 (cash paid) + 7,000 (payment still owed for construction materials) – 1,000 (bulk discount received)	44,000	
Closing inventory	(4,500)	
Cost of sales		39,500
Gross profit		120,500
Expenses		
Bad debt	2,500	
Increase in doubtful debts provision: (12,000 – 2,500) × 10%	950	
Van depreciation: (6,000 – 600) ÷ 3 years	1,800	
Van running expenses (all paid for in year)	4,000	
Equipment depreciation: (5,000 – 60) ÷ 4 years	1,235	
Wages of part time employees: 9,600 (paid) + (9,600 ÷ 12 weeks)	10,400	
Insurance: 1,800 (paid for 18 months) – (1,800 × 6/18)	1,200	
Bank charges: 400 (paid) + 75 (accrual up to 31 August 2016)	475	
Bank interest paid	200	
Total expenses		22,760
Interest received: 250 (received) + 50 (due for August 2016)		(300)
Profit for the year		98,040

Laura: statement of financial position at 31 August 2016

ASSETS	£
Non-current assets	
Van: 6,000 (cost) – 1,800 (accumulated depreciation charged up to the current year end)	4,200
Construction equipment: 5,000 (cost) – 1,235 (accumulated depreciation charged up to the current year end)	3,765
	7,965
Current assets	
Inventory: (from closing inventory in the income statement)	4,500
Trade receivables: 12,000 (invoices not paid) – 2,500 (bad debt) – 950 provision for doubtful debts	8,550
Insurance prepayment: 1,800 × 6/18	600
Interest receivable: 50 due for August 2016	50
Cash at bank: (from bank account in part (a))	13,250
	26,950
Total assets: 7,965 + 26,950	34,915
LIABILITIES	
Current liabilities	
Trade payables: 7,000 (payment still owed for construction materials supplied) – 1,000 (bulk discount received)	6,000
Accruals: 800 (wages) + 75 (bank charges)	875
Total liabilities	6,875
Net assets: 34,915 – 6,875	28,040
Capital account	
Capital introduced by Laura	50,000
Profit for the year: from income statement	98,040
Drawings: 12 × 2,500 = 30,000 + 90,000 (mortgage repayment)	(120,000)
Capital account at 31 August 2016	28,040

Notes

- Cash received and paid into the bank from cash sales is £112,000. The sales made on credit amount to £48,000. As these sales all occurred within the financial year to 31 August 2016 they, too, have to be recorded as sales, giving total sales of £112,000 (cash) + £48,000 (credit) =

£160,000. Laura has only received cash of £36,000 from her credit customers, so only this amount can be recorded as a cash receipt into her bank. The remaining £12,000 of sales (£48,000 sales – £36,000 cash paid) owed by customers who have not yet paid is recorded as a trade receivable in the statement of financial position. Remember that the accruals basis of accounting says that you must reflect the sales (and expenses) that have occurred in an accounting period regardless of when the cash for those sales was received (or when the cash was paid for expenses).

- Cash paid for construction materials amounts to £38,000. This is the total that is recorded as a payment out of the bank account for construction materials. However, £45,000 of purchases of construction materials took place during the year, so, under the accruals basis of accounting, the total purchases figure is £45,000. The £1,000 bulk purchase discount is a discount received from Laura's supplier. This discount received is deducted from purchases to give a net purchases figure of £44,000 (£45,000 expenditure – £1,000 reduction in costs). The discount relates to purchases within the financial year to 31 August 2016, so this discount is taken into account in this year rather than being taken into the accounting year in which it was received, the year ended 31 August 2017. The remaining £7,000 of amounts owed for construction materials (£45,000 total cost – £38,000 cash paid) is recorded as a trade payable less the £1,000 discount allowed, a net trade payable of £6,000.

- The known bad debt of £2,500 is deducted from trade receivables in the statement of financial position and recorded as an expense in the income statement. This bad debt is not deducted from sales, but is recorded as an expense. Net trade receivables now stand at £9,500 (£12,000 unpaid sales – £2,500 bad debt): 10% of these trade receivables is to be recorded as a provision for doubtful debts; 10% of £9,500 = £950. This amount is deducted from trade receivables and recorded as an expense in the income statement (this is not a deduction from sales). There was no provision at the start of the year as this is the first year of trading, so the income statement charge for the movement in the doubtful debt provision is the year end provision of £950 – the provision at the start of the year of £nil = £950.

- The £6,000 cost of the van is a payment out of the business bank account; £6,000 is recognised as a non-current asset on the statement of financial position. This amount now has to be depreciated. As the van is expected to do 5,000 miles each year, this indicates an even pattern for the consumption of the van's economic benefits, so straight line depreciation will be the most appropriate depreciation method to use. The annual depreciation will be (£6,000 (cost) – £600 (residual value)) ÷ 3 years = £1,800 per annum. This depreciation is deducted from the cost of the van and added as an expense to the income statement. The van now has a net book value of £6,000 (cost) – £1,800 (depreciation charged in the first year of the business) = £4,200.

- Van running expenses have all been paid from the bank account during the year, so these are recorded as a payment of cash out of the bank and an expense in the income statement. There are no adjustments to make to this cost as there are no indications of any prepaid or outstanding amounts in relation to these expenses in the question.

- The second-hand construction equipment is a payment out of the business bank account and a non-current asset. As Laura expects to make the same use of these assets in each of the four years, this equipment should be depreciated on the straight line basis. Cost of

£5,000 less residual value of £60 gives a depreciable amount of £4,940. As these assets will last for four years, the annual depreciation will be £4,940 ÷ 4 years = £1,235. Thus, £1,235 is deducted from the cost of the construction equipment and added to the income statement as an expense. The net book value of the construction equipment is now £5,000 (cost) − £1,235 (depreciation charged in the first year of the business) = £3,765.

- £9,600 has been paid out of the business bank account in respect of part time wages. However, £9,600 is not the total part time wages expense. The part time workers were employed for 13 weeks during the summer, but have only been paid for 12. The weekly part time wages were £9,600 ÷ 12 weeks = £800. Therefore, a further £800 expense needs to be recognised in the year to 31 August 2016. The additional £800 cost was incurred during this period, so it must be recognised in the financial statements for this year regardless of whether it was paid or not. The part time wages expense is thus the £9,600 paid during the year + the £800 incurred but not yet paid = £10,400. The £800 not yet paid is then recognised as an accrual, an obligation to make a payment for services received by the year end, on the statement of financial position.

- The amount paid out of the bank account in respect of insurance was £1,800. This payment covers 18 months of insurance expense. The financial year to 31 August 2016 is only 12 months long, so 6 out of the 18 months paid for has been prepaid. The prepaid element = £1,800 × 6/18 = £600. This prepayment is deducted from the £1,800 paid to leave an income statement charge for insurance of £1,200 (£1,800 paid − £600 prepayment). The prepayment is then recognised as a current asset in the statement of financial position.

- Closing inventory is a deduction in the income statement and an asset in the statement of financial position. There is no cash element in respect of this inventory, so no entry is made in the bank account.

- The payment out of the bank for bank charges is £400. This is cash paid and an expense incurred. £75 additional bank charges up to 31 August 2016 have been incurred but not yet paid. Therefore, this additional £75 has to be recognised as an expense in the year to 31 August 2016 as it was incurred in that financial year but paid in the next accounting year. An additional £75 is added to the bank charges expense in the income statement and £75 added as an accrual to the statement of financial position as an obligation validly incurred but not yet paid.

- £200 bank interest on the overdraft is the payment out of the bank. No additional bank interest is due, so there are no additional or prepaid expenses relating to bank interest. The £200 is recorded as a payment out of the bank and an expense in the income statement.

- £250 interest received from the bank is recorded as a receipt in the bank account and income in the income statement. An additional £50 interest has been earned up to 31 August 2016, so, as this income was earned in the accounting period, a further £50 is added to interest received in the income statement and a receivable of £50 recorded as a current asset, money due but not yet received from the bank.

- Laura has taken money out of the business each month for her own personal expenses as well as making a large payment off her personal mortgage at the end of the financial year. Total cash withdrawn for personal expenses was £2,500 per month × 12 months = £30,000. This is a payment out of the bank and a deduction from the capital account in the statement of financial position. Money withdrawn by the owner of a business is not a business expense, but a repayment of capital to the owner, so this £30,000 does not appear in the income statement. Similarly, the £90,000 mortgage payment is a payment out of the bank account and a deduction from the capital account, a repayment of capital to the owner of the business not a business expense or the repayment of a business liability.

- £198,250 has been paid into the bank and £185,000 paid out. Therefore £13,250 is left in the bank account. This is recorded on the statement of financial position as a current asset of the business.

Chapter 4

Question 4.1

Abi: statement of cash flows for the year ended 31 August 2016 using the direct method

	£
Cash flows from operating activities	
Cash received from sales (Note 1)	154,550
Cash payments to suppliers £3,445 + £116,328 + £6,000 (Note 2)	(125,773)
Cash payments for wages (Note 3)	(5,000)
Cash flows from operating activities	23,777
Cash flows from investing activities	
Cash paid to acquire display stands (Note 4)	(600)
Cash flows from financing activities	
Cash repaid to Abi (Note 5)	(18,000)
Net cash inflow for the year	5,177
Cash and cash equivalents at 1 September 2015	7,342
Cash and cash equivalents at 31 August 2016 (Note 6)	12,519

Notes

1. As Abi makes all her revenue (sales) for cash, this is the sales figure in the income statement. Abi paid £157,689 from cash sales into her bank, but she gave refunds of £3,789 for goods returned. She also had £650 in cash representing unbanked sales at the year end, so her total cash received from sales was £157,689 − £3,789 + £650 = £154,550.

2. Abi paid the £3,445 owing to suppliers at 31 August 2015 in the current accounting year, so this counts as a cash payment to suppliers during the financial year 1 September 2015 to 31 August 2016. She also paid £116,328 of the total purchases during the year of £120,645, so this is also a cash payment to suppliers during the financial year 1 September 2015 to 31 August 2016. During this same financial year, she paid all her rent of £6,000. Therefore, cash payments to suppliers during the financial year to 31 August 2016 were £3,445 + £116,328 + £6,000 = £125,773.

3. Cash paid for wages during the financial year was £5,000 with an accrual (cash not paid, but the expense recognised for services received by the end of the financial year together with a liability for the same amount) of £200 making up the income statement figure of £5,200.

4. The actual cash paid to acquire non-current assets (the display stands) was £600. Remember that depreciation is not a cash flow.

5. Abi withdrew £18,000 from the bank for her own personal expenses during the accounting year, so this amounts to a repayment of capital to the owner of the business.

6. Cash at 31 August 2016 is made up of the bank balance of £11,869 + cash from sales unbanked of £650 = £12,519.

Abi: statement of cash flows for the year ended 31 August 2016 using the indirect method

Cash flows from operating activities	£
Profit for the year from Abi's income statement	24,951
Add: depreciation charged for the year	190
Deduct: increase in inventory £2,382 – £4,638	(2,256)
Add: increase in trade payables £4,137 – £3,445	692
Add: increase in accruals £200 – £Nil	200
Cash flows from operating activities	23,777
Cash flows from investing activities	
Cash paid to acquire display stands	(600)
Cash flows from financing activities	
Cash repaid to Abi	(18,000)
Net cash inflow for the year	5,177
Cash and cash equivalents at 1 September 2015	7,342
Cash and cash equivalents at 31 August 2016	12,519

Question 4.2

Alison: statement of cash flows for the year ended 31 December 2016 using the indirect method

	£	£
Cash flows from operating activities		
Profit for the year from Alison's income statement		91,393
Add: depreciation charged for the year		13,255
Add: decrease in inventory £27,647 – £22,600		5,047
Add: decrease in trade payables £27,200 – £24,660		2,540
Deduct: increase in rent prepayment £2,500 – £3,000		(500)
Add: reduction in rates prepayment £1,965 – £1,865		100
Deduct: decrease in trade payables £24,962 – £30,314		(5,352)
Deduct: decrease in telephone, electricity and gas accruals £1,500 – £Nil		(1,500)
Add: increase in accountancy accrual		1,250
Cash flows from operating activities		106,233
Cash flows from investing activities		
Cash paid to acquire new computer equipment	(8,000)	
Cash paid to acquire new racks, shelving and office furniture	(9,600)	
Cash flows from investing activities		(17,600)
Cash flows from financing activities		
Cash repaid to Alison		(40,000)
Net cash inflow for the year		48,633
Cash and cash equivalents at 1 January 2016		3,682
Cash and cash equivalents at 31 December 2016		52,315

Note

Check back to Table 4.1 to remind yourself which figures to add and which figures to deduct from operating profit to determine the cash flow from operating activities when preparing statements of cash flows using the indirect method.

Question 4.3

Laura: statement of cash flows for the year ended 31 August 2016

Cash flows from operating activities	£	£
Profit for the year (Note 1)		98,040
Add van depreciation (Note 2)		1,800
Add construction equipment depreciation (Note 2)		1,235
Deduct increase in inventory (£0 – £4,500) (Note 3)		(4,500)
Deduct: increase in trade receivables (£0 – £8,550) (Note 3)		(8,550)
Deduct increase in prepayments (£0 – £600) (Note 3)		(600)
Add increase in trade payables (£6,000 – £0) (Note 3)		6,000
Add increase in accruals (£875 – £0) (Note 3)		875
Deduct interest received (Note 4)		(300)
Add interest paid (Note 5)		200
Net cash inflows from operating activities		94,200
Cash flows from investing activities		
Payment to acquire van (Note 6)	(6,000)	
Payment to acquire construction equipment (Note 6)	(5,000)	
Interest received (Note 7)	250	
Net cash outflow from investing activities		(10,750)
Cash flows from financing activities		
Cash introduced by Laura (Note 8)	50,000	
Cash withdrawn by Laura (Note 8)	(120,000)	
Payment of interest (Note 9)	(200)	
Net cash inflow from financing activities		(70,200)
Net cash inflow for the year		13,250
Cash and cash equivalents at 1 September 2015 (Note 10)		–
Cash and cash equivalents at 31 August 2016		13,250

Notes

Information from the income statement and statement of financial position in the answer to Question 3.5:

1. Profit for the year.
2. Depreciation for the year on these two non-current assets.
3. The inventory, trade receivables, prepayments, trade payables and accruals at the start of the year were all £nil as this is Laura's first year of trading. All movements in working capital figures are thus the end of year figures – £nil at the start of the year.

4. Cash inflows from interest received are dealt with under investing activities.

5. Cash outflows from interest paid are dealt with under financing activities.

6. The cash payments actually made to acquire these assets.

7. The cash flow from interest received is the actual cash received: ignore interest due for August as this is cash that has not yet been received so no cash inflow relating to this interest receivable has yet taken place.

8. Laura's cash introduced and cash withdrawn as shown in the bank account.

9. The actual interest paid to the bank during the year.

10. As this is the first year of trading, the cash balance at the start of the business' life was £nil.

Question 4.4

Potters Limited: statement of cash flows for the year ended 30 June 2016

	£000	£000
Cash flows from operating activities		
Operating profit		845
Add: depreciation		800
Deduct: profit on disposal of plant and equipment: £150,000 cash received – £100,000 net book value		(50)
Add: amortisation of trademarks		20
Add: decrease in inventory: £1,000 – £1,100		100
Deduct: increase in trade and other receivables: £1,800 – £1,550		(250)
Add: increase in trade and other payables: £1,200 – £1,000		200
Cash generated from operations		1,665
Taxation paid		(275)
Net cash inflow from operating activities		1,390
Cash flows from investing activities		
Acquisition of property, plant and equipment	(2,500)	
Proceeds from sale of property, plant and equipment	150	
Net cash outflow from investing activities		(2,350)
Cash flows from financing activities		
Proceeds from the issue of ordinary share capital £2.75 × 200,000	550	
Increase in long-term borrowings: £3,200,000 – £2,600,000	600	
Dividends paid	(100)	
Interest paid	(200)	
Net cash inflow from financing activities		850
Net cash outflow for the year		(110)
Cash and cash equivalents at 1 July 2015		310
Cash and cash equivalents at 30 June 2016		200

Question 4.5

1. Metal Bashers Limited: statement of cash flows for the year ended 30 September 2016

	£000	£000
Cash flows from operating activities		
Operating profit		1,725
Add: depreciation		1,800
Add: loss on disposal of plant and equipment: £250,000 net book value – £175,000 cash received		75
Add: amortisation of patents		20
Deduct increase in inventory: £1,400 – £1,200		(200)
Add: decrease in trade and other receivables: £2,350 – £2,400		50
Deduct: decrease in trade and other payables: £2,000 – £2,300		(300)
Cash generated from operations		3,170
Taxation paid		(375)
Net cash inflow from operating activities		2,795
Cash flows from investing activities		
Acquisition of property, plant and equipment	(5,000)	
Acquisition of intangible assets	(70)	
Proceeds from sale of property, plant and equipment	175	
Interest received	100	
Net cash outflow from investing activities		(4,795)
Cash flows from financing activities		
Proceeds from the issue of ordinary share capital £3 × 1,600,000	4,800	
Repayment of borrowings (£500 + £6,500) – (£500 + £7,000)	(500)	
Dividends paid	(1,080)	
Interest paid	(870)	
Net cash inflow from financing activities		2,350
Net cash inflow for the year		350
Cash and cash equivalents at 1 October 2015		400
Cash and cash equivalents at 30 September 2016		750

2. Metal Bashers Limited: statement of cash flows for the year ended 30 September 2016

	£000
Cash flows from operating activities	
Cash receipts from sales of goods	9,550
Cash payments to suppliers for goods and services	(5,100)
Cash payments to employees	(1,280)
Cash generated from operations	3,170

Chapter 5

Question 5.1

An oil exploration company will set itself up as a public limited company. It will need a lot of investment from a substantial number of shareholders to provide the necessary cash to purchase oil exploration equipment, to hire skilled employees and to buy exploration licences around the world. This size of investment would not be available to sole traders, partnerships or private limited companies.

A taxi driver would set up as a sole trader as driving a taxi is a straightforward operation that will require no major financing or present any other difficulties that might be overcome by adopting a different business format. The taxi driver just needs to buy a car and a hackney carriage licence, all of which expenditure can be met from personal savings. Day to day expenditure, such as petrol and repairs, can be paid for from the receipts from fares.

A family-run knitwear manufacturing business would adopt the private limited company format. As this is a family business, the family will want to maintain control of day to day operations, which would be lost if the business were to set up as a public limited company. The private limited company will be able to borrow money to buy specialised knitwear machinery and equipment while affording the family business limited liability if the business venture were to fail. As a private limited company, the family will be able to concentrate on ensuring that the business will be a commercial success without being distracted by the demands of many outside shareholders.

The business format most suited to the two friends setting up a dance school will be the partnership. Each of the two friends will want to have an equal share in running the school and in contributing to its success. Additionally, both friends will be entitled to share profits in the venture equally. The operations of the dance school will be straightforward with no complexities that would make a different format more suitable.

Question 5.2

Annual interest received on the bond: £200,000 × 5% = £10,000

Annual dividend from the investment in the 50 pence preference shares: £200,000 = 400,000 preference shares of 50 pence each × 3 pence per share = £12,000

Annual dividend from the investment in the 25 pence ordinary shares: £200,000 = 800,000 ordinary shares of 25 pence each × 2 pence per share = £16,000.

Therefore, the investor should invest in the 25 pence shares to maximise income from the £200,000 investment. The investor should also be aware that the ordinary shares are the riskiest of the three possible investments as they may generate no dividend at all and, should the company go into liquidation, the investor may lose all of the £200,000 investment. Alternatively, the dividend per share on the ordinary shares may increase and the value of the shares may also increase, potentially raising the income and capital value of the ordinary shares. The income from the bond and the preference shares, however, will remain the same for each year.

Question 5.3

Borrowing from the bank at 5% per annum: £3,000,000 × 5% = £150,000 annual cost

Ordinary shares of 40 pence each: number of ordinary shares with a par value of 40 pence each = £3,000,000 ÷ 0.40 = 7,500,000 shares × £0.019 = £142.500 annual dividend

Preference shares of 60 pence each: number of preference shares with a par value of 60 pence each = £3,000,000 ÷ 0.60 = 5,000,000 shares × £0.0315 = £157,500 annual dividend

Therefore the ordinary shares option will require the lowest cash outlay.

Alternatively, you might have compared the interest or dividend rates on each financing method. The interest on the loan is payable at 5%. The required dividend rate on the ordinary shares is equivalent to a 4.75% return (1.9 pence ÷ 40 pence) while the return on the preference shares is 5.25% (3.15 pence ÷ 60 pence). Therefore the % return on the ordinary dividend is the lowest and will provide the lowest financing cost.

Question 5.4

(a) £1 par value × 6% = £0.06 dividend per share × 100,000 shares = £6,000

(b) 100,000 ordinary shares × 10 pence + 100,000 ordinary shares × 20 pence = £30,000

(c) £45,000 retained earnings at 1 November 2015 + £50,000 profit for the year − £6,000 preference dividend − £30,000 ordinary dividends = £59,000 retained earnings at 31 October 2016

Question 5.5

(a) Amounts to be added to ordinary share capital and share premium in the statement of financial position in respect of the issue of ordinary shares on 1 May 2017:

- Par value of ordinary shares: 50 pence (Question 5.4)
- Issue price per share: £2.50 (£500,000 ÷ 200,000 shares)
- Therefore, the premium on each share issued = £2.50 (issue price) − £0.50 = £2.00
- Additional ordinary share capital: 200,000 shares × £0.50 = £100,000
- Additional share premium: 200,000 shares × £2.00 = £400,000

(b) Total dividends, both ordinary and preference, to be paid in the year to 31 October 2017:

- Preference dividends: no change as no additional preference shares have been issued, so preference dividends remain at £6,000
- Ordinary dividends paid on 15 April 2017: 100,000 shares × £0.15 = £15,000 (new ordinary shares not issued until 1 May 2017, so there were only 100,000 ordinary shares in issue on 15 April 2017)
- Ordinary dividends paid on 15 October 2017: (100,000 shares + 200,000 shares) × £0.25 = £75,000

- Total ordinary dividends for the year to 31 October 2017: £15,000 (15 April 2017) + £75,000 (15 October 2017) = £90,000

- Total dividends, both preference and ordinary, to be paid in the year to 31 October 2017 = £6,000 (preference) + £90,000 (ordinary) = £96,000

(c) Expected balance on retained earnings at 31 October 2017 after dividends for the year have been paid:

- Retained earnings at 31 October 2016 from Question 5.4 (c): £59,000

- + £90,000 (profit for the year to 31 October 2017)

- − £96,000 (total ordinary and preference dividends for the year to 31 October 2017 from (b))

- = £53,000

Question 5.6

Calculate for Halyson plc:

(a) The number of bonus shares to be issued:

- 500,000 ordinary shares currently in issue

- Seven new shares for every two held

- So 500,000 × 7 new shares ÷ 2 = 1,750,000 new shares

(b) The par value of the bonus shares to be added to ordinary share capital:

- 1,750,000 × 25 pence = £437,500

(c) The number of ordinary shares to be issued in the rights issue:

- Number of shares in issue after the bonus issue: 500,000 (original) + 1,750,000 (bonus issue) = 2,250,000 shares

- Rights issue: five new ordinary shares for every three ordinary shares currently held

- Therefore, 2,250,000 ÷ 3 shares × 5 shares = 3,750,000 new ordinary shares issued in the rights issue

(d) The amount to be added to ordinary share capital and share premium as a result of the rights issue:

- 3,750,000 new shares issued in the rights issue from answer (c)

- Par value: 25 pence

- Therefore, par value of shares issued under the rights issue = 3,750,000 × £0.25 = £937,500

- Share premium on each share issued: £0.95 − £0.25 = £0.70

- Total share premium on the issue of 3,750,000 25 pence shares at £0.95 = 3,750,000 × £0.70 = £2,625,000

(e) The preference dividend for the year to 30 June 2017:

- Preference dividend per share: £1 × 0.075 = £0.075
- Total preference dividend on 300,000 shares = 300,000 × £0.075 = £22,500

(f) The ordinary dividend for the year to 30 June 2017:

- Number of ordinary shares in issue at 30 June 2017: 500,000 (before bonus and rights issues) + 1,750,000 (bonus issue) + 3,750,000 (rights issue) = 6,000,000
- Ordinary dividend per share: £0.30
- Total dividend on ordinary shares at 30 June 2017 = 6,000,000 × £0.30 = £1,800,000

(g) The balance on the ordinary share capital account on 30 June 2017:

- 500,000 × £0.25 + £437,500 (b) (bonus issue) + £937,500 (c) (rights issue) = £1,500,000

(h) The expected balance on retained earnings at 30 June 2017:

- Balance at 1 July 2017: £5,200,000
- − £437,500 (b) (bonus issue)
- − £22,500 (e) (preference dividend)
- − £1,800,000 (f) (ordinary dividend)
- − £1,500,000 (loss for the year from the question)
- = £1,440,000

Chapter 6

Question 6.1

	2016 Calculation	2016 Ratio	2015 Calculation	2015 Ratio
Gross profit %	£18,711/£34,650 × 100%	54.00%	£15,267/£29,360 × 100%	52.00%
Operating profit %	£9,702/£34,650 × 100%	28.00%	£7,634/£29,360 × 100%	26.00%
Profit before tax %	£9,102/£34,650 × 100%	26.27%	£7,059/£29,360 × 100%	24.04%
Profit after tax %	£6,920/£34,650 × 100%	19.97%	£5,365/£29,360 × 100%	18.27%
Non-current asset turnover	£34,650/£21,655	£1.60	£29,360/£18,820	£1.56
Revenue per employee	£34,650/275	£126,000	£29,360/250	£117,440
Operating profit per employee	£9,702/275	£35,280	£7,634/250	£30,536
Earnings per share	£6,920/20,000 × 100 pence	34.6p	£5.365/18,500 × 100 pence	29.0p
Dividends per share	£4,400/20,000 × 100 pence	22.0p	£3,700/18,500 × 100 pence	20.0p
Dividend pay-out ratio	22.0/34.6 × 100%	63.58%	20.0/29.0 × 100 pence	68.97%
Dividend cover	£6,920/£4,400	1.57 times	£5,365/£3,700	1.45 times

- This will mean that sales, profits and cash flows will be generated from which to repay the long-term borrowings as they fall due.

- Gearing might look high at 116.73%, but the interest cover ratio shows that the cost of servicing the interest on the borrowings is easily affordable from the operating profits.

Question 7.2

Amounts due for repayment the day after the year end:

	Calculation	1 June 2016 £m	1 June 2015 £m
Borrowings	240/12: 216/12	(20)	(18)
Trade payables	830/24.10: 790/25.45	(34)	(31)
Other payables	150 × 20%: 140 × 20%	(30)	(28)
Dividends	Not payable until August 2016/2015	(–)	(–)
Current tax	First payment three months after year end	(–)	(–)
	Total liabilities due for payment on 1 June	(84)	(77)
	Cash and cash equivalents at year end	122	99
	Add: one day's sales on 1 June: 13,663/360: 12,249/360	38	34
	Estimated cash balance at end of 1 June	76	56

Samoco thus has more than enough cash in hand to cover any liabilities due on 1 June in each year.

Problems with relying solely on the current and quick ratios

- Current and quick ratios make the unrealistic assumption that all liabilities will be called in on the statement of financial position date.

- In reality, unless the entity is in liquidation, payment of current liabilities occurs over 12 months not all at once: individuals do not have to consider paying all their debts due over the next 12 months on the first day of the year, so why is this assumption made about business entities?

- Samoco plc is a very large company, so suppliers can be kept waiting for payment until the cash is readily available.

- Contracts govern bank loans, so, unless the company has breached the contractual terms of the loans, lenders cannot demand all their cash back until repayments are overdue.

- Other payables have been assumed to require 20% payment immediately: this is probably a serious overestimate of what is due on the day after the year end, so more cash than estimated is probably available at the end of the first day of the new financial year.

- Similarly, the current portion of long-term borrowings is more likely to be payable at the end of June not at the beginning of the month, so cash outflows on 1 June are, again, probably overestimated.

- Suppliers are happy to trade with such a large organisation and will not want to jeopardise their future trading relationships by demanding immediate payments of amounts due. They know they will be paid eventually and are willing to sacrifice cash now for the longer-term certainty of continuing trade with their large customer.

- When assessing short-term liquidity, timing of payments is everything and liabilities are paid, not immediately, but from cash left over at the end of the previous year and from subsequent cash inflows from daily trading.

- Current and quick ratios are a static measure of liquidity: in reality, the cash keeps flowing in each and every day while amounts due are paid each and every day as current trading pays off past liabilities.

Question 7.3

Ratio calculations Ted Baker plc

Ted Baker plc	Calculation	Ratio
Current ratio	159.6/91.1	1.75:1
Quick ratio	(159.6 − 111.1)/91.1	0.53:1
Inventory days/inventory turnover	111.1/152.4 × 365	266.09 days
Receivables days	25.8/387.6 × 365	24.30 days
Payables days	32.2/152.4 × 365	77.12 days
Cash conversion cycle	+ 266.09 + 24.30 − 77.12	213.27 days
Gearing %	26.2/140.6 × 100%	18.63%
Debt ratio	91.1/231.7	0.39:1
Interest cover	49.8/1.2	41.50 times

Ratio calculations Nichols plc

Nichols plc	Calculation	Ratio
Current ratio	62.7/21.3	2.94:1
Quick ratio	(62.7 − 4.7)/21.3	2.72:1
Inventory days/inventory turnover	4.7/59 × 365	29.08 days
Receivables days	21.9/109.2 × 365	73.20 days
Payables days	5.7/59 × 365	35.26 days
Cash conversion cycle	+ 29.08 + 73.20 − 35.26	+ 67.02 days
Gearing %	0.0/58.1 × 100%	0.00%
Debt ratio	27.6/85.7	0.32:1
Interest cover	N/A: zero borrowings and zero finance expense	

Ratio calculations Rolls Royce plc

Rolls Royce plc	Calculation	Ratio
Current ratio	11,188/7,685	1.46:1
Quick ratio	(11,188 − 2,768)/ 7,685	1.10:1
Inventory days/inventory turnover	2,768/10,533 × 365	95.92 days
Receivables days	4,215/13,736 × 365	112.00 days
Payables days	1,348/10,533 × 365	46.71 days
Cash conversion cycle	+ 95.92 + 112.00 − 46.71	+ 161.21 days
Gearing %	2,261/6,387 × 100%	35.40%
Debt ratio	15,837/22,224	0.71:1
Interest cover	1,390/70	19.86 times

Ratio calculations National Express plc

National Express plc	Calculation	Ratio
Current ratio	307.9/566.0	0.54:1
Quick ratio	(307.9 − 21.8)/566	0.51:1
Inventory days/inventory turnover	21.8/1084.0 × 365	7.34 days
Receivables days	105.6/1,867.4 × 365	20.64 days
Payables days	144.2/1,084.0 × 365	48.55 days
Cash conversion cycle	+ 7.34 + 20.64 − 48.55	− 20.57 days
Gearing %	797.7/836.2 × 100%	95.40%
Debt ratio	1,490.0/2,326.2	0.64:1
Interest cover	193.1/52.2	3.70 times

Question 7.4

Assessment of the cash generating ability, liquidity and solvency of each company.

Ted Baker plc

- The current ratio is very high because of the high levels of inventory maintained by the business.

- High inventories are needed in retail as no stock means no sale.

- With a financial year end at the end of January, new spring and summer season fashions will have just been delivered from suppliers, so high inventories would be expected at this time of year.

- The quick ratio is low because of the high level of inventories at the year end.

- However, this is not a cause for concern. Inventories will be sold in the stores and other outlets each day, so cash will be received on a regular basis with which to pay liabilities and other expenses as they fall due. Remember that inventory in the statement of financial position is shown at cost whereas the goods will sell for a much higher price than this cost (Ted Baker has a gross profit % of 60.68% in the 53 weeks to 3 February 2015) thereby boosting cash inflows on each and every trading day.

- Branded fashion and lifestyle goods have a shelf life of around six months, so inventories will not become obsolete and worthless within a few days of the year end.

- The cash conversion cycle is positive because of the high level of inventories.

- Receivables days are lower than payables days, but most of the sales will be made for cash.

- Payables days are high as suppliers are willing to allow high levels of credit to the business in order to retain their custom and to develop the business relationship further.

- Gearing is very low at 18.63% and a debt ratio of 0.39:1 indicates that the assets significantly outweigh the liabilities.

- Interest cover of 41.50 times indicates that borrowings are easily affordable.

- Borrowings are in the form of an overdraft rather than a loan, so the company's bank clearly sees Ted Baker as a very solid business with a very high credit rating. The possibility of the bank asking for this overdraft to be repaid immediately is very remote.

- Lenders would not be worried as Ted Baker is a very valuable global brand. This brand does not appear on the statement of financial position, so the breakup value of the group would far exceed the net assets figure as shown in the financial statements.

Nichols plc

- Current and quick ratios are very high at 2.94:1 and 2.72:1 indicating that this is a very solid company indeed.

- As a manufacturer of soft drinks, the company trades on credit with customers, hence the receivable days of 73.20.

- Payables are paid within 36 days.

- However, the very high cash balance of £34.5 million means that the company has plenty of spare money with which to finance its working capital.

- With total cash of £34.5 million and total liabilities of £27.6 million, Nichols could pay off all its liabilities at the year end and still have £6.9 million left over, so this is a company that has no financial problems.
- Soft drinks are a regular purchase for most households, so there is no danger that the business will lose its market.
- The company has no borrowings and is pretty much risk free from a financial viewpoint.

Rolls Royce plc

- A manufacturer of complex technical equipment that is sold to other companies for inclusion in their products.
- Therefore, the company will trade on credit with their customers and allow these customers a suitably long time in which to pay.
- The manufacturing cycle for complex technical equipment is lengthy and the inventory days indicate that this is well over three months.
- With receivables days approaching four months, this suggests that the group has to allow around 208 days (96 inventory days + 112 receivables days) from the start of an order to the receipt of the cash.
- Therefore, given the long working capital cycle, current and quick ratios are much higher as this working capital has to be financed by the group.
- Note that the cash conversion cycle is positive, indicating that suppliers have to be paid before inventories are turned into finished goods and before cash is received from customers.
- Customers are paying in around 96 days, while suppliers are paid after just 47 days.
- While there might be a risk of obsolete stock, finished goods are made to order for specific customers who pay a deposit when their order is placed to help Rolls Royce meet the working capital requirements for each contract.
- Gearing is low at 35.40% and interest cover of 19.85 times indicates that all borrowings are easily affordable.
- Lenders would not be worried as the group does have extremely valuable assets that do not appear on the statement of financial position, such as the company's reputation and name, the future order book and a highly skilled workforce that rivals would be willing to pay a lot of money for; therefore, the breakup value of the group would far exceed the net assets figure on the statement of financial position.

National Express plc

- As National Express is a transport operator, cash flows in daily as customers pay for their journeys as they are taken.
- This accounts for the very low current and quick ratios as the company has money flowing in up front from which to pay liabilities and the costs of running the business as they become due.

- The biggest costs in the transport sector are fuel and the wages of employees: fuel is bought on credit from suppliers (though failure to meet the payment terms might result in further supplies of fuel being cut off, bringing operations to a halt) while staff work for a month before they are paid, so the cash is received well in advance of payments being made to suppliers and employees.

- Inventory days are very low as the only inventory at the end of the year will be a few days of fuel in the vehicles and in the bus and train depots and some spares in the vehicle workshops: as long as fuel supplies are guaranteed, this is the only inventory that is required for trading in the transport sector.

- Receivables days at 20.64 days might seem high, but these trade receivables will represent money due from local and national governments for grants that are paid as subsidies to operators of bus and train services.

- These receivables are thus guaranteed and there is no risk of bad debts arising.

- The cash conversion cycle is negative, so suppliers are financing the working capital requirements of the group rather than reliance being placed on short-term bank borrowings.

- Gearing at 95.40% might seem high, but the transport sector finances the purchase of buses and trains it cannot lease by borrowings. Transport is a capital intensive sector that pays for long-term assets (buses and trains) with long-term borrowings. The costs of these borrowings (interest and loan repayments) are met from day to day cash inflows from customers, so the assets are financed by daily income from passengers.

- Interest cover at over 3.70 times indicates that borrowings are affordable.

- Transport is an essential sector and one that is likely to grow in importance as governments seek to reduce congestion in city centres and as the need to reduce reliance on other forms of transport to reduce greenhouse gases and global warming increases, so large mass transit operators should be safe companies in which to invest and with which to trade for the foreseeable future.

Chapter 8

Question 8.1

Absorption cost for one food processor

	£
Materials: £22,500 ÷ 2,000 food processors	11.25
Direct labour: £16,500 ÷ 2,000 food processors	8.25
Direct expenses: £13,000 ÷ 2,000 food processors	6.50
Overhead allocation: 4.5 machine hours × £4 per hour*	18.00
Total absorption cost of one food processor	44.00

*Overhead absorption rate: £3,000,000 ÷ 750,000 machine hours = £4 per machine hour
Selling price for one food processor: total absorption cost plus 50% = £44 × 1.5 = £66

Question 8.2

Printers Ltd print run

	£
Paper: 2,000 books × 400 pages = 800,000 pages ÷ 2,500 pages × £9 per 2,500 pages	2,880
Printing ink: 800,000 pages ÷ 20,000 × £57.50	2,300
Covers: 2,000 books × 66 pence per book	1,320
Finishing costs: 2,000 books × 50 pence	1,000
Production workers: 200 × £12.50	2,500
Overheads: £500,000 ÷ 50,000,000 pages × 800,000 printed pages	8,000
Total cost for print run of 2,000 books	18,000

Selling price for printing 2,000 books: £18,000 × 1.25 = £22,500 = £11.25 for each book (£22,500 ÷ 2,000)

Question 8.3

Applokia Limited

Part (a)	Variable cost	Fixed cost	Direct production cost	Production overhead	Period cost
Factory rent		✓		✓	
Factory manager's salary		✓		✓	
Administration salaries		✓			✓
Marketing costs		✓			✓
Plastic smart phone covers	✓		✓		
Quality control salaries		✓		✓	
Production line salaries		✓	✓		
Chip assemblies	✓		✓		
Administration office rent		✓			✓
Marketing office rent		✓			✓
Factory rates		✓		✓	
Power for production machinery	✓		✓		
Factory lighting and heating		✓		✓	
Administration lighting and heating		✓			✓
Marketing lighting and heating		✓			✓
Marketing department salaries		✓			✓
Batteries	✓		✓		
Machinery depreciation		✓		✓	

Variable costs: these are the costs that will vary directly in line with production. If you were at all unsure about which costs would be variable in this case, the way to determine if a cost is variable is to ask yourself if more of that cost will be incurred if another smart phone, another unit of production, is produced. In Applokia's case, each additional smart phone will require a plastic cover, a chip assembly, a battery and additional power for the production machinery to produce another smart phone. Therefore, these costs of production are entirely variable as they will increase or decrease directly in line with production.

Assembly line workers are paid a salary and, as it says in the question, these remain the same no matter how many or how few smart phones are produced. Thus, the assembly line workers' salaries, while being a direct cost of production (there will be no production without their input), are fixed rather than variable.

All other costs are fixed. Rent and rates will not vary in line with production and anyone paid a salary will receive the same salary no matter how many smart phones are produced or sold. Lighting and heating is best treated as a fixed cost as we noted in the case of Anna (Example 8.4) as it is not possible to allocate these costs to individual units of production.

Part (b)

	£000
Prime cost	
Plastic smart phone covers	250
Chip assemblies for smart phones produced	1,498
Batteries	242
Production line workers' salaries	500
Power for production machinery	50
Total prime cost	**2,540**
Production overhead	
Factory rent	100
Factory manager's salary	38
Factory rates	47
Production machinery depreciation	37
Factory lighting and heating	43
Quality control salaries	75
Total production overhead	**340**
Total production cost (total prime cost + total production overhead)	**2,880**
Period costs	
Administration salaries	85
Administration office rent	25
Administration lighting and heating	5
Marketing lighting and heating	4
Marketing department salaries	51
Marketing office rent	20
Marketing costs	50
Total period costs	**240**
Total costs for September	**3,120**

Part (c)

Total costs from part (b): £3,120,000

Total production in September from the question: 130,000 smart phones
Total cost of one smart phone in September: £3,120,000 ÷ 130,000 = £24
Selling price = cost + 25% = £24 + (£24 × 0.25) = £30

Part (d)

If Applokia sells its smart phones for £27, it will make a profit on total cost of £27 − £24 = £3. This is equivalent to a margin on cost of £3 ÷ £24 × 100% = 12.50%. Proof that this is the correct answer: £24 + (£24 × 0.125) = £27

Question 8.4

Part (a) Total production overheads to be allocated to the manufacturing and painting and finishing departments
The first task is to determine appropriate allocation bases for overheads. Using the information from the question, the following overhead bases would be the most suitable for each overhead:

- Machinery maintenance staff salaries and painting and finishing department employee salaries: actual cost for each department.

- Employers' national insurance contributions: these should be allocated on the basis of the salary costs in the two departments as higher salaries will mean higher employers' national insurance costs. Total salaries are £100,000 + £300,000 = £400,000. The manufacturing department is thus allocated (£100,000 ÷ £400,000) × £40,000 = £10,000 and the painting and finishing department is allocated (£300,000 ÷ £400,000) × £40,000 = £30,000.

- Rent and rates should be allocated on the basis of area as the bigger the area occupied by each department, the higher the allocated costs. Total area is 4,800 square metres + 1,200 square metres = 6,000 square metres. Total costs are £60,000, so the manufacturing department is allocated (4,800 ÷ 6,000) × £60,000 = £48,000 and the painting and finishing department is allocated (4,800 ÷ 6,000) × £60,000 = £12,000.

- Heating should be allocated on the basis of actual usage. The manufacturing department is not heated; there is not much point keeping machinery warm! As heat will be generated by the machinery as it is running to keep the manufacturing department heated, all the heating costs should be allocated to the painting and finishing department.

- Lighting is most appropriately allocated on the basis of area. Total costs are £25,000, so the manufacturing department is allocated (4,800 ÷ 6,000) × £25,000 = £20,000 and the painting and finishing department is allocated (4,800 ÷ 6,000) × £25,000 = £5,000.

- Machinery depreciation is best allocated on the basis of machinery value. Total machinery value is £360,000 + £15,000 = £375,000, so the manufacturing department is allocated (£360,000 ÷ £375,000) × £75,000 = £72,000 and the painting and finishing department is allocated (£15,000 ÷ £375,000) × £75,000 = £3,000.

- Canteen expenses should be allocated on the basis of the number of employees. The total number of employees is five in manufacturing plus 15 in painting and finishing, a total of 20 employees. Manufacturing department is allocated (5 ÷ 20) × £56,000 = £14,000 and the painting and finishing department is allocated (5 ÷ 20) × £56,000 = £42,000.

- Electricity for machinery should be allocated on the basis of the number of hours usage during the year as the number of hours of running time will determine the power that is used by that machinery. The total number of machine hours for the year is 96,000 in manufacturing and 4,000 in painting and finishing, a total of 100,000 hours. The manufacturing department is thus allocated (96,000 ÷ 100,000) × £50,000 = £48,000 and the painting and finishing department is allocated (96,000 ÷ 100,000) × £50,000 = £2,000.

- Machinery insurance should also be allocated on the basis of machinery value. Given that the total machinery value is £375,000, the manufacturing department is allocated (£360,000 ÷ £375,000) × £25,000 = £24,000 and the painting and finishing department is allocated (£15,000 ÷ £375,000) × £25,000 = £1,000.

The overheads allocated to each department can be summarised in a table along with the allocation bases used.

	Absorption basis	Total £000	Manufacturing £000	Finishing £000
Salaries	Actual cost	400	100	300
Employers' national insurance	Salaries	40	10	30
Rent and rates	Area	60	48	12
Heating	Actual usage	25	–	25
Lighting	Area	25	20	5
Machinery depreciation	Machinery value	75	72	3
Canteen expenses	Number of employees	56	14	42
Electricity for machinery	Machinery hours	50	48	2
Insurance: machinery	Machinery value	25	24	1
Total production overheads allocated to each department		756	336	420

Part (b) Most appropriate overhead recovery/absorption rate for the manufacturing and painting and finishing departments and justification for choice

- Manufacturing has a high number of machine hours and a low number of labour hours, so the most appropriate basis for the absorption of overheads in the manufacturing department will be machine hours.
- This will give an absorption rate of £336,000 ÷ 96,000 hours = £3.50 per machine hour.
- Painting and finishing has a high number of labour hours and a low number of machine hours, so the most suitable basis for the absorption of overheads in the painting and finishing department is labour hours.
- This will give an absorption rate of £420,000 ÷ 80,000 hours = £5.25 per labour hour.
- Overheads should be absorbed on bases that provide the best approximation of actual costs incurred and spread the costs over as much activity as possible. Thus, where an activity is machine intensive, overheads will be absorbed by products on the basis of machine hours consumed in that activity. On the other hand, where an activity is labour intensive, overheads will be absorbed based on the labour hours used by that activity.

Part (c) The cost of the novelty Christmas pixies will be:

Novelty Christmas pixies: 5,000 units	£
Direct materials and packaging	10,000
Direct labour	1,000
Manufacturing department 500 hours at £3.50	1,750
Painting and finishing department 1,000 hours at £5.25	5,250
Total cost	18,000
Cost per novelty Christmas pixie £18,000 ÷ 5,000	3.60

Question 8.5

Step 1: reallocate service department overheads to production departments. The servicing department overheads can be allocated using the percentage of usage of the service department.

The canteen costs should be allocated on the basis of the number of employees using the canteen as follows:

- Total employees using the canteen: 15 + 5 + 6 + 4 = 30 (canteen employees do not use the canteen so no canteen overheads can be allocated to the canteen)
- Welding department's allocation of canteen overheads: 15/30 × £60,000 = £30,000
- Painting department's allocation of canteen overheads: 5/30 × £60,000 = £10,000
- Finishing department's allocation of canteen overheads: 6/30 × £60,000 = £12,000
- Service department's allocation of canteen overheads: 4/30 × £60,000 = £8,000

Service department costs are allocated on the basis of percentage usage by welding, painting and finishing:

- Service department overhead costs are now £42,000 (given in the question) + £8,000 overhead costs allocated from the canteen = £50,000
- Welding department's allocation of service department overheads: £50,000 × 40% = £20,000
- Painting and finishing departments' allocation of service department overheads: £50,000 × 30% = £15,000 each

	Welding	Painting	Finishing	Canteen	Service
	£	£	£	£	£
Overheads from question	100,000	75,000	43,000	60,000	42,000
Canteen overheads reallocated	30,000	10,000	12,000	(60,000)	8,000
Service overheads reallocated	20,000	15,000	15,000	—	(50,000)
Total overheads allocated	150,000	100,000	70,000	—	—
Department labour hours	30,000	12,500	10,000		
Overhead absorption rate/hour	5.00	8.00	7.00		

Step 2: calculate overhead absorption rates per hour for welding, painting and finishing:

- Welding department overhead absorption rate per hour: £150,000 (total overheads) ÷ 30,000 (total hours) = £5.00 per hour
- Painting department overhead absorption rate per hour: £100,000 (total overheads) ÷ 12,500 (total hours) = £8.00 per hour
- Finishing department overhead absorption rate per hour: £70,000 (total overheads) ÷ 10,000 (total hours) = £7.00 per hour

Step 3: calculate the cost of job 12359 using the information in the question and the overhead absorption rates calculated above.

Job 12359 cost card	£
Direct materials	1,500
Direct labour	2,000
Direct expense	500
Prime cost	4,000
Overhead: welding department: 120 hours × £5/hour	600
Overhead: painting department: 50 hours × £8/hour	400
Overhead: finishing department: 25 hours × £7/hour	175
Production cost	5,175
Selling price: cost + 40% of cost: £5,175 + (£5,175 × 40%)	7,245

Question 8.6

Playthings Limited
Part (a)
First, calculate the overhead to be allocated to each product:

i.   Total machine hours: 10,000 for standard + 5,000 for deluxe = 15,000 hours in total

ii. Total overheads: £150,000

iii. Absorption rate of overheads per hour: £150,000 ÷ 15,000 hours = £10 per hour

iv. Machine hours per standard dolls house: 10,000 total hours ÷ 2,500 dolls houses produced = 4 hours per standard dolls house

v.   Overhead allocated to each standard dolls house: 4 hours × £10 per hour = £40

vi. Machine hours per deluxe dolls house: 5,000 total hours ÷ 1,000 dolls houses produced = 5 hours per deluxe dolls house

vii. Overhead allocated to each deluxe dolls house: 5 hours × £10 per hour = £50

Total absorption cost and selling price for standard and deluxe dolls houses:

	Standard	Deluxe
	£	£
Direct materials	50	76
Direct labour	30	42
Overheads absorbed	40	50
Total cost	120	168
Selling price (cost + 50%)	180	252

Part (b)
Suitable cost drivers for the four overhead cost pools:

- Machining: machine hours would be the most suitable basis for the allocation of these overheads. The allocation rate will be £45,000 ÷ 15,000 hours = £3 per hour. Machining overheads of 10,000 × £3 = £30,000 will be driven by standard and 5,000 × 3 = £15,000 by deluxe dolls houses.

- The factory supervisor costs will be driven by the number of employees supervised: the more employees supervised, the more cost is generated by this cost driver. The allocation rate will be £30,000 ÷ 15 employees = £2,000 per employee. Supervisor costs of 5 × £2,000 = £10,000 will be driven by standard and 10 × £2,000 = £20,000 by deluxe dolls houses.

- Set up-related overheads will be driven by the number of set ups: the more set ups there are the more overhead incurred in this cost pool. The allocation rate will be £50,000 ÷ 50 set ups = £1,000 per set up. Set up overheads of 15 × £1,000 = £15,000 will be driven by standard and 35 × £1,000 = £35,000 by deluxe dolls houses.

- Purchasing department costs will be driven by the number of materials orders: the more materials orders there are, the more overhead will be incurred in this cost pool. The allocation rate will be £25,000 ÷ 1,000 materials orders = £25 per order. Purchasing costs of 400 × £25 = £10,000 will be driven by standard and 600 × £25 = £15,000 by deluxe dolls houses.

Overheads allocated to each product on an activity based costing approach:

	Standard	Deluxe
	£	£
Machining	30,000	15,000
Factory supervisor	10,000	20,000
Set up	15,000	35,000
Purchasing department	10,000	15,000
Total overheads allocated	65,000	85,000
Total production	2,500	1,000
Overhead per unit of production	26	85

Part (c)
Total activity based cost and selling price for standard and deluxe dolls houses.

	Standard	Deluxe
	£	£
Direct materials	50	76
Direct labour	30	42
Overheads absorbed	26	85
Total cost	106	203
Selling price (cost + 50%)	159	304.50

Part (d)
Advice to the directors on how they might reduce the cost of deluxe dolls houses in order to compete effectively in the market:

- Under traditional absorption costing, deluxe dolls houses are not being allocated their full share of overheads and so are subsidised by standard dolls houses.
- Activity based costing now shows a much more accurate cost for each model of dolls house based on the costs incurred by the activities associated with each product.
- Under activity based costing, standard dolls houses can now be sold at a much more competitive price (£159 v. the market price of £165) than under traditional absorption costing.

- An activity based costing approach highlights activities that are causing cost with a view to helping management reduce costs in each particular cost pool, thereby reducing the costs of products in total.

- Machining costs are a necessary part of the manufacturing process and so it is unlikely that any reduction in these costs would be possible or desirable if quality is not to be compromised.

- The role of the factory supervisor could be looked at to determine whether this role is necessary. Employees could be given responsibility for their own production and quality control and incentives given to achieve zero defect production. However, any additional incentives would have to be considered in the total price of each product.

- The number of set ups in the year could be reduced to reduce total costs in this pool and in the amounts allocated to each product.

- Similarly, reducing the number of materials orders would reduce total costs in this pool and in the amounts allocated to each product.

Chapter 9

Question 9.1

(a) Contribution for one unit of production and sales is the selling price less the variable costs of production.

(b) Relevant costs in decision making are the costs that will be incurred if a certain course of action is followed. Relevant costs include opportunity costs.

(c) Irrelevant costs are those costs that will not change whatever course of action is chosen. Irrelevant costs in decision making include fixed costs and sunk costs.

(d) Sunk costs are those costs incurred in the past that have no further influence on decisions to be made in the future.

(e) Opportunity cost is the cost of choosing one alternative course of action over another.

(f) Break-even point is the point at which the revenue from sales = the total costs of the business both fixed and variable. The break-even point in sales units is given by dividing the total fixed costs by the contribution per unit of sales.

(g) The margin of safety is the current sales in units – the break-even point in sales units.

(h) A target profit is the sales in units required to generate a given level of profit. This is calculated by dividing the profit required by the contribution per unit and adding the break-even number of sales units.

Question 9.2

Podcaster University Press
Current profit: selling 200,000 text books at £30 each:

- Contribution per book: £30 selling price – £10 variable production costs = £20.
- Current profit: (200,000 sales × £20 contribution) – £3,000,000 fixed costs = £1,000,000.

Option 1: reduce selling price to £25 per book resulting in sales of 275,000 books:

- Contribution per book will now be: £25 selling price – £10 variable production costs = £15.
- Expected profit: (275,000 sales × £15 contribution) – £3,000,000 fixed costs = £1,125,000.

Option 2: reduce selling price to £21 per book resulting in sales of 360,000 books:

- Contribution per book now falls to: £21 selling price – £10 variable production costs = £11.
- Expected profit: (360,000 sales × £11 contribution) – £3,000,000 fixed costs = £960,000.

Option 1, reducing the selling price to £25 to sell 275,000 books per annum, will result in a higher profit whereas option 2 will result in a reduction in profit when compared with the current selling price of £30 and annual sales of 200,000 books. Therefore, Podcaster University Press should consider investigating option 1 further.

Question 9.3

Big Bucks University

(a) Relevant costs

- The lecturer costs are not relevant to the decision on how many students to recruit as the lecturers will be paid whether the modules run or not. The lecturer costs are thus sunk costs and irrelevant to the decision on recruitment. If new staff were to be recruited to teach these modules, then these costs would be relevant.

- The overhead costs for each room allocated to the modules are also irrelevant as these costs will be incurred whether the courses run or not. Costs that are allocated out of central overheads do not arise from the decision to run the modules and so are not relevant.

- The book and handout costs are relevant as these will vary directly in line with the number of students recruited to each module. For every additional module student recruited, a further cost of £100 for books and handouts will be incurred. These costs, along with the directly variable income from each student recruited to each module, will be relevant to the decision of how many students to recruit to each module in order to break even.

(b) Break-even point for each module

- Contribution per student: £400 module fee − £100 variable cost = £300 contribution
- Fixed costs per module: lecturer: £60 × 60 hours = £3,600
- Fixed costs per module: central overhead costs allocated: £1,200
- Total fixed costs per module: £3,600 + £1,200 = £4,800
- Break-even point: £4,800 (fixed costs) ÷ £300 (contribution per student) = 16 students

(c) Margin of safety if 25 students are recruited to each module

- 25 students recruited
- 16 students required to break even
- Therefore, margin of safety = 25 − 16 = 9 students

(d) Profit or loss at different recruitment levels

- Profit or loss at different recruitment levels will be determined by the number of students above or below the break-even point × the contribution per student
- 14 students recruited = 2 students (14 − 16) below the break-even point
- Loss incurred if 14 students are recruited = 2 × £300 = £600

- 30 students recruited = 14 students (30 −16) above the break-even point
- Profit earned if 30 students are recruited = 14 × 300 = £4,200

(e) Break-even point if the university decides to charge £340 per student per module

- Contribution per student now falls to: £340 − £100 = £240
- Fixed costs are unchanged at £4,800
- Break-even point = £4,800 ÷ £240 = 20 students

Question 9.4

Gurjit Limited

(a) Current profit made at a level of sales and production of 5,000 ink jet printers per annum

	£	£
Sales: 5,000 × £40.00		200,000
Direct materials 5,000 × £9.50	47,500	
Direct labour 5,000 × £11.25	56,250	
Direct expense 5,000 × £3.65	18,250	
Total direct costs of production	122,000	
Fixed overhead 5,000 × £5.60	28,000	
Total costs		150,000
Profit on sales and production of 5,000 ink jet printers		50,000

(b) Profit expected at a level of sales and production of 10,000 ink jet printers per annum

	£	£
Sales: 10,000 × £40.00		400,000
Direct materials 10,000 × £9.50	95,000	
Direct labour 10,000 × £11.25	112,500	
Direct expense 10,000 × £3.65	36,500	
Total direct costs of production	244,000	
Fixed overhead 5,000* × £5.60	28,000	
Total costs		272,000
Profit on sales and production of 10,000 ink jet printers		128,000

*No, this is not a misprint! Remember that fixed costs do not change, so, if the overhead absorbed is based on a level of production and sales of 5,000 units, this fixed overhead will not change if production and sales are higher. If you calculated fixed overheads to be £56,000, double the cost for 5,000 units, you should go back over the Contribution v. absorption costing section of Chapter 9 to prove to yourself that fixed costs do not change over a given period, in this case one year.

(c) Profit expected at a level of sales and production of 10,000 ink jet printers per annum and purchasing the finished ink jet printers from Anand Limited

	£	£
Sales: 10,000 × £40.00		400,000
10,000 finished ink jet printers from Anand Limited	200,000	
Additional quality control costs	40,000	
Total incremental costs of the buy decision	240,000	
Fixed overhead 5,000 × £5.60	28,000	
Total costs		268,000
Profit on sales and production of 10,000 ink jet printers		132,000

Expected profit from this option is £132,000, which is £4,000 higher than making the printers in-house. Relevant costs to take into account in this option are the costs of buying the finished products from Anand Limited and the additional quality control costs that will be incurred to make sure that the printers delivered meet the requirements of Gurjit Limited. These incremental costs (the costs that will be incurred if this option is adopted) are £240,000, which is £4,000 lower than the total direct costs of production that Gurjit Limited will incur if the company manufactures the printers themselves.

Therefore, on cost grounds, you would advise the directors of Gurjit Limited to cease in-house production of ink jet printers and transfer production to Anand Limited.

(d) Additional factors that the directors of Gurjit Limited should take into account in this decision, other than costs and profit, and points you might have included and developed further are as follows:

- Loss of internal expertise on the transfer of production to an outside party.

- Loss of control over production of ink jet printers.

- Any interruption to Anand Limited's production of printers through, for example, strikes, will mean that the products are not reaching the market and the reputation of Gurjit Limited will suffer damage.

- Additional costs to the reputation of Gurjit Limited should the products produced by Anand Limited fall short of customers' expectations.

- The additional quality control costs are only an estimate and these might be higher than the anticipated £40,000. Any increase in these costs might be greater than the total additional £4,000 profit that the directors expect to make by outsourcing production.

- Loss of confidentiality about product design and manufacture. Anand Limited could take the product and redesign and redevelop it and start producing a more advanced version itself, leading to Gurjit Limited losing all their customers and sales.

Question 9.5

Diddle Limited

Step 1: calculate the quantity of limiting factor used in the production of each product:

Clio: Material used: £30 ÷ £6 = 5 kg

Diana: Material used: £12 ÷ £6 = 2 kg

Athena: Material used: £42 ÷ £6 = 7 kg

Step 2: calculate the contribution per unit of limiting factor delivered by each product:

	Contribution per unit of key factor	Ranking
Clio	£30/5 kg per unit = £6 of contribution per unit of material used	2
Diana	£16/2 kg per unit = £8 of contribution per unit of material used	1
Athena	£35/7 kg per unit = £5 of contribution per unit of material used	3

The highest contribution per unit of key factor is delivered by Diana statues, which use just 2 kg of material in each unit and deliver a total contribution of £16 per product.

Step 3: calculate the contribution maximising production schedule:

Product	Kg of material per unit	Quantity produced	Kg of material used	Kg of material remaining	Contribution per unit	Total contribution
	Kg	Units	Kg	Kg	£	£
Diana	2	900	1,800	1,200	16	14,400
Clio	5	198	990	210	30	5,940
Athena	7	30	210	Nil	35	1,050
Total material used (kg)			3,000	Total contribution		21,390

Adopting the sales director's idea of maximising production of Athenas:

- 3,000 kg of material ÷ 7 kg per BE = 428 Athenas produced with 4 kg of material left over.
- Contribution from 428 Athenas = 428 × £35 = £14,890, well below the contribution maximising schedule above.
- As demand for Athenas is limited to 200 units, this would also mean that contribution for the month would only be 200 × £35 = £7,000 with 228 Athenas left unsold at the end of the month.

Chapter 10

Question 10.1

(a) The total expected costs of the orchard for the past year

	£
Fertiliser: 5 doses at £4.00 for 30 trees	600
Labour: 30 trees × 10 hours per tree × £7.50 per hour	2,250
Total expected costs of the orchard for the past year	2,850

(b) The actual total costs of the orchard for the past year

	£
Fertiliser: 4 doses at £4.50 for 30 trees	540
Labour: 30 trees × 9 hours per tree × £8.00 per hour	2,160
Total actual costs of the orchard for the past year	2,700

(c) Material total variance

	£
Expected cost of fertiliser	600
Actual cost of fertiliser	540
Total material variance (favourable)	60

(c) Material price variance

	£
4 doses for 30 trees should have cost: 4 × 30 × £4.00	480
4 doses for 30 trees actually cost: 4 × 30 × £4.50	540
Material price variance (unfavourable)	60

(c) Material usage variance

	Number
Expected number of doses of fertiliser: 5 × 30	150
Actual number of doses of fertiliser: 4 × 30	120
Material usage variance in number of doses (favourable)	30

	£
Material usage variance in £s: 30 × £4.00 (favourable)	120

£60 material price variance (unfavourable) + £120 material usage variance (favourable) = £60 (favourable).

(d) Labour total variance

	£
Expected cost of labour: 30 trees × 10 hours × £7.50 per hour	2,250
Actual cost of labour: 270 hours × £8 per hour	2,160
Total labour variance (favourable)	90

(d) Labour rate variance

	£
270 hours of labour should have cost: 270 × £7.50	2,025
270 hours of labour actually cost: 270 × £8.00	2,160
Labour rate variance (unfavourable)	135

(d) Labour efficiency variance

	Hours
Labour hours for 30 trees should have been: 30 × 10	300
Actual labour hours for 30 trees	270
Efficiency variance in number of hours (favourable)	30

	£
Efficiency variance in £s: 30 × £7.50 (favourable)	225

£135 labour rate variance (unfavourable) + £225 labour efficiency variance (favourable) = £90 (favourable).

Question 10.2

Fred

(a) Sales price variance

- Number of cakes sold: £14,725 ÷ £15.50 = 950.
- Sales price variance: number of cakes sold × (actual selling price per cake – the expected selling price per cake) = 950 × (£15.50 – £15.00) = £475. This variance is favourable as the actual selling price was higher than the expected selling price.

(b) Sales volume variance

- (Number of cakes sold – expected number of cakes to be sold) × the expected contribution per cake.

- $(950 - 1,000) \times (£15.00 - £6.00) = -£450$. This variance is unfavourable as fewer cakes than expected were sold.

Total sales variances: £475 favourable sales price variance – £450 unfavourable sales volume variance = £25 favourable total sales variances.

Proof that £25 favourable is the correct figure for the two sales variances

	Expected: 1,000 cakes	Actual: 950 cakes	Variances
	£	£	£
Sales: 1,000 × £15/actual sales value	15,000	14,725	275 (U)
Variable costs: 1,000 × £6/950 × £6	6,000	5,700	300 (F)
Contribution/total variances	9,000	9,025	25 (F)

Question 10.3

Sanguinary Services

(a) The profit that the centre expected to make in April, based on the original forecast of 3,000 blood tests in the month:

	£	£
Sales: 3,000 blood tests at £15		45,000
Chemicals used in blood tests: 3,000 × £5	15,000	
Laboratory workers 3,000 × £4	12,000	
Fixed overheads £72,000 ÷ 12 months	6,000	
Total costs		33,000
Expected profit for April		12,000

(b) Variances

Sales volume variance (Actual blood tests – standard blood tests) × standard contribution per blood test	Units
Actual blood tests undertaken	3,600
Budgeted blood tests	3,000
Variance (favourable)	600

	£
Sales volume variance at standard contribution 600 × £(15 – 5 – 4) (favourable)	3,600

Remember that the fixed costs are not variable but fixed and so do not form part of the calculation of contribution from each blood test undertaken. Only the costs that vary with the level of activity are deducted from the selling price to give the contribution per unit of sales.

Sales price variance (actual selling price – budgeted selling price) × number of blood tests performed	£
Actual selling price	15.50
Standard selling price	15.00
Variance (favourable)	0.50
Sales price variance at actual sales 3,600 × £0.50 (favourable)	1,800.00

Direct materials total variance

Standard quantity at standard cost v. actual quantity at actual cost	£
Chemicals for 3,600 blood tests should have cost 3,600 × £5	18,000
Chemicals for 3,600 blood tests actually cost	16,200
Direct materials total variance (favourable)	1,800

Direct materials price variance

Actual quantity at standard cost v. actual quantity at actual cost	£
33,750 millilitres should have cost (33,750 × £0.50)	16,875
33,750 millilitres actually cost (33,750 × £0.48)	16,200
Direct material price variance (favourable)	675

Direct materials usage variance

(Standard quantity – actual quantity) × standard cost	Millilitres
3,600 blood tests should have used 10 millilitres × 3,600	36,000
3,600 blood tests actually used	33,750
Direct material usage variance in millilitres (favourable)	2,250
Direct material usage variance in millilitres × standard price per ml 2,250 × £0.50 (favourable)	£1,125

Labour total variance

Standard hours at standard cost v. actual hours at actual cost	£
3,600 blood tests should have cost (900 hours × £16 per hour)	14,400
3,600 blood tests actually cost	14,985
Direct labour total variance (unfavourable)	(585)

Labour rate variance

Actual labour hours at standard cost – actual labour hours at actual cost	£
925 labour hours should have cost (925 × £16.00)	14,800
925 labour hours actually cost	14,985
Direct labour rate variance (unfavourable)	(185)

Labour usage variance

You should calculate the standard number of hours needed to complete 3,600 blood tests. Each blood test should take 15 minutes, making 4 tests per hour. Therefore, 3,600 blood tests should take 900 hours (3,600 ÷ 4)

(Standard hours for actual quantity – actual hours for actual quantity) × standard cost per hour	Hours
3,600 blood tests should have used 900 hours	900
3,600 blood tests actually used	925
Direct labour efficiency variance in hours (unfavourable)	(25)
Direct labour efficiency variance in hours × standard rate/hour 25 × £16.00 (unfavourable)	£(400)

Fixed overhead expenditure variance

Standard fixed overhead expenditure – actual fixed overhead expenditure	£
Standard fixed overhead expenditure (3,000 × £2) or (72,000 ÷ 12 months)	6,000
Actual fixed overhead expenditure	7,500
Fixed overhead expenditure variance (unfavourable)	(1,500)

(c) Statement reconciling the expected profit to the actual profit for April

	(Unfavourable)	Favourable	Profit
	£	£	£
Expected profit (part (a))			12,000
Sales price variance		1,800	
Sales volume variance		3,600	
Direct materials price variance		1,125	
Direct materials usage variance		675	
Direct labour rate variance	(185)		
Direct labour efficiency variance	(400)		
Fixed overhead expenditure variance	(1,500)	—	
Total variances	(2,085)	7,200	
Add: favourable variances			7,200
Deduct: unfavourable variances			(2,085)
Actual profit for April			17,115

Question 10.4

Smashers Tennis Club

(a) Calculation of the original expected surplus from the coaching course

	£
Revenue: 12 juniors × £70 each	840
Costs: balls: 12 × £10	120
Coach: 10 hrs × £30	300
Expected surplus	420

(b) Calculation of the expected surplus from the coaching course for 16 juniors:

	£
Revenue: 16 juniors × £70 each	1,120
Costs: balls: 16 × £10	160
Coach: 10 hrs × £30	300
Expected surplus	660

(c) Calculation of the actual surplus from the coaching course:

	£
Revenue: 16 juniors × (£70 × 90%) each	1,008
Costs: balls: 400 balls × 60p	240
Coach: 10 hrs × £33	330
Actual surplus	438

(d) Variances

(i)   Sales price variance: (£63 − £70) × 16 = £112 (unfavourable) as the price is lower than expected

(ii) Sales volume variance: additional participants: 16 − 12 = 4

Contribution per participant: £70 (price for one junior participant) − £10 (variable cost of balls for each junior member: remember that the cost of the coach is a fixed cost) = £60

Sales volume variance: £60 contribution × 4 participants = £240 (favourable) as more juniors participated than expected

(iii) Direct materials total variance: this relates to the tennis balls:

	£	
Expected cost of balls for 16 participants: 16 × £10	160	
Actual cost of balls for 16 participants 400 × 60 pence	240	
Direct materials total variance	(80)	Unfavourable

(iv) Direct materials price variance (tennis balls):

	£	
400 balls at 50 pence each	200	
400 balls at 60 pence each	240	
Direct materials price variance	(40)	Unfavourable

(v) Direct materials usage variance (tennis balls):

	Balls	
16 participants should use 20 balls × 16 participants	320	
16 participants actually used	400	
Direct materials usage variance (in tennis balls)	(80)	Unfavourable

	£	
Direct materials usage variance: 80 balls × 50 pence	(40)	Unfavourable

The unfavourable price variance of £40 + the unfavourable usage variance of £40 = the total unfavourable direct materials variance of £80.

(vi) Fixed expenditure variance (coaching costs): £300 (expected) – £330 (actual) = £30 unfavourable as more cost has been incurred than expected

Reconciliation of expected surplus to actual surplus:

	Unfavourable £	Favourable £	Surplus £
Expected surplus (part (a))			420
Sales price variance	(112)		
Sales volume variance		240	
Direct materials price variance	(40)		
Direct materials usage variance	(40)		
Fixed overhead expenditure variance	(30)		
Total variances	(222)	240	
Add: favourable variances			240
Deduct: unfavourable variances			(222)
Actual surplus for the 10-week coaching course			438

Question 10.5

Vijay Manufacturing

	(a) Sales of 2,000 garden gnomes at standard cost £	(b) Sales of 1,800 garden gnomes at standard cost £	(c) Sales of 1,800 garden gnomes at actual cost £	Variance: (b) – (c) favourable (f) or unfavourable (u) £
Sales	30,000	27,000	25,200	(1,800) (u)
Materials	9,000	8,100	8,750	(650) (u)
Labour	8,000	7,200	7,125	75 (f)
Variable overhead	6,000	5,400	5,500	(100) (u)
Fixed overhead	2,000	2,000	1,600	400 (f)
Net profit	5,000	4,300	2,225	(2,075) (u)

(d) Variance analysis and reconciliation statement:

Sales price variance

	£
(Actual selling price – budgeted selling price) × number of gnomes sold	
Actual selling price	14.00
Standard selling price	15.00
Variance (unfavourable)	(1.00)
Sales price variance of actual sales 1,800 × £1.00 (unfavourable)	(1,800)

Sales volume variance

Contribution per garden gnome sold: £15 (selling price) – £4.50 (direct materials) – £4.00 (direct labour) – £3.00 (variable overhead) = £3.50. Remember that fixed overheads are fixed and do not form part of the variable cost of production and so are not part of the contribution calculation.

Actual sales units v. standard sales units	Units
Actual units sold	1,800
Budgeted sales units	2,000
Variance (unfavourable)	(200)
Sales volume variance at standard contribution 200 × £3.50 (unfavourable)	£(700)

Direct materials total variance

	£
Standard quantity at standard cost v. actual quantity at actual cost	
Materials for 1,800 gnomes should have cost (1,800 × £2.25 × 2)	8,100
Materials for 1,800 gnomes did cost (3,500 × £2.50)	8,750
Direct materials total variance (unfavourable)	(650)

Direct materials price variance

	£
Actual quantity at standard cost v. actual quantity at actual cost	
3,500 kg of material should have cost (3,500 × £2.25)	7,875
3,500 kg actually cost (3,500 × £2.50)	8,750
Direct material price variance (unfavourable)	(875)

Direct materials usage variance

(Standard quantity – actual quantity) × standard cost	Kg
1,800 gnomes should have used (1,800 × 2 kg)	3,600
1,800 gnomes actually used	3,500
Direct material usage variance in kg (favourable)	100
Direct material usage variance in kg × standard price per kg 100 × £2.25 (favourable)	£225

Direct labour total variance

Standard hours at standard cost v actual hours at actual cost	£
1,800 gnomes should have cost (1,800 × £4.00)	7,200
1,800 gnomes actually cost	7,125
Direct labour total variance (favourable)	75

Direct labour rate variance

Actual labour hours at standard cost – actual labour hours at actual cost	£
950 labour hours should have cost (950 × £8.00)	7,600
950 labour hours actually cost (950 × £7.50)	7,125
Direct labour rate variance (favourable)	475

Direct labour efficiency variance

(Standard hours for actual quantity – actual hours for actual quantity) × standard cost per hour	Hours
1,800 gnomes should have used 1,800 × 0.5 hours	900
1,800 gnomes actually used	950
Direct labour efficiency variance in hours (unfavourable)	(50)
Direct labour efficiency variance in hours × standard rate/hour 50 × £8 (unfavourable)	£(400)

Variable overhead total variance

	£
1,800 gnomes should have cost (1,800 × £3.00)	5,400
1,800 gnomes actually cost	5,500
Variable overhead total variance (unfavourable)	(100)

Variable overhead expenditure variance

	£
Actual labour hours at standard cost – actual labour hours at actual cost	
7,000 machine hours should have cost (7,000 × £0.75)	5,250
7,000 machine hours actually cost	5,500
Variable overhead rate variance (unfavourable)	(250)

Variable overhead efficiency variance

	Hours
(Standard hours for actual quantity – actual hours for actual quantity) × **standard cost per hour**	
1,800 gnomes should have used (1,800 × 4 hours)	7,200
1,800 gnomes actually used	7,000
Variable overhead efficiency variance in hours (favourable)	200
Variable overhead efficiency variance in hours × standard rate/hour 200 × £0.75 (favourable)	£150

Fixed overhead expenditure variance

	£
Standard fixed overhead – actual fixed overhead	
Standard fixed overhead expenditure	2,000
Actual fixed overhead expenditure	1,600
Fixed overhead expenditure variance (favourable)	400

Chapter 12

Question 12.1

Podcaster University Press
Payback

	Accounting book		Economics book	
	Annual cash flows	Cumulative	Annual cash flows	Cumulative
	£000	£000	£000	£000
Investment at time 0	(450)	(450)	(600)	(600)
Net cash inflows year 1	160	(290)	240	(360)
Net cash inflows year 2	160	(130)	200	(160)
Net cash inflows year 3	160	30	160	0
Net cash inflows year 4	100	130	105	105
Net cash inflows year 5	100	230	105	210
Year 5 sale of assets	50	280	100	310

Accounting book payback period: 2 years + (130 ÷ 160) × 12 months = 2 years and 10 months
Economics book payback period: 3 years exactly

Payback: considerations

- The Accounting book is clearly preferable on the payback method of investment appraisal, although the Economics book pays back only two months later.

- The Economics book does have net cash inflows of £30,000 more than the Accounting book, although these net cash inflows do rely heavily on the sale of the assets for £100,000 at the end of year 5.

- Without this final inflow of cash from the sale of the assets, the net cash inflows of the Accounting book would be £230,000 (£280,000 – £50,000 cash from sale of the assets) compared with £210,000 (£310,000 – £100,000 cash from sale of the assets) for the Economics book.

Accounting rate of return

Accounting book

- The cost of the assets is £450,000
- The residual value of the assets is £50,000

Therefore, total depreciation is: £450,000 (cost) − £50,000 (residual value) = £400,000
Total accounting profits are £680,000 (cash inflows) − £400,000 (depreciation) = £280,000
Average accounting profit for the Accounting book: £280,000 ÷ 5 years = £56,000

Average investment in the Accounting book over its life: $\dfrac{(£450,000 \ + \ £50,000)}{2} = £250,000$

Accounting rate of return for the Accounting book: £56,000 ÷ £250,000 × 100% = 22.40%

Economics book

- The cost of the assets is £600,000
- The residual value of the assets is £100,000

Therefore, total depreciation is:
£600,000 (cost) − £100,000 (residual value) = £500,000
Total accounting profits are £810,000 (cash inflows) − £500,000 (depreciation) = £310,000
Average accounting profit for the Economics book: £310,000 ÷ 5 years = £62,000

Average investment in the Economics book over its life $\dfrac{(£600,000 + £100,000)}{2} = £350,000$

Accounting rate of return for the Economics book: £62,000 ÷ £350,000 = 17.71%

Accounting rate of return: considerations

- The Accounting book has the higher accounting rate of return so would be the preferred project on the basis of this capital investment appraisal technique.
- Average annual profits between the two book projects differ only by £6,000.
- The Economics book requires an additional average capital investment of £100,000.
- Therefore, the additional return of £6,000 per annum for this additional investment might not be considered worthwhile.

Net present value

NPV for the Accounting book

	Cash flow £000	10% Discount factor	NPV £000
Investment at time 0	(450)	1.0000	(450.00)
Net cash inflows year 1	160	0.9091	145.46
Net cash inflows year 2	160	0.8264	132.22
Net cash inflows year 3	160	0.7513	120.21
Net cash inflows year 4	100	0.6830	68.30
Net cash inflows year 5	100	0.6209	62.09
End of year 5 sale of assets	50	0.6209	31.05
		Project NPV	109.33

NPV for the Economics book

	Cash flow £000	10% Discount factor	NPV £000
Investment at time 0	(600)	1.0000	(600.00)
Net cash inflows year 1	240	0.9091	218.18
Net cash inflows year 2	200	0.8264	165.28
Net cash inflows year 3	160	0.7513	120.21
Net cash inflows year 4	105	0.6830	71.72
Net cash inflows year 5	105	0.6209	65.19
End of year 5 sale of assets	100	0.6209	62.09
		Project NPV	102.67

Net present value: considerations

- The Accounting book has the higher net present value, so this book should be accepted instead of the Economics book.
- The Accounting book breaks even on a net present value basis towards the end of year 4.
- The Economics book breaks even on a net present value basis only at the end of year 5.

Internal rate of return

NPV for the Accounting book discounted at 20%

	Cash flow £000	20% Discount factor	NPV £000
Investment at time 0	(450)	1.0000	(450.00)
Net cash inflows year 1	160	0.8333	133.33
Net cash inflows year 2	160	0.6944	111.10
Net cash inflows year 3	160	0.5787	92.59
Net cash inflows year 4	100	0.4823	48.23
Net cash inflows year 5	100	0.4019	40.19
End of year 5 sale of assets	50	0.4019	20.10
		Project NPV	(4.46)

Internal rate of return: Accounting book

$$10\% + \frac{109.33}{109.33 + 4.46} \times (20\% - 10\%) = 19.61\%$$

NPV for the Economics book discounted at 20%

	Cash flow £000	20% Discount factor	NPV £000
Investment at time 0	(600)	1.0000	(600.00)
Net cash inflows year 1	240	0.8333	199.99
Net cash inflows year 2	200	0.6944	138.88
Net cash inflows year 3	160	0.5787	92.59
Net cash inflows year 4	105	0.4823	50.64
Net cash inflows year 5	105	0.4019	42.20
End of year 5 sale of assets	100	0.4019	40.19
		Project NPV	(35.51)

Internal rate of return: Economics book

$$10\% + \frac{102.67}{102.67 + 35.51} \times (20\% - 10\%) = 17.43\%$$

Internal rate of return: considerations

- The Accounting book has the higher internal rate of return.
- This internal rate of return is higher than Podcaster University Press's cost of capital (10%), so the project should be accepted.
- The decision under IRR is consistent with the decision under the net present value appraisal method, which is to choose the Accounting book as this project has the higher net present value of the two books.

Additional considerations:

- The Accounting book is the preferred project under all the investment appraisal methods.
- The Accounting book has a lower capital outlay than the Economics book, which makes the Accounting book less risky as less capital is required to fund the project.
- The Accounting book is the chosen project as this will maximise investors' returns and increase the value of the press when compared with the Economics book.
- If the company has £600,000 to invest in a new project, choosing the Accounting book will leave £150,000, which could be invested to generate additional interest income for the company and its shareholders.

Question 12.2

Payback

	Option 1		Option 2	
	Annual cash flows	Cumulative	Annual cash flows	Cumulative
	£000	£000	£000	£000
Investment at time 0	(200)	(200)	(245)	(245)
Cash savings year 1	50	(150)	—	(245)
Cash savings year 2	70	(80)	80	(165)
Cash savings year 3	80	—	85	(80)
Cash savings year 4	70	70	86	6
Cash savings year 5	60	130	101	107
Cash savings year 6	—	—	81	188
Cash savings year 7	—	—	71	259

Option 1 has a payback period of exactly three years whereas option 2 has a payback period of just under four years. Under the payback method of capital investment appraisal, option 1 would be the chosen project.

Accounting rate of return

Total depreciation for option 1: £200,000 (cost) – £nil (residual value) = £200,000
Total depreciation for option 2: £245,000 (cost) – £nil (residual value) = £245,000
Average accounting profit for option 1: (£330,000 – £200,000) ÷ 5 years = £26,000
Average accounting profit for option 2: (£504,000 – £245,000) ÷ 7 years = £37,000
Average investment in each project over each project's life

$$\text{Option 1: } \frac{(£200,000 + £Nil)}{2} = £100,000$$

$$\text{Option 2: } \frac{(£245,000 + £Nil)}{2} = £122,500$$

Accounting rate of return: option 1: £26,000 ÷ £100,000 = 26.00%
Accounting rate of return option 2: £37,000 ÷ £122,500 = 30.20%

Under the accounting rate of return approach to capital investment appraisal, option 2 offers the higher rate of return and so would be the chosen project on this criterion.

Net present value

NPV of option 1

	Cash flow £	15% Discount factor	NPV £
Investment at time 0	(200,000)	1.0000	(200,000)
Cash savings year 1	50,000	0.8696	43,480
Cash savings year 2	70,000	0.7561	52,927
Cash savings year 3	80,000	0.6575	52,600
Cash savings year 4	70,000	0.5718	40,026
Cash savings year 5	60,000	0.4972	29,832
		Project NPV	18,865

NPV of option 2

	Cash flow £	15% Discount factor	NPV £
Investment at time 0	(245,000)	1.0000	(245,000)
Cash savings year 1	—	0.8696	—
Cash savings year 2	80,000	0.7561	60,488
Cash savings year 3	85,000	0.6575	55,888
Cash savings year 4	86,000	0.5718	49,175
Cash savings year 5	101,000	0.4972	50,217
Cash savings year 6	81,000	0.4323	35,016
Cash savings year 7	71,000	0.3759	26,689
		Project NPV	32,473

Based on our calculations of net present value, option 2 will be the preferred project as this has a higher net present value when compared with option 1.

Internal rate of return

IRR of option 1

Discounting cash flows at 19%	Cash flow £	19% Discount factor	NPV £
Investment at time 0	(200,000)	1.0000	(200,000)
Cash savings year 1	50,000	0.8403	42,015
Cash savings year 2	70,000	0.7062	49,434
Cash savings year 3	80,000	0.5934	47,472
Cash savings year 4	70,000	0.4987	34,909
Cash savings year 5	60,000	0.4190	25,140
		Project NPV	(1,030)

Internal rate of return: option 1

$$15\% + \frac{18,865}{18,865 + 1,030} \times (19\% - 15\%) = 18.79\%$$

IRR of option 2

Discounting cash flows at 19%	Cash flow £	19% Discount factor	NPV £
Investment at time 0	(245,000)	1.0000	(245,000)
Cash savings year 1	—	0.8403	—
Cash savings year 2	80,000	0.7062	56,496
Cash savings year 3	85,000	0.5934	50,439
Cash savings year 4	86,000	0.4987	42,888
Cash savings year 5	101,000	0.4190	42,319
Cash savings year 6	81,000	0.3521	28,520
Cash savings year 7	71,000	0.2959	21,009
		Project NPV	(3,329)

Internal rate of return: option 2

$$15\% + \frac{32,473}{32,473 + 3,329} \times (19\% - 15\%) = 18.63\%$$

Based on the internal rate of return criteria, the directors should choose option 1 as this has the higher internal rate of return. However, as the internal rate of return gives a different result compared with the net present value calculation, the directors should stick with option 2 as advised by the NPV decision.

Other factors in the decision

- The capital investment appraisal techniques applied favour option 2, with both the accounting rate of return and the net present value suggesting this project should be adopted, whereas only the payback method favoured option 1.

- However, seven years is a long time in technology terms and it is quite possible that better computerised supply chain systems will be developed well before option 2 has completed its useful life resulting in losses from scrapping the system and unrealised cash savings.

- Given the length of the project and the likelihood that new technology will be developed before option 2 reaches the end of its life, the directors of Zippo Drinks Limited should consider the possible obsolescence of option 2's system and any consequences arising from this.

- Cash flows from option 2 do not start until the end of year 2 and are therefore more uncertain than the cash flows from option 1: the directors of Zippo Drinks should factor in the possibility that the cash flows from option 2 do not meet expectations.

Question 12.3

Payback

	Run the restaurant		Rent restaurant	
	Annual cash flows	Cumulative	Annual cash flows	Cumulative
	£000	£000	£000	£000
Investment at time 0	(110)	(110)	(80)	(80)
Net cash inflows/Rent year 1	35	(75)	40	(40)
Net cash inflows/Rent year 2	45	(30)	40	0
Net cash inflows/Rent year 3	60	30	40	40
Net cash inflows/Rent year 4	65	95	40	80
Net cash inflows/Rent year 5	55	150	40	120
Year 5 sale of assets	2	152	—	120

Running the restaurant yourself results in a payback period of 2½ years, whereas the payback period for renting out the restaurant is just 2 years.

Accounting rate of return

Total depreciation if you are running the restaurant yourself:

£110,000 (cost) − £2,000 (residual value) = £108,000

Total depreciation if you rent the restaurant out:

£80,000 (cost) − £nil (residual value) = £80,000

Average accounting profit:

Running the restaurant yourself: (£260,000 − £108,000) ÷ 5 years = £30,400

Renting the restaurant out:

(£200,000 − £80,000) ÷ 5 years = £24,000

Average investment:

Running the restaurant yourself: $\dfrac{(£110,000 + £2,000)}{2} = £56,000$

Renting the restaurant out: $\dfrac{(£80,000 + £nil)}{2} = £40,000$

Accounting rate of return:

Running the restaurant yourself: £30,400 ÷ £56,000 = 54.29%

Renting the restaurant out: £24,000 ÷ £40,000 = 60.00%

Net present value

NPV: running the restaurant yourself

	Cash flow £000	12% Discount factor	NPV £000
Investment at time 0	(110,000)	1.0000	(110,000)
Net cash inflows year 1	35,000	0.8929	31,252
Net cash inflows year 2	45,000	0.7972	35,874
Net cash inflows year 3	60,000	0.7118	42,708
Net cash inflows year 4	65,000	0.6355	41,308
Net cash inflows year 5	55,000	0.5674	31,207
End of year 5 sale of assets	2,000	0.5674	1,135
		Project NPV	73,484

NPV: renting the restaurant out

	Cash flow £000	12% Discount factor	NPV £000
Investment at time 0	(80,000)	1.0000	(80,000)
Rent year 1	40,000	0.8929	35,716
Rent year 2	40,000	0.7972	31,888
Rent year 3	40,000	0.7118	28,472
Rent year 4	40,000	0.6355	25,420
Rent year 5	40,000	0.5674	22,696
		Project NPV	64,192

Evaluation based on purely financial considerations

- Renting the restaurant out produces a payback period of 2 years compared with a payback period of 2½ years if you run the restaurant yourself.

- Similarly, the accounting rate of return for the renting option is 60% compared with an accounting rate of return of only 54.29% if you were to run the restaurant yourself.

- The internal rate of return from renting is 41.10% compared with an IRR of 33.84% from running the restaurant yourself.

- The net present value of renting is £9,292 lower (£73,484 – £64,192) than the option of running the restaurant yourself.

- Therefore, given the superiority of the net present value investment appraisal technique, running the restaurant would seem to be the preferred option despite the preference of the other two methods for taking on the renting option.

Other factors in the decision

- Running the restaurant will be very hard work, so you might prefer to take the lower annual income from renting the restaurant out.

- If you were to rent the restaurant out, all the time you would have spent running the restaurant can now be used to undertake other activities to generate cash inflows to replace those lost from running the restaurant yourself.

- Renting the restaurant out is much lower risk as the other entrepreneur is taking on the risk of the restaurant failing to match expectations and generate the anticipated cash inflows.

- Running the restaurant yourself might have been much more profitable than you had expected, so renting it out might result in lost income.

- However, your fellow entrepreneur might not do as well as she expected and this might affect your profit share if this is not guaranteed.

- The problem you face is a common one in investment decisions: a steady, guaranteed income compared with the potentially much higher rewards that might be gained from taking a much bigger risk.

Question 12.4

Ambulators Limited
Before we can undertake any calculations to determine payback, the accounting rate of return, the net present value and the internal rate of return of the two proposed projects, we will have to calculate the expected sales and production together with the estimated net cash inflows (sales – costs) of each project.

Option 1: the new pram: sales, production and net cash inflows
The first step will be to calculate the sales from the new pram for the five years of the project's life. Sales units rise by 20% per annum, so sales units for the five years will be as follows:

Year	Calculation	Sales units
1	—	5,000
2	5,000 × 120%	6,000
3	6,000 × 120%	7,200
4	7,200 × 120%	8,640
5	8,640 × 120%	10,368

Now that the sales and production units are known, the net cash flows (receipts from sales – costs of production) from the production and sales of prams can be calculated.

- Selling price per pram: £450.

- Variable production price per pram: £150.00 + £75.00 + £25.00 = £250.

- Annual fixed overheads for prams: £50 × 5,000 = £250,000.

Remember that fixed costs are fixed and so will not change over the five-year life of the pram project.

Net cash flows per annum:

	Sales units	Gross sales value @ £450 per pram	Variable production costs @ £250 per pram	Fixed costs	Net cash flows
		£000	£000	£000	£000
Year 1	5,000	2,250.00	1,250.00	250.00	750.00
Year 2	6,000	2,700.00	1,500.00	250.00	950.00
Year 3	7,200	3,240.00	1,800.00	250.00	1,190.00
Year 4	8,640	3,888.00	2,160.00	250.00	1,478.00
Year 5	10,368	4,665.60	2,592.00	250.00	1,823.60
Totals	37,208	16,743.60	9,302.00	1,250.00	6,191.60

Option 2: the new push chair: sales, production and net cash inflows
Projected demand for the new push chair together with expected selling prices for each year is as follows:

Year	Calculation	Sales units	Selling Price
1	—	6,000	£220
2	6,000 × 110%	6,600	£230
3	6,600 × 110%	7,260	£240
4	7,260 × 110%	7,986	£250
5	7,986 × 110%	*8,785	£260

*Rounded from 8,784.6 to the nearest whole number.

- Selling price per push chair: as given in the table above with selling prices rising by £10 per annum from a starting price in the first year of £220.
- Variable production price per push chair: £80.00 + £40.00 + £10.00 = £130.
- Annual fixed overheads for prams: £20 × 6,000 = £120,000.

Remember that fixed costs are fixed and so will not change over the five-year life of the push chair project.

	Sales units	Selling price per push chair	Gross sales value	Variable production costs @ £130 per push chair	Fixed costs	Net cash flows
		£	£000	£000	£000	£000
Year 1	6,000	220	1,320.00	780.00	120.00	420.00
Year 2	6,600	230	1,518.00	858.00	120.00	540.00
Year 3	7,260	240	1,742.40	943.80	120.00	678.60
Year 4	7,986	250	1,996.50	1,038.18	120.00	838.32
Year 5	8,785	260	2.284.10	1,142.05	120.00	1,022.05
Totals	36,631		8,861.00	4,762.03	600.00	3,498.97

Payback

	Pram			Push chair	
	Cash Flow £000	Cumulative Cash Flow £000		Cash Flow £000	Cumulative Cash Flow £000
Investment	(3,300.00)	(3,300.00)	Investment	(2,200.00)	(2,200.00)
Year 1	750.00	(2,550.00)	Year 1	420.00	(1,780.00)
Year 2	950.00	(1,600.00)	Year 2	540.00	(1,240.00)
Year 3	1,190.00	(410.00)	Year 3	678.60	(561.40)
Year 4	1,478.00	1,068.00	Year 4	838.32	276.92
Year 5	1,823.60	2,891.60	Year 5	1,022.05	1,298.97
			Transfer	500.00	1,798.97

Payback period: pram: 3.28 years (3 + 410.00/1,478.00)
Payback period: push chair: 3.67 years (3 + 561.40/838.82)

Accounting rate of return

Pram
   Cost of investment: £3,300,000
   Residual value: £nil
   Total depreciation: £3,300,000
   Total accounting profits: £6,191,600 – £3,300,000 = £2,891,600
   Average accounting profit for the pram: £2,891,600 ÷ 5 years = £578,320
   Average investment in the pram: (£3,300,000 + £nil) ÷ 2 = £1,650,000
   Accounting rate of return: £578,320 ÷ £1,650,000 = 35.05%

Push chair

Cost of investment: £2,200,000

Residual value: £500,000

Total depreciation: £1,700,000

Total accounting profits: £3,498,970 − £1,700,000 = £1,798,970

Average accounting profit for the pram: £1,798,970 ÷ 5 years = £359,794

Average investment in the pram: (£2,200,000 + £500,000) ÷ 2 = £1,350,000

Accounting rate of return: £359,794 ÷ £1,350,000 = 26.65%

Net present value

	Pram			**Push chair**		
	Cash flow £000	**11% Discount factor**	**NPV £000**	**Cash flow £000**	**11% Discount factor**	**NPV £000**
Year 0	(3,300.00)	1.0000	(3,300.000)	(2,200.00)	1.0000	(2,200.000)
Year 1	750.00	0.9009	675.675	420.00	0.9009	378.378
Year 2	950.00	0.8116	771.020	540.00	0.8116	438.264
Year 3	1,190.00	0.7312	870.128	678.60	0.7312	496.192
Year 4	1,478.00	0.6587	973.559	838.32	0.6587	552.201
Year 5	1,823.60	0.5935	1,082.307	1,022.05	0.5935	606.587
Transfer	—	—	—	500.00	0.5935	296.750
	Pram: NPV		1,072.689	Push chair: NPV		568.372

Internal rate of return

	Pram			**Push chair**		
	Cash flow £000	**22%* Discount factor**	**NPV £000**	**Cash flow £000**	**19% Discount factor**	**NPV £000**
Year 0	(3,300.00)	1.0000	(3,300.000)	(2,200.00)	1.0000	(2,200.000)
Year 1	750.00	0.8197	614.775	420.00	0.8403	352.926
Year 2	950.00	0.6719	638.305	540.00	0.7062	381.348
Year 3	1,190.00	0.5508	655.452	678.60	0.5934	402.681
Year 4	1,478.00	0.4514	667.169	838.32	0.4987	418.070
Year 5	1,823.60	0.3700	674.732	1,022.05	0.4190	428.239
Transfer	—	—	—	500.00	0.4190	209.500
	Pram: NPV		(49.567)	Push chair: NPV		(7.236)

*Use the formula $1/(1 + r)^n$ to calculate the 22% discount factors.

Internal rate of return: pram

$$11\% + \frac{1,072,689}{(1,072,689 + 49,567)} \times (22\% - 11\%) = 21.51\%$$

Internal rate of return: push chair:

$$11\% + \frac{568,372}{(568,372 + 7,236)} \times (19\% - 11\%) = 18.90\%$$

Recommendation:

- On financial grounds, the pram project has the shortest payback period, the highest accounting rate of return, the highest net present value and the highest internal rate of return.
- However, the directors should consider whether sales growth of 20% each year is realistic and achievable.
- Similarly, is a 10% annual rise in the sales of the push chairs realistic and achievable?
- How realistic is the projection that the price of pushchairs will rise by £10 a year?
- The pram project requires 50% more investment than the push chair project (£3,300,000 v. £2,200,000) and returns 88.73% more (£1,072,689 v. £568,372) for this additional 50% investment.

Additional factors to consider:

- Projected birth rates over the next five years.
- If these are rising, then the projected growth rates in sales might be achievable.
- If birth rates are expected to fall, then the expected growth rate will probably not be achievable at all.
- Prams and push chairs produced by other companies and the likely demand for competitor companies' products.
- How competitor company products compare with Ambulators' prams and pushchairs.
- How effectively Amublators' products will compete with other products on the market.
- Prices charged by competitors and how these compare to the prices charged by Ambulators Limited.
- The possibility that Ambulators will have to reduce their prices in order to compete more effectively against competitors' products.
- An assumption has been made that the cost prices of each product will not change over the five years: this might not be a realistic assumption, so sensitivity analysis should be carried out on the projected results to see what effect any price rises in materials, director labour, variable overheads and fixed costs would have on the results of the calculations above.

Question 12.5

Chillers plc
Our first task will be to calculate the annual net cash flows arising from the production of the new deluxe fridge-freezer. Information that we will need to complete this task is as follows:

* Selling price of the new deluxe fridge freezer: £600.
* Variable costs per deluxe fridge-freezer: £600 × 40% = £240.
* Annual fixed costs: £1,200,000.
* Annual value of lost sales of standard fridge freezers: 2,000 × £350 = £700,000.
* Annual cost savings arising from the lost sales of standard fridge freezers: (£700,000 × 35%) + £395,000 of annual fixed costs = £640,000.

We can now calculate the annual net cash flows arising from the introduction of the new deluxe fridge-freezer:

Year	Sales units	Sales value	Variable costs	Fixed costs	Lost sales	Costs saved	Net cash flows
		£000	£000	£000	£000	£000	£000
2016	3,500	2,100	840	1,200	700	640	0
2017	4,000	2,400	960	1,200	700	640	180
2018	4,500	2,700	1,080	1,200	700	640	360
2019	5,250	3,150	1,260	1,200	700	640	630
2020	5,750	3,450	1,380	1,200	700	640	810
2021	5,500	3,300	1,320	1,200	700	640	720
2022	5,250	3,150	1,260	1,200	700	640	630
Totals	33,750	20,250	8,100	8,400	4,900	4,480	3,330

Net cash flows are calculated as follows: + sales value − variable costs − fixed costs − lost sales + costs saved. Thus, for 2016, the calculation is + £2,100 − £840 − £1,200 − £700 + £640 = £0.

Payback

	Cash Flow	Cumulative Cash Flow
	£000	£000
Investment	(2,000)	(2,000)
2016	0	(2,000)
2017	180	(1,820)
2018	360	(1,460)
2019	630	(830)
2020	810	(20)
2021	720	700
2022	630	1,330
Scrap value 2022	100	1,430

Payback period: 5.03 years

Accounting rate of return

Cost of investment: £2,000,000
Residual value: £100,000
Total depreciation: £1,900,000
Total accounting profits: £3,330,000 – £1,900,000 = £1,430,000
Average accounting profit: £1,430,000 ÷ 7 years = £204,286
Average investment: (£2,000,000 + £100,000) ÷ 2 = £1,050,000
Accounting rate of return: £204,286 ÷ £1,050,000 = 19.46%

Net present value

	Cash flow £000	13% Discount factor	NPV £000
Year 0	(2,000)	1.0000	(2,000.000)
2016	0	0.8850	0.000
2017	180	0.7831	140.958
2018	360	0.6931	249.516
2019	630	0.6133	386.379
2020	810	0.5428	439.668
2021	720	0.4803	345.816
2022	630	0.4251	267.813
2022 Scrap Value	100	0.4251	42.510
Net present value			(127.340)

Internal rate of return

As the net present value at a 13% discount rate is negative, the internal rate of return must be lower than 13%.

	Cash flow £000	11% Discount factor	NPV £000
Year 0	(2,000)	1.0000	(2,000.000)
2016	0	0.9009	0.000
2017	180	0.8116	146.088
2018	360	0.7312	263.232
2019	630	0.6587	414.981
2020	810	0.5935	480.735
2021	720	0.5346	384.912
2022	630	0.4817	303.471
2022 Scrap Value	100	0.4817	48.170
	Net present value		41.589

Internal rate of return:

$$11\% + \frac{41{,}589}{(41{,}589 + 127{,}340)} \times (13\% - 11\%) = 11.49\%$$

Should the directors undertake the project?

• Net present value at a discount rate of 13% is negative, so this project does not give a positive return to the company.

• The internal rate of return shows that the rate of return on this project is 1.51% below the required rate of return.

• The project only pays back after five years. This is a long time to wait for the return of the capital invested.

• The project is thus risky because of the length of time it takes to return the capital originally invested.

Therefore, based on the capital investment appraisal figures, this project should not go ahead.

Appendix

Table 1 Present value of £1 at compound interest $(1 \div r)^{-n}$

Periods of n	Discount rate as a percentage									
	1%	2%	3%	4%	5%	6%	7%	8%	9%	10%
1	0.9901	0.9804	0.9709	0.9615	0.9524	0.9434	0.9346	0.9259	0.9174	0.9091
2	0.9803	0.9612	0.9426	0.9246	0.9070	0.8900	0.8734	0.8573	0.8417	0.8264
3	0.9706	0.9423	0.9151	0.8890	0.8638	0.8396	0.8163	0.7938	0.7722	0.7513
4	0.9610	0.9238	0.8885	0.8548	0.8227	0.7921	0.7629	0.7350	0.7084	0.6830
5	0.9515	0.9057	0.8626	0.8219	0.7835	0.7473	0.7130	0.6806	0.6499	0.6209
6	0.9420	0.8880	0.8375	0.7903	0.7462	0.7050	0.6663	0.6302	0.5963	0.5645
7	0.9327	0.8706	0.8131	0.7599	0.7107	0.6651	0.6227	0.5835	0.5470	0.5132
8	0.9235	0.8535	0.7894	0.7307	0.6768	0.6274	0.5820	0.5403	0.5019	0.4665
9	0.9143	0.8368	0.7664	0.7026	0.6446	0.5919	0.5439	0.5002	0.4604	0.4241
10	0.9053	0.8203	0.7441	0.6756	0.6139	0.5584	0.5083	0.4632	0.4224	0.3855
11	0.8963	0.8043	0.7224	0.6496	0.5847	0.5268	0.4751	0.4289	0.3875	0.3505
12	0.8874	0.7885	0.7014	0.6246	0.5568	0.4970	0.4440	0.3971	0.3555	0.3186
13	0.8787	0.7730	0.6810	0.6006	0.5303	0.4688	0.4150	0.3677	0.3262	0.2897
14	0.8700	0.7579	0.6611	0.5775	0.5051	0.4423	0.3878	0.3405	0.2992	0.2633
15	0.8613	0.7430	0.6419	0.5553	0.4810	0.4173	0.3624	0.3152	0.2745	0.2394
16	0.8528	0.7284	0.6232	0.5339	0.4581	0.3936	0.3387	0.2919	0.2519	0.2176
17	0.8444	0.7142	0.6050	0.5134	0.4363	0.3714	0.3166	0.2703	0.2311	0.1978
18	0.8360	0.7002	0.5874	0.4936	0.4155	0.3503	0.2959	0.2502	0.2120	0.1799
19	0.8277	0.6864	0.5703	0.4746	0.3957	0.3305	0.2765	0.2317	0.1945	0.1635
20	0.8195	0.6730	0.5537	0.4564	0.3769	0.3118	0.2584	0.2145	0.1784	0.1486
21	0.8114	0.6598	0.5375	0.4388	0.3589	0.2942	0.2415	0.1987	0.1637	0.1351
22	0.8034	0.6468	0.5219	0.4220	0.3418	0.2775	0.2257	0.1839	0.1502	0.1228
23	0.7954	0.6342	0.5067	0.4057	0.3256	0.2618	0.2109	0.1703	0.1378	0.1117
24	0.7876	0.6217	0.4919	0.3901	0.3101	0.2470	0.1971	0.1577	0.1264	0.1015
25	0.7798	0.6095	0.4776	0.3751	0.2953	0.2330	0.1842	0.1460	0.1160	0.0923

					Discount rate as a percentage						
11%	**12%**	**13%**	**14%**	**15%**	**16%**	**17%**	**18%**	**19%**	**20%**	**25%**	**30%**
0.9009	0.8929	0.8850	0.8772	0.8696	0.8621	0.8547	0.8475	0.8403	0.8333	0.8000	0.7692
0.8116	0.7972	0.7831	0.7695	0.7561	0.7432	0.7305	0.7182	0.7062	0.6944	0.6400	0.5917
0.7312	0.7118	0.6931	0.6750	0.6575	0.6407	0.6244	0.6086	0.5934	0.5787	0.5120	0.4552
0.6587	0.6355	0.6133	0.5921	0.5718	0.5523	0.5337	0.5158	0.4987	0.4823	0.4096	0.3501
0.5935	0.5674	0.5428	0.5194	0.4972	0.4761	0.4561	0.4371	0.4190	0.4019	0.3277	0.2693
0.5346	0.5066	0.4803	0.4556	0.4323	0.4104	0.3898	0.3704	0.3521	0.3349	0.2621	0.2072
0.4817	0.4523	0.4251	0.3996	0.3759	0.3538	0.3332	0.3139	0.2959	0.2791	0.2097	0.1594
0.4339	0.4039	0.3762	0.3506	0.3269	0.3050	0.2848	0.2660	0.2487	0.2326	0.1678	0.1226
0.3909	0.3606	0.3329	0.3075	0.2843	0.2630	0.2434	0.2255	0.2090	0.1938	0.1342	0.0943
0.3522	0.3220	0.2946	0.2697	0.2472	0.2267	0.2080	0.1911	0.1756	0.1615	0.1074	0.0725
0.3173	0.2875	0.2607	0.2366	0.2149	0.1954	0.1778	0.1619	0.1476	0.1346	0.0859	0.0558
0.2858	0.2567	0.2307	0.2076	0.1869	0.1685	0.1520	0.1372	0.1240	0.1122	0.0687	0.0429
0.2575	0.2292	0.2042	0.1821	0.1625	0.1452	0.1299	0.1163	0.1042	0.0935	0.0550	0.0330
0.2320	0.2046	0.1807	0.1597	0.1413	0.1252	0.1110	0.0985	0.0876	0.0779	0.0440	0.0254
0.2090	0.1827	0.1599	0.1401	0.1229	0.1079	0.0949	0.0835	0.0736	0.0649	0.0352	0.0195
0.1883	0.1631	0.1415	0.1229	0.1069	0.0930	0.0811	0.0708	0.0618	0.0541	0.0281	0.0150
0.1696	0.1456	0.1252	0.1078	0.0929	0.0802	0.0693	0.0600	0.0520	0.0451	0.0225	0.0116
0.1528	0.1300	0.1108	0.0946	0.0808	0.0691	0.0592	0.0508	0.0437	0.0376	0.0180	0.0089
0.1377	0.1161	0.0981	0.0829	0.0703	0.0596	0.0506	0.0431	0.0367	0.0313	0.0144	0.0068
0.1240	0.1037	0.0868	0.0728	0.0611	0.0514	0.0433	0.0365	0.0308	0.0261	0.0115	0.0053
0.1117	0.0926	0.0768	0.0638	0.0531	0.0443	0.0370	0.0309	0.0259	0.0217	0.0092	0.0040
0.1007	0.0826	0.0680	0.0560	0.0462	0.0382	0.0316	0.0262	0.0218	0.0181	0.0074	0.0031
0.0907	0.0738	0.0601	0.0491	0.0402	0.0329	0.0270	0.0222	0.0183	0.0151	0.0059	0.0024
0.0817	0.0659	0.0532	0.0431	0.0349	0.0284	0.0231	0.0188	0.0154	0.0126	0.0047	0.0018
0.0736	0.0588	0.0471	0.0378	0.0304	0.0245	0.0197	0.0160	0.0129	0.0105	0.0038	0.0014

Table 2 Annuity table: the present value of £1 received or paid per year at a compound rate of interest
$1/r - \{1/[r(1 + r)^n]\}$

Periods of n	Discount rate as a percentage									
	1%	2%	3%	4%	5%	6%	7%	8%	9%	10%
1	0.990	0.980	0.971	0.962	0.952	0.943	0.935	0.926	0.917	0.909
2	1.970	1.942	1.913	1.886	1.859	1.833	1.808	1.783	1.759	1.736
3	2.941	2.884	2.829	2.775	2.723	2.673	2.624	2.577	2.531	2.487
4	3.902	3.808	3.717	3.630	3.546	3.465	3.387	3.312	3.240	3.170
5	4.853	4.713	4.580	4.452	4.329	4.212	4.100	3.993	3.890	3.791
6	5.795	5.601	5.417	5.242	5.076	4.917	4.767	4.623	4.486	4.355
7	6.728	6.472	6.230	6.002	5.786	5.582	5.389	5.206	5.033	4.868
8	7.652	7.325	7.020	6.733	6.463	6.210	5.971	5.747	5.535	5.335
9	8.566	8.162	7.786	7.435	7.108	6.802	6.515	6.247	5.995	5.759
10	9.471	8.983	8.530	8.111	7.722	7.360	7.024	6.710	6.418	6.145
11	10.368	9.787	9.253	8.760	8.306	7.887	7.499	7.139	6.805	6.495
12	11.255	10.575	9.954	9.385	8.863	8.384	7.943	7.536	7.161	6.814
13	12.134	11.348	10.635	9.986	9.394	8.853	8.358	7.904	7.487	7.103
14	13.004	12.106	11.296	10.563	9.899	9.295	8.745	8.244	7.786	7.367
15	13.865	12.849	11.938	11.118	10.380	9.712	9.108	8.559	8.061	7.606
16	14.718	13.578	12.561	11.652	10.838	10.106	9.447	8.851	8.313	7.824
17	15.562	14.292	13.166	12.166	11.274	10.477	9.763	9.122	8.544	8.022
18	16.398	14.992	13.754	12.659	11.690	10.828	10.059	9.372	8.756	8.201
19	17.226	15.678	14.324	13.134	12.085	11.158	10.336	9.604	8.950	8.365
20	18.046	16.351	14.877	13.590	12.462	11.470	10.594	9.818	9.129	8.514
21	18.857	17.011	15.415	14.029	12.821	11.764	10.836	10.017	9.292	8.649
22	19.660	17.658	15.937	14.451	13.163	12.042	11.061	10.201	9.442	8.772
23	20.456	18.292	16.444	14.857	13.489	12.303	11.272	10.371	9.580	8.883
24	21.243	18.914	16.936	15.247	13.799	12.550	11.469	10.529	9.707	8.985
25	22.023	19.523	17.413	15.622	14.094	12.783	11.654	10.675	9.823	9.077

					Discount rate as a percentage						
11%	**12%**	**13%**	**14%**	**15%**	**16%**	**17%**	**18%**	**19%**	**20%**	**25%**	**30%**
0.901	0.893	0.885	0.877	0.870	0.862	0.855	0.847	0.840	0.833	0.800	0.769
1.713	1.690	1.668	1.647	1.626	1.605	1.585	1.566	1.547	1.528	1.440	1.361
2.444	2.402	2.361	2.322	2.283	2.246	2.210	2.174	2.140	2.106	1.952	1.816
3.102	3.037	2.974	2.914	2.855	2.798	2.743	2.690	2.639	2.589	2.362	2.166
3.696	3.605	3.517	3.433	3.352	3.274	3.199	3.127	3.058	2.991	2.689	2.436
4.231	4.111	3.998	3.889	3.784	3.685	3.589	3.498	3.410	3.326	2.951	2.643
4.712	4.564	4.423	4.288	4.160	4.039	3.922	3.812	3.706	3.605	3.161	2.802
5.146	4.968	4.799	4.639	4.487	4.344	4.207	4.078	3.954	3.837	3.329	2.925
5.537	5.328	5.132	4.946	4.772	4.607	4.451	4.303	4.163	4.031	3.463	3.019
5.889	5.650	5.426	5.216	5.019	4.833	4.659	4.494	4.339	4.192	3.571	3.092
6.207	5.938	5.687	5.453	5.234	5.029	4.836	4.656	4.486	4.327	3.656	3.147
6.492	6.194	5.918	5.660	5.421	5.197	4.988	4.793	4.611	4.439	3.725	3.190
6.750	6.424	6.122	5.842	5.583	5.342	5.118	4.910	4.715	4.533	3.780	3.223
6.982	6.628	6.302	6.002	5.724	5.468	5.229	5.008	4.802	4.611	3.824	3.249
7.191	6.811	6.462	6.142	5.847	5.575	5.324	5.092	4.876	4.675	3.859	3.268
7.379	6.974	6.604	6.265	5.954	5.668	5.405	5.162	4.938	4.730	3.887	3.283
7.549	7.120	6.729	6.373	6.047	5.749	5.475	5.222	4.990	4.775	3.910	3.295
7.702	7.250	6.840	6.467	6.128	5.818	5.534	5.273	5.033	4.812	3.928	3.304
7.839	7.366	6.938	6.550	6.198	5.877	5.584	5.316	5.070	4.843	3.942	3.311
7.963	7.469	7.025	6.623	6.259	5.929	5.628	5.353	5.101	4.870	3.954	3.316
8.075	7.562	7.102	6.687	6.312	5.973	5.665	5.384	5.127	4.891	3.963	3.320
8.176	7.645	7.170	6.743	6.359	6.011	5.696	5.410	5.149	4.909	3.970	3.323
8.266	7.718	7.230	6.792	6.399	6.044	5.723	5.432	5.167	4.925	3.976	3.325
8.348	7.784	7.283	6.835	6.434	6.073	5.746	5.451	5.182	4.937	3.981	3.327
8.422	7.843	7.330	6.873	6.464	6.097	5.766	5.467	5.195	4.948	3.985	3.329

Table 3 Future value of £1 at compound interest $(1 + r)^n$

Periods of n	Discount rate as a percentage									
	1%	2%	3%	4%	5%	6%	7%	8%	9%	10%
1	1.010	1.020	1.030	1.040	1.050	1.060	1.070	1.080	1.090	1.100
2	1.020	1.040	1.061	1.082	1.103	1.124	1.145	1.166	1.188	1.210
3	1.030	1.061	1.093	1.125	1.158	1.191	1.225	1.260	1.295	1.331
4	1.041	1.082	1.126	1.170	1.216	1.262	1.311	1.360	1.412	1.464
5	1.051	1.104	1.159	1.217	1.276	1.338	1.403	1.469	1.539	1.611
6	1.062	1.126	1.194	1.265	1.340	1.419	1.501	1.587	1.677	1.772
7	1.072	1.149	1.230	1.316	1.407	1.504	1.606	1.714	1.828	1.949
8	1.083	1.172	1.267	1.369	1.477	1.594	1.718	1.851	1.993	2.144
9	1.094	1.195	1.305	1.423	1.551	1.689	1.838	1.999	2.172	2.358
10	1.105	1.219	1.344	1.480	1.629	1.791	1.967	2.159	2.367	2.594
11	1.116	1.243	1.384	1.539	1.710	1.898	2.105	2.332	2.580	2.853
12	1.127	1.268	1.426	1.601	1.796	2.012	2.252	2.518	2.813	3.138
13	1.138	1.294	1.469	1.665	1.886	2.133	2.410	2.720	3.066	3.452
14	1.149	1.319	1.513	1.732	1.980	2.261	2.579	2.937	3.342	3.797
15	1.161	1.346	1.558	1.801	2.079	2.397	2.759	3.172	3.642	4.177
16	1.173	1.373	1.605	1.873	2.183	2.540	2.952	3.426	3.970	4.595
17	1.184	1.400	1.653	1.948	2.292	2.693	3.159	3.700	4.328	5.054
18	1.196	1.428	1.702	2.026	2.407	2.854	3.380	3.996	4.717	5.560
19	1.208	1.457	1.754	2.107	2.527	3.026	3.617	4.316	5.142	6.116
20	1.220	1.486	1.806	2.191	2.653	3.207	3.870	4.661	5.604	6.727
21	1.232	1.516	1.860	2.279	2.786	3.400	4.141	5.034	6.109	7.400
22	1.245	1.546	1.916	2.370	2.925	3.604	4.430	5.437	6.659	8.140
23	1.257	1.577	1.974	2.465	3.072	3.820	4.741	5.871	7.258	8.954
24	1.270	1.608	2.033	2.563	3.225	4.049	5.072	6.341	7.911	9.850
25	1.282	1.641	2.094	2.666	3.386	4.292	5.427	6.848	8.623	10.835

			Discount rate as a percentage								
11%	12%	13%	14%	15%	16%	17%	18%	19%	20%	25%	30%
1.110	1.120	1.130	1.140	1.150	1.160	1.170	1.180	1.190	1.200	1.250	1.300
1.232	1.254	1.277	1.300	1.323	1.346	1.369	1.392	1.416	1.440	1.563	1.690
1.368	1.405	1.443	1.482	1.521	1.561	1.602	1.643	1.685	1.728	1.953	2.197
1.518	1.574	1.630	1.689	1.749	1.811	1.874	1.939	2.005	2.074	2.441	2.856
1.685	1.762	1.842	1.925	2.011	2.100	2.192	2.288	2.386	2.488	3.052	3.713
1.870	1.974	2.082	2.195	2.313	2.436	2.565	2.700	2.840	2.986	3.815	4.827
2.076	2.211	2.353	2.502	2.660	2.826	3.001	3.185	3.379	3.583	4.768	6.275
2.305	2.476	2.658	2.853	3.059	3.278	3.511	3.759	4.021	4.300	5.960	8.157
2.558	2.773	3.004	3.252	3.518	3.803	4.108	4.435	4.785	5.160	7.451	10.604
2.839	3.106	3.395	3.707	4.046	4.411	4.807	5.234	5.695	6.192	9.313	13.786
3.152	3.479	3.836	4.226	4.652	5.117	5.624	6.176	6.777	7.430	11.642	17.922
3.498	3.896	4.335	4.818	5.350	5.936	6.580	7.288	8.064	8.916	14.552	23.298
3.883	4.363	4.898	5.492	6.153	6.886	7.699	8.599	9.596	10.699	18.190	30.288
4.310	4.887	5.535	6.261	7.076	7.988	9.007	10.147	11.420	12.839	22.737	39.374
4.785	5.474	6.254	7.138	8.137	9.266	10.539	11.974	13.590	15.407	28.422	51.186
5.311	6.130	7.067	8.137	9.358	10.748	12.330	14.129	16.172	18.488	35.527	66.542
5.895	6.866	7.986	9.276	10.761	12.468	14.426	16.672	19.244	22.186	44.409	86.504
6.544	7.690	9.024	10.575	12.375	14.463	16.879	19.673	22.901	26.623	55.511	112.455
7.263	8.613	10.197	12.056	14.232	16.777	19.748	23.214	27.252	31.948	69.389	146.192
8.062	9.646	11.523	13.743	16.367	19.461	23.106	27.393	32.429	38.338	86.736	190.050
8.949	10.804	13.021	15.668	18.822	22.574	27.034	32.324	38.591	46.005	108.420	247.065
9.934	12.100	14.714	17.861	21.645	26.186	31.629	38.142	45.923	55.206	135.525	321.184
11.026	13.552	16.627	20.362	24.891	30.376	37.006	45.008	54.649	66.247	169.407	417.539
12.239	15.179	18.788	23.212	28.625	35.236	43.297	53.109	65.032	79.497	211.758	542.801
13.585	17.000	21.231	26.462	32.919	40.874	50.658	62.669	77.388	95.396	264.698	705.641

Glossary

Absorption costing The cost of products including all the direct costs of production and a proportion of the indirect costs of production based on normal levels of output.

Acid test ratio See quick ratio.

Accountability Managers provide an account of how they have managed resources placed in their care. In this way, those appointing managers can assess how well their managers have looked after the resources entrusted to them.

Accounting The summarising of numerical data relating to past events and presenting this data as information to managers and other interested parties as a basis for both decision making and control purposes.

Accounting equation Assets – liabilities = equity or assets = liabilities + equity.

Accounting rate of return An investment appraisal technique that averages the projections of accounting profit to calculate the expected rate of return on the average capital invested.

Accruals Expenses incurred during an accounting period but not paid for until after the accounting period end are still recognised as a liability in the statement of financial position and as an expense in the income statement.

Accruals basis of accounting All income and expenditure are recognised in the accounting period in which they occurred rather than in the accounting period in which cash is received or paid.

Activity based costing Overhead costs are allocated to products on the basis of activities consumed: the more activities that are associated with a particular product, the more overhead is allocated to that product and so the higher its cost and selling price will be.

Actual v. budget comparisons A comparison of forecast outcomes with actual outcomes on a monthly basis as a means of exercising control over operations.

Adverse variances Unfavourable variances.

AGM Annual general meeting.

Annual general meeting A meeting held every year by limited liability companies at which shareholders consider and vote on various significant resolutions affecting the company.

ARR See accounting rate of return.

Articles of Association A document that covers the internal regulations of a company and governs the shareholders' relationships with each other.

Assets Defined by the IASB as 'a resource controlled by an entity as a result of past events and from which future economic benefits are expected to flow to that entity'.

Attainable standard A standard that can be achieved with effort. This standard is neither too easy nor so difficult as to be unattainable.

Bad debts Trade receivables from which cash will not be collected. Bad debts are an expense in the income statement and are not a deduction from sales.

Balance sheet Another term for the statement of financial position.

Bond A long-term loan to an organisation with a fixed rate of interest and a fixed repayment date.

Bonus issues An issue of shares to shareholders from retained earnings. A bonus issue does not raise any cash.

Budget The expression of a plan in money terms. That plan is a prediction or a forecast of future income, expenditure, cash inflows and cash outflows.

Budgetary control Comparisons between budgeted and actual outcomes to determine the causes of variances between forecast and actual results. The causes of differences are then identified to enable remedial action to be taken.

Budgeting The process of drawing up the budget.

Business entity Any organisation involved in business. Businesses may be sole traders, companies with limited liability or partnerships.

Business entity convention The business is completely separate from its owners. Only business transactions are included in the business' financial statements.

Capital account The equity part of the statement of financial position for sole traders. The capital account is the sum of the opening capital balance plus the profit for the year (minus a loss for the year) plus any drawings made by the sole trader during the year.

Capital investment The acquisition of new non-current assets with the aim of increasing sales, profits and cash flows to the long-term benefit of a business.

Capital investment appraisal An evaluation of the long-term cash generating capacity of capital investment projects to assist decision makers in allocating scarce investment capital resources to projects to maximise long run profits.

Cash conversion cycle Inventory days + receivables days – payables days. Also known as the working capital cycle.

Cash flow cycle The time it takes a business to convert inventory into a sale and to collect cash either at the point of sale or from trade receivables with which to pay trade payables.

Cash flow forecast A detailed summary on a month-by-month basis of budgeted cash inflows and cash outflows.

Cash flows from financing activities One of the three sections in the statement of cash flows. This section represents the cash raised from the issue of share capital and loans and the cash spent in repaying borrowings and interest paid and received.

Cash flows from investing activities One of the three sections in the statement of cash flows. This section represents the cash spent on buying new non-current assets and the cash received from selling surplus non-current assets.

Cash flows from operating activities One of the three sections in the statement of cash flows. This section represents the cash generated from sales less the cash spent in both generating those sales and in running the organisation.

Comparability A quality of accounting information. To be useful, accounting information has to be presented in such a way that it can be compared with information from different accounting periods. Accounting measurements have to be made on a consistent basis in order for accounting information to be comparable.

Consistency The presentation or measurement of the same piece of accounting information on the same basis each year.

Contribution Selling price less the variable costs of making that sale.

Cost allocation The process of allocating costs, both direct and indirect, to products or services.

Cost centre A division of an entity to which attributable costs are allocated.

Cost drivers The level of activity associated with each cost pool used to allocate costs to products under activity based costing.

Cost pools The allocation of indirect costs of production associated with particular activities in an activity based costing system.

Cost of capital The level of return on an investment that is acceptable to a business given the level of risk involved. Also known as the hurdle rate of return.

Cost of sales The direct costs attributable to the sale of particular goods or services.

Cost-volume-profit analysis A management accounting technique used to determine the relationship between sales revenue, costs and profit.

Costing The process of determining the cost of products or services.

Creditors Persons to whom entities owe money. See also payables.

Creditor days See payables days.

Credits A term used in double entry bookkeeping. Credits represent liabilities and income as well as reductions in assets and expenses.

Current assets Short-term assets that will be used up in the business within one year. Examples include inventory, trade receivables, prepayments and cash.

Current liabilities Short-term liabilities that are due for payment within one year. Examples include trade payables, taxation and accruals.

Current ratio Current assets divided by current liabilities. Used in the assessment of an entity's short-term liquidity.

CVP See cost-volume-profit analysis.

Debenture A long-term loan to an organisation with a fixed rate of interest and a fixed repayment date.

Debits A term used in double entry bookkeeping. Debits represent assets and expenses as well as reductions in liabilities and income.

Debt ratio Total liabilities divided by total assets. An indicator of how reliant an entity is upon external parties to fund its assets.

Debtors Persons who owe money to an entity. See also trade receivables.

Debtor days See receivables days.

Depreciation The allocation of the cost of a non-current asset to the accounting periods benefiting from that non-current asset's use within a business. Depreciation is *not* a way of reflecting the market value of assets in financial statements and it does not represent a loss in value.

Direct cost The costs of a product or service that vary exactly in line with each product or service produced. Direct costs reflect the additional costs incurred by a business in producing one more unit of a product or service. Also known as the variable or marginal cost of a product or service.

Direct labour efficiency variance The time taken to make the goods actually produced compared with the standard time that should have been taken to make those goods multiplied by the standard rate per hour.

Direct labour rate variance What labour hours actually cost compared with what the labour hours should have cost for the actual level of production achieved.

Direct material price variance What the materials for actual production cost compared with what the standard says they should have cost for that level of production.

Direct material usage variance The actual quantity of materials used to make the goods actually produced compared with the standard quantity that should have been used to make those goods multiplied by the standard cost per unit of material.

Direct method An approach to preparing the statement of cash flows that involves disclosing the gross cash receipts from sales and the gross cash payments to suppliers.

Directors Persons appointed by the shareholders at the annual general meeting to run a limited company on their behalf.

Discounting Future cash inflows and outflows are discounted to their present value using an entity's cost of capital.

Discounts allowed An allowance given to trade receivables against amounts owed to encourage early payment of amounts owed or as a reward for buying in bulk. Discounts allowed are treated as an expense of running the business and a deduction from trade receivables, not as a deduction from sales.

Discounts received Suppliers reward their customers with discounts for early payment or bulk purchases. Discounts received are a source of income in the income statement, a deduction from cost of sales and a deduction from trade payables.

Distributable reserves Retained earnings available for distribution to shareholders as a dividend.

Distributions The distribution of retained profits to shareholders as a dividend.

Dividend A distribution of profits to shareholders.

Dividend cover A comparison of the total dividend for an accounting period to the profit after taxation. This ratio is used to assess the expected continuity of dividend payments. The higher the ratio, the more likely the dividend payment will continue into the future.

Dividend per share The total dividend for a period divided by the number of ordinary shares in issue multiplied by 100 to give a figure of dividends per share in pence.

Dividend yield The dividend per share as a percentage of the current share price.

Double entry An accounting methodology which recognises that every transaction has two effects on the figures in the financial statements.

Doubtful debts Trade receivables from which cash might not be collected. Doubtful debts are not bad debts.

DPS See dividends per share.

Drawings Amounts taken out of a business by a sole trader for personal rather than business use. Drawings are in effect a repayment of the amounts owed by the business to the owner. Drawings are not permitted in limited liability companies.

Dual aspect The recognition that each accounting transaction has a double effect on the amounts stated in financial statements.

Earnings per share The profit after taxation and after preference dividends divided by the number of ordinary shares in issue multiplied by 100 to give a figure of earnings per share in pence.

Efficiency ratios Measures of non-current asset turnover and revenue and profit per employee to determine how well an organisation has used its resources to generate profits.

EPS See earnings per share.

Equity The capital of an entity on its statement of financial position. Equity is, in theory, the amount the owners of the business would receive if all the business assets and liabilities were sold and settled at the amounts stated in the statement of financial position.

Exceptional income Income and expenditure that arises from transactions that are not in the ordinary course of business.

Expenses Defined by the IASB as 'decreases in economic benefits during the accounting period'.

Fair value The amount at which an asset could be sold or a liability settled in the open market.

Favourable variances Differences between actual and forecast results arising from higher income or lower expenditure.

Financial accounting The reporting of past information to parties external to the organisation.

Fixed cost A cost that does not vary in line with production or sales over a given period of time.

Fixed overhead expenditure variance The difference between the actual fixed overhead expenditure incurred and the forecast level of fixed overhead expenditure.

Gearing ratio Long and short-term borrowings divided by the total statement of financial position equity figure × 100%. A measure designed to help financial statement users assess whether an entity has borrowed too much money. The gearing ratio should be used in conjunction with the interest cover ratio in making this assessment.

Going concern A business that has sufficient demand for its products and sufficient sources of finance to enable it to continue operating for the foreseeable future.

Gross profit Sales less the direct costs of making those sales.

Gross profit % The gross profit of an organisation divided by the sales figure × 100%.

Historic cost The original cost of an asset or liability at the time it was purchased or incurred.

Ideal standard The best that can be achieved. Ideal standards tend to be unrealistic and unachievable as they would only ever be attained in a perfect world.

Income Defined by the IASB as 'increases in economic benefits during the accounting period'.

Income statement A statement of income and expenditure for a particular period of time.

Indirect cost Costs that cannot be attributed directly to units of production. Also known as overheads.

Indirect method An approach to preparing the statement of cash flows that ignores total inflows and outflows of cash from operations. Instead, the operating profit for a period is adjusted for increases or decreases in inventory, trade receivables, prepayments, payables and accruals and for the effect of non-cash items such as depreciation in order to determine the cash flows from operations.

Insolvency The inability of an entity to repay all that it owes to its creditors.

Interest cover Trading profit divided by finance cost (interest payable). This ratio shows how many times interest payable on borrowings is covered by operating profits. The higher the ratio, the more likely entities will be able to continue paying the interest on their borrowings.

Internal rate of return The discount rate applied to the cash flows of a capital investment project to produce a net present value for the project of £nil.

Inventory A stock of goods held by a business.

Inventory days Inventory divided by cost of sales × 365 days. The ratio measures the average stockholding period, the length of time an entity holds goods as stock before they are sold.

Inventory turnover = Inventory days.

IRR See internal rate of return.

Key factor = Limiting factor.

Liabilities Defined by the IASB as 'a present obligation of an entity arising from past events, the settlement of which is expected to result in an outflow from the entity of resources embodying economic benefits'.

Limiting factor A scarcity of input resources, such as materials or labour, is referred to as a limiting factor in the production of goods or services. When input resources are scarce, entities calculate the contribution per unit of limiting factor to maximise their profits in the short term.

Liquidity The ability of entities to meet payments to their creditors as they become due.

Management accounting Cost and management accounting is concerned with reporting accounting and cost information to users within an organisation to assist those internal users in making decisions and managing the business.

Marginal cost The additional cost incurred in producing one more unit of product or delivering one more unit of service. Also known as the variable cost of production.

Materiality The IASB Framework defines materiality thus: 'Information is material if its omission or misstatement could influence the economic decisions of users taken on the basis of the financial statements.'

Memorandum of Association This document covers a limited company's objectives and its powers and governs the relationship of the company with the outside world.

Money measurement The measurement of financial results in money terms.

Net book value Cost or fair value – accumulated depreciation.

Net present value The total of the discounted future cash inflows and outflows from a project. Projects with a positive net present value are accepted, while projects with a negative net present value are rejected.

Net profit The surplus that remains once all the expenses have been deducted from sales revenue.

Non-current assets Assets held within the business long term for use in the production of goods and services. Non-current assets are retained within the business for periods of more than one year and are not acquired with the intention of reselling them immediately or in the near future.

Non-current asset turnover Revenue is divided by non-current assets to determine how many £s of sales are generated from each £ of non-current assets.

Non-current liabilities Liabilities due for payment more than 12 months from the statement of financial position date.

Normal level of production The expected level of production achievable within an accounting period. This level is used as the basis for allocating fixed overhead costs to products and in the valuation of inventory at the year end.

Normal standard What a business usually achieves.

NPV See net present value

Operating profit The profit that remains after all the costs of trading, direct (cost of sales) and indirect (distribution and selling costs and administration expenses), have been deducted from sales revenue.

Operating profit % Determines profitability on the basis of revenue less all operating costs before taking into account the effects of finance income, finance expense and taxation.

Ordinary share capital The most common form of share capital issued by companies conferring on holders the right to receive all of a company's profits as dividends and to vote at company meetings.

Par value The face value or nominal value of a share.

Payables Amounts owed to suppliers and other creditors for goods and services supplied on credit.

Payables days Trade payables divided by cost of sales × 365 days. The ratio measures the average period taken to pay outstanding liabilities to trade suppliers.

Payback The number of years it will take for the cash inflows from a capital investment project to pay back the original cost of the investment.

Performance ratios Ratios of particular interest to an entity's shareholders as they measure the returns to the owners of the business.

Period costs Fixed costs incurred in the administration, marketing and financing of an entity relating to the period in which they are incurred.

Periodicity The preparation of financial statements for a set period of time, usually one year.

Pre-emption rights The rights of existing shareholders to subscribe to new issues of share capital before those shares can be offered to non-shareholders.

Preference share capital Preference shares receive a fixed rate of dividend that is paid before the ordinary shareholders receive any dividend. Preference share capital is returned to preference shareholders before any amounts are returned to ordinary shareholders on the winding up of a company. However, preference shareholders have no right to vote in company general meetings.

Prepayments Amounts paid in advance for goods and services to be provided in the future. These amounts are recognised as prepayments at the statement of financial position date and as a deduction from current period expenses.

Present value The discounting of future cash inflows and outflows to express all cash flows in the common currency of today, thereby facilitating a fair comparison of projected cash inflows and outflows for evaluating different capital investment proposals.

Price/earnings ratio The current market price of a share divided by the latest earnings per share figure. The ratio provides an indication of how long it would take for that share to pay back its owner in earnings if the share were purchased today and earnings remained the same for the foreseeable future.

Prime cost The total direct cost of producing one product or one unit of service.

Production cost The total direct costs of producing one product or one unit of service plus the proportion of fixed production overheads allocated to products and services on the basis of the normal level of production.

Profit The surplus remaining after all expenses are deducted from sales revenue.

Profit after tax The profit that remains once all the expenses and charges have been deducted from sales revenue and any other income for the accounting period added on.

Profit after tax % Profit for the year (= profit after tax) divided by revenue x 100%.

Profit before tax Sales – cost of sales – distribution and selling costs – administration expenses + finance income – finance expense.

Profit before tax % Profit before tax divided by revenue × 100%.

Profitability An assessment of the profits made during an accounting period by comparing current period profits and profitability %s to those of previous periods.

Profit for the year Profit after tax.

Profit per employee Calculated by dividing the number of employees during an accounting period into the operating profit for the period.

Provision for doubtful debts The provision for doubtful debts is calculated as a percentage of trade receivables after deducting known bad debts.

Prudence The process of exercising caution in the production of financial statements in the expectation of less favourable outcomes.

Purchase returns The cancellation of a purchase by returning goods to suppliers. The accounting effect of purchase returns is to reduce purchases in the income statement and trade payables in the statement of financial position.

Quick ratio Also known as the acid test ratio. The quick ratio compares current assets that are readily convertible into cash with current liabilities as a measure of an entity's short-term ability to pay what it owes over the next 12 months. This ratio should be used with caution in the evaluation of an entity's liquidity.

Ratio(s) The expression of the relationship(s) between two different figures.

Realisation Profits should not be anticipated until they have been earned through a sale.

Receivables Amounts of money owed to an entity by parties outside the organisation.

Receivables days Trade receivables divided by sales × 365 days. The ratio measures the average period taken to collect outstanding debts from credit customers.

Reducing balance A method of allocating depreciation on non-current assets to accounting periods benefiting from their use. This method uses a fixed percentage of cost in the first year of an asset's life and then applies the same percentage to the net book value of assets in accounting periods subsequent to year 1. The reducing balance method allocates a smaller charge for depreciation to each successive accounting period benefiting from a non-current asset's use. Residual value is ignored when calculating reducing balance depreciation.

Relevance A requisite quality of financial information. To be relevant, information must possess the ability to influence users' economic decisions and be timely. Relevant information may be predictive and assist users in making predictions about the future or it may be confirmatory by assisting users to assess the accuracy of past predictions.

Reliability A quality of accounting information. Accounting information should be free of significant error or bias. Information is reliable if it can be depended upon to represent faithfully the transactions or events it claims to represent.

Residual value The amount which the original purchaser of a non-current asset thinks that the asset could be sold for when the time comes to dispose of it.

Return on capital employed Operating profit (profit before interest and tax) divided by the equity of an entity plus any long-term borrowings × 100%.

Revenue Sales of goods and services made by an entity in the ordinary (everyday) course of business.

Revenue per employee Calculated by dividing the revenue for an accounting period by the number of employees employed during that accounting period.

Rights issues An issue of shares to existing shareholders at a discount to the current market price. This is not the issue of shares at a discount, which would be illegal under the Companies Act 2006.

ROCE See return on capital employed.

Sales = revenue.

Sales price variance The difference between the standard selling price and the actual selling price multiplied by the actual quantity sold.

Sales returns The cancellation of a sale by a customer returning goods. The accounting effect of sales returns is to reduce sales in the income statement and trade receivables in the statement of financial position.

Sales volume variance The actual sales – budgeted sales in units multiplied by the standard contribution per sale.

Sensitivity analysis Changing the assumptions on which forecasts are based to determine the effect of those changes on expected outcomes.

Share capital A source of very long-term financing for limited companies. All limited companies must issue share capital that will remain in issue for as long as the company exists.

Shareholders Owners of share capital in limited companies. Shareholders may be either ordinary shareholders or preference shareholders.

Share premium The amount subscribed for shares in a limited company over and above the par value of each share.

Standard costing The costs and selling prices of products are estimated with a reasonable degree of accuracy. Comparisons of actual and standard outcomes are then undertaken to determine the variances between expected and actual outcomes with a view to revising standards where necessary.

Statement of cash flows A summary of the cash inflows and outflows of an entity for a given period of time.

Statement of financial position A summary of the assets and liabilities of an entity at a particular point in time.

Stewardship The process of looking after resources entrusted to a person.

Stock A different term for inventory.

Stock days See inventory days.

Stock turnover See inventory turnover.

Straight line A method of allocating the cost of non-current assets to the accounting periods benefiting from their use. The straight line method allocates the same charge for depreciation to each accounting period benefiting from a non-current asset's use within a business.

Time value of money Money received today is worth more than money received tomorrow due to the impact of inflation and the uncertainty surrounding the receipt of money in future time periods.

Trade receivables Amounts owed to an entity by customers for goods and services supplied on credit

Turnover The term used in financial statements in the UK to represent sales or revenue.

Understandability A requisite quality of accounting information. Accounting information should be presented in such a way that those making use of it can understand what it represents. Readers of financial reports are assumed to have sufficient knowledge of business and economic events in order to make sense of what they are presented with.

Unfavourable variances Differences between actual and forecast results arising from lower income or higher expenditure.

Unsecured Loans for which no assets of an entity have been pledged in the event that the entity fails to repay the loan.

Variable cost The costs of a product or service that vary directly in line with the production of a product or delivery of a service. Also known as the marginal cost of a product or service.

Variable overhead efficiency variance The time taken to make the goods actually produced compared with the standard time that should have been taken to make those goods multiplied by the standard variable overhead rate per hour.

Variable overhead expenditure variance The variable overhead actually incurred in the production of goods compared with the standard expenditure that should have been incurred for the level of actual production.

Variances Differences between expected, forecast or budgeted and actual financial results.

Working capital Current assets less current liabilities.

Working capital cycle See cash conversion cycle.

Index